Race and Renaissance

A JOHN D. S. AND AIDA C. TRUXALL BOOK

RACE and RENAISSANCE

African Americans in Pittsburgh since World War II

JOE W. TROTTER and JARED N. DAY

University of Pittsburgh Press

Portions of this text previously appeared in Joe William Trotter Jr., *River Jordan: African American Urban Life in the Ohio Valley* (Lexington: University Press of Kentucky, 1998, and are used with permission of the University Press of Kentucky.

Published by the University of Pittsburgh Press, Pittsburgh, Pa., 15260
Copyright © 2010, University of Pittsburgh Press
All rights reserved
Manufactured in the United States of America
Printed on acid-free paper
10 9 8 7 6 5 4 3 2 1

Library of Congress Cataloging-in-Publication Data

Race and renaissance : African Americans in Pittsburgh since World War II / edited by Joe W. Trotter and Jared N. Day.
        p.   cm.
    Includes bibliographical references and index.
    ISBN-13: 978-0-8229-4391-4 (cloth : alk. paper)
    ISBN-10: 0-8229-4391-3
    1. African Americans—Pennsylvania—Pittsburgh—History. 2. African Americans—Pennsylvania—Pittsburgh—Social conditions. 3. African Americans—Pennsylvania—Pittsburgh—Economic conditions. 4. African Americans—Pennsylvania—Pittsburgh—Intellectual life. 5. City and town life—Pennsylvania—Pittsburgh. 6. Community development—Pennsylvania—Pittsburgh. 7. Pittsburgh (Pa.)—History. 8. Pittsburgh (Pa.)—Race relations. 9. Pittsburgh (Pa.)—Biography.   I. Trotter, Joe William, 1945– II. Day, Jared N., 1963–
    F159.P69N473 2010
    305.896'073074886—dc22   2010011308

Dedicated to Pittsburgh's African American Historians

Laurence Glasco

Dennis C. Dickerson

Rob Ruck

Edna McKenzie

Ralph Proctor

John Brewer

Patricia Pugh Mitchell

CONTENTS

ILLUSTRATIONS

ACKNOWLEDGMENTS

We are grateful for the assistance, generosity, and encouragement of numerous individuals, colleagues, institutions, family, and friends for making this book possible. This study draws from a broad pool of both primary and secondary sources. Moreover, federal, state, and local government reports and census accounts provide essential statistical documentation. In addition to the Pennsylvania papers of the federal Fair Employment Practice Committee (located at the Region III National Archives and Records Administration in Philadelphia), the principal archival sources include the local Pittsburgh branch files of the National Urban League and the National Association for the Advancement of Colored People (NAACP), both at the Library of Congress in Washington DC.

In addition, archival materials at the Senator H. John Heinz III Regional History Center in Pittsburgh and at the Archives of Industrial Society at the University of Pittsburgh proved significant. The staff of the H. John Heinz III Regional History Center in Pittsburgh deserves special thanks not just for their assistance in working through their extensive collections but also for their sponsorship of the Pittsburgh History Roundtable. These sessions were always thought provoking, and they urged us on in our own research efforts. We are also indebted to the Heinz History Center's African American Advisory Committee (AAAC), along with its diversity subcommittee, for ongoing support and promotion of African American history in Pittsburgh and western Pennsylvania. In addition to President and CEO Andrew Masich and Senior Vice President Betty Arenth, special thanks go to Samuel Black, curator of African American collections, and committee members Nancy Bolden, John and Tina Brewer, Andrea Mahone, Paulos Afeworki,

Frieda Williams, Thelma Lovette Morris, Sala Udin, Emily Davis, and Olga Burks Duff.

The ongoing observations of contemporary journalists for the *Pittsburgh Post-Gazette* and *Pittsburgh Courier*, such as Carl Morris, Alvin Rosensweet, Jim McKay, Debran Rowland, Vivienne Robinson, George E. Barbour, Clarke Thomas, Sonya Haynes, and Ervin Dyer, among many others, provided key contextual details. The University of Pittsburgh's Hillman Library and Carnegie Public Library, Oakland branch, also contained important primary reports, news clippings files, and surveys from the Pittsburgh Housing Authority and other city agencies and private organizations such as Action Housing, Incorporated. Along with the research staff of Hillman Library, we want to thank Marilyn Holt, Barry Chad, Gilbert Pietrzak and other staff persons in the Pennsylvania room of the Carnegie Library of Pittsburgh in Oakland. We are also indebted to the excellent reference and interlibrary loan staff at Carnegie Mellon University's Hunt Library, especially Gloriana St. Clair, Dean of University Libraries, Erika Linke, Associate Dean, Gabrielle Michalek, Ona Taylor, Sue Collins, Joan Stein, Barry Schles, and Andrew Marshall.

Another primary resource was the Remembering Africanamerican Pittsburgh Oral History Project (RAP) developed by the Center for Africanamerican Urban Studies and the Economy (CAUSE) at Carnegie Mellon University in Pittsburgh. Of special relevance were the oral interviews conducted by students in Benjamin Houston's Oral History class in spring 2007 and by participants in the Pittsburgh African American History workshop coordinated by Johanna Fernandez during the summer of 2007. Professors Houston and Fernandez codirected RAP during its first year of operation, with Houston serving as director for the remaining three years of the four-year project. We are grateful to more than one hundred individuals who provided oral interviews for the oral history project. Together, these interviews form the basis for future studies on all facets of African American life in Pittsburgh, but we wish to offer special thanks to Gail Austin, Morton "Mo" Coleman, Dave and Cecelia Epperson, Wendell Freeland, Gerald Fox, Philip Hallen, Marva and Gene Harris, Robert Lavelle, Thelma Lovette, Tim Stevens, Betty J. Tillman, Sala Udin, and Judge Warren Watson.[1] Under grants from the Allegheny Regional Asset District and the Pennsylvania Council on the Humanities, this book and the oral history project also benefited from collaboration with the August Wilson African American Cultural

Center. In particular, we wish to thank Neil Barclay, former CEO and President, Shay Wafer, Vice President of Programs, Ada Gay Griffin, Director of Annual Giving, and T Keaton-Woods, Program Manager. As part of our collaboration with the August Wilson Center, local historian Patricia Pugh Mitchell served as an interviewer for RAP during the summer of 2009 and helped to expand the base of interviews into the community of African American artists in the city of Pittsburgh.

In addition to providing interviews for RAP, members of the larger Pittsburgh community have encouraged our work on this book in a variety of ways. For their ongoing commitment to the role of history as a resource in helping to rebuild Pittsburgh's post-industrial African American community, we are indebted to Bev Smith, Chris Moore, Lynn Hayes Freeland, Connie Portis, and many other media professionals in the Pittsburgh metropolitan area. Among countless others, we thank Michael Creighton, Fred Logan, and S. K. Woodall for their regular attendance and participation in the annual CAUSE public lecture series on African American urban, political, and social history. Also, for the opportunity to work with public school teachers on some of the ideas presented in this book, we wish to express our gratitude to Linda Lane, deputy superintendent of the Pittsburgh Public Schools, Anita Ravi, high school and social studies curriculum specialist, and Kenneth Smith, course developer, as well as to Helen Faison, director of the Chatham University Pittsburgh Teachers Institute (PTI) and the 2008 PTI fellows in the "African American History in Pittsburgh Since World War II" seminar including Vivienne Bartman, Ashley Coudriet, Kipp Dawson, Carleton Heywood, Merrie Luna, Janelle Price, and Dana Williams.

Scholarly studies of pivotal significance to our work include those by Lori Cole, Dennis Dickerson, Laurence Glasco, Peter Gottlieb, Samuel Hays, John Hinshaw, Maria Lee, Ancella Livers, Roy Lubove, Ralph Proctor, and Michael S. Snow. In addition, we benefited from ongoing conversations with Ralph Proctor and Larry Glasco. At the University of Pittsburgh, the School of Education and the School of Social Work nurtured a generation of graduate students in the 1960s and 1970s whose wide-ranging dissertations on Pittsburgh's African American community proved very useful. Exceedingly helpful, too, in recent years were the "State of Black Pittsburgh Reports" by President and CEO Esther Bush of the Urban League of Pittsburgh, and the benchmark studies of the Center for Race and Social Problems under the leadership of Dean Larry Davis and economist Ralph Bangs at the University of Pittsburgh.

Dissertations from the departments of history at the University of Pittsburgh and at Carnegie Mellon University made critical contributions as well.

Graduate students also added to the success of this project through their participation in seminars and as interviewers for the Remembering Africanamerican Pittsburgh oral history project. Specifically, we wish to thank Erika Barrington, Jessica Brazier, Kevin Brown, Fidel Campet, Kate Chilton, Lisa Johnson, Jessica Barber Klanderud, Kathleen McLean, Syed Kaaz Naqvi, Rachel Oppenheimer, Russell Pryor, Diana Rodgers, Jennifer Schuitema, Christina Strellec-Simpson, Germaine Williams, and Kalem Wright. We owe a special thanks to Heinz College interns Jessica Brazier and others for their service to the project over the years. Undergraduate students also advanced work on this book through their enthusiastic engagement with the subject in our courses on African American and U.S. urban history. These include among others Brianna Agyemang, Sterling Berliant, Nathaniel Dixon, David Dominique, Amelia Nichols, Dominique Davis, Allison Deasy, Robert Jefferson, NaSheena Porter, Chlotilde Taylor, Michael Tyson, Victoria Ward, Monica Ware, and Shayna Watson.

Colleagues within and outside Carnegie Mellon facilitated this project through their encouragement and support. At Carnegie Mellon, these include Caroline Acker, Edda Fields Black, Wendy Goldman, Terrance Hays, Yona Harvey, Richard Purcell, Joel Tarr, David Miller, and Shawn Alfonso Wells. Over the years, our scholarship has also benefited from the scholarship and friendship of Earl Lewis (Emory), Tera Hunter (Princeton), Darlene Clark Hine (Northwestern), Curtis Stokes, Richard Walter Thomas, and Joe T. Darden (Michigan State University); Stanlie James (Arizona State), Craig Werner, and the late Nellie McKay (Wisconsin); Kevin Gaines, James Jackson, Matthew Countryman, and Stephen Ward (Michigan); and Rhonda Williams (Case Western Reserve); Robin D. G. Kelley (Southern California), Laurence Glasco and Ted Muller (University of Pittsburgh), Myra Young-Armstead (Bard College), Quintard Taylor, and James N. Gregory (University of Washington), to name only a few.

Former graduate students, CAUSE postdoctoral fellows, and visiting faculty members also reinforced work on this book. In addition to Johanna Fernandez (Baruch College, City University of New York), we are grateful to Luther Adams (University of Washington-Tacoma),

Richard Pierce (University of Notre Dame), Eric S. Brown (University of Missouri), Lisa G. Hazirjian (Case Western Reserve), Derek Musgrove (University of the District of Columbia), Lisa Levenstein (University of North Carolina-Greensboro), and John Wess Grant (University of Arizona); Sherie Mershon (independent scholar, Pittsburgh), Carolyn Carson (University of Pittsburgh), and Robert Gleeson (Northern Illinois State University), to name a few.

Senior university administrators and local foundations provided indispensable support to this project. We are especially grateful to Carnegie Mellon's President Jared Cohon, Provost Mark Kamlet, and Dean John Lehoczky for ongoing financial support for CAUSE. Among local foundations, we extend special thanks to the Maurice Falk Fund for a three year grant covering research on the postwar years, particularly the history of black Pittsburgh; the Mellon Financial Corporation for endowing the Mellon Bank Professorship (1996–2007); and the Giant Eagle Foundation for endowing a new Giant Eagle Professorship of History and Social Justice (2007–) to facilitate this work and the larger mission of CAUSE.

Closely interrelated with university and foundation support has been ongoing encouragement from our CAUSE advisory board: Milton L. Cofield, Associate Teaching Professor of Business Management, Tepper School of Business, Carnegie Mellon University; John P. Lehoczky, Dean, College of Humanities and Social Sciences and Lord Professor of Statistics, Carnegie Mellon University; James P. McDonald, First Vice President, Corporate Affairs Mellon Financial Corporation; Susan Williams McElroy, Associate Professor of Economics and Education Policy, University of Texas-Dallas; Kerry O'Donnell, President, Maurice Falk Fund; Everett L. Tademy, Assistant Vice President for Diversity and Equal Opportunity Services, Carnegie Mellon University; and Mark Wessel, former Dean of the H. John Heinz III School of Public Policy and Management at Carnegie Mellon University. We also wish to thank Gail Tooks, business manager of the department of history and former and current CAUSE assistants Nancy Aronson, Donna Konias, and Michelle Wirth for providing valuable administrative service in connection with this book.

For providing permission and enabling us to reproduce several photographs from the Charles H. "Teenie" Harris Collection, we offer special thanks the Carnegie Museum of Art, especially Louise Lippincott, chief curator of Fine Arts, Kerin Schellenbarger, photo archivist, Laurel Mitchell, coordinator of rights and reproductions, and Ayanna Burrus, former Fine Arts department assistant.

For photographic use and permission, thanks are also due to independent photographers Clyde Hare and Carlos Peterson as well as Eric Gaines, advertising sales manager, and John Brewer at the New Pittsburgh Courier; Kathleen Kornell of the University of Illinois Press; Sarah Becker, Sales and Service Representative at Getty Images; Sharon M. O'Neill, the Assistant General Counsel of the Urban Redevelopment Authority of Pittsburgh; and John Ciroli, Esq., the Counsel of the Legal Department at the Housing Authority of the City of Pittsburgh. Special thanks also to Linda Parker, Assistant to the Editors at the *Pittsburgh Post-Gazette*, for her efficiency in dealing with our many requests. For permission to use portions of previous publications, the authors also wish to thank the University Press of Kentucky.

We also wish to express our deep gratitude to the University of Pittsburgh Press for its commitment to this project. Special thanks go to both our anonymous readers and to Cynthia Miller, director of the University of Pittsburgh Press, and her staff, particularly Deborah Meade, David Baumann, and Ann Walston, for helping us to bring this book to completion.

As always, we owe our greatest debt of gratitude to family and friends. Jared Day wishes to thank his parents, Jon and Dorothy Day, as well as his brother and his family, Jon and Pam Day and J.J., Sydney and Sam. He also wishes to thank Steven Corey (Worcester State College), Joe Spillane (University of Florida), and Tim Haggerty (Carnegie Mellon University) for years of provocative academic camaraderie. Joe Trotter extends special thanks to Nancy Bolden, Nancy and Milton Washington, Eric and Cecile Springer, and Justin and Florence Johnson for their abiding confidence in this project and the work that we are undertaking at the Center for Africanamerican Urban Studies and the Economy. Most of all, in addition to the Trotter-14, Joe Trotter thanks his wife, H. LaRue, for her love and ongoing intellectual engagement with this book.

Finally, as a small token of our appreciation for their contributions to the study of Pittsburgh's black experience, we dedicate this book to the city's African American historians.

INTRODUCTION

African American urban history since World War II is an emerging field of scholarship. This research is helping to transform our understanding of numerous topics and themes—the origins and significance of the second Great Migration, the second ghetto, the contemporary urban crisis, deindustrialization, and the modern Civil Rights and Black Power movements, to name only a few. Scholars have published detailed case studies of New York, Philadelphia, Oakland, Los Angeles, Baltimore, Detroit, Greensboro, and Atlanta, but the city of Pittsburgh is largely absent from the historiography of the postwar city and the heated debates that it has generated.[1]

This book aims to address this gap in our knowledge and add Pittsburgh to recent discussions of post–World War II black urban history. It draws upon existing secondary sources, supplemented by primary archival accounts, newspapers, and oral histories to document the persistence of Jim Crow into the postwar years; the rise of the modern black freedom struggle; deindustrialization; and the city's effort to create a postindustrial renaissance. By focusing on the development of Pittsburgh's postwar African American community, this volume also seeks to pinpoint areas for future research and establish the conceptual foundation for a broader and more comprehensive study of the city's black community during the second half of the twentieth century. As such, this book is primarily a work of synthesis rather than a detailed case study of postwar African American urban life.

Equally important, this book is an interpretive account of the connection between contemporary life and historical change. It seeks to illuminate how African Americans in Pittsburgh arrived at the present moment in their history, as well as the history of the city, the region, and the nation. In 2007, the University of Pittsburgh's Center for Race and Social Problems published a report titled "Pittsburgh's Racial Demographics: Differences and Disparities," which documents striking gaps in employment, education, and quality of life for African Americans and whites in the Pittsburgh metropolitan region. In this book, we underscore what racial disparities mean in the day-to-day lives of black people and the diverse strategies that they deployed to address persistent inequities along the color line. As such, we hope to encourage ongoing discussions between contemporary social researchers, historians, policy makers, students, teachers, and activists.

A focus on Pittsburgh is not only justified by a dearth of research on the post–World War II years, but by the unique history of the city's black population. As the principal urban symbol of the nation's industrial history, the Steel City offers an unusual opportunity to capture the racial and class dimensions of an era that is rapidly fading from historical memory. During the industrial era, contemporaries often called Pittsburgh capitalism's first city. Organized around steel production, the economy of the Pittsburgh region underlay much of the nation's urban-industrial expansion. The area attracted large numbers of European immigrants, African Americans, and American-born whites from declining agricultural areas. A variety of racial and ethnic groups perceived Pittsburgh as one of the best places for work in the industrial sector. The dynamic interplay of blacks, whites, unions, employers, the state, and a plethora of private institutions all make Pittsburgh a site with profound regional, national, and international significance for the post–World War II era.

The Steel City continues to struggle with the long-term consequences of the collapse of its old industrial infrastructure. By the late 1980s, the city had undergone a first and second renaissance and was prepared for a third. In 1985 and 2007, Rand McNally selected Pittsburgh as the nation's "most livable city," and helped to enhance the reputation of an urban center that had successfully made the transition from manufacturing to high technology service industries. Yet the fruits of economic revitalization movements were unevenly distributed. The city's black population became widely dispersed across several neighborhoods, all of which experienced difficulties gaining access to jobs in the vibrant, higher-paying sectors of the service economy. Thus, Pittsburgh provides an exceedingly important example of a place in which historical scholarship bears on issues of contemporary social change, particularly those of class and race within the larger context of an evolving global economy.

Pittsburgh's historic African American community influenced the history of class and race relations in the state and nation from its origins during the late eighteenth and early nineteenth centuries through the closing decades of the twentieth century. Founded during the early twentieth century, the daily newspaper called the *Pittsburgh Courier* not only helped to transform African Americans' relationship to the predominantly white press, but also facilitated the African American struggle for full citizenship on a national scale. While employed by the *Pittsburgh Courier*, photojournalist Charles "Teenie" Harris produced a collection of images that is now considered the premiere depiction of African American urban life during the peak of the industrial era and the early onset of deindustrialization.[2]

Black Pittsburgh gave to the United States and the world not only two of the most well-known baseball teams of the professional Negro Leagues (the Homestead Grays and the Pittsburgh Crawfords), but also a disproportionately large number of renowned jazz musicians. These include Mary Lou Williams, Earl Garner, Grover Mitchell, and Earl Fatha Hines, to name only a few. Pittsburgh is also the birthplace of the late August Wilson, the internationally known playwright who selected the city as the principal setting of his prize-winning plays on black urban life. Stretching from the Civil War through the turn of the twenty-first century, Wilson's plays represent the major source of knowledge of Pittsburgh and African American urban history and culture for many people around the globe.[3] One recent study refers to the city's Hill District as "pound for pound" the "most generative" black community in the United States.[4]

Integral to the history of African Americans in Pittsburgh was the rise of black communities in Homestead, Braddock, Duquesne, McKees Rocks, Clairton, and other towns and cities along the Monongahela, Allegheny, and Ohio rivers. More so than the city of Pittsburgh, however, there is little systematic historical research on black communities in these smaller towns and cities. Thus, in addition to drawing upon available evidence from these areas to illuminate connections between the city and region, our study accents the need for more systematic scholarship on African American life in the numerous mill towns and cities along the three rivers of western Pennsylvania.

Pittsburgh's black community has transformed against the broader backdrop of industrial capitalism, on one hand, and the spread of the segregationist system on the other. The dynamics of class and racial inequality in interwar Pittsburgh set the stage for the emergence of more intense movements for social change in the postwar era. Scholars have used a variety of specific conceptual models—including emphases on residential segregation, migration, working-class formation, cultural change, and the dynamics of sex and gender relations—to describe and explain these transformations in African American life.[5] We build on each of these overlapping ways of thinking about black urban history while accenting the impact of demographic and economic forces on the politics, institutions, and culture of the city's black community. We also enhance recent efforts to push our understanding of the modern black freedom movement back in time before the well-known milestones of the 1950s and early 1960s—i.e., pre–*Brown v. Board of Education*, the Montgomery Bus Boycott, the Birmingham movement, and others.[6]

Following World War II, the city's African American population increased, gained a larger share of the city's total population, and made substantial material and social progress. This period dovetailed with what some scholars call the second Great Migration, the second ghetto (i.e., new forms of residential segregation), and the escalation of the modern Civil Rights movement. Compared to scholarship on the first great wave of black population movement into U.S. cities during and after World War I, the second Great Migration is often treated as a movement of despair more than a movement of hope, partly because of the intensification of technological, political, and social forces pushing blacks off the agricultural lands of the South in the years after World War II. These forces included the mechanization of production; government supplements to farmers for reducing crop acreage; and the continuation of disfranchisement, racial violence, and unequal access to social services in southern states.[7] Similarly, in accounting for the expansion of racially segregated residential areas and the rise of new ones during the 1940s and 1950s, the notion of a second ghetto accents the role of racially biased federal housing policies as a new force, along with persistent white hostility against blacks in the housing market.

While chapters 2 and 3 show how each of the foregoing developments unfolded in Pittsburgh, our account also underscores the role that African Americans, particularly poor and working-class blacks, played in bringing about these changes.[8] We also highlight the significance of Pittsburgh as part of a broader northern Civil Rights movement. Until very recently, post-World War II northern civil rights and political movements received little attention in historical scholarship on the subject.

As historians Jeanne F. Theoharis and Komozi Woodard have noted, "The dominant civil rights story remains that of a nonviolent movement born in the South during the 1950s that emerged triumphant in the early 1960s but then was derailed by the twin forces of Black Power and white backlash when it sought to move North after 1965."[9] The Pittsburgh experience suggests the emergence of grassroots civil rights struggles in the urban North at the same time and even earlier than some of the most dramatic encounters in the postwar urban South.[10] These chapters also show how the early onset of deindustrialization and the downside of the city's aggressive urban renewal programs nearly cancelled out gains of the postwar years and precipitated the expansion of the modern Civil Rights and Black Power movements during the 1960s and early 1970s.

Chapters 4 and 5 examine the impact of deindustrialization and the loss of industrial jobs on the city's African American community from the mid-1970s through the turn of the new century. On the national level, these developments paralleled what some scholars have called the "urban crisis" and the growth of a new "underclass" in the wake of the modern black freedom struggle. According to this body of scholarship, post–Civil Rights era changes resulted in the rapid spread of poverty, social disorder, and the unraveling of a more cohesive industrial age black urban community.[11] Over the past decade, however, a growing number of studies present a more complicated portrait of these changes. While such studies focus mainly on the first three decades after World War II, they suggest the ways that a process of community rebuilding proceeded alongside a destructive process of global social change.[12]

In Pittsburgh, chapters 4 and 5 show how some well-educated and well-trained blacks moved into higher echelon positions in the emerging post-industrial economy and gradually left the city for predominantly white neighborhoods in the suburbs. At the same time, deindustrialization and the intensification of class and racial inequality weakened the city's African American community and underlay the spread of urban poverty during the final decades of the twentieth century. Growing numbers of young people responded to declining opportunities by leaving Pittsburgh for other cities, but most African Americans stayed within the city and worked to create their own renaissance to counteract some of the destructive impacts of Pittsburgh's predominantly white urban revival. The book ends with reflections on the place of Pittsburgh within the larger story of African American history since World War II.

Race and Renaissance

1

War, Politics, and the Creation
of the Black Community

Pittsburgh's African American community had its origins in the late colonial and revolutionary struggles to build a new republic in North America. African American men and women played an important role in the early national and antebellum growth of Pittsburgh as a commercial center in western Pennsylvania and the Ohio Valley. While some black men gained jobs as strikebreakers and made inroads into the steel industry during the late nineteenth and early twentieth centuries, the years between the world wars witnessed the Great Migration, the dramatic growth of the city's black population, and an increase in manufacturing employment. African Americans transformed themselves into a predominantly urban-industrial working class, which facilitated the expansion of the black middle class; they also built their own city within the city and escalated their fight for full citizenship rights. Pittsburgh's black community made the transition from an alliance with industrial elites and the Republican Party at the end of the nineteenth century to an alliance with the organized, predominantly white, labor movement and the Democratic Party by the end of World War II.[1]

Steel Making, Class, Ethnicity, and Race

The foundation of the African American experience in Pittsburgh has always been employment, and this employment has shifted over time, reflecting the changing character of Pittsburgh's distinct worlds of work and social relations. Between the Civil War and World War I, Pittsburgh emerged at the center of industrialization in western Pennsylvania and the nation. Located at the confluence of the Monongahela, Allegheny, and Ohio rivers, Pittsburgh offered a wealth of water power, iron ore, and coking coal for steel making. By the turn of the twentieth century, industrialists in western Pennsylvania operated nearly a thousand coal mines and more than thirty thousand beehive coke ovens. In 1901, industrialists and bankers consolidated their holdings; formed the giant U.S. Steel Corporation; and transformed the Pittsburgh district into the industrial capital of the United States. Pittsburgh manufacturers built dozens of new plants and established the Pittsburgh stock exchange by 1911. Known locally as "Pittsburgh's Wall Street," the Pittsburgh stock exchange enabled industrialists and financiers to invest in a variety of businesses—including aluminum, oil, chemicals, steel, ship-building, and construction—that served local, regional, and national markets. Before the onset of World War I, the Pittsburgh region alone produced over 40 percent of the nation's steel.[2]

Industrialists exploited the region's resources not only through an aggressive program of capital investments, but through an equally energetic campaign of recruiting European immigrants to fill their industrial labor needs. Although industrialists like Andrew Carnegie made generous contributions to southern black colleges and developed close relations with black leaders like Booker T. Washington, they maintained a view of black workers as "inefficient, unsuitable, and unstable" to meet the labor requirements of machine production.[3] Instead, people from south, central, and eastern Europe fueled the city's industrial expansion. Pittsburgh's population rose from fewer than 50,000 in 1860 to an estimated 534,000 by 1917. The Polish population increased from less than 3,000 in 1890 to over 20,600 in 1910, while the number of Italians rose from just over 2,000 to over 14,000 in the same time period. For the Poles and Italians, respectively, this population growth represented an increase of 318 and 219 percent between 1890 and 1900, and another 74 and 117 percent between 1900 and 1910. Because so many of these people disembarked at the Pittsburgh terminal of the Pennsylvania Railroad, some scholars

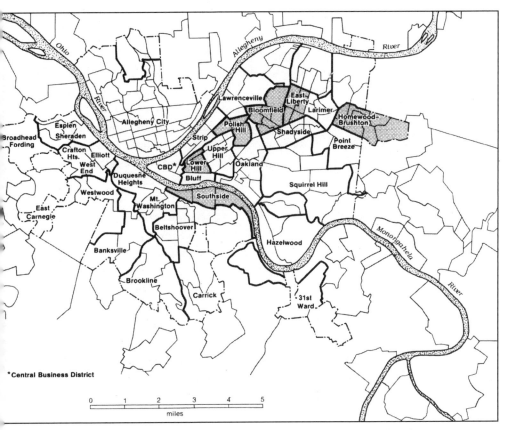

Map of early-twentieth-century African American communities in Pittsburgh.

Source: John Bodnar, Roger Simon, and Michael P. Weber, *Lives of Their Own: Blacks, Italians, and Poles in Pittsburgh, 1900–1960* (Urbana: University of Illinois Press, 1982), 12.

later described the area around the Pennsylvania station and the three rivers as "Pittsburgh's Ellis Island."[4]

Immigrants and their children increased the city's manufacturing workforce from 24,000 in 1859 to nearly 155,000 in 1899. By 1900, an estimated 40 percent of the city's male workforce held jobs in manufacturing; 27 percent in trade and transportation; and 28 percent in domestic and personal service. As the industrial workforce expanded, ethnic and racial stratification intensified. By 1907, compared to their American-born and Irish and German counterparts, the new workers entered the least skilled, most difficult, and lowest paid segments of the Pittsburgh and western Pennsylvania labor force. At U.S. Steel's Homestead mill, 40 percent of American-born whites, 46 percent of British-born whites,

51 percent of Scots, and 24 percent of Irish workers occupied skilled jobs. Conversely, only 2 percent of the Polish, 1 percent of the Italians, and less than 2 percent of other immigrant groups worked in skilled positions.[5]

In the early postbellum years, the iron industry had become increasingly specialized, as blast furnaces, forges, and rolling and finishing mills had moved away from small, centralized shops to larger establishments specializing in one or another operation. During the late nineteenth and early twentieth centuries, however, Pittsburgh's industrial and financial elites—Andrew Carnegie, Henry Clay Frick, Henry Phipps, James Hillman, and Richard and Thomas Mellon—increased capital investments in blast furnaces and rolling mills; applied new mass production technology; and introduced labor-saving cost accounting and management techniques. New processes like the Bessemer converter, open hearth furnace, and steam and electric power enabled manufacturers to reintegrate diverse production processes. Management also hired more foremen and supervisory personnel and increased oversight of the workplace from the top down.[6]

As manufacturers heightened their control over the work process, white employees challenged management's authority at the point of production and increased their demands for economic justice: higher wages, better working conditions, and more equitable treatment in the workplace. Building upon their antebellum experience in the Sons of Vulcan union (formed in 1858), iron puddlers joined other craftsmen and organized the Amalgamated Association of Iron and Steel Workers in 1876. In their negotiations with owners, workers adopted the strike as their principal weapon in the struggle for economic democracy. Dramatic and violent conflicts broke out in the "Railroad War" of 1877 and the Homestead Steel Strike of 1892.[7]

White workers gradually bridged their ethnic and nationality differences and waged a unified struggle for their rights, but the Sons of Vulcan and the Amalgamated Association of Iron and Steel Workers unions restricted membership to whites only. Seasoned, skilled black men could not obtain union cards and young black workers could not gain access to apprenticeship and training programs. According to one white steel unionist, compelling whites to work with black men "was itself cause sufficient to drive . . . [white workers] into open rebellion."[8]

African Americans sought a measure of control over their own labor through the instrument of strikebreaking. As early as 1880, *Harper's*

New Monthly Magazine featured Pittsburgh's black steelworkers in all phases of the steel-making process.[9] Employers understood how slavery had offered black men training in the art of iron making. At the Tredgar Iron Works in Richmond, Virginia, the number of slaves increased from less than one hundred in 1860 to nearly one thousand during the Civil War. Black iron- and steelworkers mastered skilled jobs as puddlers, rollers, roughers, and iron and steel heaters. When U.S. Steel took over the Tennessee Coal and Iron Company in 1907, African Americans made up about 25 to 30 percent of its labor force in the Birmingham District of Alabama. As early as 1881, the steel employers' magazine *Iron Age* commented favorably on the skills of southern black boilers, heaters, and rollers in the steel industry. Less than ten years later, the magazine noted, "wherever the Negro has had a chance to acquire the necessary skill . . . he has shown himself capable."[10]

The first black workers arrived at the Pittsburgh Bolt Company on 3 March 1875. Puddlers had been on strike for several months. In late February, the *Pittsburgh Leader* commented on the southern recruitment efforts of local companies, "A short time ago, the Pittsburgh Bolt Company sent representatives to Virginia, and other firms are doing likewise. An executive of theirs said an abundance of colored puddlers could be had." Upon arrival of the black puddlers, some four hundred angry white men and boys marched on the mill. Local policemen refused to disperse the crowd, claiming they were not empowered to act unless violence occurred, but the company soon gained cooperation of the police chief and the governor of Pennsylvania, who threatened to bring in the infantry. The crowd dispersed and black workers remained on the job. Black workers also crossed the picket lines at the Black Diamond Steel Works (1875), the Solar Iron Works (1887–1889), Carnegie Steel, later U.S. Steel (1892, 1901), and the McKees Rocks Pressed Steel Car Company (1909). Most of these men had been trained in the mills of the South.[11]

The number of black steelworkers in Pittsburgh and Allegheny City (now Pittsburgh's North Side) increased from virtually nil at the end of the Civil War to nearly eight hundred by 1910. During that time span, Pittsburgh's overall black population jumped from under three thousand to nearly twenty-six thousand, an increase of about 3 percent of the region's total population to about 5 percent (see appendix to this volume, table 1; hereinafter, all table references in appendix). In 1901, an overly enthusiastic writer for the *Colored American Magazine* concluded, "Na-

African Americans at the Black Diamond Steel Works, Mill #1, c. 1901.
Source: Oliver G. Waters, "Smoky City: Part I," *Colored American Magazine* 3, no. 6 (Oct. 1901): 419.

tionality and color probably play less part here in the matter of employment than in any other city. The prime questions are: Do you want work? And can you put out the goods."[12]

Although African Americans entered the iron and steel industry as strikebreakers, they were not anti-union; they balanced their strikebreaking activities with efforts to organize their own labor unions or to join predominantly white ones on their own terms. Black boilers formed the Garfield Lodge No. 92 at the Black Diamond Steel Works. Complementing the Pittsburgh local was the formation of Sumner Lodge No. 3 in Richmond, Virginia. When black workers struck the Black Diamond Works in 1881–1882, employers turned to Richmond for replacement workers, but the Sumner Lodge foiled the effort.[13]

During the 1880s, African Americans joined the Knights of Labor assembly of Pittsburgh. One African American, Jeremiah Grandison, later represented the group at the founding convention of the American Federation of Labor in 1886. In his speech before the group, Grandison focused attention on the fundamental principles of the labor movement. "Our object," he said, "as I understand it, is to federate the whole laboring element of America. I speak more particularly with the knowledge of my own people, and declare to you that it would be dangerous to mechanics to exclude from this organization the common laborers." Grandison warned white union men that employers might employ black workers in a variety of "positions they could readily qualify to fill."[14] After he became editor and partner of the black weekly newspaper called the *Pittsburgh Courier*, Robert L. Vann regularly urged black workers to form their own unions to counteract discrimination by organized white labor. "The Colored," he said, must "organize themselves into a substantial union of their own . . . and thus get control of their own labor."[15]

Pittsburgh's first generation of black iron and steel men worked in a variety of skilled as well as general labor steelmaking occupations. By 1910, well-educated and skilled blacks made up about 27 percent of Pittsburgh's black iron and steel workforce. The Black Diamond Steel Works and the Clark Mills employed African Americans as plumbers, engineers, die grinders, rollers, roughers, finishers, puddlers, millwrights, and heaters. John Harley, a black graduate of the University of Pittsburgh, became a draftsman at the Crucible Steel Company. William Dennon, also a graduate of the University of Pittsburgh, joined the engineering department at the Farrell plant of U.S. Steel. William Nelson Page, another early employee in the steel industry, served as private secretary to W. G. Glyde, general manager of sales for Carnegie Steel. Some skilled black workers supervised their less skilled white counterparts. Richard R. Wright, a close contemporary observer of African American life in Pennsylvania, noted that the two chief rollers at one plant were blacks and that several white men worked under their supervision. Indeed, for a brief moment, according to a 1910 survey of wages in the Pittsburgh district, African American iron and steelworkers earned a higher average weekly wage at $14.98 than their Polish counterparts who earned $12.21 per week.[16]

Despite making substantial inroads into the industrial sector during the late nineteenth and early twentieth centuries, blacks made up only 3 percent Pittsburgh's total workforce by the onset of World War I. American-born whites made up 29 percent and immigrants accounted for 68 percent of all steelworkers, some 300,000 by 1910. Most black men and women worked in general labor, domestic, and personal service jobs in Pittsburgh and the outlying mill and coal towns of western Pennsylvania. Manufacturing, transportation, and trade provided employment for fewer than 50 percent of black men and less than 8 percent of black women (see table 2). In 1897, African Americans joined immigrant workers in helping to construct Andrew Carnegie's Pittsburgh, Bessemer, and Lake Erie Railroad. African Americans made up the majority of workers who excavated the huge Bessemer tunnel near the town of Unity, eight miles east of Pittsburgh. Following completion of the tunnel and the railroad project, African Americans took a variety of "odd jobs" to make ends meet. In an interview with Bettie Cole, Mattie Rucker Braxton, born in 1885 in Amherst, Virginia, described such work among blacks in western Pennsylvania: "I came to Sewickley in 1907. . . . When I came here, colored people worked in private famil[ies], worked on the roads and the dams, and drove horses. Wasn't no millwork for colored folks then."[17]

Some pre–World War II blacks parlayed their expertise and earnings in domestic service and general labor into prosperous business enterprises. John T. Writt, for example, was born in Winchester, Virginia, before the Civil War. Writt's family migrated to Ohio shortly after his birth, and Writt moved to Pittsburgh as a young man in 1864. He obtained work with a wealthy white family and, by the turn of the twentieth century, operated his own catering business and owned his own home in the suburb of Homewood. Cumberland "Cum" Posey Sr. developed the commercially successful Posey Coal Dealers and Steam Boat Builders Company. His father's employment in the household of a large river boat owner provided Posey access to work on the boat. There, he acquired the

This late 1890s river steamer, *Tornado*, was built by the African American engineer and entrepreneur Cumberland ("Cum") W. Posey Sr.
Source: Thomas S. Ewell, "The Smoky City, Part III: Social and Business Life," *Colored American Magazine* 3, no. 9 (Dec. 1901): 144.

initial skills, knowledge, and motivation necessary to become an engineer and launch his own lucrative business venture.[18]

Women figured prominently in the development of black businesses. In his analysis of turn-of-the-century black businesses, Thomas S. Ewell, a writer for the *Colored American Magazine*, noted that African American women were "a constant inspiration to the life and work" of pre-war black entrepreneurs. Indeed, though less commercially successful than men, some women operated their own beauty, restaurant, and boarding house service establishments.[19] Nonetheless, before World War I, few African Americans, men or women, transformed domestic and general labor jobs into lucrative businesses. Such opportunities increased during the industrial growth of the 1920s. The pattern of African American household and general labor, supplemented by a comparatively small number of steel industry jobs, increasingly gave way to work in the industrial sector with the onset of the Great Migration.

The Great Migration and the African American City within the City

The first Great Migration fueled Pittsburgh's black population growth and community development. Strikebreaking as a mode of labor recruitment declined during the interwar years as higher wages in the steel industry, networks of family and friends, and the labor demands of two world wars attracted increasing numbers of southern blacks to Pittsburgh and western Pennsylvania. The city's African American population rose from under 27,000 at the onset of World War I to over 82,000 by the end of World War II. This represented an increase from 4.8 to 9.3 percent of the city's total population (see table 1). Nonetheless, black workers helped to break the Great Steel Strike of 1919. In fact, according to the Interchurch World Movement's account, a major cause of the strike's dismal failure "was the successful use of strike breakers, principally negroes, by the steel companies, in conjunction with the abrogation of civil liberties." Some company officials bluntly stated that black workers "did it."[20]

While strikebreaking remained a big source of work for African Americans, industrial firms intensified their regular recruitment of black workers during and after World War I. In August 1923, eleven plants of the Carnegie Steel Company employed some 6,000 black workers. Other area firms also hired significant numbers of black workers, among them: Jones and Laughlin (3,000 black employees), Pressed Steel Car Company (1,700), Westinghouse Airbrake (465), and Pittsburgh Plate Glass Company (350). By 1930, unlike in the pre–World War I years, over 65 percent of African American men worked in the manufacturing, transportation, or trade sectors of the economy (see tables 3 and 4). The percentage of black men in the region's steel industry labor force increased from less than 3 percent of the region's steel industry labor force before World War I to a peak of 14 percent during World War II. By the late 1920s, over 300 black women also worked in manufacturing and mechanical industries. They labored mainly in the garment industry as dressmakers and seamstresses, and in selected occupations in the iron and steel industry as well.[21] During the war years, black industrial workers earned between $3.50 to over $5.00 per eight-hour day compared to no more than $2.50 per twelve-hour day in southern cities, and little more than $1.00 per day for southern agricultural workers. Black household workers also sometimes earned over $3.50 per day. One employer of domestic labor complained that: "Hundreds of [domestic] jobs go begging at $15 per week."[22]

In addition to the labor recruitment efforts of manufacturing companies, networks of family and friends helped to pave the way for black migration to Pittsburgh. One woman persuaded her husband to move to Pittsburgh instead of Cincinnati: "I wrote him a letter back. My older sister had come to Pittsburgh, and I took her as a mother because I had lost my mother. And I wrote him back, and said, 'I don't want to stay in Cincinnati. I want to go to Pittsburgh.' Next letter I got, he had got [a] job in Pittsburgh and sent for me."[23] In a letter to the Pittsburgh Urban League, one man wrote for himself and seven others seeking jobs in the industrial North, "We Southern Negroes want to come to the north . . . they [white southerners] ain't giving a man nothing for what he do . . . they is trying to keep us down." From South Carolina, a woman wrote for her two sons: "[I have] two grown son[s] . . . we want to settle down somewhere north . . . wages are so cheap down here we can hardly live."[24]

African Americans who arrived in Pittsburgh had acquired substantial urban experience in other southern and northern cities. In his pioneering study of the Great Migration to Pittsburgh, historian Trent Alexander found that most black migrants came to Pittsburgh from "multiple-generation urban roots—both they and their parents were born in urban areas. Most of the rest of the migrants (almost a third) came from multiple-generation rural families." According to marriage certificates in Allegheny County, nearly 55 percent of African Americans who applied for marriage licenses during the 1930s had migrated to Pittsburgh from towns of over ten thousand people, and more than a quarter arrived in Pittsburgh from towns of one hundred thousand or more.[25]

While most blacks in Pittsburgh had grown up in poverty in the rural and urban South, they often expressed shock and disappointment at the physical environment and geography of their current home. In the words of one migrant, "Man, it was ugly, dirty," the "streets were nothing but dirt streets." While the hills made walking and travel difficult, clouds of smoke and soot blanketed the city during peak work hours. In a letter to his pastor back home, another migrant wrote, "Some places look like torment [hell] or how they say it look." Still another newcomer declared the South "is clean. Everything is white, beautiful. . . . Everything was black and smoky here." Some were struck by the technology of steel making: "One thing [that] impressed me very much was to look at the steel, the iron. All that I had seen in previous years was all finished and hard and everything. To come [to Pittsburgh] and see it running like water—it was amazing." A migrant from the iron and steel city of Birmingham, Alabama, had a different response: "I felt very much at ease. . . . Pittsburgh wasn't strange. It was like Birmingham. They're both mineral towns. There's lots of coal and steel in both of them."[26]

Despite earning higher wages in the industrial sector, African Americans took jobs at the bottom of the labor force and faced an ongoing pattern of "last hired" and "first fired." Employers placed over 90 and sometimes 100 percent of the new workers in jobs classified as "unskilled." This pattern prevailed at Carnegie Steel, Jones and Laughlin, National Tube, Crucible Steel, and others. African Americans worked in the most difficult, dangerous, low-paying, and dirty categories of industrial labor. They fed the blast furnaces, poured molten steel, and worked on the coke ovens.[27]

Black workers' jobs exposed them to disproportionate levels of heat, deadly fumes, and disabling and serious injuries. In 1919, blacks made up 4.6 percent of the state's iron, steel, and manufacturing employees, but registered 8.5 percent of all victims of accidents. While 26 percent of blacks in metal industries suffered severe injuries or death, the figures were 24 and 22 percent, respectively, for immigrants and American-born whites. By 1930, laborer jobs accounted for the top ten occupations among Pittsburgh's black men. Not a single white-collar, professional, clerical, skilled craft, or even "semi-skilled" operative position figured among the top ten occupations for black men (see table 5). Conversely, among all

men, the top ten jobs included clerks (ranking first), salesmen, retail dealers, semi-skilled operatives, carpenters, and machinists (see table 6).[28]

Although some African American women gained access to jobs in
the industrial sector, manufacturing offered limited opportunities for
black women. In 1920, over 87 percent of black women continued to work
in jobs defined as domestic and personal service. This figure increased to
90 percent as the Depression got underway (see tables 3 and 4). Moreover, African American women had the highest labor force participation rate of any women in the city. Whereas 32 percent of black women
worked outside the home, only 16 percent of immigrants and 27 percent
of American-born white women entered the wage earning labor force by
the late 1920s. In 1930, personal service occupations accounted for seven
of the top ten occupations among black women (see table 7). For their
part, white women gained increasing access to jobs as teachers, social
workers, telephone operators, typists, receptionists, and office secretaries
(see tables 3 and 8). In 1930, although personal service was the leading occupation for all women, it accounted for only one of the top ten occupations among white women (see table 8).[29]

Black workers endured frequent layoffs and found it exceedingly difficult to make ends meet. Facing the industrial downturn of the early
1920s, one Pittsburgh migrant sought to get his old southern farm labor
job back: "I want you to save me my same place for me, for I am coming
back home next year, and I want my same farm if you haven't nobody
on it."[30] In 1928 and 1929, following the reemployment boom of the mid-
1920s, the Pittsburgh Urban League discouraged black migration to the
city, emphasizing "how difficult it is to find work in Pittsburgh today." By
1931, while black men accounted for only 7 percent of Allegheny county's
male population, they made up 22 percent of the men seeking employment at the County's Emergency Association.[31]

The color line in the workplace encouraged and was in turn encouraged by racial discrimination in the larger residential, institutional, and
community life of the city. At the height of the Great Migration, Pittsburgh realtors converted railroad cars, basements, boathouses, and ware-
houses into living quarters for black workers and their families. Moreover,
steel companies often housed single young men in bunkhouses or segregated camps, where they occupied rooms with so-called "hot beds," i.e.,
two, three, or four men to a bed on double or triple shifts. In his study of
the impact of World War I on housing among blacks in Pittsburgh, sociologist Joe Darden concludes that blacks, "regardless of income, had great

difficulty either renting or buying good houses in non-segregated areas."[32] A national representative of the YWCA observed poor housing conditions and congestion as nearly "universal" and "critical" in Pittsburgh's black community. Similarly, Abraham Epstein, in his pioneering study of African American migration to Pittsburgh during the era of World War I, described black neighborhoods "as congested beyond capacity by the influx of newcomers." Consequently, new black settlements had opened up "in hollows and ravines, on hill slopes and along river banks, by railroad tracks and in mill-yards."[33]

The Hill District rapidly expanded as the primary residence of the city's black population. During World War I and the industrial boom of the 1920s, the third and fifth wards gained nearly 14,000 new black residents, but lost about 7,600 European immigrants and their children. New zoning laws reinforced the racially segregated housing market and made it increasingly difficult for blacks to inhabit structures defined as "fit for human habitation." At the time, however, both white proponents and opponents of zoning legislation downplayed the racial implications of such laws. In 1923, for example, public hearings on the Pittsburgh zoning measure focused on issues of height limitations for buildings, the effects of crowding on public health, and "individual rights" as they related to class, but not on racial discrimination. Predominantly "colored areas" also emerged in Braddock (Port Perry), Duquesne (Castle Garden), and other surrounding mill towns of western Pennsylvania.[34]

Pittsburgh's public school system had abandoned de jure segregation in 1881. Nonetheless, only a handful of schools in the Hill District and elsewhere allowed black and white students to attend the same schools. In 1926, out of 106 elementary schools in the city, only 20 admitted any black students. Between 1881 and 1933, no black teachers were hired even on a part-time basis. In 1934, when Hill District resident Thomas Harrison inquired about the employment of black teachers, N. R. Criss, solicitor for the board, replied in no uncertain terms, "colored teachers never will teach white children in the City of Pittsburgh. Such a step would be suicidal and would bring upon the Board of Education the condemnation of the entire community."[35] Frank Bolden, a *Pittsburgh Courier* correspondent and a 1937 graduate of the University of Pittsburgh, recalled, "if you wanted to teach on any level and you were black, you left Pittsburgh. If you didn't want to leave Pittsburgh, you didn't teach."[36]

Racial inequality in other aspects of the city's culture and politics mirrored discrimination in the schools, housing, and labor market. During the 1920s, an estimated 125,000 whites enrolled in newly founded chapters of the Ku Klux Klan in Pittsburgh, Homestead, Wilkinsburg, Carnegie, and other towns along the Ohio, Monongahela, and Allegheny rivers. The Klan's application for membership asked prospective members to enlist as a "soldier" in "the Pennsylvania State Klavaliers." Some recruits had as much as twelve years of military experience. In an official communiqué, the KKK Realm of Pennsylvania later cited this period as a high-water mark of Klan activities in the state and region: "Klansmen and former Klansmen from every section of this Province . . . express the desire to see the Klan regain the position that it held [in] 1926, 27 and 28."[37]

Local law enforcement officials reinforced racial hostility through disproportionately high rates of arrests and incarceration of African American residents. In the steel town of Duquesne, for example, when white residents called police about the conduct of blacks in a local boardinghouse in 1926, police soon raided the place and arrested and fined black workers for "shooting craps." The local newspaper, *Duquesne Times,* further inflamed racial hostility in the community by suggesting, "white citizens should physically retaliate against the colored *visitors* [our italics] and their offensive acts."[38] On another occasion, in 1926, the police sought to enforce a 10:00 p.m. curfew at one Jones and Laughlin plant. According to an "incident report" on the matter in the papers of the Urban League of Pittsburgh, "police drove them [black men] to bed with guns."[39]

In 1933, police arrested thirty black men and women in the town of Industry, Beaver County. When those arrested could not pay the fines levied, they were placed in the county jail overnight. The next day they were loaded onto three trucks and transported some one hundred miles south, just short of the West Virginia border. Authorities forced the men and women off the trucks "in a driving rain" and ordered them to walk across the state line into West Virginia. One contemporary observer described this incident as the "Beaver Shanghai episode of 1933."[40]

Virtually every institution serving the public discriminated against blacks in some form or fashion. Public accommodations and commercial establishments—restaurants, theaters, swimming pools, department stores, and skating rinks, to name only a few—either excluded African Americans from service altogether or offered provisions on a segregated and unequal basis. Downtown Pittsburgh department stores denied black patrons the customary courtesy of trying on garments, for example.

Banks, insurance companies, hospitals, and medical facilities, including the University of Pittsburgh Medical School, also restricted services to the city's black community. During the 1930s, one woman told a WPA interviewer that it made her "blood boil" to observe how white physicians treated black patients. "They don't seem to think our people have any feelings . . . there was one woman lying in a bed, and they all stood around her and questioned her so everybody in the ward could hear, and they laughed and they pointed at her." [41] Leading insurance companies not only maintained segregated black and white offices in the city, but restricted black clients to a narrow range of services. One company provided only two types of insurance for black people, while offering whites some thirty distinct services and options. Moreover, the company sold policies to black clients at "higher than normal rates." [42]

As the wall of segregation and racial discrimination spread across the city and region, African Americans intensified their community-building activities. During the early to mid-twentieth century, they built one of the nation's most vibrant urban communities in Pittsburgh's Hill District. In their pioneering historical documentary of the area, filmmakers and journalists Chris Moore, Nancy Levin, and Doug Bolin described the Hill as Pittsburgh's "Little Harlem." Contemporary residents often referred to the Hill as a "dynamic," "thriving," and "bustling" area. Some called it "the crossroads of the world," where there was "never a dull moment" and where "people never went to bed." In other words, African Americans in Pittsburgh constructed their own "black metropolis" and transformed "segregation," a mean experience, into "congregation," a sense of brotherhood, sisterhood, and community. [43]

Religious, fraternal, business, and professional institutions proliferated under the impact of the Great Migration. The city's Euclid Avenue AME church increased from just over 300 members before World War I to 1,500 in 1926. Membership at the Ebenezer Baptist Church leaped from 1,500 at the outset of the period to an estimated 3,000 by the late 1920s. Central Baptist Church enrolled 500 new members during the war years; John Wesley AME Zion Church added some 1,200 new parishioners during the 1920s. By the late 1920s, African Americans maintained forty-five churches in the Hill District alone. These churches included seventeen Baptist denominations and eighteen storefronts serving a diverse constituency. Twenty-five of these churches counted a membership of 12,400; twenty-one owned an estimated $1.62 million in church property; and, together, the total of forty-five black churches recorded an an-

Founded in the early nineteenth century, Pittsburgh's Old Bethel African Methodist
Episcopal Church was the first AME body organized west of the Allegheny Moun-
tains. This building served the church through the early twentieth century and was
finally demolished in the 1950s.

Source: Carnegie Museum of Art, Charles "Teenie" Harris Collection, photo #2001.35.14520.
Photograph © 2009 Carnegie Museum of Art, Pittsburgh.

nual collection of $175,422 in 1928. At twenty-five of these Hill District
churches, some 10,000 people regularly attended Sunday services.[44]

Christianity was not the only religious tradition forged by African
Americans in Pittsburgh. In 1913, Timothy Drew, a North Carolina–
born African American, adopted the name Noble Drew Ali and established the Moorish Science Temple in Newark, New Jersey. During the
war and early postwar years, Noble Drew Ali aimed to link black people
to the Koran and the teachings of Allah in Pittsburgh and other cities of
the East and Midwest. By the mid-1920s, however, the Moorish Science
Temple increasingly gave way to the influence of the Ahmadiya Movement in Islam, which spread to the United States from India. As historian Laurence Glasco notes, compared to the Moorish Science Temple,
the Indian Ahmadis "introduced more traditional Muslim rituals into

The Ohio, Monongahela, and Allegheny rivers served as sites of baptism, a key rite of passage in the African American community. Such ceremonies would increasingly move to inside pools during the years after World War II. Here, two deacons assist Rev. James M. Allen of Calvary Baptist Church to conduct a baptism in the Allegheny River, 1969.

Source: Carnegie Museum of Art, Charles "Teenie" Harris Collection, photo #2001.35.21609. Photograph © 2009 Carnegie Museum of Art, Pittsburgh.

the services" of Pittsburgh's black Muslim community. Other influences on Pittsburgh's black Islamic community included the Islamic Mission of America and later the Nation of Islam.[45]

Fraternal orders, mutual benefit societies, and social clubs included the Grand United Order of Odd Fellows, the Knights of Pythias, the Grand United Order of True Reformers, the Masons and Elks, and local chapters of the National Association of Colored Women (NACW), to name only a few. These organizations and their auxiliaries provided helpful sickness and death benefits for members and their families and education opportunities for their children. Under their motto, "Lifting as We Climb," the NACW provided one- to four-year college scholarships; achievement awards to encourage academic excellence; and study groups to analyze and address the social and political conditions of the city's

Opened in 1899, as the Hill District branch of the Carnegie Library, this building would later house the First Mosque of Pittsburgh as the African American population increased.

Source: Pittsburgh History & Landmarks Foundation, African American Historic Sites Survey of Allegheny County. Courtesy of Pittsburgh History & Landmarks Foundation, James D. Van Trump Library.

black population. In his study of social conditions in the Hill District, Ira DeAugustine Reid identified over a dozen active black women's clubs and concluded, in "proportion to their membership," that these clubs had done more "in a community way than any other group."[46]

A group of men's clubs—the Loendi Club, the Frogs, and others—complemented the cultural, economic, and community development work of black fraternal orders and the women's clubs. Fraternal orders and social clubs also offered African Americans crucial centers of leisure time pursuits, cultural expression, and political autonomy. Contemporary observers often commented on the role of such organizations within the larger context of a Jim Crow social order. A WPA interviewer summarized the significance of these groups for Pittsburgh's black community: "In them, large numbers of people find opportunities to achieve eminence, a desire and a need deep-seated in every human being. In these groups a man may become a Grand Patriarch, a Grand Sword-Bearer, a Noble Grand, or a Grand Pursuivant, a most worshipful Grand Master,

Alongside churches and fraternal organizations, Pittsburgh's early twentieth-century African American community established a variety of secular organizations with their own separate facilities. This is a photograph of the original building of the Loendi Club.

Source: Carnegie Museum of Art, Charles "Teenie" Harris Collection, photo #2001.35.5514. Photograph © 2009 Carnegie Museum of Art, Pittsburgh.

or Thrice Potent Grand Master, and in the auxiliaries a woman may be a Daughter Grand, or a Worthy Councilor . . . such things are for many members, to touch glamour and to achieve exaltation." [47]

Various entrepreneurial activities symbolized the emergence of a more cohesive and self-sufficient black community. The *Pittsburgh Courier* vigorously promoted the growth of Pittsburgh's black "city within the city." Originally from North Carolina, Robert L. Vann attended the University of Pittsburgh Law School and became its first African American graduate in 1909. A year later, he became editor and part owner of the *Courier*. Like other black newspapers during the period, the *Courier* repeatedly urged blacks to "concentrate" their earnings, "make capital," and hire, produce, and sell for themselves. In Vann's view, capital accumulation, businesses, and professional enterprises represented the keystones of African American institutional, intellectual, cultural, and community development. During the late 1920s, the *Courier* moved into a new $54,000 office building on Centre Avenue in the Hill District. *The WPA History of the Negro in Pittsburgh* praised the *Courier* as a "successful, well-managed business," providing jobs for some eighty skilled and professional employees.[48]

African Americans also founded the Home Finders League, the Mutual Real Estate Investment Company, and the Steel City Bank. Formed in 1919 under the leadership of Rev. J. C. Austin, pastor of Ebenezer Baptist Church, the Steel City Bank claimed some five thousand depositors before it collapsed in 1925. The Home Finders League, closely aligned with the Steel City Bank, purchased nearly $300,000 in real estate and enabled some blacks to move into their own homes before its demise. Following the collapse of those two, Hill District blacks formed the Mutual Real Estate Investment Company and purchased a three-story apartment complex at the intersection of Wylie Avenue and Morgan Street just months before the stock market crash of 1929.[49]

Cumberland "Cum" Posey Jr. and W. A. "Gus" Greenlee, manager and part owner of the Homestead Grays, spearheaded the growth of professional black baseball in Pittsburgh. Gus Greenlee also operated a lucrative numbers game during the 1920s and purchased another black team, the Pittsburgh Crawfords, in 1930. Greenlee recruited star players like Josh Gibson and Satchel Paige and built his own stadium on Bedford Avenue in the Hill District. At a time when the Pittsburgh Pirates excluded black players, Greenlee not only helped to transform baseball into a major leisure-time and cultural activity for the African American community, but a significant employer of black workers as well. In an interview with historian Ancella Livers, Harold C. Tinker Sr., who played professional and sandlot baseball, underscored the double-duty role that black baseball played in Pittsburgh's black community: "We had a pride underneath. . . . We were helping people. That's what my pride came from. We used to make people rejoice who were down. During the era of

The Pittsburgh Crawfords and the Homestead Grays emerged as outstanding teams in the National Negro League. The Crawfords won the 1935 Negro National League World Series. Here are the Pittsburgh Crawfords outside the Crawford Recreation Center, n.d.

Source: Carnegie Library of Pittsburgh, Pennsylvania Department.

the Crawfords that was the bad time, '27, '28, and I used to see people at baseball games forget all about their troubles. They were turning hand-springs and jumpin', hollerin.' And just the fact that people were making people happy for a few hours, it did something to me. And I was just as proud as if I was making a thousand dollars a week."[50]

Hill District residents fondly recalled the positive role of the policy game in the community life of the city. Some ministers, and later historians like Rollo Turner and Rob Ruck, described the city's black "numbers kings" as "honest," "dynamic, generous, and compassionate" human beings. They helped a lot of people. As one black woman recalled, the policy operators were not men "who made money and kept it in their pockets." Similarly, historian Rob Ruck concluded, the Grays and Crawfords "prospered within a black community that supported them with cheers and spare change and looked to them for recreation and a source of identity."[51]

Nightclubs and after-hours spots rounded out the cultural life of black Pittsburgh during years between the World Wars. African American musicians performed at clubs like the Hurricane Lounge, the Musicians Club, and the renowned Crawford Grill on Wylie and Centre avenues in the Hill District. In addition to a variety of popular local bands, nationally acclaimed black artists like Duke Ellington, Lena Horne, Count Basie, Cab Calloway, and others also performed in the city's black community. One local musician, Judge Warren Watson, later explained the appeal of Pittsburgh's black night life: African Americans in Pittsburgh "were hard-working mill workers five days a week. On Friday night, they wanted to go out and get a single and a beer and have a good time, something maybe Saturday, and sober up on Sunday and get ready to go back to the mill and breathe in all this heat [and] dust."[52]

Buoyed by their expanding network of community-based institutions and informal cultural interactions, African Americans increased their demands for full citizenship rights. From the end of the Civil War through the Great Depression, the Republican Party retained a commanding sway over politics in Pittsburgh, western Pennsylvania, and the state. The powerful partnership of Republicans Christopher Magee and William Flinn, the so-called Magee-Flinn machine, attracted black votes not only because of the Republican reputation as the party of Lincoln and African American freedom, but because it also delivered lower-rung patronage jobs to African American supporters. As early as 1911, the Magee group "broke all precedents" and appointed a black man, William Randolph Grimes, as the assistant solicitor for the city of Pittsburgh. This position represented the highest political post blacks had ever occupied in the city's history. A year later, African Americans gained significant employment as laborers removing "the HUMP," a three-block-long hill that obstructed vehicular and pedestrian traffic in the triangle area of the Central Business District.[53]

Despite evidence of material gain through their alliance with the Republican machine, African Americans expressed increasing dissatisfaction with the party's record on civil rights and took steps to elect members of their own group to public office. In 1919, African Americans elected Robert H. Logan to city council. While he served only one term, his victory accented the efforts of Pittsburgh blacks to transform segregation into a base of political empowerment and counter the Republican Party's neglect of its black constituency. According to Robert Vann of the *Pittsburgh Courier*, Logan's election represented "a solid bloc" effort of black voters. After suffering defeat in his own bid to become judge of the

Court of Common Pleas of Allegheny County in 1921, Vann expressed even greater urgency for black voters to mobilize in their own interests: "It is better to elect a Negro generally speaking than ANY white man ... [far] better to have a Negro speaking in [the race's] behalf than any white man." By 1927, Pittsburgh blacks had formed the Third Ward Voters' League under the leadership of Walter C. Rainey, and soon claimed a membership of some five thousand black voters. Black people outnumbered whites in the third ward and expressed a determination to create more jobs and public offices for blacks through aggressive participation in electoral politics.[54]

The civil rights campaigns and programs of the NAACP and Urban League strengthened the electoral activities of the African American community. Established in 1915, the Pittsburgh branch of the NAACP had its origins in local and national protests against screenings of the racist film, *Birth of a Nation*. The local branch waged struggles against racial injustice in all areas of African American life in the Pittsburgh region. In 1921, Rev. J. C. Austin, pastor of Ebenezer Baptist Church, became president of the Pittsburgh branch of the NAACP. Under Austin's leadership, the group pushed for the employment of black teachers, the admission of black students to previously all-white schools, passage of new state civil rights laws, an end to labor union discrimination, and termination of police harassment of black workers. Police arrested migrants as vagrants, the branch protested, for the purpose of forcing them "back to the flames of the torturing South."[55]

Formed in 1918, the Urban League of Pittsburgh (ULP) took the lead in helping black workers make the transition to life in the industrial city. John T. Clark directed the ULP from 1918 to 1926. He had earned his bachelor of arts degree from Ohio State University, taught high school in Louisville, Kentucky, and headed the housing department of the National Urban League headquarters in New York City. Alonzo Thayer, who served as director from 1927 to 1930, received degrees from Avery Normal Institute in Charleston, South Carolina, and Fisk University in Tennessee. Before coming to Pittsburgh, he also served as director of the Atlanta Urban League. The ULP not only played a mediating role in the black workers' relations with employers, landlords, and the schools, but also with law enforcement institutions as well. Local courts sometimes employed ULP staffers to investigate cases of criminal misconduct among southern newcomers and helped to reduce the number of African Americans incarcerated for certain crimes.[56]

From the outset of the Great Migration, black women influenced the political and civil rights struggles of the black community. As president of the Negro Women's Equal Franchise Federation, Daisy Lampkin influenced the political life of blacks in Pittsburgh and the nation. Born in Washington DC in 1883, Daisy Adams Lampkin moved to Pittsburgh in 1909. She married restaurant proprietor William Lampkin and soon became active in local politics. By 1912, she had launched her political career as part of the suffrage movement. Lampkin participated in street-corner campaigns designed to organize black women into political clubs and, in 1915, she became the third president of the Negro Women's Equal Franchise Federation, founded in 1911. After participating in the campaign to gain women's suffrage, Lampkin held positions as local chair of the Allegheny County Negro Women's Republican League, vice-chair of the Negro Voters League, and vice-chair of the Colored Voters Division of the Republican National Committee. As historian Edna McKenzie has noted, "Only six years after American women gained the vote, she was elected as an alternate delegate at large to the national Republican Party convention, a stellar achievement for any black or woman of that era." In 1929, the national office of the NAACP praised Lampkin for her "outstanding" work with the Pittsburgh branch. Lampkin helped to make the Pittsburgh chapter "one of the strong branches of the association." Under her leadership, the branch had added two thousand new members in a recent membership campaign.[57]

Despite substantial racial solidarity in their civil rights and political struggles during the 1920s, African American community-building activities entailed significant internal social and political conflicts. The Methodist and Baptist churches absorbed growing numbers of newcomers and experienced rising internal class and cultural tensions and conflicts. While the city's black elite (including disproportionate numbers of light-skinned blacks) most often belonged to the Congregational, Presbyterian, and Episcopalian bodies, they were also prominent in the city's oldest black church, the Bethel Methodist Episcopal Church, located in the Hill District. Under the leadership of college- and seminary-trained black ministers, old elite residents also dominated Homestead's black Clark Memorial Baptist Church. Clark Memorial built a new church and a community center; adopted the newest techniques in administering the religious, social, and business affairs of the church; and experienced increasing cleavage between old and new residents. Even before the onset of World War I, some of the church's newcomers had articulated the need for a place of worship of their own and founded the Second Baptist Church.[58]

Unlike Clark Memorial, the ministers at Homestead's Second Baptist were not seminary trained. The church adhered closely to matters of the spirit in its worship services and it did not have a community center. While sermons at Clark Memorial stressed both spiritual and temporal issues, including "God's Idea of Segregation," those at Second Baptist talked about the church as a "Blessing in the World," a "New Heart," and the "Character of the Holy Spirit." Southern migrants shared stories about the cold treatment they received in established churches. Only in the churches with "down home" preaching and ways of greeting did newcomers feel comfortable or at home. As one woman put it, "The women, especially the older women—they were so friendly—they put their arms around me and made me feel so welcome." Another said he liked "the way they do, talk, and everything—so I joined." One college-educated black woman later told a Works Progress Administration field worker how old elite residents of the city refused to "mix with the new families. They weren't good enough. I remember my mother telling about her and her sisters peeking out the windows to see Southern people going by to church."[59]

In the Civil Rights and political movements of the black community, the Universal Negro Improvement Association (UNIA) and, to some extent, the Communist Party offered African American workers alternatives to the Urban League, NAACP, and Republican Party. As early as 1928, black steelworker Ben Careathers took a prominent part in a labor rally for William Z. Foster, presidential candidate of the Communist Party. Handbills advertising the event also highlighted Careathers as one of the featured speakers. The *Pittsburgh Courier* explained the Communist Party's appeal to black workers: "The Communist stand on the Negro question differs from the one taken by the rest of the parties . . . [T]hey make the Negro question a special issue demanding full social and racial equality, for the Negroes, the abolition of all Jim Crow laws . . . [and] the removal of all discriminations against Negroes in the trade unions."[60]

The UNIA proved even more attractive to African Americans than did the Communist Party. Under the banner of "Race First," Marcus Garvey and the UNIA advocated the unity of black people across geographical and national boundaries. Garvey visited Pittsburgh on several occasions and delivered speeches to sizable crowds. Following Garvey's visit to the city in September 1919, the *Negro World* reported, the UNIA had "captured" Pittsburgh during a mass meeting at the Rodman Street Baptist Church, located at the intersection of Sheridan and Collins Avenue. Less than a year later, Garvey came to Pittsburgh again and soon told a New York assembly about his visit. In his words, he had yet to witness "in any section of the U.N.I.A. anything to beat the enthusiasm of Pittsburgh."[61]

In the postwar years, after hearing Marcus Garvey speak on the need for race pride and independence for people of African descent, Matthew Dempsey, an unemployed steelworker, organized a local chapter of the UNIA in Aliquippa, Pennsylvania. The Klan had recently burned crosses, held marches, and delivered inflammatory speeches against blacks and immigrants in the town. Dempsey also hoped to use the UNIA to combat discriminatory hiring practices in the steel industry. When the Jones and Laughlin Steel Company discovered the Garvey-inspired activities of Dempsey and another steelworker, management fired the two men. According to R. B. Spencer, an FBI agent from the Pittsburgh district, steel management officials were "very anxious to see Garvey tried and convicted in order that his influence among the Negroes at the Jones and Laughlin plant will disappear."[62]

While some black leaders actively discouraged the UNIA in the Pittsburgh region, others boldly supported the organization. Rev. J. C. Austin became the most prominent clergyman supporting the Garvey cause. He not only allowed members to use his church for meetings, but invited UNIA leaders to speak from his pulpit at the Ebenezer Baptist Church. In 1923, Austin also delivered the opening address at the UNIA's International Convention, where he "received a loud and enthusiastic greeting" when he addressed the gathering as "my beloved yoke fellows in tribulation and co-partners in this struggle for freedom and justice."[63] Despite advice from some of his fellow black clergymen to bar Garveyites from his church, Rev. G. W. Gaines at John Wesley AME Zion Church supported the activities of the UNIA and explained, "If radicalism meant telling the truth, he was glad to have Garvey with him."[64]

Intra-racial conflicts also played out in the leisure-time life of the African American community. Black professional and business people often criticized black wage earners for the way they used their newfound earnings and time off. One Urban League report blamed single men "with money to spare" for the spread of prostitution among urban blacks. In 1924, John T. Clark, executive director of the local Urban League, described the same group of men as "the more irresponsible type." These men made "more money than they ever have in their life," Clark said, but they lacked proper "cultural wants for which to spend their money." Therefore, in his view, they engaged in unhealthy leisure-time pursuits, including gambling and excessive drinking. In a column titled "Wylie Avenue," the *Pittsburgh Courier* identified unlicensed night clubs as perhaps the most dangerous spots for "fights, brawls, and the worst form of disorders."[65]

Gender divisions also punctuated the community building, civil rights, and political activities of African Americans in Pittsburgh. In her study of gender conventions within Pittsburgh's black community during the early to mid-twentieth century, Ancella Livers documents extensive evidence of gender discrimination within the black urban community. Black women sometimes openly remarked about the constraints black men placed on their efforts to assume leadership positions. In October 1929, in a letter to Walter White of the national office of the NAACP, Daisy Lampkin protested "men holding the leadership in the branches, and they [women] having all of the work to do." She also said, "the men seem to have no interest, and function only when the women force them. The more I see of our men throughout the country, the more I wonder as to the future of our race." The Pittsburgh Urban League developed numerous programs targeted to meet the special needs of black women. In its own professional staff positions, however, women received significantly less pay than their male counterparts. Similarly, the *Pittsburgh Courier* praised black women's achievements but sometimes presented sexual stereotypes of black women in its columns.[66] Intra-racial tensions and conflicts persisted throughout the interwar years, but, during the Depression and World War II, African Americans bridged their differences and created their own New Deal in the city of Pittsburgh.

Forging a New Deal

During the Great Depression, white workers insisted that their interests take precedence over those of African Americans. Skilled tradesmen pledged to introduce for membership only, "sober, industrious white person[s]." In 1933, at Montefiore Hospital, an assistant superintendent trained a crew of white women elevator operators and dismissed black women for "gross inefficiency," although some of the women had worked there since the facility opened in 1929, and none had worked there for less than a year. A year later, the Allegheny Steel Company in Breckenridge replaced its black workers with whites. The company argued that black workers' gambling, bootlegging, and disturbances justified the decision.[67]

In February 1934, African Americans made up 40 percent of the county's unemployed workers, and had over 43 percent of their numbers on relief compared to 15.7 percent for whites. At the same time, employers of household labor expressed a growing preference for white women and weakened African American women's access to traditional avenues of female employment. In a report to the national office, the Metropolitan YWCA of Pittsburgh acknowledged how young women from Centre Avenue in the Hill District "felt the full brunt of the depression. Low pay, long hours, discrimination and the ever present formula 'last to be hired, first to be fired.'" Among black Depression-era workers who retained their jobs, a Duquesne worker declared: "The colored has a hard way to go. They . . . bawl you out and make you work fast [!]"[68]

The Urban League of Pittsburgh urged employers to retain black women domestic workers by setting up a four- to eight-week course designed to train young black women "how to cook, serve, tend children, drive a car, and in general to make the job of houseworkers attractive and respectable." Following graduation from high school during the mid-1930s, Thelma Lovette Sr., recalled taking a job as a dishwasher at the Ruskin Avenue Apartments in Oakland. She earned $10 per week for over twelve hours of work per day. She washed dishes by hand for over one hundred people. Lovette soon moved out of dishwashing to "salad girl" and finally to "pastry cook." From her father, she said, "I learned that hard work will make you learn a lot of things."[69]

Pittsburgh blacks complained along with their brothers and sisters across the country that they received a "Raw Deal" rather than a "New Deal" from their government. The Federal Housing Administration refused to guarantee mortgages in racially integrated neighborhoods, and New Deal economic and labor legislation—the Social Security Act, National Recovery Act, and the Wagner Labor Relations Act—excluded general laborers and domestic service employees from benefits like the minimum wage and hour codes. When African American workers, the NAACP, and National Urban League protested the exclusion of unskilled and semiskilled workers and proposed a nondiscriminatory clause in the new labor law, white labor leaders defeated the measure. According to Wagner's assistant, Leon Keyserling, "The American Federation of Labor fought bitterly to eliminate this clause and much against his will Senator Wagner had to consent to elimination in order to prevent scuttling of the entire bill."[70] As late as 1939, the Allegheny County Works Progress Administration programs continued to discriminate against African Americans. According to Reginald A. Johnson, secretary of the ULP's department of industrial relations, decisions made by foremen and minor supervisory staff for WPA projects "proved a handicap to the employment of Negroes" in Pittsburgh and Allegheny County. In addition to establishing a domestic service training project for black workers, the ULP pushed for a quota or "percentage clause" for black employment on federal projects, particularly public housing projects.[71]

By the late 1930s, several factors enabled African Americans to transform what they called a "Raw Deal" into a "New Deal." These forces included the emergence of the CIO, the Communist Party, increasing social services of New Deal programs, and the growing political unity of the black community itself. Although the Communist Party in Pittsburgh claimed only a few hundred members at the height of its influence during the late 1920s and early 1930s, a few blacks joined the party and took highly visible positions in party affairs. During the mid-1930s, the CIO's Steel Workers Organizing Committee (SWOC) turned to the Communist Party for organizers, including black workers from the Pittsburgh district. In a rally on Pittsburgh's North Side, Phillip Murray, director of the Steel Workers Organizing Committee and vice president of the United Mine Workers of America (UMWA), urged black workers to pour their heart, mind, body, blood, and soul into the "great crusade to organize the colored workers employed in the great steel industry."[72]

For its organizing drive in steel, the CIO soon recruited black Communists Ernest McKinney, Ben Careathers, and William Scarville. During the early Depression years, Ernest McKinney, the grandson of an active member of the UMWA, joined a splinter group of the Communist Party and participated in demonstrations on behalf of unemployed workers in Pittsburgh. Originally from the Chattanooga, Tennessee, area, Ben Careathers migrated to Pittsburgh before World War I; in succession he worked as a janitor and helper on the railroads, opened an upholstery shop, and joined the Socialist and then the Communist Party by the early 1930s. He also participated in the Communist Party's unemployed councils. The black Pullman porter William Scarville also joined the Communist Party in Pittsburgh and became well known in the circle of white communists in western Pennsylvania. As Croatian immigrant and Communist Steve Nelson recalled: "One of the things about the Pittsburgh Party that impressed me most was the small group of black

Communists there. . . . It was out of respect for workers like Scarville that young Communists in Pittsburgh developed a fuller understanding of racism."[73]

African American Communist Party members believed Communists offered the best hope for obtaining important leadership positions and overcoming racial injustice in America. In their view, compared to the two mainstream parties, the Communist Party was more committed to the eradication of racism and the extension of equal opportunity to black people. The Communist Party, Benjamin Careathers later recalled, provided blacks a strong platform for advocating for "peace, economic security, Negro rights, extension of democratic rights and the need for a Socialist reorganization of society." Careathers also gave the party credit for offering African Americans meaningful opportunities for leadership. With pride, he said, "Phillip Murray placed me on the staff of the Steel Workers Organizing Committee. . . . In that capacity, I led the movement which broke through the company rule in Aliquippa which built the union there. I recruited into the union some 2,000 steel workers while I was an organizer."[74]

The Communist Party's unique willingness to publicly expel members for "anti-Negro" and "anti-Semitic" bias also caught the attention of potential black recruits. For these and other reasons, the *Pittsburgh Courier* concluded, the Communist Party's "stand on the Negro question surely deserves attention and support on the part of every Negro worker." Partly inspired by the Communists, the National Negro Congress (NNC), formed in 1935, brought together a broad cross-section of black religious, civic, and political organizations. In 1936, the Pittsburgh chapter of the NNC sponsored a planning conference, including national leaders like T. Arnold Hill of the Urban League and A. Philip Randolph of the Brotherhood of Sleeping Car Porters (BSCP), as well as Pittsburghers Robert L. Vann, Bishop William J. Walls of the Allegheny Annual Conference of the AME Zion Church, and Reverend T. J. King, then pastor of Ebenezer Baptist Church. Black religious leaders offered their churches as a base for organizing black workers and promoting their movement into unions, while Robert L. Vann "pledged the full support of the *Pittsburgh Courier* to the steel drive and declared that it would expose in its pages those Negroes who betrayed the best interests of their people by supporting the bosses."[75]

Vann captured the changing political consciousness of African Americans in Pittsburgh and the nation when he penned his renowned

1932 editorial urging blacks to abandon the party of Lincoln. "My friends," he said, "go turn Lincoln's picture to the wall. That debt is paid in full." Two years earlier, African Americans had already escalated their push for elective office in the city's Hill District when they rallied behind attorney Theron B. Hamilton for election to the state legislature from the city's first district on the Republican ticket, but Republican mayor Charles Kline rejected Hamilton. In order to counteract this growing challenge from blacks within the party, Republican leaders supported another black candidate, Walter E. Tucker. Hamilton remained on the ballot as an independent candidate, but both African American candidates lost to their white opponents, Joseph Marcus and J. R. Lynch, respectively, in the primary. The combined total of votes received by the black candidates, however, exceeded the votes for the two white candidates. In his assessment of the election, sociologist Rollo Turner described the election as an illustration of the "long-standing tactic of 'divide and conquer' used innumerable times by white politicians when their power or authority is challenged or threatened by a unified group of blacks." When the victorious white candidate for the legislature died just after the primary, the Republican Party endorsed Tucker who won in the general election. Thus, Tucker became the city's first black state representative. He covered the predominantly black third and fifth wards.[76]

In 1931, the Robert H. Terrell Law Club passed a resolution (endorsed by the Keystone Civic and Political League of the Thirteenth Ward) urging African Americans to vote only for candidates who supported the interests of the black community, including the election of blacks to public office as aldermen, employment as policemen, and access to training in the medical field as physicians and nurses. During the same year, in the fifth ward, African Americans challenged Irish and Italian control of the ward and won. Robert H. Logan gained election to city council and Earl Sams became constable on the Republican slate.[77]

In 1934, NAACP president and attorney Homer S. Brown was elected to the state legislature from the Hill District's third and fifth wards. A graduate of the University of Pittsburgh's Law School, Brown ran as an Independent, but he soon declared himself a Democrat, joined forces with Democratic governor George Earle, and pushed for a "Little New Deal for Pennsylvania" and its black citizens, particularly black workers. When the state legislature passed the McGinnis Labor Relations Bill, which sanctioned the provisions of the National Labor Relations Act (or Wagner Act), Brown did what national leaders had failed to do; he obtained an amendment that penalized unions excluding members on the basis of color or race. Although the AFL put up a vigorous fight to defeat the amendment, the Brown provision gained support from the CIO and passed into law in May 1937.[78]

Under Brown's leadership, the Pennsylvania legislature enacted a new equal rights law in 1935. The new law banned discrimination on the basis of color in a wide range of institutions: hotels, motels, and barrooms; public parks, bathhouses, and resorts; theaters, orchestras, and dance halls; libraries, schools, and colleges. According to a Pittsburgh WPA Project writer, one black attorney declared the bill was not only "a Declaration of Rights" for black people in the state, but also a victory for all minorities. This law, he said, "may yet be cited as much by Jews and aliens as by Negroes."[79] In February 1937, Brown spearheaded the state legislature's investigation of the hiring policies of the Pittsburgh Board of Education. Subpoenaed members of the board denied discriminating against blacks on the basis of race, but numerous testimonials showed otherwise. In May 1937, Homer Brown vigorously questioned Marcus Aaron, president of the board, about discrimination against qualified black teachers. Aaron denied any wrongdoing and sought to avoid discussing the question of race and employment:

Q: Do you know as a matter of the board's knowledge that there were colored students going through the college and none were appointed?

A: I do know that no colored teachers were appointed.

Q: Do you know that there were some who graduated but were never appointed?

A: No.

Q: Why were none of them appointed?

A: Because they were not recommended to the board for appointment. The statement I read makes the situation clear and I repeat that I have tried to bring out the point that public discussion on this point is harmful to those you are trying to help.

Representative Alfred E. Tronzo, a white member of the state legislature, followed on Brown by questioning Aaron with an equally pointed inquiry designed to expose racial injustice in public education:

Q: Do I get from that colored people should be more interested in making friends than in getting teaching positions?

A: Yes. I think there are a lot more important questions for them to discuss.

Q: Do you think that colored teachers would teach in mixed schools?

A: It depends on the number of white children in the schools and the attitude of the parents. I understand from the investigation which Dr. Graham has made in other cities that if colored teachers are placed in the schools, the parents ask for a change of schools for the children.

Q: Don't you think that that is a matter of education in itself?

A: I think it could be done but it cannot be done in a day.

Q: Should it not have been done back in 1917?

A: I guess it should have been but I cannot tell you that the result would have been satisfactory.[80]

In addition to state and local efforts to end discrimination against black teachers, the National Education Association (NEA) helped to create a climate for change. At its annual meeting, the NEA passed a resolution affirming that teachers should not be discriminated against on the basis of "race, color, belief, residency or economic or marital status." In 1937, under increasing local and national pressure from African Americans and their white supporters, the Pittsburgh Board of Education relented and hired its first black full-time teacher since 1881. The ULP's Committee on Teacher Appointment enthusiastically announced the school board's plans to appoint two black teachers to posts in the Pittsburgh Public Schools during the fall term. Observing a change of attitude on the part of the school board toward the hiring of black teachers, the ULP now believed its principal task would be to locate "properly qualified applicants," and to expand opportunities for teacher training for black students. A similar battle developed in the health field. Unlike the struggle for black teachers, however, the ULP's Health Committee concluded with a call for the development of "a Negro-controlled hospital" as "the most urgent need of our people in Pittsburgh."[81]

African Americans merged their local struggle for economic democracy with the national "Don't Buy Where You Can't Work" campaign. This movement aimed to harness black consumer power to a broader demand for jobs and citizenship rights. In 1933, blacks in Pittsburgh participated in a selective buying campaign against the Atlantic and Pacific (A&P) and Butler grocery stores. Three years later, they formed the

Housewives Cooperative League and continued to pursue "Don't Buy Where You Can't Work" actions. Although two male Urban League officials, William E. Hill and Roy Garvin, initiated the formation of the organization, black women such as Daisy Lampkin, Frances Stewart, and Alma Illery soon took leadership of the organization. The Housewives League urged Pittsburgh's black community to boycott businesses that excluded blacks from employment and/or provided segregated and unequal services. According to the minutes of the organization, the boycott would "open up new avenues of employment in the way of clerks and white collar jobs, and some skilled jobs, break down 'Jim Crowism' in Pittsburgh [and] abolish discourteous discrimination."[82]

Grassroots black activism strengthened African Americans in the electoral arena and enhanced their access to New Deal social programs. By the late 1930s, blacks in Pittsburgh enjoyed disproportionately more benefits from government social programs than whites. Although African Americans made up less than 10 percent of the population, black men and women, respectively, accounted for 23 and 18 percent of all workers receiving emergency relief employment. At the national level, nearly forty-five blacks held appointments in various New Deal agencies and cabinet departments. President Franklin D. Roosevelt appointed Robert L. Vann to a post in the office of the attorney general. Although Vann felt ill at ease in FDR's administration and soon resigned, the "Black Cabinet," as these black advisers were popularly known, enabled African Americans in Pittsburgh and elsewhere to improve their position on a variety of New Deal projects.[83]

World War II and the Struggle for Full Citizenship Rights

Although African Americans in Pittsburgh gained increasing access to the fruits of New Deal social programs in the late 1930s, only the labor shortages of World War II allowed African Americans to regain and expand their foothold in the urban economy. More so than during World War I, African Americans resolved to fight injustice at home and overseas. Their determination received potent expression in the *Pittsburgh Courier's* "Double V" campaign for "Victory Abroad and Victory [Against Discrimination] at Home."[84]

Beginning in the fall of 1941 and continuing through the war years, African Americans in Pittsburgh fought to break down discrimination in all areas of the city. The *Courier* regularly printed front-page stories on the struggle and often compared the fight in Pittsburgh to developments in other cities. In August 1942, for example, the paper called attention to the movement to hire black conductors on street railway cars: "People of Pittsburgh: Do you know that in New York, Negroes are motormen on the city-owned subways? Do you know that Negroes act as motormen and conductors of public vehicles in Detroit, Cleveland, and other large centers?—Yet, in Pittsburgh—especially on Bedford and Centre Avenue cars, where a large percentage of the commuters are colored—NO NE-GROES are being employed for these jobs!"[85]

World War II veterans later remembered the shock of racial segregation below the Mason-Dixon Line. When the train carrying new recruits from Pittsburgh and other northern cities pulled out of Washington DC, one African American veteran recalled, black and white soldiers were segregated, although some of them had grown up together and were friends. "We put up a fuss but we had to do it." Moreover, as the train

In Pittsburgh and elsewhere, World War II heightened the contradiction between black soldiers fighting for freedom overseas and facing the realities of Jim Crow at home. This photo shows members of the uniformed and armed Ninth U.S. Calvary at a train station, ca. 1941.

Source: Carnegie Museum of Art, Charles "Teenie" Harris Collection, photo #2001.35.6691. Photograph © 2009 Carnegie Museum of Art, Pittsburgh.

Tuskegee Airman James T. Wiley, wearing his light-colored U.S. Army uniform, c. 1944.

Source: Carnegie Museum of Art, Charles "Teenie" Harris Collection, photo #2001.35.38389. Photograph © 2009 Carnegie Museum of Art, Pittsburgh.

neared the town of Rocky Mount, North Carolina, the officer told black soldiers to lie down on the floor, warning them local whites would soon throw "bricks and pop bottles" through the windows, "and sure enough they did." In a letter to the Homestead *Daily Messenger*, another black serviceman from Pittsburgh described on- and off-base discrimination at a southern military installation. In addition to harassment from local whites, the black soldier confronted racial segregation in public transportation facilities, as well as in hotels, theaters, restaurants, and other places of amusement and business. The editor of the *Daily Messenger* articulated the soldier's frustration: "These boys, whether white or black, are Americans. They are willing and eager to take up arms so that freedom and democracy may come through victoriously against our enemies. Yet, . . . how democratic are southern states [?]"[86]

Racial segregation and conflict also punctuated the streets, schools, and workplaces of wartime Pittsburgh, Homestead, and other towns and cities along the three rivers. Despite passage of the state's equal rights law of 1935, Pittsburgh owners of commercial establishments and public accommodations resisted enforcement of the measure. In the city's fifth ward alone, between 1939 and 1949, some twenty-seven cases of discrimination reached municipal and county courts. According to legal historian Martha Foy, the defendants in these cases included twelve combined drinking and eating places; six restaurants; two beer gardens; one swimming pool; one skating rink; and the bar of a hotel. Some proprietors of these establishments defended themselves by declaring "there would be trouble if white waitresses were called to wait on Negro diners." There were no convictions in these cases and plaintiffs often had to pay court costs or split costs with the accused.[87]

One large amusement park openly defied public accommodation laws against racial discrimination. Management announced that it would "positively not allow Negroes" to use the dance halls or swimming pools, "except when there are Negro picnics." The proprietor expressed confidence there was not a jury in the state that would find him guilty. Within a year of the law's passage, the city council of Avalon, north of Pittsburgh, passed a law designating certain days for African American use of the municipal pool. Councilmen defended their actions on the premise the pool was not a public facility. The owner of a Pittsburgh skating rink not only continued to bar African Americans from use of the facility, but threatened violence against any blacks who attempted to use the rink. While judges generally upheld the state's equal rights law when such cases reached the courts, a visiting judge dismissed the skating case, arguing that the plaintiff, supported by the American Youth Council, a liberal, left-wing organization, had unlawfully instigated the confrontation as a test case. According to *The WPA History of the Negro in Pittsburgh*, while African Americans frequently won judgments against small establishments, the larger and more expensive places of leisure remained openly segregated or refused service to black people. Visiting black conventioneers invariably had to find housing in private homes and black-owned or -operated hotels and boarding houses.[88]

The Hill District continued to be a predominantly black community, and just after World War II, nearly 97 percent of Lower Hill residents rented their homes compared to about 75 percent in the Polish Hill area and just over 50 percent for Italians in Bloomfield. Most wartime newcomers, however, crowded into an area on the city's South Side called Beltzhoover, where the housing was poor for whites and even more so for blacks. By the end of World War II, the percentage of housing through-out Pittsburgh described as substandard stood at 30 percent of all black units compared to 12.3 percent of white ones.[89]

Steel plant expansion projects forced black and white workers to seek homes elsewhere under the pressure of wartime production. In Homestead, most blacks lived in the path of company plans to add sev-eral open-hearth furnaces, a plate mill, and a forge and machine shop to its operations. In January 1942, the company demolished more than 60 percent of the 1,200 homes in the area, and only about 10 percent of the 10,000 residents of the area remained. Similarly, in Duquesne, African Americans in the town's Castle Garden community were disproportion-ately affected by plans to add three electric furnaces, a conditioning plant, and a heat-treating mill. An estimated 2,900 people lost their homes. The unequal displacement of black workers from these areas placed tremen-dous pressure on the existing housing market.[90]

The emergence of federally funded low-income housing projects al-leviated some of the housing problems of Pittsburgh blacks, but rein-forced racially segregated neighborhoods. Through the "neighborhood composition rule," federal policy makers sanctioned racially separate public housing projects for blacks and whites. Federal Housing Admin-istration (FHA) guidelines prohibited the financing of racially integrated housing until the U.S. Supreme Court declared such rules unconstitu-tional in 1948. By 1945, African Americans made up about 40 percent of Pittsburgh's federally funded public housing projects, including Bed-ford Dwellings, Addison Terrace, Allequippa Terrace, and Wadsworth Terrace, among others. While some of these projects housed both black and white families, from the late 1930s through the 1950s, the Pittsburgh Housing Authority (PHA) maintained segregated housing within the projects. Thus, a building or set of buildings was set aside in each devel-opment for African American families while other buildings were set aside for white families. Despite this segregation, public housing repre-sented a significant improvement for many black families over the old, dilapidated housing available for rent in the Hill District and other black enclaves during the Depression years.[91]

Institutional and residential segregation strengthened the spread of racially segregated schools. During World War II, African Americans made up about 10 percent of all public school children, but experienced increasing separation from their white counterparts. At the city's Watt, McKelvey, and Franklin Elementary schools, for example, black children made up nearly 99 percent of the total. Yet, by the end of the war, the Pittsburgh Board of Education had hired only two full-time black teachers. In June 1940, a recent graduate of the predominantly white Westinghouse High School said teachers were fair for the most part, although, as he put it, they "naturally liked the white children better." At the Heron Hill Junior High School, a teacher discouraged another black student from preparing for a career in business and commerce, "because there was no opportunity for Negroes in Pittsburgh in that field and he would have to go south to get a job."[92]

African Americans routinely hit glass ceilings, no matter what kind of employment they pursued. One particularly revealing case was that of Gerald Fox, who spent most of the 1930s and 1940s working in almost every sector of Pittsburgh's low-paid service and industrial jobs. After dropping out of high school, Fox became, in turn, a drugstore porter, a restaurant bus boy, a hotel bus boy and shoe shine, a fry cook, a country club bus boy, waiter, room service provider, and then bartender. During World War II, Fox got work in a munitions plant, working twelve hours a day in very hot temperatures. He eventually had to leave this industrial job because it was so physically debilitating.[93]

In 1942, according to the Commonwealth of Pennsylvania's *Final Report of the Pennsylvania State Temporary Commission on the Conditions of the Urban Colored Population*, 50 percent of Pittsburgh firms barred blacks from employment or relegated them to the lowest rungs of their employment ladder. These firms included the Pennsylvania Bell Telephone Company, the U.S. Chromium Company, Westinghouse Air Brake Company, and the Pittsburgh Street Railway Company.[94] By war's end, nearly 40 percent of all Allegheny County employers continued to bar black applicants. After Superior, Columbia, Bethlehem, and other area steel plants turned down black applicants in 1942, the Pittsburgh Urban League lamented, "there are still plants in this area which refuse to hire Negroes even at common labor."[95] As late as May 1945, at the United Bronze Casting Company, a personnel manager turned a black applicant away, saying that white workers would not work with a black person because of "a prejudice among white workers which the company had not been able to overcome." In 1942, the Pittsburgh Steel Band Company openly confined African Americans to jobs as "janitors and window washers."[96]

As alluded to previously, the city's railway and bus system routinely denied African Americans jobs as motormen and drivers. In December

1944, in a meeting with civil rights organizations, Charles D. Palmer, transportation manager, told the group "flatly" that the company "would not hire Negroes." For its part, the Pittsburgh Railways Union also resisted the employment of blacks on the premise that some 300 of its 2,400 men would immediately walk out on strike in protest. In March 1945, the War Manpower Office ceased to refer job seekers to the Pittsburgh Railway Company until the firm agreed to hire operators "regardless of race, creed, or color."[97]

African American women observed white women entering defense industry work, while they remained unemployed. In a letter to FDR, a Pittsburgh woman described the employment practices of two nearby defense industry plants, "They will hire the white girls but when the colored girls go there they always refuse them."[98] In a letter to Patrick T. Fagan, area director of the War Manpower Commission, George E. Denmar, secretary of the Urban League of Pittsburgh, criticized the American Bridge Company for steadfastly refusing to employ black women in production jobs, even as growing numbers of white women gained training and employment in such jobs as "welders and burners." Several black women—Thelma Oldston, Lillian Williams, Mildred Tucker, and Naomie Smith—had visited the company's office three or more times but were disappointed that: "White women by the dozens of all ages, shapes, and sizes were being employed but there was no place for Negro women [except to clean lavatories]."[99] About forty black men in production jobs at the facility signed a petition urging the company, "to employ women of the Colored race." The petition stated, "There are many Colored women equipped to perform duties in your company and also eligible for the training that you are giving to white [female] job applicants . . . Negro women . . . can do other jobs beside clean lavatories. They should be in production, too."[100]

Pittsburgh blacks responded to wartime injustices by joining the national March on Washington Movement (MOWM). Under the leadership of A. Philip Randolph of the Brotherhood of Sleeping Car Porters, the MOWM emerged in 1941 following a meeting of civil rights groups in Chicago. The critical moment came when a black woman angrily addressed the chair: "Mr. Chairman . . . we ought to throw 50,000 Negroes around the White House, bring them from all over the country, in jalopies, in trains and any way they can get there, and throw them around the White House and keep them there until we can get some action from the White House." A. Philip Randolph not only seconded the proposal but offered himself and the BSCP as leaders: "I agree with the sister. I will be very happy to throw [in] my organization's resources and offer myself as a leader of such a movement."[101]

By early June, the MOWM had established march headquarters in Harlem, Brooklyn, Washington DC, Detroit, Chicago, St. Louis, San Francisco, and Pittsburgh, among other metropolitan areas. The Brotherhood of Sleeping Car Porters listed only about two hundred Pittsburgh-area porters among its membership, but the movement soon joined forces with local NAACP and Urban League chapters, churches, and fraternal orders. The *Black Worker*, the official organ of the BSCP, became the official newspaper of the MOWM. The paper's May issue reprinted the official call to march: "We call upon you to fight for jobs in National Defense. We call upon you to struggle for the integration of Negroes in the armed forces . . . of the Nation. . . . We call upon you to demonstrate for the abolition of Jim Crowism in all Government departments and defense employment. . . . The Federal Government cannot with a clear conscience call upon private industry and labor unions to abolish discrimination based upon race and color so long as it practices discrimination itself against Negro Americans."[102]

President Franklin D. Roosevelt resisted the movement as long as he could, but the MOWM finally produced results. Roosevelt met A. Philip Randolph and Walter White of the NAACP on 18 June 1941. A week later, on 24 June 1941, FDR issued Executive Order 8802, banning racial discrimination in government employment, defense industries, and training programs. The order also established the Fair Employment Practice Committee (FEPC) to implement its provisions. The government empowered FEPC to receive, investigate, and address complaints of racial discrimination in the national defense program.[103]

In Pittsburgh, under the influence of FEPC and wartime production, African Americans exceeded their previous standing in the industrial labor force, gradually gaining greater access to skilled and semiskilled production jobs in industry with government contracts. In February 1943, the FEPC established an office in Pittsburgh and helped to make an even more diverse range of jobs available to black people. When the office opened, Walter S. Buchanan, cochairman of the committee, suggested that the FEPC would open up new areas of employment to African Americans, including jobs as motormen for the Pittsburgh Railway Company. The following year, in April 1944, Patrick T. Fagan announced that this goal had indeed been achieved. By August, five African Americans operated "regular runs" for the company, with several more "in training." At the Carnegie-Illinois Steel Company, in March 1944, Milo Manley, an FEPC examiner, enthusiastically reported the promotion of blacks "into jobs never before held by Negroes" in some departments.[104]

The wartime black freedom struggle gained significant support from a small group of liberal white allies. Executive Order 8802 linked blacks in the Pittsburgh region even more closely to the Democratic Party and helped to situate blacks more firmly within the predominately white labor-liberal coalition. The CIO often supported the FEPC claims of black workers and helped them to break many barriers to higher-level employment. At its annual convention in 1941, for example, the CIO denounced racial discrimination as a "direct attack against our nation's policy to build democracy in our fight against Hitlerism." A year later, the organization established its own Committee to Abolish Racial Discrimination and urged its affiliates to support national policy against discrimination: "When a decision to employ minority group workers is made, the union must be prepared to stand behind it."[105]

In addition to participation in the civil rights and political activities of the NAACP, Urban League, and CIO, white activists also helped to spearhead the formation of new civil rights organizations and initiatives such as the Pittsburgh Interracial Action Council (PIAC) and the race work of the Citizens Coordinating Committee of the National Defense Program. In 1941, according to Edward D. Porter, PIAC and NAACP member, white students at the University of Pittsburgh formed the PIAC after they observed the exclusion of a black veteran from service at a local restaurant. By the end of World War II, the organization claimed credit for helping to end racial discrimination at about twenty-five Pittsburgh-area restaurants.[106]

As early as 1943, the Citizens Coordinating Committee of the national defense program urged the city's railway system to employ African American workers as motormen. During his campaign for mayor in 1945, David L. Lawrence promised to establish a special council to foster peace and cooperation among the city's diverse population. "When elected Mayor of Pittsburgh," Lawrence said, "I shall immediately establish a Pittsburgh Unity Council with representatives of the Protestant, Catholic and Jewish faiths, of labor and management, of Negroes, of youth, of education and of social and civic affairs." Shortly after taking office, Lawrence kept his promise and set up the Civic Unity Council with power to investigate cases of discrimination and offer remedies "so that conditions which cause racial tensions may be eliminated."[107]

At the end of World War II, the U.S. Congress failed to renew the FEPC. As the war came to a close, African Americans experienced a revival of explicitly racial advertising for job openings. Many area firms reverted "to type" and reestablished prewar hiring practices. Such industrial plants adopted, as the *Pittsburgh Courier* reported, "a 'white only' or 'Christian' only policy" following termination of their war contracts. The *Courier* also lamented, "many of these plants are in the process of reconversion and apparently have decided to ignore thousands of workers of various racial or religious creed who worked so faithfully during war production." S. Chapman Wright, assistant War Manpower director for the region, confirmed that some war contractors had returned to their old policies. They could now "hire at the gate and [since they] hold no war contracts, they can tell us they don't need us and there's nothing we can do." At the same time, the United States Employment Service (USES) decided to respect such "white only" requests from employers.[108]

Labor and civil rights activism persisted through the war years, but its intensity waned as plans for demobilization got underway. By war's end, according to activist Sophia B. Nelson, the Pittsburgh branch of the NAACP had declined, "from an active one which entertained the Nat[ional] N.A.A.C.P. Conference in 1931" to one that could hardly convene a board meeting. In 1944, Edward Porter, chair of the NAACP's local membership drive, blamed inactivity and lack of cooperation among officers of the organization for failure of the year's membership campaign.[109] Two years later, when the federal government failed to renew the FEPC and the Pittsburgh branch office closed, an important pillar of the city's interracial alliance for social justice disappeared. Labor and civil rights activists found it increasingly difficult to sustain their activities as the city and nation moved toward the cold war era.[110]

2

New Migrations, Renaissance I, and the Challenge to Jim Crow

Pittsburgh entered a prolonged period of economic and population decline during the years after World War II. The city lost increasing numbers of jobs and people to the suburbs, the South, the Southwest, and to overseas expansion of manufacturing production. During this time, Pittsburgh's black population increased and gained a larger share of the city's total, but African Americans confronted the persistence of racially biased employment policies; structural limits on their economic mobility; and enduring barriers to where they could live and educate their children. The city's black residents responded to these constraints by intensifying their demands for equal access to jobs, housing, education, and a variety of human services and public accommodations. Their postwar movement for social change gained increasing focus in the rise of the modern Civil Rights and Black Power movements.[1]

Migration, Industrial Decline, and Economic Inequality

Global competition, technological change, and shifting federal investment policies transformed Pittsburgh's socioeconomic, class, ethnic, and race relations during the 1950s and 1960s. The U.S. share of the world's steel market, dominated by the Pittsburgh region, plunged from 54 percent at the end of World War II to 20 percent in 1970. The city's value added from manufacturing employment dropped from 47 to 38 percent during the same period.[2] Pittsburgh's total population decreased from nearly 700,000 in 1950 to just over 500,000 in 1970. This represented a loss of about 11 percent during the 1950s and 14 percent during the 1960s. Young people between the ages of twenty and thirty-nine left the city and region in growing numbers, while the city's immigrant population continued to drop—from 85,000 during the 1940s to just over 45,000 during the 1960s (see table 1). In June 1963, a local housing study concluded that Pittsburgh needed more than forty thousand new jobs annually in order to arrest economic decline and maintain its current population level.[3]

The city's largest employers confronted increasing foreign competition for their products. European producers already created competition for steel made in the United States, but during the postwar years, Taiwan, Korea, and Brazil became major steel-producing countries as well. At the same time, the Basic Oxygen Furnace (BOF) and electrical steel-producing processes displaced older, labor-intensive "open-hearth" furnaces. The BOF produced a batch of steel in less than one hour and dramatically reduced the demand for industrial labor. Conversely, the open-hearth process required six to twelve hours to perform the same job. During the late 1940s and early 1950s, open-hearth methods had accounted for over 90 percent of U.S. steel production. By 1970, the United States produced some forty-eight million tons of steel using the open-hearth methods, while steel produced by BOF and electrical processes together increased from only a few million tons in 1958 to 83.5 million tons by the late 1960s.[4]

Government investment policies also weakened the steel industry and the manufacturing sector of the Pittsburgh region. Whereas the federal government favored steel producers during the interwar years, it now increasingly favored aerospace, electronic, computer, and similar firms relying on synthetic rather than metal products. The West Coast and South emerged as major centers of these new industries. During the 1950s alone, California increased its share of defense spending by 21 percent, while the southern region showed an increase of 13 percent. Meanwhile, the Pittsburgh-based U.S. Steel Corporation diminished its own vitality by opening up expensive new sources of iron ore in northern Canada at a time of steady decline in market demand for steel and metal products.

The city's other major employers (most notably H. J. Heinz Company, Alcoa, Gulf, and Westinghouse) responded to escalating global competition and technological change by internationalizing large portions of their operations. By the 1960s, the international units of these corporations accounted for about 35 percent of their profits.[5]

In order to arrest economic and demographic decline, the city initiated an ambitious urban redevelopment program known as Renaissance I. Beginning in 1943 and running through the 1960s, Renaissance I was a public-private partnership led by Democratic mayor David L. Lawrence and banker Richard King Mellon. The Allegheny Conference on Community Development (ACCD) became the central planning agency for the city's revival, and focused first and foremost on rebuilding the central business district. The city granted the ACCD permission to demolish numerous buildings and undertake a vigorous reconstruction program. By the late 1960s, the city's Urban Redevelopment Authority (URA) had completed or initiated nineteen renewal projects, particularly the cluster of buildings at the confluence of the three rivers called the "Golden Triangle."[6]

As Pittsburgh's Renaissance I gradually took hold, the second Great Migration stimulated the rapid expansion of Pittsburgh's black population. The African American population in the city increased from 82,500 in 1950, about 12 percent of the total population, to 105,000 in 1970, about 20 percent (see table 1).[7]

Many Pittsburgh families have recollected the period of the Second Great Migration and their arrival in a new city. In the summer of 1941, Will C. Philan, his wife, Ina Mae, and their five-year-old daughter, Ruth, left Lynch, Kentucky, for Pittsburgh. As an adult, Ruth Ward described herself as "a skinny little thing," "wearing Shirley Temple curls" and a cotton dress when she entered the Pennsylvania Station in Pittsburgh with her stepfather and mother. David Blakely said he did not know anything about "a Great Migration," but he got tired of second-class citizenship in the Deep South and moved to Pittsburgh to enjoy a greater measure of freedom. "All I know," he said later from his home in the Homewood-Brushton neighborhood of Pittsburgh, "is I left [Pensacola, Florida] because I was tired of not being able to vote and not being treated like a citizen." Blakely moved first to Manhattan in 1947 and then to Pittsburgh after only a year in New York.[8]

Some postwar African American migrants found Pittsburgh less promising than the places they left. When Betty J. Tillman moved to

Pittsburgh's Redevelopment and Public Housing Program in 1953. This Urban Redevelopment Authority map shows how Renaissance I's economic redevelopment program targeted traditionally minority communities with large-scale development that either created new facilities for nonresidents or internally segregated, later overwhelmingly black, public housing projects.

Source: Housing Authority of the City of Pittsburgh, "A Report to the People: Public Housing in Pittsburgh, 1938–1953" (Pittsburgh: HACP, ca. 1954).

Pittsburgh from Washington DC during the 1960s, she expressed surprise at the small number of blacks in professional and business occupations. She also recalled how some newcomers expressed their keen disappointment by referring to Pittsburgh as the "Mississippi of the North."[9]

The new arrivals had help from the children of the first Great Migration in swelling the size of Pittsburgh's black community during the 1950s and 1960s. Nate Smith, the youngest of four children born to Alabama migrants Luvenia and Noble Smith, was born in the city's Hill District in 1929. At the age of twelve, he ran away from home and joined the Navy, serving for over eighteen months before he returned to Pittsburgh and took a job with his father at the Dormont Theater. Smith later became a professional prizefighter and used his influence as a boxer to break the color barrier in the Operating Engineers Union. In 1948, at the age of eighteen, he got married and started a family of four children with his wife, Minnie. Smith told an interviewer that he enjoyed fatherhood: "Being a father was a great thing to me. I wanted to be somebody; I couldn't be somebody without taking my family with me. I enjoyed being a father, very much so."[10]

Partly because the black population increased at the same time jobs in the steel industry declined, the second Great Migration posed significant challenges to the city's African American community. Whether migrant or Pittsburgh-born, African Americans occupied the cellar of Pittsburgh's declining postwar economy. According to the white recording secretary of one United Steel Workers (USW) local: "The range of jobs now open to minority groups has not changed one bit since our plant organized [during the 1930s]. In fact, the negroes are worse off now, in some respects, than they were before the plant organized."[11] Black steelworkers dominated the low-wage jobs in the coke ovens, and in furnace, masonry, janitorial, and track gang departments. Employers refused to hire black workers, African Americans often remarked, in any position where they could not overwork and underpay them. Oliver Montgomery, a research analyst at the U.S. Steel Workers union headquarters, later described black workers' positions in the mills as "man-killing jobs." "They ate up all that smoke and dust." On one occasion, a team of men wore goggles and alternated stints on a job within the flue of a hot coke oven. When one man emerged from the flue, he removed his goggles and layers of skin peeled off into the goggles. Black men themselves often succinctly referred to their jobs as "hard work, just hard work."[12]

African Americans found it exceedingly difficult to gain access to apprenticeship programs and move into the more highly skilled maintenance and managerial positions. Some superintendents openly declared that "no blacks" would gain access to skilled positions so long as they were in charge. In 1950, only 21 blacks worked as blacksmiths, forgemen, and hammermen in Pittsburgh-area steel mills and foundries out of a total of nearly 1,500 such workers. A mere 12 blacks worked as millwrights out of a total of nearly 3,300 workers in this category.

At its South Side plant, Jones and Laughlin (J&L) excluded black workers from its crews of bricklayers and carpenters until the 1970s. Although Daniel Brooks, a migrant from Fairfield, Alabama, came to J&L with two years of college education, the company hired him as a laborer. Only slowly did he advance within the separate, predominantly black, open-hearth shop.[13] At the Irwin works, without a furnace department, blacks made up less than 1 percent of the labor force. The J&L Aliquippa plant employed only four blacks in managerial positions and only eight in clerical and office jobs, though they made up 8 percent of the firm's total workforce. Blacks made up nearly 33 percent of the National Tube Company's blast furnace department but less than 2 percent of its skilled maintenance workers. Moreover, African American furnace hands received lower wages and benefits than white open-hearth workers who occupied the higher echelon steelmaking jobs.[14]

Otis King trained hard to become a brickmason at the U.S. Steel Homestead works. He attended school during the day and worked at night. When his shift changed to days, he attended school at night. When he finally completed his course of study and took the test to become a bricklayer with the company, officials informed him that the company "was not quite ready" to employ blacks as bricklayers. "That was a big letdown," King painfully recalled, because he felt certain that he would get the job after demonstrating his sacrifices, knowledge, and training.[15] According to a 1957 report of the Urban League of Pittsburgh (ULP), U.S. Steel received the organization's lowest grade on the promotion of black workers into plant, office, and technical positions.[16]

In predominantly black departments, African American men trained white men to become their bosses. Pittsburgh reminded some black workers of the Alabama steel industry, where a new white hire would enter a department, receive on-the-job training from black workers, and in "the next two weeks . . . he is your boss." In Clairton, a black steelworker remarked, U.S. Steel would "take a white man right out of the street and make you teach him and after you teach him they give him your job or make him your foreman.[17] At Carnegie-Illinois Steel, when the company instituted labor-saving machinery and reduced the number of Carrie Furnaces in Rankin from six to four, some veteran black workers retained their jobs as the new equipment eased the labor intensity of their work. As they retired from the company, however, young white men rather than young black men replaced the retirees in the previously all-black department. At Jones and Laughlin, former iron ore loader William Wayte related how, when he had six years' experience, the company placed a "white high school boy" over his crew when the white foreman called in sick one day: "What chance do I have to be a foreman, when they put a high schooler in the job over me?"[18]

Seniority provisions of union contracts protected the jobs of some black workers and improved their position compared to the nonunion era, but labor contracts instituted department-wide rather than plant-wide seniority procedures and limited the long-term economic mobility of African American workers. Black workers referred to the seniority system as "room service," because African American employees entered a room at the outset of their careers and usually stayed there until they retired, no matter how much seniority they compiled.[19] Veteran black workers could only bid on jobs within their own disproportionately black general labor departments; bidding outside these departments meant risking loss of seniority. When mechanization eliminated their jobs, long-time black workers could not take positions in other departments in which white employees with less seniority continued to work.

Moreover, labor-management agreements placed laid-off workers from various departments in a plant-wide "labor pool." Departments with labor shortages could select anyone from the pool for temporary employment without regard to seniority. Under this arrangement, so-called temporary employees might work within a particular department for long periods of time, but the company computed their seniority only within the context of the labor pool.[20] Some union and company officials acknowledged racial discrimination and openly expressed their concerns. The chairman of Clairton's civil rights committee acknowledged that labor pool arrangements prevented blacks from moving into departments with better jobs and higher pay. As he put it, "longer service [Negro] employees are being denied seniority rights . . . there are a number of Units and Departments which employ no Negroes." According to E. C. Myers, assistant vice president of industrial relations administration for

U.S. Steel, many company managers had not "kept pace with changing times" on questions of race and equal employment opportunities. John Murray, director of the USWA District 16 in Pittsburgh, confirmed that most white steelworkers "don't want to work with colored people." Even so, most rank-and-file white workers and union officials downplayed the persistence of racial discrimination in the workplace. At the A. M. Byers Company, for example, the president of USWA Local 1268 claimed that the local had "never been confronted with a discriminatory problem in as much as there have never been Negroes employed" at his mill. At H. K. Porter, the recording secretary of USWA Local 1592 stated that his union "had no blemishes on its racial record."[21]

Whereas the steel industry restricted blacks to lower-rung jobs, the building trades largely excluded African Americans altogether; Pittsburgh's unions in this field made little effort to conceal their desire to maintain a "lily-white" field. During the 1950s, blacks made up less than 5 percent of all employees in Pittsburgh's construction industry. In 1960, blacks accounted for nearly 65 percent of laborers and plasterers and cement occupations in the nation, but they constituted only about 14 and 11 percent of these categories of work in Pittsburgh, the lowest percentage of all the major cities in the United States. As late as 1964, only one black apprentice entered the operating engineers program; two in the sheet metal field; one lather; four carpenters; one bricklayer; and three painters. There were no black union apprentice electricians, pipefitters, ironworkers, or plumbers at this time.[22] The city's 1,400-member Brotherhood of Electrical Workers Local 5 had only one black member in the early 1960s. For three years during the late 1950s and early 1960s, James Williams, a U.S. Army veteran and registered electrician, was denied work with the city of Pittsburgh. The Democratic chairman of the twelfth ward told the *Courier* the city could not hire any man in craft positions without the union's consent because: "No politician wants [white] labor against him."[23]

In addition to the color line in the steel and construction industries, utility companies, department stores, hotels, and grocery chains placed limits on African American employment. Duquesne Light, Kaufmann's, Sears Roebuck, Gimbels, Horne's, Union Switch and Signal, Penn Sheraton Hotel, and the Giant Eagle grocery chain all developed racially discriminatory employment policies. Obstacles also prevailed in the most lucrative lines of business, education, and medicine; in real estate, banking, and finance; in the Pittsburgh public schools and area colleges and universities for positions as teachers, administrators, and counselors; and in the medical field for jobs as nurses, physicians, technicians, and administrators.[24]

At the outset of the postwar years, the expanding nursing field offered a promising opportunity for young high school–educated women. Indeed, African American women expressed increased interest in entering this work. In June 1946, Harriet Black, a senior at Fifth Avenue High School, attended an open house for prospective nurses at Montefiore Hospital. Speakers for the event emphasized the shortage of nurses and urged high school–aged girls to consider enrolling in nursing school and preparing for careers in the nursing field. When Black inquired about admission procedures for the program, the director of the hospital's nursing program informed her that the policy of the hospital "simply does not allow us to take colored girls as nurses." The *Pittsburgh Courier* pressed the organization about discriminating against African Americans, and Montefiore's director of nursing responded, "some larger local hospitals should break the ice in admitting them. Then, perhaps Montefiore would follow suit." By the end of World War II, the Pittsburgh chapter of the National Association of Colored Graduate Nurses identified about forty graduate nurses in Pittsburgh, but only five worked in private hospitals.[25]

Moreover, white women entered the labor force in growing numbers in the postwar years and competed with black women for the attenuated range of jobs available for women. At the national level, the percentage of black women in the labor force remained relatively stable at about 44 percent, while white women's labor force participation rates increased from 30 percent in 1948 to nearly 40 percent during the 1960s. In Pittsburgh, however, the predominantly male steel industry continued to prevail, and the city's white women had only 30 percent of their numbers in the workforce in 1960 compared to well over 40 percent for black women.[26]

African American men with requisite training and skills found it equally difficult to break the color line in the rapidly expanding electronic and computer industries. The U.S. armed services offered training to some black men for these jobs, but employers rejected highly trained black veterans, arguing that they did not hire people "with only military experience." When area firms denied Air Force veteran David E. Ellis employment despite four years of military training in computer technology, the Pittsburgh NAACP and Urban League investigated his case and confirmed that he had been denied employment on the basis of race. White men with identical qualifications (trained in the military without civilian experience) routinely gained jobs in technical fields requiring computer training.[27]

From the early 1950s through the 1960s, the unemployment rate of African Americans nearly doubled and sometimes trebled the rate of whites. Peacetime layoffs reduced the black steel workforce from a wartime peak of 11,500 (14 percent of the total) to about 8,200 (6.5 percent of the total) during the 1960s. In June 1963, the *Pittsburgh Press* estimated "three times" as many blacks out of work as whites, with few blacks employed as professionals, managers, clerks, salespeople, technicians, or skilled office workers. White-collar jobs in Pittsburgh had increased 40 percent over the past decade, but less than 13 percent of African Americans were so employed compared to nearly 37 percent of all whites. Moreover, 65 percent of black families in Allegheny County earned less than $5,000 a year compared to about 33 percent of white families. African American incomes rose by 22 percent between 1949 and 1959. During the same decade, white incomes jumped by nearly 50 percent. Thus, even as African Americans made progress, it was far less dramatic than for their white brothers and sisters. As one newcomer recalled, "I came to Pittsburgh hoping for better things. It just didn't turn out that way."[28]

African Americans were unable to offset their job losses by taking advantage of expanding employment opportunities in downtown Pittsburgh's Central Business District (CBD). While Renaissance I benefited from what urban historian Roy Lubove has dubbed the "reverse welfare state," the few urban renewal programs targeted toward the African American community rarely got past the planning stages. Although federal investment allowed for extensive urban infrastructure, of the total 1,500 acres of land involved in the construction of the Golden Triangle, most went to commercial and industrial development. Some projects benefited the Jones and Laughlin Steel firm, while others served the interests of educational and medical institutions like the University of Pittsburgh, Duquesne University, and Allegheny General Hospital. Few blacks gained employment through these construction projects or their spinoff opportunities.[29]

In its 1962 report, the Urban Redevelopment Authority (URA) celebrated the improved "business climate" and the creation of hundreds of new employment opportunities. Whereas before 1949, fewer than four thousand employees worked "under inconvenient, overcrowded and dismally run-down conditions" in Gateway Center, the URA now counted more than seventeen thousand men and women working in "uncongested and pleasantly-landscaped Gateway Center." In its 1965 report called "A Changing City," the URA declared that "urban redevelopment was put to work as a basic tool in industrial job and general economic development."[30] By 1967, the firms in renewal areas employed some fifty-five thousand people, but few hired African Americans except as domestics and general laborers. Moreover, modest economic growth on the suburban periphery did little to improve job prospects for black Pittsburghers.[31]

Most African Americans continued to work in what some analysts called "occupational traps," but they did not accept this situation without a fight. Black workers continued to deploy a broad range of strategies for changing the terms of their labor. Sometimes white steelworkers stood together with their black brothers. In 1946, for example, when a white foreman ordered a black steelworker at Jones and Laughlin to remove bricks from an oven in repair, white union members supported the black worker's refusal to act on the basis that this work was not part of his job classification. In the steel strike of 1946, black men walked out with their white brothers to improve their pay, time off, and access to pensions and benefits. The *Pittsburgh Courier* celebrated interracial working-class solidarity as evidence of integration and cooperation across the color line that "the most extreme anti-Negro propaganda" could not erase.[32]

Black workers also used the union's grievance machinery to fight racial bias among their fellow white workers. In 1957, over one hundred black workers at the Homestead Works voiced their complaints at a meeting of USWA Local 1397. A former grievance committeeman who had recently lost his job complained that the black worker "either works as a general laborer for the rest of his life or else moves over to the track department." Black workers criticized white union officers for failing to process the grievances of black workers in a timely manner. Despite several "packed" union hall meetings to resolve these issues, African Americans failed to gain satisfactory resolution of their complaints.[33]

When the union failed to address their grievances, black workers staged their own independent work stoppages to achieve their goals. In one case, a black worker clearly articulated the group's motivation for walking off the job: "The men knew that they were risking their jobs in this walkout . . . but they had got worked up to the point where this didn't seem so important . . . they were tired of never getting promoted, and they were tired of being treated like dogs by . . . white foremen."[34] In 1946, Boyd Wilson investigated conditions at J&L and concluded that black work stoppages "seem to indicate a final resort after long periods of efforts to find fair settlements for just grievances." Some of the grievances, he said, had "never reached top management or top union officials." Wilson promised to make the entire corporate and union hierarchy aware of injustices against the black worker. J&L, he said, had a disproportionately larger number of complaints than other area companies.[35]

Partly as a result of white rank-and-file resistance to their demands for equity and fair play, African Americans in Pittsburgh helped to form new all black labor unions to advance their interests. In October 1951, several African Americans from Pittsburgh traveled to Cincinnati to help found the National Negro Labor Council (NNLC). They joined delegates from twenty-two other cities representing every region of the country. The assembly elected as president William R. Hood, recording secretary of the United Automobile Workers Local 600 of Detroit. The NNLC's statement of principles and program of action called for the creation of one hundred thousand new jobs for black men and women nationwide; establishment of a new federal Fair Employment Practice Committee; and full citizenship rights for blacks in all parts of the country.[36]

Under increasing Cold War repression of radical political movements, the NNLC declined by the mid-1950s. During this time black and white labor leaders and Communists were convicted on charges of "un-American activities." Although the government's case rested on flimsy evidence, a federal court jury found Ben Careathers, Steve Nelson, and three other Pittsburgh Communists guilty of violating the Smith Act, which prohibited "advocating and teaching violent overthrow of the government." These convictions were later overturned. The FBI employed former Communists as spies for the government during and after World War II. One of these men, African American Alex Wright, offered his services as an informant for the FBI after he failed to gain a job when he moved to Pittsburgh in 1941.[37]

Black unionists in Pittsburgh and elsewhere regrouped and formed the Negro American Labor Council (NALC) in 1959, under the national leadership of A. Philip Randolph. In Pittsburgh, Clarence L. (Larry) Huff spearheaded the NALC's participation in a broad-based coalition of civil rights organizations to demand jobs for black workers at Pittsburgh's new Civic Arena. The $22 million domed Civic Arena, completed in 1959, was a combined convention and sports facility built alongside luxury high-rise apartments. This construction in the Lower Hill destroyed 1,300 buildings and forced the removal of some 400 businesses

This protest took place outside the Civic Arena in October 1961. Similar to earlier protests at the facility, this one sought to erase the color line in employment, with placards reading: "Job opportunities for us too; We just want our God-given rights; The soundness of our cause should prick your conscience." The march included local leaders like Jim McCoy, Byrd Brown, and Rev. LeRoy Patrick.
Source: Carnegie Museum of Art, Charles "Teenie" Harris Collection, photo #2001.35.6295. Photograph © 2009 Carnegie Museum of Art, Pittsburgh.

and 1,551 families (8,000 residents), mostly African Americans (1,239 black compared to 312 white families).[38] Composed of the NAACP, ULP, the Greater Pittsburgh Improvement League, and the NALC, the coalition staged a march through the streets of East Liberty, Homewood, and the Hill District, where "thousands of Negroes viewed the spectacle—Negroes in a united move to accomplish a specific job." The march ended at the Civic Arena, where pickets surrounded the facility, displaying signs, "Remember Forgotten Man," "Be Civil With Our Rights," and "Open Arena for Jobs."[39]

Following the protest, representatives of the Civic Arena met with coalition leaders and agreed to immediately open jobs to black workers. The arena hired two black guards with the promise of six additional openings for African Americans in technical fields as engineers, electricians,

A youth protesting in front of Civic Arena, c. 1960–1970, holds a sign that reads "Give to all, all at once, jobs."
Source: Carnegie Museum of Art, Charles "Teenie" Harris Collection, photo #2001.35.7071. Photograph © 2009 Carnegie Museum of Art, Pittsburgh.

or utility men. Although arena officials claimed that nondiscrimination clauses existed in all contracts, at the time of the demonstrations the arena had employed only five African American "ushers out of a total of 86; no Negroes among the 25 ticket-takers; no colored among the six engineers and six electricians; some colored janitors; no Negroes employed by the concession owners; no Negroes in the office staff, which includes four persons; no Negroes on the four member watchman's staff."[40]

Throughout the early postwar years, black workers in Pittsburgh and elsewhere pushed for greater representation at all levels of the labor movement, particularly the United Steel Workers of America. At the 1948 convention, Boyd Wilson and black delegates from Pittsburgh and elsewhere proposed the creation of a civil rights department within the USWA. Although in greatly modified and weakened form, the national board approved the establishment of a civil rights department under the white leadership of Tom Shane of Detroit as chairman and his brother Frank as executive director. Despite Boyd Wilson's extensive experience with black workers across the nation over the previous eight years, the union passed over him for membership and created an all-white commit-tee. Tom Shane, according to Wilson, "knew absolutely nothing about the Negro problem and had no interest in it." The committee remained all white until black protests changed its composition in 1952. At that time, the union appointed black unionist Joseph Neal of Baltimore to the civil rights committee.[41]

Pittsburgh's major department stores regularly advertised for help but refused to hire black workers, except as custodians, even as tem-porary help during the busy Christmas holiday season. Moreover, area stores routinely denied African Americans the courtesy of trying on gar-ments while shopping for clothes. In December 1946, a coalition of nearly a dozen civil rights organizations, including the ULP, NAACP, CIO, and the Pittsburgh Interracial Action Council (PIAC), launched a cam-paign to desegregate the city's department stores and end discrimina-tion against blacks as both customers and prospective employees. With a combined membership of over five thousand people, these groups flooded downtown Pittsburgh with handbills calling for an end to racist employ-ment practices. One handbill angrily highlighted the contradiction be-tween the city's claim to freedom and democracy for white residents and the absence of full citizenship rights for African Americans: "We're mad! How about you? . . . PITTSBURGH is a progressive, vital AMERICAN city . . . [but] THIS FREEDOM IS NOT THEIRS!"[42]

Mayor David Lawrence asked demonstrators to delay pickets until he could convene a meeting of store managers and so-called "cooler heads." Rev. Raymond Custer, president of the PIAC, expressed the sentiments of the coalition when he urged the city and area stores to act quickly or risk the emergence of a more militant group: "We are here with you as an orderly group composed of leaders of the city. . . . We are sitting on a steam-kettle trying to hold the thing down. If you don't do some-thing now; and I am not trying to threaten you . . . some less responsible persons might attempt to work this thing out in less orderly fashion."[43] Religious organizations like the Catholic Diocese of Pittsburgh also sup-ported swift employment of black clerks: "Catholics concerned for the application of right principles of interracial relations have a duty to tell the stores that their present policy is a serious disservice to the general welfare."[44]

When national news media picked up the story of the Pittsburgh department store demonstrations, negotiations with area department stores entered a more promising phase. In early February 1947, after

nearly two years of protests, the city's Retail Merchants Association issued a nondiscrimination policy statement: "There will be no discrimination in upgrading and employing of negroes from this day forward." Five
major stores—Kaufmann's, Horne's, Frank and Seder, Rosenbaum, and
Gimbels—endorsed the policy and promised to employ blacks as clerks.
Representatives of the coalition's negotiating committee included K. Le-
Roy Irvis and Maurice Moss of the ULP; P. L. Prattis of the NAACP;
and Mrs. Robert L. Vann of the *Pittsburgh Courier*.[45]

When loss of the federal Fair Employment Practice Committee
(FEPC) weakened the grievance machinery available to black workers, as
elsewhere in postwar black America, African Americans in Pittsburgh
responded in a variety of ways. Adopting wartime rhetoric and describing their efforts as the "Battle for Democracy," they joined the nationwide movement to renew the federal law and helped to launch vigorous
campaigns for local- and state-level fair employment practices legislation.[46] State representative Homer Brown introduced a fair employment
practice bill into the Pennsylvania legislature in 1945. In its original form,
the Brown bill prohibited racial discrimination in employment and provided significant sanctions against guilty parties. In advance of hearings
on the proposed law, the *Pittsburgh Courier* predicted a mass convergence
of African Americans from Pittsburgh and across the state on the capital city of Harrisburg: "More than two hundred supporters of the bill
are expected to attend from Pittsburgh, while reliable reports indicate
that more than a thousand delegates will come from Philadelphia and
the remaining number will come from smaller communities and cities
throughout the state, resulting in one of the largest legislative caravans in
history." The *Courier* later estimated some two thousand Pittsburghers
at a hearing on the measure.[47]

Republican members of the state legislature blocked passage of the
Fair Employment Practice (FEP) law on five different occasions between
1945 and 1955. A considerably weaker version of the measure became law
in 1955. Like many other states, Pennsylvania followed the New York
model (the first state FEP law in the nation) by making it "unlawful for
employers, employment agencies, or labor organizations to discriminate
against a person in hiring, promotion or termination on the basis of
his or her race, color, religion, national origin, or ancestry."[48] The state
charged the Pennsylvania Human Relations Commission with enforcement of the law. At the time of the law's passage, the ULP recalled nearly
a dozen years of state and local activism on behalf of the measure: "For

the past eleven years, the Urban League, along with many other agencies and organizations, has supported the effort for a state-wide Fair Employment Practices Act, attending planning sessions in the western end of the state and in Harrisburg and helping to interpret the importance of such legislation to the community generally."[49]

The movement for a Pittsburgh FEP law unfolded alongside the push for state legislation. At the local level, Alma Illery, president of the Housewives Guild, initiated the campaign for a municipal FEP. She believed a municipal law would reinforce the movement for state and federal FEPC laws. Rev J. O. Williams, pastor of the Warren Methodist Church, also supported passage of a local law, arguing that such an ordinance "would guarantee the right of all people to work at their level of skills regardless of color or religion" and "help to remove the traditional concept that the employment of Negroes should be limited to certain categories, such as that of menial laborers, porters, and domestics."[50] Some proponents of the state law, however, such as Homer Brown and Maurice Moss, opposed the movement for a city FEP law, fearing that an aggressive city campaign would undermine efforts for statewide legislation. For its part, however, the National Council for a Permanent FEPC endorsed both local and state movements as mutually beneficial, and helped to reconcile these two different approaches to FEP laws among blacks in Pittsburgh.[51]

In 1953, the city of Pittsburgh passed a municipal fair employment practices ordinance and established its own Fair Employment Practice Committee to oversee enforcement of the law. When the state passed its FEP measure two years later in 1955, Pittsburgh renamed its local committee on fair employment the Mayor's Commission on Human Relations and treated complaints within the context of new statewide legislation. In 1957, the Pennsylvania Human Relations Commission considered 144 cases and ruled discrimination had indeed taken place in 31 cases; 76 cases remained open; and another 37 were dismissed. The Pittsburgh area office accounted for nearly 25 percent of all cases statewide.[52] According to historian Thomas Sugrue, during the agency's first five years, it processed nearly 1,200 cases of employment discrimination but ruled in favor of complainants in only about a third of the cases and failed to prosecute any employers for wrongdoing.[53]

Postwar black workers continued to develop their own day-to-day strategies for improving the terms of their labor. Many black men continued to move from job to job, piecing together a living through employment in a variety of odd jobs within and outside the industrial sector. Often described as "hustling to make a living," such work entailed, for example, short stints operating pool rooms, bartending, hanging wall paper, and a plethora of general labor jobs requiring lifting, cleaning, and hauling for commercial and industrial establishments.[54]

In a recent biographical account of his life, Rev. Archie Dennis recalls how his father worked as a sanitation worker. Dennis grew up on the North Side and later moved to a housing project on the South Side. His father worked in the city's sanitation department during the 1950s. Although the city offered higher wages and steadier hours than private employers of sanitation workers, it was nonetheless the same arduous labor. Dennis describes how his father's work "involved going into people's backyards and turning the contents of an oil drum into a burlap bag, grabbing four corners of the sack and hoisting it over his shoulder and walking the plank leading into an open-bed truck. . . . The garbage drum served as breeding grounds for flies and maggots, which often fell out of the bag as it was slung over the worker's shoulder."[55] In order to help address the difficulties of such work, in 1959, under the leadership of Emmanuel Phillips, president, and Madelaine Hightower, secretary, African Americans formed the Independent Refuse Haulers Association. This organization aimed to connect men who hauled "rubbish and garbage," under the motto: "Fair Compensation, Harmony, and Friendly Relations."[56]

In the building and construction trades, some black workers combated the color line by taking work in the nonunion sector. The Pittsburgh Urban League noted that many self-employed skilled black workers "did not really want to join a union." Others filled numerous small jobs as "independent contractors." According to the Urban League, "these Negro workers had plenty of work, [because] work tends to be continuous in the nonunion sector and there is less risk of layoff."[57] Thelma Lovette Sr., who grew up in the Hill District, confirmed the Pittsburgh Urban League's observations. Lovette recalled how her father, a self-taught plumber, got "lots of work" putting bathrooms in Hill District homes without toilet facilities.[58]

Poor and working-class blacks also created an underground "jitney" transportation service in underserved areas such as the Hill District. The jitney service provided fulltime employment for some and part-time employment for many area residents. In their careful study of the jitney service in Pittsburgh, urban economists Otto Davis and Norman Johnson

Renowned
Pittsburgh-born
playwright
August Wilson.
Source: Scott Olson/
Getty Images News.

estimated that this underground industry was probably twice as large as the city's commercial taxi service. Playwright August Wilson conceived the idea of his prize-winning play, "Jitney!" (1971) following a visit to his boyhood home in Pittsburgh. Jitney stations were an important part of the cultural landscape of black Pittsburgh, and their meaning in the lives of black people struck a deep chord in the creative imagination of August Wilson. Despite persistent discrimination by licensed taxi services and inadequate public transportation, local cab companies and the Port Authority Transit (PAT) conducted ongoing efforts to drive jitney operators out of business.[59]

Other black workers broke the color barrier in the labor force through their own ingenuity and resolve. In exchange for membership in the union, Nate Smith gave local labor leaders ringside seats to the world heavyweight boxing championship (between Ezzard Charles and Jersey Joe Wolcott) at Pittsburgh's Forbes Field. "I said, Mr. Snyder, are you going to see the fight? We ain't got no tickets . . . I said if I give you two tickets for the fight, will you give me my one ticket for the union? Basically, a fair exchange, no robbery. And the tickets I gave them were right next to me, at that ringside. . . . He [Snyder] thought I would drop out and not keep my dues up, and I did the opposite. I worried them half to death till they gave me a job." When white workers tried to force him to quit, Nate retaliated. "What I done was, I hit one of the operating engineers [who] called me a nigger, and this and that . . . I took my bulldozer, with a big blade on it, and pushed it right up against his roller and was pushing him backwards, because I had a lot of power in that machine. And he jumped off the thing . . . He said, What are you doing? You're trying to kill me. I said, You call me another name, I'm going to kill you. And word got out, you better not call Nate Smith a nigger."[60]

Another black worker, Henderson Thomas, aspired to become a crane operator, but U.S. Steel's Duquesne works refused to train and hire blacks for that job. Thomas observed crane operators at work on a daily basis, often staying after hours to do so and to document the company's racial hiring practices. He noted how the firm systematically passed over veteran black workers while employing several new white crane operators. For over a year, he regularly confronted managers with his request for transfer to the job of craneman. Finally, one day the foreman relented and asked him to demonstrate his ability to operate the crane. Usually new recruits received instruction from a veteran crane operator, but Thomas had to prove his ability without the benefit of help. Based solely upon his observation of crane operators from the ground, Thomas demonstrated that he could do the job. In an interview with filmmakers Ray Henderson and Tony Buba, Thomas recalled, "By eating and sleeping crane, I became as good as anybody, and, seriously, I was determined, and I did it."[61]

Many black women pieced together work by taking a series of jobs as waitresses, seamstresses, dishwashers, and cooks within and outside private homes. African American women also developed strategies for moving into clerical, health, and social welfare services. Lorraine Poindexter left household labor to become a caseworker for the county department of welfare. She explained how her case work job built upon her skills as a household worker. Initially, her wages as a caseworker were so low she received a supplement from the welfare department. Moreover, she also helped her clients with light housework. Gradually, however, higher wages enabled her to leave welfare altogether. Marion Harper also recalled how she made the transition from "day work" to "caseworker" for the welfare department in the community of Turtle Creek. For her part, Thelma Lovette moved out of food service into a job as elevator operator at the Bell Telephone Company; from there she took a clerical job in the law offices of African American attorney Byrd Brown and his partner. She later entered the field of social work and eventually earned a master's degree from the University of Pittsburgh's School of Social Work.[62]

The social service and civil rights programs of the Urban League of Pittsburgh and NAACP complemented the day to day, grassroots, workplace, and union-based activities of black workers. Executive director Alexander J. Allen Jr. as well as industrial relations secretaries Louis Mason (1951–1952) and Richard Dowdy (1952–1959) took the grievances of black workers to black welfare officers at area steel mills and to local and international officers of the USWA itself. In addition to working with the Pittsburgh branch of the NAACP, the ULP maintained close ties with attorney Boyd Wilson, who served on the boards of both the international steel union and the local Urban League. As early as 1948, the Pittsburgh chapter of the National Urban League had launched its local Pilot Placement Project, designed to open doors for black professionals, including teachers, in a variety of jobs heretofore closed to them.[63]

The ULP also formed the Defense Manpower Project in 1951 and the Management Council by 1958, both of which helped to open up new positions to black workers. The Management Council attracted executives from some twenty-four area firms, including the vice president of U.S. Steel, president of A. M. Byers, and vice president of Allegheny Ludlum Steel. However modest the progress, the ULP regularly praised certain firms for hiring blacks in entirely new capacities: an engineer at Westinghouse; a clerk in the shipping department of J&L's central office; and a research chemist at U.S. Steel's Monroeville Research Center, for example. In 1955, the ULP's annual report on new placements included a note of appreciation from Regis Bobonis, the first full-time African American reporter for the *Pittsburgh Post-Gazette*. Bobonis praised the Urban League for assembling a substantial roster of qualified black journalists for the *Post-Gazette* job and opening the door to his employment.[64]

Housing Discrimination and Residential Segregation

Efforts to combat the color line in the labor force were closely intertwined with the struggle for better housing. Pittsburgh's black population inhabited the most dilapidated sections of the city's residential market. Just before the end of World War II, Pittsburgh city councilman George E. Evans described 90 percent of the buildings in the Hill District as "substandard" structures that had "outlived their usefulness." Nearly 98 percent of Lower Hill residents rented their homes compared to 75 percent in Polish Hill and over 50 percent in the largely Italian neighborhood of Bloomfield.[65]

In the early postwar Hill District, Italian, Jewish, and African American families continued to live side by side. Near the birthplace of playwright August Wilson, located at 1727 Bedford Avenue, the Italian Butera family ran a watch and shoe repair business on one side. On the other, a Jewish family ran Bella's Market, a grocery and general store. Just down the street, people worshipped at a Syrian Orthodox church and shopped at a Syrian-run candy store.[66]

Racial differentiation soon increased, however, and conditions for African American housing deteriorated. By 1960, under 6 percent of black families in the Lower Hill area owned their own homes compared to over 25 percent for whites in the same community. An estimated 40 percent of the structures in the Lower Hill's third ward had been built before 1900; 60 percent were in need of major repairs or private bath or both; and nearly 15 percent had 1.5 or more persons per room. The city of Pittsburgh had issued nearly 3,000 building permits between 1945 and 1949 for an estimated 5,700 family dwelling units, but only about 6 of these units were built in predominantly African American neighborhoods. Many more African American than white dwelling units lacked adequate water supply, heat, bath, and toilet facilities, with fewer than half of black families inhabiting units meeting the "minimum standards for health, sanitation and privacy." By the early 1950s, according to the Pittsburgh Housing Association, a large part of the African American community remained in "overcrowded, disease and crime-breeding ghetto homes." The organization also concluded that nearly 6,000 units were needed "to house adequately the Negro population."[67]

African Americans continued to pay larger proportions of their total incomes for housing than their white counterparts. Some 50 percent of blacks paid more than a quarter of their annual earnings for housing, whereas only about 30 percent of white families paid that much. Partly because the demand for housing among African Americans greatly exceeded the supply, landlords and realtors regularly charged blacks, renters, and home buyers alike higher prices for lower quality housing. Geographer Harold Rose has called this phenomenon "the color tax."

Based on 1960 data, a ULP survey concluded that Pittsburgh's black population was indeed "color taxed."[68]

The real estate industry and private homeowners blocked African American access to housing outside predominantly black enclaves. As early as 1946, a careful study of the city's housing market found a nearly inverse relationship between the number of blacks in a community and the ratio of units available for sale or rent. Census tracts with a high percentage of blacks had the lowest vacancy rate, while those with the lowest percentages of blacks had the highest vacancy rates. In 1951, according to the Pittsburgh Housing Association: "the highest vacancies, 14.7%, corresponds to zero negroes in the tract, 13.0% vacancies to 0.2% negroes; conversely the high negro percentages, 95.2% for instance, corresponds to 1.1% vacancies, 86.4% to 0.9% vacancies, and so on." Moreover, "Daily, without exception, Negro families—large and small—of low, middle, or high income, receive negative replies from the vacancy secretary of the [Housing Authority of the City of Pittsburgh]. There are no vacancies for the negro, neither for rent, sale, nor exchange."[69]

Until the 1960s, advertisements in the city's white-dominated newspapers reinforced discrimination by identifying properties by race. The city's leading dailies routinely carried "for colored" listings of property for sale or rental to black people. In 1959, for example, the *Pittsburgh Press* advertised an apartment as follows: "Homewood—Colored: 3 rooms, bath, apt. bldg. $62.50 Ch-2–3200." Similarly, the *Pittsburgh Sun-Telegraph* advertised houses for sale to blacks: "Homes for Colored— Reasonable Good Location, Terms Jacob L. Phillips, Broker, 6286— Broad Street MO-1–2061."[70]

While African Americans protested such discriminatory advertising in the white press, the absence of such "colored ads" in outlying metropolitan areas highlighted the exclusion of blacks from the suburban housing market. In Mt. Lebanon, an overwhelmingly white suburb in the South Hills, real estate agents simply refused to show homes to blacks and Jews. Ruth Reidbord, a charter member of the city's Community Relations Board, recalled, "A black person couldn't buy [or rent] a house in Mt. Lebanon. It was very much a closed community." Mt. Lebanon was by no means an exception. Such was the case in many other suburban communities, including Fox Chapel, Deer Lakes, Keystone Oaks, and Bethel Park.[71]

Land companies, banks, and private homeowners stood at the center of racially biased housing policies and business practices. During the late 1950s and 1960s, nearly 80 percent of African American housing complaints targeted homeowners and realtors either failing to process their application (30.4 percent) or refusing to accept their applications for rental or sale (48.9 percent). Such complaints were most prominent in areas adjacent to established or newly expanding black communities. Oakland and Shadyside topped the list, followed by East Liberty, Larimer, the North Side, Squirrel Hill, Homewood-Brushton, Point Breeze, and Hazelwood-Greenfield. The Greater Pittsburgh Board of Realtors (GPBR) and the powerful East End Multilist, Inc. (EEM, later renamed the Greater Pittsburgh Multilist, Inc.) controlled access to multilisting resources in the city.[72]

The East End Multilist was a powerful, nonprofit, membership organization formed in 1958 and an affiliate of the Greater Pittsburgh Board of Realtors. The organization consolidated and distributed to its members all the real property listings of other members. As such, it regulated the activities of listing and selling offices in its membership territory, which included the area of the city bounded on the west by the CBD, on the south by the Monongahela River, on the north by the Allegheny River and on the east by the city line. This area included over one-half of the land and more than 50 percent of the population of the city of Pittsburgh.[73]

The EEM excluded African Americans from membership, effectively blocking black brokers from showing customers properties listed by the organization. In May 1965, African American realtor Robert Lavelle applied for membership in the EEM. The organization quickly informed Lavelle that he needed the endorsement of two current members in good standing in the all-white organization. When Robert Lavelle secured the necessary sponsorship, he applied again, but the EEM nonetheless rejected his application. Lavelle then requested information on the basis of the organization's decision and the EEM bluntly replied, "the one and only reason [for rejection] was that your office simply did not receive the required three-fourths affirmative vote for acceptance." This matter, the EEM emphatically declared, was "conclusively closed." The matter, however, was by no means settled. Later in this book we will tell the story of how Lavelle took the matter to court and won. Despite hostile and sometimes violent reactions to his efforts to place blacks in homes in previously all-white neighborhoods, Lavelle would continue to challenge the color line in the housing market in Pittsburgh and western Pennsylvania.[74]

Most white brokers also "disapproved" or "strongly opposed" fair

Robert Lavelle, realtor and banker, was the plaintiff in a landmark civil rights case that forced real estate organizations to open their memberships and organization resources to African Americans. This case gave black homebuyers much wider access to homes in white neighborhoods.
Source: Carnegie Museum of Art, Charles "Teenie" Harris Collection, photo #1996.69.55349. Photograph © 2009 Carnegie Museum of Art, Pittsburgh.

housing laws. In explaining their position, local realtors invoked the National Real Estate Board's "1965 Statement of Policy," which held, "No realtor should assume to determine the suitability or eligibility on racial, creedal, or ethnic grounds of any prospective mortgager, tenant, or purchaser."[75] In other words, only the property owner would have the final decision on the "suitability" or "eligibility" of a prospective buyer or renter. Partly because few African Americans were able to engage in home buying and financing, relatively few formal complaints named banks and home-building companies. Still, complaints that financial and building institutions require applicants to provide their race on mortgage applicants made up 1.2 percent of the total complaints against these establishments. Moreover, banks and builders were deeply implicated in the exclusion of blacks from the suburban home-building boom. Based on census tract data, the city's index of residential segregation by race increased from 64.3 percent during the 1940s to 74.5 percent by the late 1960s.[76] Pittsburgh's urban redevelopment programs would reinforce this pattern.

Urban Renewal and Public Housing

Federal, state, and municipal housing policies deepened the discriminatory impact of private real estate practices on the African American community. In the Housing Act of 1949, the federal government provided funds for the twin processes of urban redevelopment and public housing. By the 1960s, buoyed by huge infusions of federal money for

Renaissance I, Pittsburgh's Urban Redevelopment Authority had initiated and/or completed nineteen renewal projects.[77] A variety of public entities approved measures designed to demolish buildings in the city's poor, working-class, and increasingly African American neighborhoods. These measures included the passage of state legislation in 1953; creation of the municipality's Public Auditorium Authority in 1954; and the city council's approval of the Pittsburgh urban renewal plan in 1955.[78]

In Pittsburgh and western Pennsylvania, as in other urban centers across the country, urban renewal programs destroyed whole communities, especially those dominated by low-income families, and the businesses that sustained their neighborhoods. Renewal authorities granted land for the private development of high-income luxury housing, cultural centers, hotels, and sporting arenas. Such policies benefited non-local commercial interests and high-income communities located in other parts of the city and in the middle-class suburbs. By 1966, as historian Roy Lubove has noted, at least 5,400 families in Pittsburgh had been displaced by urban renewal, while only 1,719 new dwelling units had been constructed or were slated for construction. Even these new units tended to be upscale, high-rent apartments: 594 in the Lower Hill; 311 in Gateway Center; and 350 in Allegheny Center. To supplement the 296-unit Pennley Park North Apartments in East Liberty, another 1,273 units were in the planning stages.[79]

Three urban renewal projects would have the most profound impact on the city's African American population. In addition to the Lower Hill's Civic Arena, the North Side's Allegheny Center and the East End's Penn Circle ignored the wants and needs of Pittsburgh's black community and resulted in the displacement of large numbers of African American families, institutions, and social services. In locating urban renewal and public housing projects, professional planners and policy makers sought the cheapest land and the path of least resistance from neighborhood residents. Planners also used both the natural and built environment to reinforce segregation along class and racial lines. The city's bridges, roads, buildings, parking lots, and open spaces became instruments in the separation of human beings on the basis of income, wealth, and color. Construction of the Civic Arena, for example, included the creation of a wide vacant space, which served as "a buffer zone" between the central business district and the expanding African American Middle and Upper Hill communities.[80]

On the East Side, the Penn Circle urban renewal project spurred

Aerial photo of proposed urban renewal plans in the predominantly African American Lower Hill District in 1956.
Source: Carnegie Library of Pittsburgh, Pennsylvania Department.

the rise of East Liberty's segregated black community. Penn Circle reoriented the major roadways through the area, most notably along the east-west arteries of Penn Avenue and Frankstown Avenue. Urban redevelopment authorities also erected a major housing project straddling Penn Avenue in the heart of East Liberty's business district. Rather than facilitating commercial development, reviving local property values, or revitalizing the local economy, the Penn Circle project helped to impoverish the neighborhood. Penn Circle, designed to facilitate traffic around East Liberty's business district, strangled the area's commerce, leaving it cut off from pedestrian traffic south of Penn Avenue. The area became a nightmare for vehicular traffic, providing ample incentive for customers to move around the district rather than stopping to shop there.[81] In Homewood-Brushton, a railroad also helped to separate black and white neighborhoods.[82]

African Americans found it hard to relocate from urban renewal areas to better housing in other communities within and outside the city limits. For the most part, African Americans were conspicuously absent

Aerial photo of the Lower Hill District following redevelopment in 1961.
Source: Carnegie Library of Pittsburgh, Pennsylvania Department. All rights reserved.

from the detailed day-to-day planning and relocation stages of urban renewal. Displaced residents received little relocation compensation and
minimal benefits from the local, state, and federal governments. In the
Lower Hill Redevelopment Area, 53 percent of black families and 6 percent of white families relocated to public housing; 7 percent of blacks
and 51 percent of whites purchased private housing, while 21 percent of
blacks and only 1 percent of whites relocated to "substandard" private
rental housing. The Hill District increased from about 60 percent black
in 1940 to over 80 percent black in 1950 and to nearly 100 percent black
in 1960. Area residents later bitterly recalled, the "most devastating
thing that ever happened to the black community was to tear out the

Lower Hill . . .people went in all directions settling where they could find a place."[83]

East Liberty's older white residents, caught in the vise of inflation, falling property values, and rising taxes, looked to redevelopment as a means of maximizing property values so they could quickly sell and move out. In disproportionate numbers, white residents refused to take advantage of new rental housing in the area, leaving it largely to lower-income black families displaced by urban renewal in other parts of the city. Tenants in at least one new housing project were two-thirds black. As a result of these changes, East Liberty's black population rose from less than 30 percent of the total at the end of World War II to just over 70 percent in 1960.[84]

Homewood-Brushton also attracted growing numbers of African Americans in the wake of urban renewal. A neighborhood of approximately one and one-half square miles near the eastern edge of the city, Homewood-Brushton's black population increased from about 13 percent in 1940 to an estimated 70 percent in 1960. Similar to developments in other large urban areas, Pittsburgh neighborhoods absorbed the huge migration of blacks by breaking up "single-family" structures into "multiple-family" living units. Sometimes as many as four or five families crowded into a one-family house. Cut off from most of the area by the railroad, only the southern section of Homewood-Brushton remained predominantly white. Many of these white families no longer considered themselves part of the Homewood-Brushton community. By 1970, some of the most racially segregated housing tracts in the city had shifted from the Hill to Homewood-Brushton.[85]

Urban renewal also transformed the city's lower North Side into an increasingly working-class and poor black community. The major North Side renewal projects included the Community College of Allegheny County; the East Street Valley Expressway (designed to link downtown to the city's northern suburbs and Interstate 79 at Cranberry); Allegheny General Hospital; and Three Rivers Stadium. In 1954, the Allegheny Conference on Community Development (ACCD) and the Pittsburgh Regional Planning Association (PRPA) concluded the North Side was a "blighted" area and recommended the clearance of major residential areas in the predominantly African American Manchester district, and along the rivers, to be developed for industrial use.[86]

Many North Side homeowners, fearing that their properties would be taken over by eminent domain and torn down, lost interest in making needed repairs. Speculators began buying properties at low prices by telling owners that Pittsburgh's URA would pay even lower prices. As these processes unfolded, according to lower North Side residents, the city also reduced police, fire, and garbage services. Consequently, property values plunged throughout most of the lower North Side, and vandalism and other incidence of crime significantly increased. Although the North Side renewal projects did not start until the mid-late 1960s, the area's population dropped from twenty-one thousand in 1950 to about five hundred in 1965. By 1970, the lower North Side had become a predominantly poor and African American community. By the late 1960s, African Americans in Pittsburgh lived in several widely dispersed, segregated neighborhoods, supplemented by smaller pockets of black settlement elsewhere in the city.[87]

As urban renewal took its toll on the city's housing stock and as African Americans entered previously all-white or predominantly white communities, interracial and interethnic conflict intensified. Old residents feared the establishment of what they called Lower Hill Districts in their neighborhoods. As early as August 1957, one Homewood-Brushton resident described changes in the area of Frankstown Avenue between Braddock and Brushton avenues, accenting the presence of "loiterers," "drunks," and "gamblers," broken "glass and debris." Furthermore, he said there was a lack of police protection: "My wife and children used to shop in this section, but now I'm afraid to allow them to come down."[88]

One of the key areas where racial tensions showed up was in local churches and synagogues where predominantly white congregations confronted an increasingly black neighborhood. An ACTION Housing report noted that B'nai Israel, a Jewish synagogue in Homewood-Brushton, took little action to ameliorate poverty in the neighborhood, and that many members in fact looked forward to renewal and the removal of low-income black families. Likewise, the white Brushton Methodist Church reinforced the idea that a religious body could not remain racially inclusive. White Methodists tended to give in easily to the notion that institutional segregation was inevitable. Similarly, white members of St. Stephens Roman Catholic Church hoped to retain the racial composition of the area, even as the congregation developed social service programs designed to encourage community improvement and interracial cooperation.[89]

While blacks and whites were clearly divided by race, class emerged as the most divisive issue within the black community itself. Established middle-income black families became divided against low-income African Americans. Some middle-class black residents referred to more transient, low-income blacks as "half-brothers." Longtime residents and neighborhood leaders often seemed embarrassed meeting with newcomers, especially when visits to downtown agencies were involved. Even in neighborhood meetings, according to ACTION-Housing officials, "the poorly dressed, often inarticulate half-brother is not listened to by his more fortunate neighbors."[90]

Black homeowners took strong steps to address what they perceived as the deleterious impact of rising numbers of low-income families on their community. In 1954, African Americans spearheaded formation of the Homewood Community Improvement Association (HCIA), "to preserve the property evaluation of homeowners in the Homewood district, 13th Ward of the City of Pittsburgh, and to prevent, through educational and legal means, the deterioration of property in the section." The organization formed ninety local block community clubs by the early 1960s. In 1956, 350 people attended the annual meeting, and some 500 attended in 1961.[91] According to *Courier* reporter Toki Johnson, "Black clubs were organized, officers selected committees which functioned as monitors of their block. Residents, whose homes were marred by broken shutters with front and back yards cluttered with junk, were warned. And when the period of grace was over, the community moved in and took over."[92] In his report at the third annual banquet of the HCIA, president William Howell lamented the decline of police protection, rising delinquency among youth at Westinghouse High School, and the spread of neighborhood bars. Within a five-block area on Frankstown Avenue, Howell identified eleven liquor establishments.[93]

Only a small portion of blacks lived in Pittsburgh's public housing projects during the late 1940s and 1950s. By the 1970s, however, an estimated 25 percent of the city's black population occupied public housing units. African Americans increased from nearly 42 percent of all public housing tenants during the late 1940s and early 1950s, to an estimated 47 percent in 1960 and to over 70 percent by 1970. Civil rights and social service organizations battled the Housing Authority of Pittsburgh regarding strict limits on the ratio of black to white tenants, and by the mid-1960s open occupancy became the norm. Over time, what had been mixed-race complexes (but segregated buildings) made the transition to overwhelmingly black occupancy throughout.[94]

Formed in 1937, the Housing Authority of the City of Pittsburgh (HACP) had built eight public housing projects by the early 1960s. The late Depression and wartime developments included Bedford Dwellings in the Upper Hill District, Addison Terrace in the Middle Hill District, Allequippa Terrace in the Hill-Oakland area, Arlington Heights on the upper South Side, Allegheny Dwellings on the central North Side, Glen-Hazel Heights in upper Hazelwood, and Broadhead Manor on the West End. These developments were followed in the postwar period by such public housing projects as St. Clair Village in St. Clair and Northview Heights on the upper North Side. In locating these projects, the HACP favored relatively isolated, undeveloped hilltops rather than established community settings. Allegheny Dwellings, on the North Side, occupied a mountainous site, according to one researcher, "with perpendicular rock cliffs rising higher than the buildings." Constructed during the 1950s, St. Clair Village, on the South Side, was "originally . . . two hills separated by a ravine with the entire area of 107 acres surrounded on three sides by steep slopes."[95]

Northview Heights, completed in 1961, was located on the outskirts of the city. The project's 999 units overlooked the East Street Valley at the east end of the Swindell Bridge, built in 1929 to spur development. However, the site was so rocky and secluded that, even after the bridge construction, developers ignored it for more than twenty years. Bedford Dwellings and Allequippa Terrace and Addison Terrace (known collectively as Terrace Village) in the Middle Hill District were exceptions. Completed in 1941, they were also located on hilltops, but unlike the other projects they were built within existing communities and were convenient to the Wylie Avenue commercial corridor, Oakland, Downtown, and industrial jobs in the mills along the Monongahela River.[96]

Although the HACP denied using "color" or "racial" factors to determine "eligibility or priority" in selecting public housing tenants, municipal and county housing authorities practiced racial segregation and exclusion both in hiring and in renting. HACP executive director Alfred Tronzo had supported desegregation of the schools and the hiring of black teachers during the interwar years; under his leadership, however, the HACP remained an overwhelmingly white agency until the late 1960s. Beginning in the late 1930s, the HACP adopted a "checkerboard system" with respect to renting. So, in a group of three townhouses, one was set aside for African American families. This scheme broke down in the face of immediate opposition from white families. Yet the HACP used this one-third ratio of black families when the public housing development St. Clair Village opened in 1949. White resistance was still for-

Alfred Tronzo, deputy administrator, and later executive director, of the Housing Authority of the City of Pittsburgh (HACP). Tronzo helped design the agency's entrance, placement, and hiring policies in the 1950s. These policies were challenged in the late 1960s, ultimately leading to Tronzo's removal in 1970. *Source:* Housing Authority of the City of Pittsburgh, "A Report to the People: Public Housing in Pittsburgh, 1938–1953" (Pittsburgh: HACP, ca. 1954).

midable; HACP executive director Alfred Tronzo later noted that white families "would see the black families there and would either walk out without giving an excuse or say thanks, we don't want to view the apartment, we don't think we're ready for integration." The housing authority received some version of this response from over four hundred white families before the units were finally filled.[97]

The HACP refused to integrate a building that already had a large black population. The housing authority concluded, "you didn't just integrate with families but with the proper type of families [meaning double-headed rather than single-parent families with children]." The authority experimented with integrating some complexes with carefully selected and prescreened black families. Indeed, officials actively sought out those "better" black families from their existing tenant rolls and would try coaxing them into relocating to new complexes they wished to integrate. These families heard phrases such as, "would you like to live in a lovely three-bedroom home in lovely St. Clair Village, we will transfer you and will help in every which way."[98]

The HACP maintained a racial quota of about 70:30 for those buildings designated as "integrated"—even as they maintained many buildings that were still exclusively white or exclusively black. Similar to the situation in private housing, what emerged in public housing was a pattern of high vacancy rates in predominantly white buildings (a product of resistance to black occupancy in such units) and zero or low vacancy rates in complexes open to black families (a consequence of consistently high demand for housing among low-income African Americans). From mid-1955 through late 1956, for example, vacancies in the predominantly white Arlington housing project ranged from 10.2 to 15.5 percent compared to 0.0 to 2.0 at Bedford Dwellings, even though the latter included the addition of a new wing. A similar pattern characterized the Addison and Allequippa Terrace residences. African Americans could not easily fill vacancies in predominantly white units. In 1970, one former ten-year resident of the Bedford Dwellings recalled "an insensitive [public housing] administration that neither sought nor accepted the advice of the [black] people who had to live in public housing." According to this former resident, "when black people were pleading to live next to whites," the HACP "was practicing segregation."[99]

The attitudes and behavior of white residents reinforced racial separation in the city's public housing community. In his psychological study of Glen-Hazel Heights, Richard Hessler interviewed one sixty-six-year-old Hungarian-born woman who declared that she did not like Glen-Hazel because of the "dangerous colored" who lived there. A thirty-nine-year old white woman noted: "I like it here myself, but the only thing I don't like is we are so close. . . . The porches are so small here. You know . . . you have to sit, and . . . now we have one (a Negro woman) in there. . . . I doubt if I'll be out this summer. I'll probably stay in all summer. I hardly get out anyway. The rent is cheap; that's the only reason I'm here."[100]

Many white residents believed that black occupancy, even in small numbers, led to the deterioration of the neighborhood, despite the existence of long-run economic and demographic processes predating the arrival of blacks into a particular neighborhood. Whites who opposed integrated public housing also cited notions that blacks were "dangerous," less educated, and more criminal than whites. On the contrary, however, public housing initially brought large numbers of elderly whites together with young blacks with more formal years of schooling than their white neighbors. At Glen Hazel, blacks made up nearly 73 and 61 percent, respectively, of all inhabitants ages 16 to 25 and 26 to 40. Conversely, whites made up 57, 49, and 56 percent, respectively, of all residents ages 41 to 50, 51 to 65, and 66 and up. In addition, blacks made up nearly 80 percent of all tenants reporting more than a high school education; 63 percent of all high school graduates; and 58 percent of those with high school education. Glen Hazel's black tenants also made up a larger proportion of Glen Hazel's wage earners—61.3 percent—than whites—38.7 percent.[101]

Wedged between the ravages of urban renewal and stiff restrictions in the private housing market, many African Americans perceived public housing as their most viable option for obtaining access to new housing. In 1966, some 81.5 percent of blacks in the Glen Hazel community described their previous housing as worse or the same as public housing. Only 17.6 percent of blacks revealed a decline in living conditions when they moved into public housing, which for most blacks was not only more affordable, but "cleaner" and "safer" than residences they had left behind. The incidence of African American drug use, infant mortality, teen pregnancy, and violent crime escalated in public housing over time, but the first wave of public housing tenants occupied meaningful new space.[102]

African Americans in Pittsburgh often recalled "good memories" of their lives in the city's new public housing projects. In her recollections of African American homeownership and the advent of public housing, Gail Austin recalled how at one time her family lived with her uncle in a house that he owned, but it lacked hot running water and was by no means "always a comfortable situation." Thus, she said, when public housing opened, "we were happy to move there [Bedford Dwellings]. . . . [It] was not a bad situation. It really wasn't." Similarly, Sala Udin, whose family moved to Bedford Dwellings during the 1950s, recalled the family's delight in occupying new and better housing: "One day my dad came home and said, we're moving. . . . We went to this new, shiny new place. Now, the apartment that we had on the second floor at Fullerton and Epiphany Street was very old . . . we were constantly having to turn out the lights because the light bill was too high. We would only turn up the heat just enough . . . to prevent frostbite because the heating bill was too high. So my dad managed that kind of stuff. 'Turn the lights off!' 'Turn that heat down.' 'Close that window!'" Other interviewees who occupied their own homes or rental units during the period accented the poor quality of such housing. Lorraine Poindexter 's family never lived in the projects but occupied "substandard housing where the roof would leak" and the family kept big buckets on hand to catch the water when it rained.[103]

While African Americans frequently celebrated the material gains of new public housing, they also expressed the pain of being uprooted from their old neighborhoods. Neighborhood displacement generated deep and painful memories among the city's black residents. The artist Carlos Peterson, a resident of the Lower Hill, later recalled seeing the bulldozers from the third floor of his building: "I was young and did not fully understand what was happening. I only knew this process was coming

The destructive impact of urban renewal on the city's black community is depicted in artist Carlos F. Peterson's photograph, "Hill-o-Phobia," showing the exposed roots of a huge tree left in the wake of the demolition and clearing of the area for the Civic Arena.

Source: Copyright © 1992 by Carlos F. Peterson. Printed with the permission of the artist.

towards us. Coupled with the sense of personal loss of friends and neighborhood, this event had quite an influence on my life." Peterson later captured the pain of removal in a photograph entitled, "Hill-o-Phobia," which showed the Civic Arena just behind an uprooted tree. In an interview with Mindy Thompson Fullilove, Tamanika Howze also recalled the pain of urban renewal: "I remember so well what was going on. I saw chunks of the Hill taken, destroyed, and in some places replaced with other structures." When asked how he felt about moving from his Hill home to Bedford Dwellings, Howze's son, former Pittsburgh councilman Sala Udin, expressed that he was: "Happy and anxious. Anxious because we were going to an unknown area. Happy because the old conditions of the housing that we lived in were being replaced by new facilities. Sad also that the old, old, old friendships that bound people together were broken. See it was a bittersweet experience."[104]

The destruction of black neighborhoods in Pittsburgh and the pain that it engendered were part of a larger national pattern of urban social change. Between 1949 and 1973, federally supported urban renewal programs destroyed some 2,500 neighborhoods in nearly 1,000 American cities of various sizes in all regions of the country. Nearly a million people lost their homes and had to move to other locations. By 1972, the destruction of the Pruitt-Igoe housing project in St. Louis symbolized the limits of urban renewal and the promise of low-income public housing in large metropolitan areas like Pittsburgh.[105]

African Americans developed numerous strategies for improving their living spaces. Even under the worst of circumstances, black people resented the definition of their homes as "blighted." In an interview with Melvin Williams, one former Hill District resident recalled "the small details" of a house that his family moved into: "He remembered the several months of labor that his father, his brother and he put into a five-room brick house before it was fit for human habitation. Even with these efforts it was still a modest house with two bedrooms on the second floor and a frame kitchen set off from the house . . . the kitchen was the coldest room during the winter. Often the water was left running to keep it from freezing and bursting the pipes."[106]

Similar to the fight against employment discrimination, the struggle for better housing also included a campaign for new legislation to ensure fair housing in both the private and public sectors. In the fall of 1957, African Americans and their white supporters intensified their call for a municipal fair housing ordinance. Following Mayor Lawrence's reelection, some twenty civic and political organizations joined the NAACP in a campaign for a municipal housing law. Charles C. Holt, chair of the NAACP's housing committee, reported that nearly a dozen states and twenty-two cities had enacted some form of fair housing legislation but not Pittsburgh. Holt urged the mayor to extend his "personal ACTIVE leadership to the problem of obtaining equal and unsegregated" housing for the city's black population.[107]

Whereas Pittsburgh had enacted a fair employment practice ordinance at the outset of the postwar years, only in 1958 did Pittsburgh pass its fair housing ordinance, which prohibited discrimination in the "rental, sale, purchase or financing of residential housing because of race, color, religion, ancestry or national origin." Similar to the city's FEP law, the fair housing ordinance empowered the city's Human Relations Commission to move beyond investigating cases of wrongdoing and prosecute offenders, including brokers, salespersons, banks, and private owners of five or more living units. In 1959, African Americans filed twenty-five real estate discrimination complaints with the Mayor's Human Relations Commission. The annual number of such cases nearly doubled by the mid-1960s.[108]

When the Stanton Land Company denied Dr. Oswald Nickens access to its development, Nickens filed a suit against the company under the city's Fair Housing Ordinance. During *Nickens v. Stanton Land Company* (1963–1964), state and countywide civic, political, labor, and civil rights organizations—including the Pennsylvania Equal Rights Council (PERC) and the Allegheny County Council on Civil Rights (ACCCR)—submitted exceedingly strong "friend of the court" briefs on behalf of Oswald Nickens. These briefs contested the claim of the Stanton Land Company that the city and state's fair housing laws were unconstitutional. The ACCCR and PERC forcefully argued that the real issue in this case was whether the Stanton Land Company was "free to create a socially segregated all white residential community by refusing to sell a home site to a Negro family in contravention not only of the Pittsburgh Ordinance but the public policy of the Commonwealth of Pennsylvania as declared in the Pennsylvania Fair Housing Law."[109] The Allegheny Court of Common Pleas upheld the constitutionality of the city's fair housing law and ordered the company to accept Nickens's application and admit him to the development.[110]

Education, Social Services, and Politics

As the city's black population and residential segregation increased, black children constituted an even greater proportion of students in the Pittsburgh public schools. Pittsburgh's African American student population increased from less than 13,500 in 1945 to over 27,500 in 1964. By the mid-1960s, African Americans composed over 40 percent of the public school population compared to less than 20 percent at the end of World War II. At the same time, the number of white students in public schools dropped by nearly 25 percent from nearly 63,000 in 1945 to under 48,500 in 1964, partly because they gained greater access to parochial or private schools. In 1960, for example, blacks represented only about 19 percent of all school-aged children in Pittsburgh, but they made up over 30 percent of all public school students.[111]

Despite the U.S. Supreme Court's 1954 decision in *Brown v. Board of Education*, which ended de jure segregation in public schools, racially segregated schools increased in Pittsburgh and other parts of the urban North during the postwar years. White Pittsburghers declared the sanctity of "neighborhood schools," which, in their view, represented the logical outcome of their own local customs, traditions, and "rights" to educate their children as they saw fit. The Pittsburgh Board of Education endorsed these views and developed policies that reinforced segregation. The African American student population rapidly increased and became concentrated within a relatively small number of schools. Most black students attended schools in the third and fifth wards (Hill District); twelfth ward (East Liberty); thirteenth ward (Homewood-Brushton); eighteenth ward (Beltzhoover); and the twenty-first ward (North Side, Manchester). The Pittsburgh public schools developed a series of small, community-based elementary schools that fed into larger middle and/ or junior and senior high schools and maintained patterns of nearly all-white or predominantly black schools.[112]

Black children bore the brunt of de facto segregation in public education. The city had built its last high school in 1927. In 1965, the board adopted an "extended school day, with staggered schedules" to alleviate overcrowding. The board itself described schools in the black community as "badly overcrowded," and, "in some cases old, uneconomical and ugly schools." While the city failed to construct new high schools in the two decades after World War II, it built several new elementary schools. All but one of these schools initially served predominantly white student bodies. In 1955, the city constructed the Philip Murray School with a black student population of 35 percent, but the African American enrollment reached over 55 percent ten years later. By 1960, six predominantly black elementary schools had emerged in Homewood-Brushton.[113]

Predominantly black schools suffered increasing overcrowding and soon exceeded their capacity. By contrast, the nearby Regent Square School, a predominantly white facility near Homewood-Brushton, operated at just 25 percent of its capacity, and resisted the enrollment of black students from the overcrowded Homewood schools. Other predominantly black and increasingly overcrowded schools included Westinghouse High School in Homewood-Brushton; Fifth Avenue High in the Upper Hill District; and Schenley High in the Oakland/Squirrel

Hill area. In addition, Allegheny, Gladstone, and Oliver High Schools had about 40 percent black student enrollment, Langley High School approximately 20 percent, and the remaining fourteen middle schools and high schools had less than 10 percent African American student enrollments. The number of predominantly black schools increased from nine in 1955 to nineteen in 1965.[114]

An even more hostile learning environment greeted black students as the number of nearly all black schools increased. At the Fifth Avenue High School, black teacher Alice Bernice Wade recalled how administrators often enlisted the police to discipline black children. Policemen took black male students into the alley to beat them for reportedly misbehaving in school. The administration was well aware of this practice and did nothing to stop it. On another occasion when she took over a white fellow teacher's class, she noted that each student's name was followed by certain letter designations. N students received grades of C, D, or F, while W students received grades of B or A. White teachers and guidance counselors encouraged black male and female students to pursue careers in domestic service or the manual trades rather than professions requiring college degrees. Conversely, counselors urged white students to attend college and made applications and scholarship information readily available to them.[115]

Historian Ralph Proctor, who grew up in Pittsburgh, later recalled that white counselors denigrated black culture. In his words, they "insisted upon treating Black youngsters as some aberrant form" of white childhood. The author recalls quite vividly being advised to take shop courses and go to a trade school rather than take academic courses or to think about college."[116] Despite these fundamental inequalities in black and white education in Pittsburgh, students later also recalled many "fond memories" of black and white teachers and their learning experience in predominantly black schools, especially during the elementary years. One former student of the Robert L. Vann Elementary School in the Hill District, for example, recalled, "There was not a bad apple in the whole bunch."[117]

Even as several elementary and some high schools became predominantly black, African American teachers found it difficult to gain jobs in the Pittsburgh public schools. By the end of World War II, only about a dozen black professionals (about four teachers) had gained employment in the Pittsburgh public schools. Qualified black teachers regularly took other jobs because they could not secure employment in the Pittsburgh schools. Before Hazel Stallings got her job in 1946, for example, she left the city and taught in North Carolina for several years. Another black teacher refused to seek employment in the Pittsburgh public schools because her knowledge of the color line was so pervasive and discouraging. Ollie May Guice, an experienced Spanish teacher, left the city when her mentors at the University of Pittsburgh told her she "would never get a job teaching in Pittsburgh, let alone teaching Spanish on the secondary level" as she proposed to do. Indeed, the personnel director of the Pittsburgh Board of Education informed Guice that the city's high schools were not prepared for "her kind." Still another black teacher recalled that the same director urged a certified high school teacher to go back to school for an elementary certificate because the Board "can't put blacks in high school."[118]

In 1950, the *Pittsburgh Courier* celebrated the placement of black teachers outside the Hill District. According to the *Courier*, the Board finally "abandoned the policy of using Negro teachers only in Hill District schools, a practice followed since the first appointment of Negro teachers in 1936." In 1955, the first African American principal in Pittsburgh was appointed, and in 1960, the first African American guidance counselor followed suit; like the first black teachers, both worked in the predominantly black Hill District. Following World War II, blacks made up no more than 2 percent of the city's professional education staff, but by the late-1950s, the number of black professionals had increased to 137 or 5.3 percent of all public school professionals.[119]

African Americans also pushed for representation on the Pittsburgh Board of Education. Until 1977 the Commonwealth Court Judge appointed Pittsburgh Board of Education members and invariably overlooked potential black appointees. Attorney Byrd Brown, became president of the NAACP in 1958 and served at that post until 1971, declared the school board selection process violated the "one man, one vote" principle of the U.S. constitution and deprived blacks of their rights. Pittsburgh's black community not only vigorously assaulted the color line in the representation of black people on the board of education but also demanded a study of textbooks to detect racial bias, expansion of "extracurricular activities," and the improvement of "vocational training programs" for black students.[120]

Pittsburgh's black community challenged racial inequality in the medical establishment, as well. In July 1963, the ULP charged the city's medical profession with discriminating against black physicians, patients, and potential students. The University of Pittsburgh's medical school enrolled only 2 black students out of a total of 400; there were only 26 blacks listed among the city's 1,749 physicians; and only 22 dentists among 855 total were black. According to Eric Springer, member of the ULP board and the Health Law Center at the University of Pittsburgh, a black doctor could practice in Pittsburgh so long as "he does so quietly in his own neighborhood. But he may have trouble advancing to key positions consistent with his abilities . . . in a predominantly white hospital." When admitting patients, area hospitals routinely asked white patients if they would object to sharing a room "with a Negro." Moreover, some physicians segregated patients by race, while others simply refused to accept blacks in their private practice. Chaired by Dr. Earl E. Smith, the ULP health committee concluded, the city had "a long way to go in wiping out discrimination in medicine."[121]

African Americans also pressed for greater influence in the city's dominant Democratic Party and its control over city and county government. They complained that Mayor Lawrence worried more about preserving the appearance of racial peace than he did about achieving equal opportunity and social justice for black people. When African Americans launched protests against the discriminatory practices of downtown department stores, Lawrence invited K. LeRoy Irvis to his office to head off what he called "this damn fool thing."[122] Moreover, in cases involving police brutality against black Pittsburghers, the Lawrence administration invariably sided with the police, despite clear evidence of police misconduct in some cases.[123]

Despite resistance from city hall, African Americans increased their influence in third, fifth, and thirteenth ward politics. Following World War II, the Republican Party sought to regain its black constituency by endorsing black candidates for alderman: Cornell Talley in 1947 and William Young in 1953. These candidates garnered most of the black votes, but failed among both white Republican and white Democratic voters. Partially due to their exceedingly strong races, however, Lawrence and the Democratic Party feared the loss of black support and initiated the endorsement of their own black candidates for alderman. According to C. B. "Knowledge" Clark, a *Courier* columnist and resident of Pittsburgh from 1926 through the early postwar years, David Lawrence and his Democratic colleagues established "what was referred to as the 'Balkan Succession,' meaning that the party would maintain one black member of council." In 1954, the mayor chose and council approved the appointment of Paul Jones, a former workmen's compensation referee, to fill a vacant aldermanic seat. In 1955, Jones also received the party's endorsement as an incumbent in the primary and won in the general election. In 1960, when Councilman Jones died in office, Mayor Barr selected James Jordan, an attorney for the Koppers Corporation.[124]

K. Leroy Irvis's rise to power in the state legislature symbolized the growing impact of the black freedom struggle on electoral politics in Pittsburgh and Pennsylvania. In 1958, Irvis gained election to the state legislature from the Hill District on the Democratic Party ticket. According to Irvis's biographer, historian Laurence Glasco, he achieved this feat by joining forces with the white legislative candidate James Clark, which enabled him to win necessary white votes in the Oakland area and defeat two veteran incumbents. Irvis also benefited from a Hill District election team that included *Pittsburgh Courier* reporter Frank Bolden and attorney Paul Jones, among others. Most important, however, according to Glasco, Irvis gained the enthusiastic and energetic support of African American women like Alma Ilery, who headed a network of achievement clubs, and helped to mobilize people from all walks of life, including numbers runners and tenants of the area's housing projects. Irvis's constituents sent him back to the legislature fourteen times.[125]

Civil rights and political figures like K. Leroy Irvis owed many of their successes to ward-level political activists like Robert E. "Pappy" Williams. A graduate of Schenley High School and Carnegie Institute of Technology (later Carnegie Mellon University), Williams served on the executive committee of the fifth ward organization of the Allegheny County Democratic Party. He later received credit for helping to elect black candidates to influential public offices, including Homer S. Brown as the first African American judge of the Court of Common Pleas; Paul Jones to the city council; and Irvis to the state legislature. Williams also advocated for blacks in municipal jobs, including appointments as police lieutenants, patrol car officers, and as fire captains. Grassroots, political activists in the wards would play an even greater role in the city's black community as the Civil Rights and Black Power movements escalated during the 1960s.[126]

Efforts to desegregate Pittsburgh in the postwar years extended to every facet of life, including recreational venues. In August 1948, the Urban League of Pittsburgh and white members of the Progressive Party launched protests against the exclusion of blacks from the Highland Park pool on the city's east side. An estimated six hundred to one thousand

A small but influential core of black political leaders worked hard to expand the scope of Pittsburgh's Civil Rights movement during the 1950s. A voter registration meeting in 1958 included (from left to right): Councilman Paul F. Jones, Constable Thomas J. "Tommy" Smith, Robert E. "Pappy" Williams, Alderman Harry Fitzgerald, and K. Leroy Irvis, standing on right.

Source: Carnegie Museum of Art, Charles "Teenie" Harris Collection, photo #2001.35.325. Photograph © 2009 Carnegie Museum of Art, Pittsburgh.

angry white residents met the protesters and tried to turn them back. Only the presence of some 160 police officers prevented a violent assault on activists. Established in 1946, the Mayor's Civic Unity Council (which included the heads of a variety of civic, education, religious, and community organizations) gained credit for identifying potential points of violent conflict and for deploying the police force to those areas of growing tension. In the Highland Park swimming pool protests, for example, the city spent an estimated $8,000 in 1949 to help prevent the outbreak of violence.[127]

During the early 1950s, interracial swimming teams again challenged the "all white" rule at the Highland Park pool and the Paulson Avenue pool in East Liberty. In June 1951, two black men, Joe Allen of the Ur-

Men protesting swimming pool segregation on Grant Street sidewalk with signs reading "We want democracy at Highland Park Pool, Mayor Lawrence, what do you want?" and "We fought together, why can't we swim together," c. 1949.

Source: Carnegie Museum of Art, Charles "Teenie" Harris Collection, photo #2001.35.13770. Photograph © 2009 Carnegie Museum of Art, Pittsburgh.

ban League and Gaines Bradford, sought to swim in the Highland Park pool. According to local historian Rollo Turner, guards and local policemen did little to prevent "a gang of a hundred whites" from ejecting Allen from the pool and "hurling epithets at him and Bradford." When Allen later returned to the pool, white swimmers again hurled "insults" and "stones" at him.[128] At the same time, Wendell Freeland, Richard Jones, and other black attorneys filed a lawsuit against the City of Pittsburgh. The suit charged the city with operating the pool "as a public nuisance," and sought "to enjoin the city from operating the pool unless it was safe for black patrons." For more than two weeks, under the leadership of Rev. LeRoy Patrick, demonstrators converged on these swimming pools to exercise their right to swim regardless of the color of their skin. The court ruled in favor of the African American plaintiffs, and by late summer 1952, the city had desegregated the Highland Park and Paulson Avenue

Headline from the *Pittsburgh Courier:* "URBAN LEAGUE HEAD EJECTED FROM HIGHLAND PARK POOL."

Source: *Pittsburgh Courier,* 30 June 1951.

pools. As African Americans gained increasing access to a previously all white pool, it was sometimes pejoratively referred to as, "the inkwell," as was the Washington Boulevard pool. At the same time, some swimming pools and places of amusement resisted orders to desegregate. According to *Pittsburgh Courier* writer George E. Barbour, Pittsburgh's famous Kennywood amusement park diverted its swimming pool into a lake rather than permit blacks to swim there with whites. The city of Pittsburgh also filled in its West Park swimming pool to avoid racial integration.[129]

It would take nearly a decade of protests to desegregate the city's roller rinks. Judge Livingstone Johnson later vividly recalled discrimination at a roller rink in East Liberty. As a youth, Johnson had skated with whites at a rink in Wilkinsburg. When he attempted to do the same in East Liberty, he faced the color line in no uncertain terms: "One day I went to a rink in East Liberty with five white students. The ticket taker told me, 'get out of here; these people will kill you.' I got out. My father felt futility and frustration when I told him." Johnson credited his experience with such incidents as a youth for his activism during the 1950s and 1960s. "This is why I'm on the United Negro Protest Committee. I don't intend to stand for this kind of thing."[130]

3

Pittsburgh's Modern Black Freedom Movement

Inspired both by their own history of social struggle and the rapid growth of the Civil Rights movement in the South, African Americans in Pittsburgh escalated their efforts for social change during the 1960s. The emergence of new organizations reinforced and expanded the ongoing activities of the Pittsburgh Urban League and NAACP. Until the late 1960s, "nonviolent direct action" defined Pittsburgh's black free-dom struggle. In the wake of Martin Luther King Jr.'s assassination and the Eight-Day Riot of 1968, however, Black Power emerged at the fore-front of Pittsburgh's African American liberation movement. The black freedom struggle dramatically exposed the class and racial limitations of Pittsburgh's Renaissance I. While the 1960s and early 1970s brought about substantial improvements in the lives of African Americans, such changes failed to eradicate the fundamental underpinnings of Jim Crow, class, and racial inequality in the city's life. Consequently, African Americans would soon face the brunt of deindustrialization as Pittsburgh pre-pared for Renaissance II.[1]

Nonviolent Direct Action

As the Civil Rights movement expanded and dissatisfaction with Jim Crow in the urban North grew, African Americans in Pittsburgh formed a variety of new grassroots nonviolent direct action organizations to fight for social justice. These organizations included the United Negro Protest Committee (UNPC), the Black United Movement for Progress, Operation Dig, and the Black Construction Coalition (BCC). In alliance with the NAACP, Urban League, and their white supporters, the mass marches and protest activities of these groups targeted discrimination in a broad cross section of private and public institutions: area department stores, hospitals, and schools; the construction trades, the steel industry, and other industrial firms; utility companies, real estate firms, banks, and other financial institutions. Numerous people played a pivotal leadership role in the civil rights and political struggles of Pittsburgh's black community during the period, including, but not limited to: Byrd Brown, attorney and president of the local branch of the NAACP; Jim McCoy, organizer for the United Steel Workers of America (USWA); William "Bouie" Haden, community activist; Alma Fox, executive director of the Pittsburgh branch of the NAACP; Nate Smith, labor activist; and Donald McIlvane, Catholic priest.[2]

Established in 1963, the United Negro Protest Committee forged a grassroots coalition of interracial civil rights, religious, and civic organizations, including the NAACP and the Greater Pittsburgh Civic League. Under the leadership of Jim McCoy, who was not only a paid organizer for the USWA but also a volunteer chairman of the NAACP's labor and industry committee, the UNPC gathered statistics on black employment in area firms and initiated talks with discriminatory companies. Over the next five years, the organization launched vigorous job discrimination protests against a broad range of area employers, including the A&P grocery chain, Isaly's dairy stores, the Duquesne Light utility company, the Pittsburgh Brewing Company, and the Bell Telephone Company.[3]

Following meetings with Rev. Charles E. McFadden, chairman of the UNPC's subcommittee on groceries and chain stores, A&P hired an African American in its personnel department. Isaly's also signed an agreement with the UNPC, promising to hire a black manager at one of its stores and to increase the number of blacks in production and office jobs. By the late 1960s, the Pittsburgh Brewing Company, and the city's

Women and men march around Duquesne Light Company Building, some wearing armbands reading, "Let's March," 1963.

Source: Carnegie Museum of Art, Charles "Teenie" Harris Collection, photo #2001.35.10675. Photograph © 2009 Carnegie Museum of Art, Pittsburgh.

advertising industry reached similar hiring agreements with UNPC. The Bell Telephone Company also agreed "in principle" with the UNPC's proposal to hire one thousand additional black workers, including more African Americans in its employment office, but the company refused to sign an agreement on the premise that it had already reached a "Plans for Progress" accord with the federal government. Nonetheless, under mounting pressure from the UNPC, Bell promised to meet with the organization on a regular basis to monitor the firm's progress on the hiring and promotion of black workers.[4]

In 1963 and again in 1967, the UNPC targeted Duquesne Light for failure to employ black workers. When Duquesne Light failed to respond to initial inquiries, scores of protesters picketed the company's headquarters at Sixth Avenue and William Penn Way. Livingstone Johnson, attorney and chairman of the UNPC bargaining team, announced that pickets would continue until satisfactory results emerged from negotiations with the company.[5] During the protests, when demonstrators violated a local ordinance by using a loudspeaker-equipped automobile to address the crowd, authorities arrested Jim McCoy, Byrd Brown, and Lain Lee, organizing chairman of the interracial Greater Pittsburgh Civic League. Following the arrests, nearly two hundred pickets chanted, "We want Byrd Brown, we want Byrd Brown" and "Let's all go to jail, Let's all go to jail."[6] Duquesne Light gradually opened up employment opportunities for blacks, and by 1967 the utility company signed a hiring agreement with the UNPC.

As elsewhere during the civil rights era, the Pittsburgh movement engaged the African American religious community. During demonstrations to open up public service jobs in Allegheny County, activist Rev. W. D. Petett, a migrant from Georgia and moderator of the Allegheny Union Baptist Conference, urged black churchmen to join Byrd Brown and other pickets at the Allegheny County Courthouse. Demonstrators sat on the floor of the courthouse corridor praying and singing, "We Shall Not Be Moved." In one demonstration, two women carried a UNPC sign protesting discrimination by labor unions while singing "My Heavenly Father Watches Over Me." In November 1966, Martin Luther King Jr. visited Pittsburgh. When he arrived at the University of Pittsburgh Student Union, Jim McCoy "officially welcomed" him to the city and worked to cement the city's ties to the national civil rights struggle. McCoy later summed up his perspective on black religious beliefs and culture in creating the movement as a "self-generating" phenomenon: "I feel that a person does not get into this movement; the movement is in the person. . . . We have in us a mechanism that is self-generating. We'll never become disillusioned in our journey up the road toward total equality."[7]

Local observers often referred to Pittsburgh's black activism during the time as the "Marching Season." As such, the Pittsburgh movement reinforced the words of A. Philip Randolph on the eve of the historic mass March on Washington for Jobs and Freedom in 1963: "Demonstrations are the hallmark of every revolution since the birth of civilization. . . . [T]here is no way . . . to stem these demonstrations until the cause is removed; and the cause is racial bias, the cause is exploitation and oppression, the cause is second-class citizenship in a first-class nation."[8]

In June 1967, the Homewood-Brushton activist William "Bouie" Haden spearheaded the formation of the United Movement for Progress. A loose coalition of neighborhood activists, this organization soon demanded managerial jobs at neighborhood grocery stores, including Giant Eagle and the A&P chain. Although Homewood business establishments had hired blacks since the end of World War I, few hired African Americans beyond custodial or general labor positions. When owners refused to upgrade black employees, the United Movement for Progress staged a boycott of the Frankstown Avenue Giant Eagle Store. As Pittsburgh's "Black Fist," Haden symbolized the growing militance of the black community. Initially Haden's efforts to negotiate with employers were "respectable." In the *New Pittsburgh Courier*, Carl Morris noted, "He wore a suit and tie when he made his personal visits along Homewood Avenue." When his efforts proved "fruitless," "He took off his suit, removed his tie, and went to the streets. That hot June Friday morning found him replete in khaki pants, runover shoes, and a plaid shirt, which since has become his trademark, his street uniform."[9] When Giant Eagle hired its first black manager in July, the United Movement for Progress increased pressure on other neighborhood groceries, especially A&P, which hired its first black manager a few months later.

At about the same time, Operation Dig emerged on the city's North Side. A grassroots, pre-apprenticeship training program, Operation Dig aimed to break down racial barriers in the building and construction trades. Under the leadership of Nate Smith, the former boxer and the lone black member of the city's Operating Engineers Union, Operation Dig trained young black men on the use of heavy equipment and placed increasing pressure on the Master Builders Association (MBA) and constituent unions to admit black trainees into the building trades. The MBA soon adopted resolutions supporting equal opportunity for black workers, but failed to open the door to black apprentices. One prospec-

African Americans in Pittsburgh targeted a variety of retail establishments for discriminatory employment practices by the early 1960s. In this photo, protesters marched in front of an A&P food store wearing signs that read, "Don't Buy at A&P Until They Hire Negro Cashiers," c. 1950–1970.

Source: Carnegie Museum of Art, Charles "Teenie" Harris Collection, photo #2001.35.10722. Photograph © 2009 Carnegie Museum of Art, Pittsburgh.

tive apprentice rejected by the Operating Engineers program, opined, "The only thing that will convince Negro boys that it makes sense to apply is for them to see some Negroes operating those machines."[10]

David Epperson, a member of the Mayor's Committee on Human Resources and Professor of Social Work at the University of Pittsburgh, facilitated Operation Dig's efforts to create construction jobs for black workers. Formed in 1963, the Mayor's Committee on Human Resources addressed issues of poverty and economic deprivation, whereas the earlier Commission on Human Relations focused on eradicating all forms of discrimination based on religion, nationality, and color. Epperson later recalled how Nate Smith and two other men came to his office and asked that he drop what he was doing and go with them. Epperson said that he had no idea where they wanted to take him, but he complied. Smith and

Homewood-Brushton activist William "Bouie" Haden (pictured here on the left with Phil Carter). Under Haden's leadership, the Black United Movement for Progress escalated demands for equal access to employment opportunities for Pittsburgh's black population.
Source: Ulish Carter, "News Media Draws Wrath of Angry Black Leaders Who Support Kohlman," *New Pittsburgh Courier,* 12 Jan. 1974.

his comrades walked Epperson to their car and drove over to a construction site on the North Side, where some fifty black workers had gathered to express their grievances with the construction industry and the city's toleration of racism in employment practices. [11]

Smith urged the men to speak their mind and asked Epperson to take their job demands to the mayor's office. It was a tense meeting. The men expressed a desire to reach their goals by peaceful means if possible but by violence if necessary, mainly because white construction workers regularly expressed their determination to use violence to keep blacks out. Epperson recalled that it was clear (even before a revolver fell out of the pocket of one man) that these men were determined to take aggressive steps to secure a livelihood. Epperson returned to his office and helped to persuade the Mayor's Committee on Human Resources (which evolved into Pittsburgh's War on Poverty Community Action Program in 1967) to provide financial support for Operation Dig's training program. [12]

Federal equal employment opportunity agencies reinforced the economic demands of Pittsburgh's black community. Following President John F. Kennedy's assassination in 1963, his successor, Lyndon Baines

Pittsburgh's black leaders, such as Nate Smith (pictured here), were involved in the integration of the building trades in 1969–1970.
Source: Carnegie Museum of Art, Charles "Teenie" Harris Collection, photo #2001.35.7578. Photograph © 2009 Carnegie Museum of Art, Pittsburgh.

Johnson, responded to the escalating Civil Rights movement by initiating his "Great Society" program. A centerpiece of Johnson's economic reforms was the "War on Poverty" as reflected in the Civil Rights Act of 1964, particularly Title VII, which established the Equal Employment Opportunity Commission (EEOC) to investigate and remedy racial discrimination by both companies and unions. At about the same time, Johnson's Executive Order 11246 (1965) required that federal contractors take "affirmative action" to ensure equality of employment opportunities.[13]

In 1964, the Office of Economic Opportunity under Joseph Barr, Lawrence's successor as mayor, mandated "maximum feasible participation" of citizens in municipal decision making. Accordingly, Barr established an independent Committee on Human Resources that focused community organizing in eight neighborhoods with the highest concentrations of poverty and welfare cases in the city. Target communities included the Hill District, East Liberty, Homewood-Brushton, and the North Side. Each of these neighborhoods elected a citizens committee to encourage grassroots participation and decision making.[14] Under the leadership of David G. Hill, executive director, Pittsburgh's War on Poverty Community Action Program (CAP) received the highest per capita funding of any urban program in the nation. Mayor Barr agreed to a decentralization of funding so that neighborhoods could exercise a great deal of control over resources and programs in employment, education, family services, and legal aid. CAP collaborated with the Allegheny Conference on Community Development (ACCD), and supported a variety of community-based organizations to facilitate the growth of grassroots initiatives. These efforts continued under the new model cities program set up under the federal Demonstration Cities and Metropolitan Development Act of 1966. Faculty and students at the University of Pittsburgh's School of Social Work encouraged these activities and helped to open the way for grassroots challenges to the established Democratic machine.[15]

As early as 1963, the Pennsylvania Human Relations Commission (PHRC), strengthened by recent federal legislation, cited seven all-white craft unions for racial discrimination and ordered them to admit black workers to membership and apprenticeship programs. Rather than contesting the ruling, the offending unions—the Steamfitters Local 449; IBEW Local 5; Iron Workers Local 3; Plumbers Local 27; Elevator Construction Local 6; Painters Local 751; and Asbestos Local 2—accepted the commission's order to enroll qualified black journeymen; permit neutral observers to oversee written, oral, and/or performance examinations; and to provide written reports on the status of nonwhite applicants for apprenticeship programs.[16]

Local courts upheld the city's fair employment practices ordinance in the *City of Pittsburgh vs. Plumbers Local No. 27* (1965). The court fined the IBEW union $400 for barring two black nonunion journeymen from membership on the basis of race. In the meantime, in early 1964, the Master Builders Association adopted resolutions supporting equal opportunity for black workers and agreed to provide jobs to all "card-carrying Negro carpenters." Nearly one hundred black men acquired jobs as heavy equipment operators, but this effort was not enough to offset the impact of years of exclusion from this vital industry.[17]

African Americans also continued their relentless struggle to break down barriers in public education. Activist students, teachers, and civil rights organizations protested racial segregation and discrimination in the education of black children and the employment of black educators. In August 1965, nearly 150 people picketed the Pittsburgh Board of Education building in Oakland, calling for an end to de facto segregation and overcrowding at Westinghouse High School in Homewood. Byrd Brown told school board officials, "We want action now—not in five or ten years."[18] Movement leaders also warned the board, "The temper of the residents of Homewood-Brushton is short and seething . . . this community has been considerate and patient . . . but it and the collaborating organizations are at the point of exhaustion and frustration." When the school board dragged its feet, picketing continued sporadically through 1966 and 1967. Crowds of pickets circled the Board of Education offices on Bellefield Street in Oakland, opposing the board's policy of "voluntary transfers" and demanding "compulsory busing" to achieve racial balance in the schools.[19]

The Pittsburgh chapter of the NAACP insisted that the Board of Education immediately desegregate all elementary schools in order to create equality of education across the color line over time. Conversely, "the Great Schools" idea of Superintendent Sidney Marland accented what he called "compensatory education" rather than desegregation. It called for the construction of five large high schools for the city, each located in their respective district. Assuming substantial funding from state and federal sources, each school would accommodate a student population of between three thousand and five thousand. Marland's plan aimed to integrate the schools by drawing upon diverse neighborhoods, including predominantly black ones, but it would not disrupt existing patterns of white power at the local level. As the board put it: "To remove a child by government action from his neighborhood and locate him in a different neighborhood solely to accomplish an enforced integration which may be contrary to his family's wishes is as serious affront to freedom as enforced segregation." At the same time, Marland misread the force of the African American social revolution. He told the Allegheny Conference on Community Development that the "poor are not yet the initiators and agenda makers of the revolution, therefore it [the "Great Schools"] is still a revolutionary effort by our society for them."[20] Yet black students would soon expose flaws in Marland's judgment regarding the African American community's commitment to social change.

The Pittsburgh Board of Education responded to the demands of African Americans partly by forging bonds with federal agencies, philanthropic organizations, and leading institutions of higher education. The National Defense Education Act of 1965 financed the city's compensatory education programs; the Ford Foundation funded the board's "Team Teaching Project" for inner-city schools; the local Buhl Foundation funded the board's Negro Education Emergency Drive (NEED) program to aid prospective black college students; and David Lewis, the Andrew Mellon Professor of Architecture and Urban Design at Carnegie Institute of Technology (later Carnegie Mellon University) conducted research supporting Marland's "Education Park" idea. The of impact of such programs on African American children was very helpful, but the Board of Education estimated that its desegregation programs would call for a 15 to 20 percent increase in its budget. Only by receiving federal funds and local and national foundation support, the board believed, could it initiate and sustain special programs in inner-city neighborhoods; instead, de facto segregation in the Pittsburgh schools proceeded apace.[21]

In 1961, the legislature expanded the Pennsylvania Human Relations Commission's jurisdiction to include education as well as employment and housing discrimination. Buoyed by the federal Civil Rights Acts of 1964 and 1965, the PHRC cited many local school districts (including Pittsburgh's) for maintaining racially imbalanced schools. The commission also initiated proceedings against Pittsburgh and other urban school districts to force the adoption of appropriate remedies. In *Pennsylvania Human Relations Commission v. Chester School District* (1967), the Pennsylvania Supreme Court upheld the commission's mandate. This ruling made it possible for the PHRC to compel compliance and, in theory, force districts to adopt meaningful desegregation plans. On 2 February 1968, the PHRC ordered the Pittsburgh Board of Education to desegregate its schools. The order required Pittsburgh to "submit plans to eliminate the racial imbalance and . . . to implement this plan, together with a timetable."[22]

In 1965, Pittsburgh public schools issued a statement deploring "the segregation of children for reasons of race, religion, economic handicap, or any other difference." The board now clearly stated its belief in the justice of school integration. "We have stated without qualification that we believe in integrated schools. This works at cross purposes with those who seek to preserve all-white neighborhoods."[23] The school board also linked the city's "best hope for an integrated society" to the allocation of additional resources for the education of black children. The number of black education professionals increased from 137, or 5.3 percent of all professionals in 1955, to 301, or 9.8 percent, in 1964. The number of black public school teachers, supplemented by nurses, social workers, and retail salespersons, signaled the gradual emergence of a new black middle class. Moreover, the number of black nonprofessional staff—clerical, kitchen staff, and custodial services—increased even more rapidly than professional positions. In 1963, African Americans made up 315 (about 20 percent) of the total 1,541 nonprofessional employees; in the following years, they also took a large proportion of the new nonprofessional jobs opening up (24 percent of 167 new positions in 1963 and 34 percent of 236 new positions in 1964).[24]

Educational integration was further advanced by the selection of two African Americans to the Pittsburgh Board of Education. In 1966, attorney Richard F. Jones became one of two vice presidents of the board. At about the same time, Gladys McNairy became the first African American woman to serve on the board. In 1971, McNairy also became the first black president of the Pittsburgh Board of Education. Following the selection of black members to the board, African Americans waged a relentless campaign to open up board meetings for discussion and action on a broad range of issues involving black children and the schools. The United Movement for Progress placed representation in the school system and input on policy making at the top of its list of demands. As African Americans among other groups (including the Teachers Union) escalated their demands for representation, the influential Pittsburgh Council on Public Education concluded that a major problem confronting the board was its detachment from the larger Pittsburgh public. Accordingly, the council encouraged the board to "listen to and talk with the community." Partly through the mediating role of the council, the board instituted a system of regular Tuesday public hearings before each monthly meeting, and a parent representative system to aid in gathering input from the community.[25]

Larger numbers of black teachers, counselors, administrators, and board members helped to gradually improve certain aspects of black education. Students at Vann, Westwood, Madison, and Beltzhoover schools scored higher than the national average in reading and mathematics. African American principals Doris Brevard, Janet Bell, Vivian Williams, and Louis Vernon gained a good deal of credit for such successes. Black students gained greater access to opportunities for college preparatory courses, athletics, clubs, and curriculum that featured black people in a positive light. The board also initiated plans with the University of Pittsburgh and Duquesne University to develop a new teachers' program, the Urban Teacher Project, which proposed to add a fifth-year of training to prepare a new generation of teachers for service in poor urban communities.[26]

Black students won a rising number of prestigious college scholarships. In 1964, seventy-four black students from nine of the city's high schools received college scholarships; one third of those came from Westinghouse (sixteen students) and Schenley (eight students). These graduates not only attended historically black colleges and universities like Howard, Fisk, Morgan State, Lincoln University, and Central State, but Harvard, Princeton, University of Pennsylvania, Northwestern, and the University of Pittsburgh. Moreover, the National Achievement Scholarship Program cited the accomplishments of twenty-two black high school graduates from Pittsburgh, and now-famous writer John Edgar Wideman, a graduate of Peabody High School and the University of Pennsylvania, was "the only recent Rhodes scholar" from the Pittsburgh region.[27]

Alongside escalating marches and protests for jobs and education, African Americans intensified their push for open housing. In early 1967, the city enacted a new fair housing ordinance. Unlike the 1958 law, the new ordinance instituted a penalty of $300 or ninety days imprisonment for persons found guilty of breaking the law, whereas the earlier statute mandated a fine of only $100 or 30 days imprisonment for each violation.[28] Under the new fair housing law, African American realtor Robert Lavelle filed suit against the Greater Pittsburgh Multilist, Inc. In the case of *Robert R. Lavelle v. The Greater Pittsburgh Multilist, Inc. and P. J. Ricca* (1967), black realtors won a landmark decision. The U.S. District Court for the Western District of Pennsylvania ruled that the exclusion of Lavelle from GPM membership constituted "a conspiracy" by white members—to illegally constrain interstate commerce and to deprive black brokers of a livelihood. In the wake of Lavelle's suit, banks and building and loan associations went on record as willing to lend "to any qualified" applicant and to finance housing "in any area," without regard to color, race, or religion.[29]

Black public housing residents and renters of substandard housing also increased their demands for more and better places for poor and working-class people to live. Under the leadership of Dorothy Richardson, a North Side resident, African Americans and their white allies formed Citizens Against Slum Housing (CASH). Pennsylvania's Rent Withholding Act of 1965–1966 (PRWA) strengthened grassroots organizations like CASH by enabling tenants to stop payment for apartments in the face of housing code violations. Encouraged by the provisions of this new legislation, CASH pushed for code enforcement, the construction of new public housing to absorb the city's expanding black population, and a housing court to compel landlords to make necessary repairs and ensure that residences were fit for human habitation. By August 1967, the city had established such a housing court and had escalated efforts to improve housing for the city's poor and working-class residents.[30]

The Rise of Black Power

Despite the escalation of marches, protests, and legal actions against racial inequality in the city's economy, housing, and schools, the color line persisted, and the slow pace of change heightened the racial consciousness of black Pittsburghers. As early as 1964, during the presidential election in Pittsburgh, signs appeared urging whites to "vote white—vote Goldwater," and to "Vote White—Vote Republican." By the end of 1966, the Mayor's Commission on Human Relations described "definite signs of progress" for African Americans "in employment and public accommodations and a limited extent in housing," but concluded, "more Negroes are worse off educationally, economically, and socially than they were 12 years ago at the beginning of the Civil Rights movement."[31]

Pittsburgh's nonviolent direct action campaigns encountered stiff white opposition, particularly in the hiring, promotion, and upgrading of blacks into jobs heretofore reserved primarily for whites. In 1967, the *Pittsburgh Courier* bitterly declared that Renaissance I had passed over the city's poor black community: "Hidden in the shadows of the city's Renaissance are the slums and ghettoes of Negroes. Negroes have not benefited from the resurgence fostered by the city fathers. They have been ignored and overlooked in the planning of their neighborhoods, their communities, their health and welfare."[32] The *Courier* not only captured the pain of urban renewal in the city's North Side black community, it also highlighted their exclusion from work on the urban renewal building boom. African Americans resented employment discrimination on projects that sprang up on the ground of their old homes, businesses, and cultural institutions. Black people witnessed material progress in their old neighborhood and did not like what they saw. Young people were especially disappointed by the evidence of progress that seemed to leave African Americans behind: "They saw white men working on the projects while their fathers stood on street corners and their mothers went to work in Miss Anne's kitchen. Black people [observed] . . . urban renewal for the benefit of Whitey, and they don't like it. . . . Their reactions are sporadic and violent."[33]

Violence had already erupted in cities across the urban North and West between 1964 and 1967. Government officials called these outbreaks of violence civil disorders or spontaneous riots, but they also exhibited features of African American rebellion and revolt, rooted in dissatisfaction with class and racial inequality. African Americans warned city officials that the persistence of racial inequality meant the risk of violence in the streets. In a meeting with church leaders, Rev. James J. (Jimmy Joe) Robinson declared, "All we're asking for is a spirit of commitment. If not, there's going to be bloodshed." In a speech at the Pittsburgh Plate Glass Foundation, Whitney Young, head of the National Urban League made the same point, concluding, "If responsible Negro and white Americans do not act together, black and white demagogues could drive a wedge between them which may serve to keep them permanently apart."[34]

In March 1968, the *Pittsburgh Courier* revealed that blacks in Pittsburgh were planning a "B-Day" ("Burn Day") for May. On 5 April 1968, the day after Martin Luther King's assassination, violence erupted in Pittsburgh's Hill District a month earlier than predicted. Beginning at a meat market on Centre Avenue, looting and fire bombing spread over eight days to nearby Wylie, Dinwiddie, and Fifth avenues; Webster, Elmore, Bedford, Hillman, and other adjacent streets; to the nearby neighborhoods of Oakland, Herron Hill, Hazelwood, and Lawrenceville; to the North Side–Manchester area; to Homewood-Brushton; and to the outlying river towns of Duquesne and Braddock.[35]

While the rebels targeted the usual predominantly white-owned retail establishments like groceries, liquor stores, pharmacies, and bakeries, African American shopkeepers also felt compelled to camp out overnight to protect their property from the torch. Realtor Robert Lavelle had just completed the redesign of his building using a black architect and black

Violence broke out in 1968 following Dr. Martin Luther King Jr.'s assassination.
Police in riot gear lined up downtown near Washington Plaza, 1968.
Source: Carnegie Museum of Art, Charles "Teenie" Harris Collection, photo #2001.35.4646.
Photograph © 2009 Carnegie Museum of Art, Pittsburgh.

contractor, but black people, he said, "were equating me with white. I
wore a necktie and represented the status quo. I got calls all that night
that Saturday saying they were going to bomb my building." The following morning, someone came to the church where Lavelle taught Sunday
School and told him that most of the other buildings were on fire, but his
remained intact.[36]

As the violence spread into Homewood-Brushton, the governor
dispatched some 4,500 National Guardsmen and 350 state troopers
to supplement the city's 1,400-person police force. Five nights of arson
and looting resulted in 1,300 arrests; one death; 515 fires; and $620,000
in property damage. African American policeman William "Mugsy"
Moore, head of the city's police community relations unit, recalled,
"Youngsters were very angry. You could feel the hatred and hostility."
Rev. LeRoy Patrick, former pastor of the Homewood Bethesda Presbyte-

Police officers in riot gear pursuing individuals in crowd, c. 1960–1975.
Source: Carnegie Museum of Art, Charles "Teenie" Harris Collection, photo #2001.35.4644.
Photograph © 2009 Carnegie Museum of Art, Pittsburgh.

rian Church, later described the warlike atmosphere in the neighborhood of his church: "I went out to look at the troops standing on Homewood Ave. I could hardly believe this in Pittsburgh. Troops with combat gear, big boots, khaki, helicopters overhead. That kind of thing is indelibly impressed on your mind."[37]

On the morning of the rebellion, Alma Fox, then executive director of the NAACP and later chair of the Mayor's Commission on Human Relations, remembered that the organization had planned a peaceful march from Freedom Corner, at Centre and Crawford avenues, to Downtown, but was confronted by the police tactical squad, "lined up with their legs spread and touching shoe to shoe. They held their nightsticks in front, and they looked 10 miles long. You have to picture this scene with flames up Centre Avenue and the line of police facing us." Fox nonetheless somehow penetrated police lines and got arrested: "I was in the front line . . . so I just crawled through. They threw me bodily into the paddy wagon." Although safety director David Craig and Lieutenant Moore of the Pittsburgh police pleaded for her to get out of the vehicle, she refused, saying, "Not unless we can march."[38]

Partly because of Fox's determination, the NAACP won the right to march downtown to Point State Park. Craig, who later became a commonwealth court judge, recalled why the city tried to cancel the NAACP's march permit: "There was literally smoke from buildings rising from the Hill. The National Guard was moving in on Bigelow Boulevard as we stood there. . . . Should we revoke the parade permit at that time? . . . Some suggested I revoke it. Mayor Barr left the decision to me. I decided not to revoke the permit on the faith that it could be conducted without injury. It was." In Craig's view, Pittsburgh's employment of a civilian safety director, who exercised authority over the fire and police departments, made it possible to mediate conflicting interests and curtail violence between demonstrators, rioters, and police. According to Craig, "Not a shot was fired by police that weekend. Not one policeman injured. Thousands were arrested, but there was a remarkably low level of complaints about how arrests were handled."[39] Race relations in Pittsburgh nonetheless remained tense through the summer of 1968, when a group of black men physically assaulted John P. Kelley, assistant police superintendent, during a protest involving police brutality in the city council chambers.[40]

Compared to other cities, a variety of factors curtailed the extent of violence in Pittsburgh in the aftermath of King's assassination. By heavily patrolling the borders between black and white areas, police contained the violence within the boundaries of local black communities. Nearby establishments in Downtown, the East End, and the predominantly white communities of Squirrel Hill, Shadyside, and Regent Square escaped the violence. On the city's North Side, Rev. Jimmy Joe Robinson, black policeman Harvey Adams, James "Swampman" Williams, and Lieutenant Mugsy Moore joined forces and worked with youth gangs, including gang leader Percy Trevillion's "Black Rangers," to squash a possible shootout between black youth and police.[41] In the Hill District, state legislator K. LeRoy Irvis and other black leaders took to the streets, talking to large crowds, and urging them to disperse. On one occasion, Irvis prevented attacks on two policemen and later recruited young participants themselves to help keep the peace. Young men responded to Irvis's request and posted guards around his Centre Avenue apartment. In a subsequent meeting with public officials, one hundred predominantly white Hill District businessmen criticized the city for failing to protect their property in black neighborhoods. Irvis reminded the men that some had benefited immensely from the Hill but had not reinvested in the community. "It is time," Irvis said, "for you to examine your consciences, you have taken and not given." He also took the men to task for failing to communicate with him except on an emergency basis. "The only time you come to talk with me is when you're in trouble. You have a board of trade in the Hill. Get together among yourselves and come to me with some concrete plans."[42]

In Homewood-Brushton, at a meeting convened by Lieutenant Moore, grassroots black leaders met with the Pittsburgh police department and the National Guard. They urged law enforcement officials to withdraw from Homewood and allow the community to patrol its own streets. This meeting included African Americans Nick Flournoy, Bouie Haden, Nate Smith, and others; David W. Craig, safety director, and James Slusser, police superintendent, among others from Mayor Joseph Barr's office; and John K. Tabor from the governor's office. During an extremely heated discussion on the matter, Slusser said that he opposed giving authority to "hoodlums and tiny criminal elements fomenting riots," but Haden retorted, "We're all hoodlums with records but we can stop the riots." The meeting nearly collapsed following Slusser's statement, but city police and the National Guard agreed to allow twenty special community-based deputies to patrol the neighborhood to help prevent violence.[43]

The postwar proliferation of interracial organizations in Pittsburgh also helped to alleviate interracial conflict and curtailed the incidence of violence. In addition to white participation in the work of the Pittsburgh NAACP, Urban League, and civil rights departments of USWA locals, a variety of predominantly white ethnic, religious, denominational, and civic organizations developed programs designed to address the social implications of Pittsburgh's expanding black population. Protestant, Catholic, and Jewish organizations all established special committees or organizations to alleviate racial tensions and prevent the outbreak of violence. Rev. Donald McIlvane, the priest at St. Richards Parish in the Hill District, spearheaded the creation of the Citizen-Clergy Coordinating Committee, an umbrella organization of some thirty community groups, to work with the NAACP and grassroots organizations like CASH.[44]

Despite evidence of interracial cooperation in the wake of King's assassination and the violence of 1968, the Black Power movement emerged at the center of Pittsburgh's African American freedom struggle during the late 1960s and early 1970s. Helping to fuel the rise of the Black Power movement on both the local and national levels was the spread of the Nation of Islam. In 1945, African Americans established the First Muslim Mosque of Pittsburgh, Incorporated, on Wylie Avenue in the Hill

District. This mosque became the first in the United States to be char-
tered by American-born blacks. In the years after World War II, as Islam expanded its influence, the *Pittsburgh Courier* regularly carried Elijah
Muhammad's weekly column, "Muhammad Speaks."[45] Influential civic
leaders urged the *Courier* to discontinue the column and take out ads
condemning Elijah Muhammad and the Nation of Islam. Derrick Bell,
executive secretary of the Pittsburgh branch of the NAACP, resisted
such calls. He explained that efforts to drive the Muslims from public life
would camouflage the underlying social injustices that fueled the growing militance of the city's black population: "Many, many Negroes did
not need Elijah Muhammad and his Muslim doctrine [to attribute] . . .
their lowly position in the American social and economic scale to whites.
A lengthy tour through . . . the dark alleys of Pittsburgh's Lower Hill will
be beneficial to those who are surprised that bitterness exists."[46]

The teachings of Minister Malcolm X captured the imagination of a
young generation of urban blacks in Pittsburgh and elsewhere. Malcolm
X regularly spoke in Pittsburgh and other large metropolitan areas in
the country. Before and especially after his break with Elijah Muhammad, his message of black nationalism helped to change the political
landscape of Pittsburgh and the nation. Advocates of Black Power such
as Stokely Carmichael of the Student Nonviolent Coordinating Committee (SNCC) and Huey P. Newton and Bobby Seale of the Black
Panther Party, inspired by the ideas of Malcolm X, helped to usher in
a more militant phase of the black freedom movement. When African
Americans formed the United Movement for Progress in 1967, *Courier*
journalist Carl Morris announced the arrival of the "Black Fist" in Pittsburgh, "ushering in the era of militant civil rights protests, the beginning
of blackness in a city where color prejudice was rampant. Black is here,
Baby!" The line between nonviolent direct action and the Black Power
movement was not drawn so starkly in Pittsburgh as suggested by some
accounts. Gail Austin, a student activist at the University of Pittsburgh
at the time, later described the modern Civil Rights and Black Power
movements as the "same movement," but "two wings." Austin recalled
visits to Pittsburgh by both Martin Luther King Jr. and Stokely Carmichael. In her words, both men "validated" aspects of her emerging political consciousness, but the ideas of the Student Nonviolent Coordinating
Committee and the burgeoning ideology of Black Power exercised a more
profound influence on Austin's thinking than did the philosophy of King
and the Southern Christian Leadership Conference. Along with many

In November 1966, Dr. Martin Luther King Jr. spoke at the student union of the University of Pittsburgh. James McCoy of the NAACP and the United Negro Protest Committee "officially welcomed" King to Pittsburgh as he entered the union.
Source: Carnegie Museum of Art, Charles "Teenie" Harris Collection, photo # 2001.35.5829. Photograph © 2009 Carnegie Museum of Art, Pittsburgh.

other black Pittsburghers, Gail Austin heard Stokely Carmichael speak at both the University of Pittsburgh and in the Hill District. She later recalled that Carmichael's eloquence, logic, and determination to help forge a black liberation movement attracted her to the ideology of Black Power.[47]

The Vietnam War also helped to transform the political consciousness of Pittsburgh's black community. The Hill District and Homewood-Brushton provided a large number of recruits. Richard Craddock of the Hill District served tours of duty with two of his brothers in Vietnam. Craddock recalled preoccupation with the day-to-day demands of war until the assassination of Martin Luther King Jr. He later told Samuel W. Black, curator of the nationally acclaimed museum exhibit, "Soul Soldiers: African Americans and the Vietnam Era," that he willingly served in the Vietnam War but he questioned the war against the liberation struggles of black people in Pittsburgh and across the United States.[48]

Whereas the Craddock brothers volunteered for the armed services,

Stokely Carmichael (Kwame Touré) visited Pittsburgh and spoke at both the University of Pittsburgh and within the African American community. He is shown here speaking at a church with a WAMO microphone, c. 1960–1975.
Source: Carnegie Museum of Art, Charles "Teenie" Harris Collection, photo #2001.35.8843. Photograph © 2009 Carnegie Museum of Art, Pittsburgh.

others were drafted. Hill District veteran David Alonzo Shelton recalled his induction into the military as a "kidnapping" experience. "They had to jump on me to hold me down," he said. Before induction into the military, Shelton explained, "I wasn't exposed to a lot of athleticism, because I was in church for practically at least three nights a week and Saturday. And then we had to go out and do field service where we just went to people's homes." Although Shelton went on to serve in a combat unit and received numerous military honors, including a Bronze Star and Purple Heart, he recalled his induction as a coerced experience that embittered him during his entire tour of duty in Vietnam.[49]

In Pittsburgh, as elsewhere, government officials targeted young black civil rights activists for military service during the Vietnam War. The Pittsburgh-area draft board cooperated with Louisiana officials in drafting Michael Flournoy, although he was twenty-six years of age at the time, due to his civil rights activities in rural Louisiana and other parts of the South. Flournoy later recalled that his induction into the military, and subsequent service in Vietnam, represented a shift "from one war to another." In their struggle for equal rights within and outside the military, black Vietnam veterans also gave to the black freedom movement one of its most powerful symbols of unity, the "dap," a Black Power handshake. Writer Wallace Terry described the "dap" as having over fifty variations.[50]

In 1970, the NAACP's United Negro Protest Committee reconstituted itself as the United Black Protest Committee (UBPC) and renewed its push for better jobs. The NAACP-UBPC organized a boycott of Sears stores to protest low numbers of African American employees (see table 19). Designating a "Black Monday" boycott of stores in the Pittsburgh area in November 1969, the NAACP-UBPC promised that the boycott could extend to "Tuesdays, and every day [Sears] chooses to open its doors to the public." Following nearly four years of petitions, Sears signed a new agreement, including a deposit of $10,000 into the African American owned Dwelling House Savings and Loan Association.[51]

Pittsburgh's Black Power movement would gain its most articulate expression with the emergence of the Black Construction Coalition (BCC) and the rise of the Black Student Movement. In 1969, following two years of resistance from the building and construction trades, African Americans established the BCC to fight discrimination in the construction industry. A grassroots umbrella organization, the BCC included Operation Dig, the NAACP, the Bidwell Training Center, the Democratic Association of Black Brothers (DABB), and a host of community-based organizations and anti-poverty agencies. Under the leadership of Clyde Jackson, the coalition, with strong support on area campuses, charged the city's building trades with systematic discrimination against blacks. The BCC gained a major victory when the building trades agreed to the Pittsburgh Plan, a volunteer program designed to increase the training and hiring of blacks for construction jobs. Under this plan, blacks gradually gained access to the building and construction trades. The road to achieving this goal, however, was difficult and violent.[52]

In the summer of 1969, the BCC staged marches at nearly a dozen construction sites over two weeks and demanded an end to discriminatory employment and labor practices (see table 20). The organization also called for equal access to apprenticeship training and jobs for black workers upon completing their training. Over a three-day period between what activists called "Black Monday" (25 August) and Wednesday (27 August) 1969, African Americans and their white allies picketed sites including Three Rivers Stadium on the North Side; the U.S. Steel Building downtown; and the Western Psychiatric Institute and WQED television station in Oakland. On the first day of protests, well over one thousand demonstrators gathered for a march across the Manchester Bridge to the Three Rivers Stadium construction site. At the outset of the gathering, attorney Byrd Brown set the tone. Although the demonstrators had already forced authorities to close down all major construction sites in the city "to avoid violence" during the impending mass marches, Brown told the gathering, "This is not a victory. They are shut down only for one day. We of the BCC do not have a one-day goal. We do not intend to get bogged down in negotiations while they continue to work on these jobs. We are going to march."[53]

The BCC defied a court injunction to limit the number of marchers to twenty people. Marchers not only crossed the bridge en mass to the Three Rivers Stadium site, but paraded through Downtown to the site of the U.S. Steel Building. The demonstrators chanted, "Jobs now, jobs now" and "more jobs now for black men." When demonstrators discovered white men working on the U.S. Steel building in violation of the city's order to close, they chanted "Close it down, close it down," and forced white workers off the job. During the BCC demonstrations, one white truck driver for the Calig Steel Drum Company responded to chants for employment and jobs by yelling out the window of his truck, "Want a job niggers? Join the army!" Some black activists recalled confronting members of the John Birch Society anti–civil rights marchers on Downtown streets. In some cases, members of white crowds wore Nazi symbols.[54]

Police exercised restraint on the first day of protests but aggressively confronted, beat, maced, and arrested demonstrators on the second day. These actions resulted in twelve injuries among police and thirty among demonstrators, including NAACP president Byrd Brown, Rev. Jimmy Joe Robinson of Bidwell Presbyterian Church, and Eugene Robinson of the community employment program on the city's South Side. In beating and arresting one demonstrator, a policeman declared, "I'm gonna kill you nigger." Police arrested 180 demonstrators on "disorderly conduct" charges, and the municipal court fined each person $25 and ordered each to pay $11 for cost of court. Authorities charged another 9 of the marchers with "inciting a riot" and placed each under $10,000 bond.[55]

"Black Monday" demonstration on behalf of the Black Construction Coalition, near the Civic Arena and Chatham Center, with WIIC-TV Channel 11 car in foreground, 1969.
Source: Carnegie Museum of Art, Charles "Teenie" Harris Collection, photo #2001.35.10587. Photograph © 2009 Carnegie Museum of Art, Pittsburgh.

The *Pittsburgh Courier* bitterly protested police conduct on the second day of the protests. The police not only maced black leaders, but knocked women and children to the ground, denied black people the right to peaceably assemble, and conducted "mass arrests, and mass convictions." Attorney Wendell Freeland observed and commented on the city's violation of the demonstrators' civil rights and called the proceedings a "kangaroo court." Freeland also later sadly recalled how the city's bar association refused to help prevent the mistreatment of poor and working-class people by the legal system. Only the presence of African American policemen on the front lines of subsequent marches helped to curtail the incidence of police harassment and arrests of protesters.[56]

Police brutality and misconduct within the black community also fueled the rise of a Pittsburgh chapter of the Black Panther Party. In the wake of the 1 April 1970 police shooting of Robert Lowery, a black teenager, African Americans formed the Black Panther Party and opened

Members of the paramilitary Democratic Association of Black Brothers holding dogs face policemen at the U.S. Steel Building during the Black Construction Coalition demonstrations of 1969.

Source: Photo by Ross Catanza. Copyright ©, *Pittsburgh Post-Gazette*, 2009, all rights reserved. Reprinted with permission.

local headquarters at 574 Brushton Avenue. Following the lead of Black Panther units across the nation, the Pittsburgh chapter not only protested police brutality, but also established a free breakfast program for needy families and made plans for a free health clinic and a free clothing project. The local Panthers also organized among high school students and staged a few highly visible marches and parades through the streets of Pittsburgh, targeting particularly the issue of police brutality. In an interview with the *Courier,* Harold Wright, a spokesman for the local chapter, declared that "Raymond Lowery was unarmed at the time of the shooting, therefore we feel that there cannot possibly exist any justification for this attempted, almost successful, murder . . . of a black teenager."[57] Describing the actions of the Pittsburgh Police Department as "criminal," the Black Panther Party concluded that shooting of Lowery placed "the life and safety of every teenager in the black community in serious jeopardy."[58]

The Pittsburgh chapter of the Black Panther Party emerged within the larger context of growing federal repression of radical political organizations nationwide. In early 1968, the Federal Bureau of Investigation

In April 1970, the Pittsburgh Black Panther Party opened headquarters in
Homewood-Brushton. In this street demonstration, c. 1970–1975, a banner shows a
fist breaking a chain inscribed "Blood."
Source: Carnegie Museum of Art, Charles "Teenie" Harris Collection, photo #2001.35.7015.
Photograph © 2009 Carnegie Museum of Art, Pittsburgh.

had named the Black Panther Party as the greatest threat to the internal
security of the United States. During the final years of the decade, FBI
attacks on Panther headquarters largely removed the organization as an
effective force for socioeconomic and political change. By May 1970, U.S.
Attorney General John Mitchell reported that militant groups like the
Black Panther Party no longer represented "a real threat to the United
States" as far as its established institutions were concerned. At the same
time, the *New Pittsburgh Courier* lamented that the city's Black Panther
Party had opened up an office that promised to impact the social welfare
of poor and working-class black people, but had disappeared from public
view even more swiftly than it had emerged.[59] Partly because the Pittsburgh office of the Black Panther Party opened late, amid rising government repression of radical political organizations on a national scale, its
accomplishments and degree of local activism was less extensive than its
counterparts in other major U.S. cities.

Following the outbreak of violence in 1968, white business, social welfare, and political leaders expressed greater sensitivity to the needs of the black community. Tim Stevens, youth director of the NAACP at the time, recalled, "It was frustrating to those of us who didn't believe in violence, but the riots of 1968 did bring things to focus." The Allegheny Conference on Community Development gradually shifted its focus from improvements in physical space to the development of social welfare programs to benefit the poor. The organization provided some $14 million in loans and loan guarantees to prospective black entrepreneurs over the next five years; initiated an aggressive program to hire more black people in the central business district and business establishments throughout the city; and established job training programs for unemployed black youth. The ACCD also supported Forever Action Together (FAT), a coalition of some sixty neighborhood groups formed in 1968 and headed by Episcopalian minister Rev. Canon Carter of Holy Cross Church in Homewood-Brushton, to coordinate the activities of over seventy different citizen groups in the Homewood-Brushton community. Headed by civil rights activist Clyde Jackson, the United Black Front (UBF) also gained grants for economic development in the Hill. Formed in 1968, following the MLK revolt, the UBF established a community food mart, a nail factory (the only black-owned one in the country), and job training programs, including business education for running the food mart. Under K. Leroy Irvis's leadership, African Americans also gained state funds for job training programs such as Opportunities Industrialization Centers (OIC), Bidwell Training Center, and the Hill Phoenix Shopping Center, which stimulated the return of businesses, including a larger grocery store, to the area.[60]

Area companies during this period developed aggressive campaigns to promote their image as equal opportunity employers. In addition to sending letters to civil rights and social service organizations like the NAACP and Urban League that confirmed their commitment to nondiscriminatory hiring policies, steel companies like U.S. Steel and J&L regularly paid for advertisements in the black press. Such ads featured photos of black employees and assured black readers that the steel industry stood for "quality people, for a quality product."[61]

At the same time, the USWA escalated its support of national civil rights organizations like the NAACP and the National Urban League. As early as 1961, president David McDonald joined civil rights groups in urging an end to discrimination "in all its open and hidden forms." A year later, the USWA inserted nondiscrimination clauses into its contracts with steel companies. Such provisions promised to help black workers gain access to apprenticeship and training programs as well as promotions within the steel industry. At the same time, McDonald expanded the number of black representatives on the USWA's national civil rights committee from one in 1952 to four in 1965. Subsequently, most locals formed civil rights committees and by the 1968 convention, twenty-eight of the union's thirty district offices had employed civil rights coordinators. Under the impact of African American protests against job discrimination, the number of blacks in Pittsburgh area steel mills increased from 8,231 in 1960 to 10,975 in 1963 and to 11,762 in 1964.[62]

Education, Housing, and Social Services

Following Martin Luther King Jr.'s assassination in 1968, African Americans in Pittsburgh intensified their demands for desegregation of the public schools. In the summer of 1968, the Black United Movement for Progress interrupted the board's public hearings at the Frick School in Oakland. Bouie Haden and his group, including some whites, staged a mock trial to determine responsibility for the criminal neglect of black children's education. Rev. LeRoy Patrick, chairman of the NAACP's education committee, criticized the superintendent of schools for ignoring the results of his own research: "The Superintendent's own figures show that the Negro child is not getting quality education." Similarly, Eric Springer, president of the city's Human Relations Council, challenged the sanctity of neighborhood schools. "Under no circumstance," Springer said, "should a neighborhood school be considered exclusive. It is the property of all citizens." The United Movement for Progress held a mock trial in which they found the Pittsburgh Board of Education guilty. Accordingly, the group gave the board an ultimatum to transfer, by September 1968, a large number of inner-city black youth from predominantly black and overcrowded schools to predominantly white schools with lower occupancy rates and few or no black students.[63] While the city dragged its feet on desegregation, by September the board responded to increasing protests by opening its meetings to greater public participation.

African Americans not only demanded desegregation of the schools, but transformation of the schools' curriculum, culture, and learning environment as well. In May 1968, attorney Byrd Brown, president of the NAACP, criticized the Pittsburgh Board of Education for misrepresenting black culture and history in its curriculum, which was taught by predominantly white teachers. Brown expressed this growing nationalist consciousness of Pittsburgh's black community when he said: "We can no longer allow a Black child to feel shamed and humiliated because of his race." Furthermore, Brown called for the removal of school officials who permitted the denigration of black people: "A superintendent of schools with his old guard staff and a Board of Education which permits these racist lies to poison our children must be removed or forced to resign."[64] The NAACP and the Black United Movement for Progress also called for the "elimination of racist textbooks" and changes "in school board rules to render bigoted remarks or actions of ethnic, racial, or poverty, grounds for dismissal even for teachers with tenure." The African American media—particularly the *Pittsburgh Courier*, WAMO radio station, and a new pioneering WQED show called "Black Horizons," produced by historian Ralph Proctor—reinforced pressure on the board to transform the culture of the public schools.[65]

Black Pittsburghers expressed increasing disapproval of one-way busing to achieve racial balance in the schools, declaring invariably African American children had to board buses bound for white neighborhoods rather than vice versa. In March 1967, Mattie Addis, coordinator of the Hill District's antipoverty program explained: "There's something psychologically negative about always being bused out and nobody ever being bused in." Likewise, at a meeting of the Urban League in the Hill District, Frankie Pace reinforced the views of Addis: "Why is it that we always have to be bused? . . . Why can't they put something fine in our neighborhood and bus other people in here?"[66]

Norman Johnson, director of research for the Mayor's Commission on Human Resources, offered an extended critique of one-way busing. He urged city officials to recognize "that the problem will not be resolved by insisting that the poor, particularly the black poor, do all the sacrificing" and excoriated the board for supporting "a plan of complicity, by taking black youngsters to the white man rather than as a minimum requiring that black and white youngsters come traveling relatively equal distances to receive an education." Johnson concluded that the city's busing plan represented an affront to the intelligence of black parents and students: "These black children are not dumb. They will come to know that not one single white child in the five-school scheme is being bused to get to another. . . . The white man remains stationary and once again is made to feel that the problem was not created by him."[67]

On the campuses of Pittsburgh area colleges, universities, and high schools, students helped to link changes in the educational institutions of the city to larger movements to transform the black community. Alongside the public schools, local institutions of higher education—the University of Pittsburgh, Carnegie Mellon University, Duquesne University, and Community College of Allegheny County—came under increasing scrutiny by African American students and community activists, and their white allies. In 1968, black students staged sit-ins at the computer center of the University of Pittsburgh. Under the leadership of Jack Daniel and Curtiss Portis, they presented the university with a list of demands that not only included the recruitment of more black students, faculty, and staff, but the development of a black studies program.[68] In the same year, at Carnegie Mellon, representatives of the Citizens Committee of the Pittsburgh Community Action Project (CAP) urged the university to increase the recruitment of minority students. Following this meeting, the university agreed "to increase the number of black students; give them full financial support; institute changes in the curriculum; and allow African American students to carry a course load designed to ensure their success." [69]

At Westinghouse High School, black students launched a strike that soon spread to other schools across the city. Supported by FAT, Westinghouse students presented the administration with a list of demands that included improvement of the lunchroom, institution of a black history course, and dismissal of the white principal. According to Robert Wideman, brother of Rhodes scholar and author John Edgar Wideman, the principal "was a mean nasty old dude. Hated niggers. No question about that. He wouldn't listen to nobody. Didn't care what was going on. Everybody hated him. We told them people from the school board his ass had to go first thing or we wasn't coming back to school."[70]

Strikes spread from Westinghouse to Langley, Perry, Fifth Avenue, and Schenley high schools. Once students shut schools down across the city, the Board of Education met at Westinghouse to hear the students' grievances. The board accepted all the students' demands, and the strike ended. Students and members of the community retired to Westinghouse Park and held an all night celebration of their victory, unmolested by the police. As Robert Wideman recalled:

> Cops sat out in them squad cars and Black Marias, but wasn't nothing they could do. We was smoking and drinking and carrying on all night, and they just watched us, just sat in the dark and didn't do

a thing. We broke into the park building to get us some 'lectricity for the bands and shit. And get us some light. Broke in the door and took what we wanted, but them cops ain't moved an inch. It was our night, and they knew it. [K]new they better leave well enough alone. We owned Westinghouse Park that night. Thought we owned Homewood.[71]

Wideman was especially proud of the strike, although the momentum slipped away over the summer: "We lost it over the summer, but I still believe we did something hip for a bunch of kids. The strike was citywide. We shut the schools down. All the black kids was with us. The smart ones. The dumb ones. It was hip to be on strike. . . . We lost it, but we had them going, Bruh. And I was in the middle of it."[72]

Despite progress under the impact of the modern Civil Rights movement, *Courier* writer Diane Perry noted that African Americans made up only about 13 percent of Pittsburgh Public School teachers, while accounting for 40 percent of all students in 1968–1969. Moreover, the majority of black teachers and principals took positions in predominantly black schools, including Vann, Baxter, Beltzhoover, Crescent, Leo Weil, and other elementary schools and Westinghouse, Fifth Avenue, and Herron Hill high schools.[73]

Alongside jobs and education, African Americans increased their demands for more and better housing for poor and working-class blacks. Between 1944 and the early 1970s, the percentage of African Americans among all public housing residents increased from just over 40 percent to 76 percent (see table 21). In 1967, the UNPC met with the Housing Authority of the City of Pittsburgh (HACP) to protest severe deterioration, segregation, and employment discrimination in the public housing projects. The head of the HACP confessed that he had not visited a housing project location in years. In frustration, the UNPC group promptly demanded his resignation along with many other members of the authority, remarking that "they have no concern for Negroes."[74]

The NAACP, the Urban League, and the Metropolitan Tenants Organization (MTO) challenged policies that threatened to harm public housing residents. In the fall of 1971, when the housing authority announced a new policy designed to screen out persons with previous records of misconduct, delinquency in payment of rent, and inability to "maintain a home in a manner that would meet average or acceptable standards," the MTO argued that the new policy "would more easily

Churchill Kohlman, first African American director of the Housing Authority of the City of Pittsburgh (HACP). Under Kohlman's leadership, the HACP expanded the number of housing units available to black families, initiated an ambitious equal opportunity hiring program, and increased the number of African American employees.
Source: New Pittsburgh Courier, 18 Aug. 1973.

harm poor people than help them." Moreover, the MTO released a statement noting the policy did not include "a clear statement of admission standards required by law" and provided applicants no opportunity to appeal a negative decision. Thus, the policy violated both the "equal protection clause of the constitution" and the screening procedures of the U.S. Housing Act. [75] Public housing residents also moved increasingly toward rent-withholding strategies for improving conditions in the project. [76]

When tenants escalated their protests against the HACP, Mayor Peter Flaherty not only fired housing authority director Alfred Tronzo, but expanded the HACP board of directors from five to seven members and appointed two African Americans to these new posts, including the public housing activist Rev. Charles Foggie. After a brief interlude, Flaherty also appointed Churchill Kohlman, an African American assistant housing director, to head the HACP in 1972. Kohlman soon emerged as an outspoken advocate for Pittsburgh residents. As executive director, Kohlman was not only the most powerful black public official in Pittsburgh, but also the country's first African American head of a major metropolitan public housing authority.[77]

Kohlman immediately launched an aggressive campaign to expand social services in the HACP. By the early 1970s, public housing had started to lose its image as a new, safe, environment to young black families to live. In September 1971, interviews with the *Pittsburgh Press* revealed that black residents of the city's public housing projects had reached a consensus on conditions facing tenants: "everyone agrees the most serious social problem in public housing is crime." A large number of black public housing residents conceded the projects "are literally armed camps" where young and not so young people "daily prey on the helpless." Herman Wolson, a maintenance clerk at Addison Terrace in the Hill District, reiterated, "Most of our tenants are the nicest people you'll want to find but there's enough bad ones to make it bad for everybody." Catherine McGee, an eight-year resident of Addison Terrace, lamented, "Maybe management should do things like they used to. . . . In the old days, a tenant who didn't keep his place up would get fined. Things were much better then."[78]

Partly in response to the growing demands of black public housing residents, the HACP initiated a security force for the city of Pittsburgh. Supported by a $2 million federal grant, Kohlman moved to create an HACP police force, separate from the municipal police, which would be responsive to the specific needs of black residents of public housing. He established a public employment agency; a credit union; an "ancillary program" with a staff of 111 designed to provide senior citizens with homemaking, health, and recreational services; and a newspaper entitled *Speaker of the House* to address the needs and interests of HACP residents. During Kohlman's brief tenure, he expanded overall HACP annual spending from $1.1 million in 1969 to $1.7 million in 1972.[79]

When staffing these various new programs, Kohlman looked to compensate African Americans for decades of exclusion by significantly reforming the hiring and personnel practices at the HACP. He increased black employment at the HACP by 75 percent and adopted policies to equalize pay scales for blacks and whites. Kohlman stated in early 1973 that his goal was "that anyone can be considered for a job no matter what their race, religion or political affiliation."[80] He also aggressively sought new sources of funding from the U.S. Department of Housing and Urban Development to pay for these initiatives and attempted to make the HACP the central social service agency for residents.[81]

Security and public safety became growing concerns for HACP residents. In 1972, police statistics showed that the crime rate in public housing was more than double of that in the city as a whole. Of the approximately 30,000 residents of the city's eighteen public housing communities, 2,242 were victims of major crimes. Public housing residents represented 6 percent of the population but 20 percent of the city's recorded murders, 15 percent of the rapes, 10 percent of the robberies, and 35 percent of the assaults. This rise in crime was especially troubling because the projects were increasingly populated by females with young children. As early as 1967, a study of Northview Heights described the complex as "a woman's world." Viewing the lack of security in public housing as an "emergency," Kohlman authorized a dramatic increase in spending for policing, from $5,000 in 1969 to $581,000 in 1972. In May 1973, Kohlman hired African American Leo Anderson to lead the proposed one-hundred-person HACP security force.[82]

In concert with the battle for public housing, the struggle for better private housing continued. Following his entry into the Greater Pittsburgh Multilist in 1967, Robert Lavelle's real estate firm sold an average of forty homes per year to black buyers, including homes in predominantly white areas within the city (Point Breeze, Squirrel Hill, Beechview, and Oakland) and outside of it (Monroeville and Penn Hills). Formed in 1951, the Hill District's Dwelling House Savings and Loan had granted only 132 mortgages by 1970. In the brief period from May to November 1970, however, the firm extended fifty-five new mortgages. The following year, the company made seventy-three mortgage loans, all FHA or VA insured, seventy-two of which were contracted with black clients. By 1972, the firm claimed assets of nearly $3 million.[83]

After joining the Multilist in 1971, Oliver Jackson also helped to expand the sale of houses to African Americans in the city neighborhoods of Point Breeze, Bloomfield, Homewood, and East Liberty, as well as Penn Hills, Wilkinsburg, and Monroeville in outlying areas. In his study of African American housing in postwar Pittsburgh, Joe Darden concluded that the black broker was "the most effective potential channel" through which residential segregation in owner-occupied housing could be substantially reduced. In 1971 interviews, eight of the ten black realtors in the city expressed the sense of possibility they saw after the 1967 lawsuit: "little or no discrimination would exist in the area of 'house sells' if black home seekers make use of black brokers who are members of the Multilist. Multilist makes it possible for a black real estate broker to sell any house listed be it in a white area or not."[84]

The fight against unfair housing practices not only stimulated business for black realtors, but also helped to reduce the degree of residential segregation and increase the proportion of black homeowners. Although modest, African Americans experienced a decrease in racial segregation in the decades 1950 to 1970. The index of dissimilarity dropped, respectively, by 2.8 percent between 1950 and 1960 and by 2.4 percent between 1960 and 1970. Black homeownership increased by 147 percent—compared to 40 percent for whites—between 1940 and 1950. The percent of African American owner-occupied units increased from 8.9 percent of all units in 1940 to almost 16 percent by 1960. Still, in a study of blacks who moved into predominantly white areas, only 4 percent said that they "wanted integrated neighborhoods." Most emphasized efforts to improve the space, size, sanitation, and safety of their current homes. They also invariably cited the prior existence of black people in a neighborhood (however small the numbers) as a major factor in their decision to move into a predominantly white community. The following comments were common: "Negroes have lived here for years," "Colored lived here previously (the agent) had more reason to rent to colored," and "One Negro family moved in and opened up the neighborhood."[85]

Integral to the struggle for jobs, housing, and education was the fight for equal access to medical services and equal protection under the law. Harvey Adams recalled that the Pittsburgh police would "abuse anyone [particularly black people] who dared challenge their authority." When Adams became chief of police for the HACP, he emphasized training a police force that would treat public housing tenants with "respect and care." After a series of mass meetings in 1974 to protest police brutality in the Homewood-Brushton area, African Americans formed Citizens Opposed to a Police State (COPS). Founded at Bethesda Presbyterian Church in Homewood, COPS represented a coalition of churches, civic, civil rights, and political organizations. According to coordinator Sala Udin of the Congress of Afrikan People, COPS aimed to end the mistreatment of black people by "hysterical policemen and set the record straight in the minds of people."[86]

Following the killing of a patrolman in the Homewood-Brushton area in July 1974, COPS reported that the police "kicked in the doors of at least 24 homes there and physically abused and threatened scores of other persons." Tense police-community relations preceded the officer's death. Between November 1972 and April 1973, the Pittsburgh-Community Relations Project, a coalition of eighteen religious and social activist organizations, conducted a study of "citizen attitudes towards the police in Pittsburgh" as a basis for formulating more effective government policy on policing the city. The report offered a litany of incidents that occurred between black citizens and police between about 1968 and early 1973. Incidents included civil rights violations by the city's tactical police force (TPF); the so-called "blue flu," in which white officers reported sick rather than abide by certain affirmative action decisions;

Black Power–era portrait of political activist and later city councilman Sala Udin (Sam Howze), c. 1963–1975.

Source: Carnegie Museum of Art, Charles "Teenie" Harris Collection, photo #2001.35.4656. Photograph © 2009 Carnegie Museum of Art, Pittsburgh.

and the "mistaken identity shooting of a black youth by a white police officer and subsequent shooting of the black youth's brother following a high speed auto chase in downtown Pittsburgh."[87] In the East Liberty area, six city policemen were well known for engaging in five categories of "clearly illegal behavior" against African Americans. Following two days of graphic testimony from area residents, a U.S. district court judge issued an injunction against the officers for "Stopping persons without cause, beating plaintiffs and other Blacks residing in the area while they conducted themselves lawfully, using excessive force during arrests, harassing or intimidating, and unlawful search and seizure."[88]

When queried about police behavior in an interview with *Pittsburgh Magazine*, police superintendent Robert J. Coll Jr. emphasized the difficulty of gaining convictions against police for misconduct. He accented the role of the police peer review trial board as a fundamental obstacle in holding police responsible for their conduct. The trial board rarely convicted their own members. Coll concluded, "It's difficult to change without authority. I need a hammer."[89] Louis Mason, African American city council president, believed that police behavior was difficult to control because police were "too ingrained with racism to change their ways." Similarly, a study by the American Friends Service Committee Pre-Trial Justice Program concluded that African American in Pittsburgh were more likely than whites to be charged with a minor offense, confront higher bail amounts, and spend more time in jail awaiting trial. As black students attended predominantly white high schools in larger numbers, they frequently cited instances of police harassment and or lack of police protection in the face of attacks by white students. In one incident, according to the *New Pittsburgh Courier*, only the appearance of black policeman Lieutenant Moore "prevented dozens of fully armed white policemen from clubbing en masse a small group of black students."[90]

Racial discrimination in police services also affected African Americans' access to health care in Pittsburgh. After World War II, when municipal authorities placed emergency ambulance service in the hands of the police department, African Americans lamented the lack of emergency care for their communities. In 1968, in an effort to improve emergency health care services for the Hill District community, Freedom House Enterprise, a nonprofit organization devoted to economic development in the Hill District, founded the Freedom House Ambulance Service. Financed by the Maurice Falk Medical Fund, under the leadership of director Philip Hallen, Freedom House Ambulance Service set out to train a core of community based emergency workers. About 50 percent of the initial Freedom House recruits had not completed their high school education before entering training for emergency medical care, and many believed that they were "untrainable." Yet through the services of Dr. Peter Safar of Presbyterian University Hospital, these workers gained instruction in the techniques of "emergency care in the streets" and soon entered the field, where they mitigated suffering and saved lives.[91]

Despite the successes of the Freedom House Ambulance Service, Pittsburgh police and city health officials failed to accord the unit appropriate respect and support. According to Philip Hallen, "racism prevented elements of the police and city government from appreciating Freedom House for the unparalleled asset it was." When one Freedom House worker arrived at a local hospital emergency room with a patient and described the patient's condition along with measures taken to stabilize the patient, the attending nurse "laughed at him and walked away before he could finish" his report. Moreover, although the city awarded Freedom House a contract to serve the emergency needs of the target community, local police continued to see themselves as the appropriate recourse for emergency medical assistance; in answering calls, they often refused to cooperate with Freedom House.[92]

A study that compared Freedom House Ambulance to police services revealed that 62 percent of patients in police care received improper treatment compared to only 11 percent of those under Freedom House care. Understandably, when whites in the area called for emergency care, they would sometimes tell the dispatcher to "send Freedom House." In 1975, the city of Pittsburgh terminated its contract with Freedom House and established its own Emergency Medical Services (EMS). The city failed to follow through on assurances that employees of Freedom House would gain jobs with the new service. "If this was a mostly white organization," one disappointed paramedic told the *Post Gazette*, "I don't think this thing would be happening."[93]

Confronting the Limits of Urban Politics

Municipal, corporate, small business, and labor responses to the needs of Pittsburgh's growing black population were fundamentally inadequate. Only federal intervention enabled African Americans to break through the color line in Pittsburgh's economy. The job demands of Pittsburgh's black steelworkers (particularly at Jones and Laughlin and U.S. Steel's

Homestead Works) increasingly converged with those of their counterparts across the country, including Sparrows Point, Maryland; Gary, Indiana; and Birmingham, Alabama. Between 1970 and 1973, a series of federal court decisions defined department-based seniority systems in the steel industry as racially discriminatory and mandated the institution of new plant-wide seniority procedures. In April 1974, the U.S. Equal Employment Opportunity Commission filed a consent decree with nine steel companies and the USWA. Six of the nine firms cited in the consent degree operated in the Pittsburgh district: U.S. Steel, Jones and Laughlin, Allegheny-Ludlum, Armco, Bethlehem Steel, and Wheeling-Pittsburgh. The consent decree affirmed that women and minority group steelworkers "were systematically assigned to lower-paying jobs with little opportunity for advancement, denied training opportunities, and judged by more stringent qualification criteria than were white males."[94]

Pittsburgh's industries and organized labor accepted the decree, and admitted that their policies and practices had discriminated against blacks, women, and Latino/a workers. The decree abolished departmental seniority; implemented plant-wide seniority programs; and established a more equitable basis for layoffs, recalls, promotions, and demotions. Moreover, both company and union officials agreed to set specific goals and timetables for the promotion of women and minority group workers, particularly African Americans, into technical, clerical, supervisory, and managerial posts.[95]

While industrial barriers were being broken down, grassroots white opposition to school integration became more hostile. In 1971, when the Pittsburgh Board of Education approved the transfer of white sixth- and seventh-grade students to the predominantly black Knoxville Elementary School, located on the city's South Side, white parents from the Bon Air and Concord neighborhoods initiated a boycott of the Knoxville Elementary School and filed a lawsuit in the Common Pleas Court to prevent the transfers. The Veterans of Foreign Wars, the Eagles, the Fraternal Order of Police, various business establishments, and civic organizations from the neighborhood of Northview Heights all supported the demands of white parents. In making their case for halting the transfers, the parents argued that the Knoxville Elementary School was unsafe and represented an endangerment to their children. Judge Charles D. McCarthy issued a ruling in favor of the parents and stopped the transfers.[96]

The Pittsburgh Board of Education appealed the Knoxville case to the Pennsylvania Supreme Court, which overturned the local court's ruling and allowed the school board's busing order to stand. Over the next two years, white parents and students from Carrick, Concord, Roosevelt, and Grandview boycotted the Knoxville school. In spring 1972, some 24,000 of the city's 70,000 students vacated the schools when antibusing groups staged a citywide school boycott. For their part, both black and white teachers and students at Knoxville staged counter-protests against the boycotts and the Common Pleas Court's decision that Knoxville was an unsafe environment for some white children, but acceptable for black children. However, as increasing numbers of white parents tired of the boycott and sent their children back to school, boycott organizers (particularly the Carrick Citizens Council) negotiated the return of all white students to the classroom. Despite substantial absenteeism, the school board agreed to promote white students pending satisfactory completion of summer school classes. [97]

In 1975, Homewood-Brushton's black parents fought to preserve their own neighborhood schools in the wake of mounting disciplinary problems at Westinghouse High School. As early as fall 1968, in the aftermath of the citywide black student strike, Robert Wideman recalled how Westinghouse became an armed camp: "Locks on the doors, cops in the halls. Big cops with big guns. . . . . We had a black history class, but wasn't nobody eligible to take it. Had a new principal, but nobody knew him . . . everybody had to have an I.D. Yeah. That was a new one. Locks and I.D.s and cops. Wasn't never our school. They made it worse instead of better."[98]

In order to defuse conflict at Westinghouse, the school board moved the eighth grade to Baxter Elementary School, an older, all black school. In turn, the kindergarten through sixth grade students at Baxter were relocated to Crescent, Homewood, Belmar, and other elementary schools, which were already overcrowded and in need of renovation. At the same time, the city planned to open the Florence Reizenstein Middle School, a new, fully integrated school of approximately 1,600 students. Although 1,800 eligible black children lived in the area, only 800 would be admitted to Reizenstein. African American parents of students at Baxter opposed the removal of their children from one overcrowded and inadequate setting to another. Black parents organized protests and blocked access to Baxter, complaining that their children would have to endure longer walks to schools outside their neighborhoods and that the school board had mandated the changes without consultation with the community. "It's the same old story all over again," one protester remarked, while an-

Black parents and students protest inadequate schools for black children in the Homewood-Brushton community.
Source: New Pittsburgh Courier, 19 July 1975.

other declared, "Blacks are getting the short end. Our children are being shoved into schools that are already overcrowded. Well, we are here to say that they are not." Another black parent remarked, "The people from the board underestimate the parents. They think we are a bunch of ghetto folk, and it's a piece of cake dealing in black areas."[99]

When talks with the school board and picketing failed, black parents took their case to the Common Pleas Court. They argued that the conversion of Baxter into a middle school would result in their children occupying an all black and substandard facility. Judge John P. Flaherty permitted the school to open as scheduled, though he enjoined parents and school officials to meet on a regular basis and develop a plan for resolving inequities. In February 1976, under increasing pressure from the African American community, along with failure of the school board to comply with his preliminary order to meet regularly with representatives of the black community, Judge Flaherty ruled that the Baxter Middle School Center indeed discriminated against blacks by perpetuating racially divided education in the public schools.[100]

In the meanwhile, white and, to some extent, African American resistance to busing intensified. From the outset of the Pennsylvania Human Relations Commission's 1968 desegregation order, the Pittsburgh public school system had dragged its feet on implementation. Initially, the city promised to respond to the "maximum" of its ability, but asked for and received a thirty-day extension. When the board finally submitted its plan, the PHRC rejected several elements and ordered the board to submit another supplementary plan by 1 February 1969. The Pittsburgh Board of Education requested and received additional deadline extensions. On 7 June 1971, however, the PHRC issued its "Final Order" demanding an acceptable plan within thirty days. The board circumvented the "Final Order" by requesting that the Commonwealth Court prevent any legal action against the board until the court acted. The court granted the board's request. A year later, in a vote of seven to three, the board denounced the use of "forced busing for racial balance purposes" and directed its staff to exclude "forced busing solely for racial balance purpose, in their reorganization plans." Mayor Flaherty also opposed busing and wrote a letter of opposition to the school board president, African American Gladys McNairy.[101]

In fall 1975, the superintendent of schools proposed a $45 million desegregation and building plan. Through selected busing of students, this plan promised to reduce racial segregation in the city's schools by decade's end, but representatives of some twenty-seven black and white civic, civil rights, and political organizations firmly rejected the plan at a public hearing. Residents of Homewood-Brushton declared that the measure would not only fail to meet the needs of black children, but would perpetuate what they called "inferior, antiquated, and old" facilities for black children.[102]

The PHRC had established that any school with a ratio of black to white students greater or less than between 32 and 66 percent was not in compliance with school desegregation orders. In 1976, the Pittsburgh public schools, including twelve high schools, remained racially segregated. Located in the central city and east end, two high schools— Westinghouse and Schenley—had black student enrollments greater than 66 percent. By contrast, in the western portions of the city, and in the South Hills, five of the twelve high schools had fewer than 32 percent black student enrollment; these included South Hills, Langley, South, and Carrick. Similar demographics characterized the city's elementary and middle schools (see tables 22 and 23). District-based rather than region-based desegregation plans made it difficult to ensure a more even distribution of the races in the Pittsburgh public schools.[103] In 1976, Pittsburgh's antibusing campaign gained substantial national support due to the formation of the National Organization for Neighborhood Schools (NONS), which defined desegregation as "social engineering that undermined school choice." Norene Beatty, president of the Pittsburgh chapter of NONS, argued that antibusing efforts violated the state code by dealing with children on a racial, ethnic, or religious basis.[104]

The efforts to truly integrate Pittsburgh's schools corresponded to continuing efforts to grant equal access in the city's private housing market. Despite the city's Fair Housing Ordinances (1958 and 1967) and the federal Civil Rights Act of 1968, enforcement of open housing laws remained problematic through the mid-1970s. Limitations were most discernable in Pittsburgh's predominantly white suburbs. In Mt. Lebanon, for example, when the municipality established a Community Relations Board in 1966 to help address the problem, independent realtor Elaine Wittlin was the first agent to sell homes to African Americans and Jews in the previously all-white Virginia Manor development. Wittlin recalled that one homeowner, due to economic difficulties, needed to sell quickly, but when she tried to get a black family inside to see it, the listing agent would not schedule a walk-through. Wittlin broke with accepted practice and called the homeowner directly. The owner agreed to show the home to the black family and the sale went through. She then received threatening phone calls, and one of the neighbors moved out over the sale. As a result of such continuing limits on where blacks could live, some observers described the city's fair housing laws as "little more than a force of 'pacification' rather than a significant anti-discriminatory force."[105]

Discrimination also continued in public housing. The bold changes initiated by Churchill Kohlman during his tenure as director of the Housing Authority of the City of Pittsburgh were short-lived. Conservative white reactions to the gains of the city's modern Civil Rights and Black Power movements impacted public housing with a vengeance. Under the leadership of HACP board member Harold Tweedy, the board increasingly blocked Kohlman's programs, challenged his directives, and micromanaged the agency by interjecting their views into what formerly had been routine matters left largely to the director. In short order, Kohlman found himself under attack from his predecessor Tronzo and others for overspending, improbable connections with underworld figures, nepotism, waste, fraud, and abuse. After only eighteen months in office and despite widespread support within the black community for him and his programs, Kohlman resigned in August 1973. His replacement quickly fired over one hundred of Kohlman's recent hires (mostly African Americans) and drastically scaled back the programs Kohlman had started.[106]

Following Kohlman's resignation, black community activists Bouie Haden and Phil Carter cochaired a meeting at the Hill House to defend Kohlman against unfair media reporting. In an opening statement, conveners of the meeting stated, "When the news media decided to destroy a black man no one came to his rescue. They are assassinating you [Black people] in the newspapers."[107] Some 250 supporters crowded into the office of the HACP to show their support of Kohlman. In response to the HACP's cutbacks in public housing security and other changes, a group of tenants sought to take over management of the 999-unit Northview housing complex. As a spokesperson noted at the time, "It's a move to control our own destiny, to select our own residents, to manage our own community." This was the first time in the city's history and, according to the *Pittsburgh Press*, the first time in U.S. history that public housing tenants had made such a request. The continuing transformation of public housing into predominantly African American living spaces would accelerate during the late twentieth century.[108]

Pittsburgh's African American community was by no means entirely united in its demands for equal rights. In 1968, African Americans spearheaded the formation of the Homewood-Brushton Neighborhood Health Center. This drug treatment facility was renamed in honor of neighborhood activist Alma Illery in 1977. Dr. George McClomb later recalled that when he took over as head of the center at the height of the black freedom struggle in 1977, "there was absolute war between community organizations" in the Homewood-Brushton neighborhood.[109] There were significant ideological and class-based conflicts over policy decisions and the direction that the movement for full citizenship rights and economic democracy should take. One of the most potent internal disputes emerged over the use of federal poverty funds to support birth control clinics within the Homewood-Brushton area. In 1965, Pennsylvania joined other states that made public funds available for support of family planning clinics and the purchase of contraceptive devices.[110]

Under the influence of the Black Power movement of the late 1960s, a militant anti–birth control movement developed among a small number of blacks in Pittsburgh and other urban areas of the country. In Pittsburgh, activist Bouie Haden and physician Charles Greenlee, chair of the local NAACP's health committee, allied with the Catholic priest Father Charles Owen Rice, defined the birth control movement as a form of genocide aimed at the African American population. In their view, the government preferred to eliminate black people rather than allot necessary resources for jobs, health care, and education to ensure the survival and development of the group. In the words of Dr. Greenlee, the white power structure would not "spend a dime to kill the rats that eat up your babies, but they'll spend thousands to make sure you can't have any babies." Likewise, Haden said, "You can't call what the blacks have planned parenthood. It's planning for no parenthood."[111]

In their campaign to block federal funds earmarked for organizations offering birth control services, the anti–birth control forces targeted the Homewood-Brushton Medical Center, including its home visitor program and family planning clinic. When this movement resulted in the closing of the family planning clinic, black women in the Homewood-Brushton community mobilized to reopen the facility. One woman spoke for many when she said, "Let Mr. Haden mind his own business. This is something that should be kept between a husband and wife." Another woman agreed: "Some things must be left up to the woman. Like how many children you think you can feed, clothe and send to school." Under the determined efforts of these women, poverty fund authorities reversed their decision and restored birth control and family planning services to the Homewood-Brushton community.[112]

Other internal conflicts emerged over strategies for improving the education of black children. When the city proposed to build two middle schools and one elementary school in Homewood-Brushton in 1964, the Pittsburgh NAACP argued that the Homewood site would perpetuate racial segregation in the schools. Instead, the NAACP recommended East Liberty, where there was a lower concentration of blacks. For its part, however, the Homewood-Brushton Renewal Council supported the Homewood site for the new buildings. The council argued that the larger question of racial integration was important, but the neighborhood needed immediate relief from overcrowding and that a new facility would boost the morale of the community, teachers, and students, while also improving the quality of education at the neighborhood level. As they put it, "We the residents, feel that these schools must be built if we are to get better education and relief for overcrowded conditions which exist today. Racial balance is desirable, but not at the expense of our children's education. . . . We go on record as of this date, and with the full vote of the Association, that we are against any alternate plan that would not put the new schools in (our) area."[113]

Once middle-class black families moved into previously all white areas, they sometimes resisted, along with whites, the encroachment of low-income public housing projects upon their neighborhoods. In October 1967, when the Pittsburgh Housing Authority proposed locating a thirty-seven-unit housing development on a vacant lot near Chartiers Avenue in the West End, both white and black homeowners rushed to the city council to protest. Leroy Hatcher, a black homeowner, declared, "Other public housing projects with mostly Negroes have been allowed to deteriorate. Most of these thirty-seven new families will be Negro and the same thing will happen. That means that the value of the home I've fought and scraped for will go down." A white homeowner later stated, "Our area has been integrated for years by well-to-do families. We like the Negro families but you will just turn the place into a slum with $35-per-month families in a housing project." In 1966, in a middle-class East Hills neighborhood that was predominantly African American, the city proposed locating a ninety-one-unit federally subsidized project for lower-middle-income families. Established black homeowners blocked the project for more than a year, leaving proponents of the project to accuse the owners of injecting "class prejudice" into the situation.[114]

Desegregation and the emerging ethos of integration represented mixed blessings for the city's black population. In fact, large numbers of African Americans later recalled that, "integration was the worst thing that ever happened to us." From the onset of urban renewal, African Americans found it even more difficult to move their businesses as opposed to their homes from the Lower Hill to other areas of the city. In November 1957, Reese Williamson, operator of a barbecue establishment, hoped to move his business from Fullerton Street in the Hill District to Davenport Street further east toward the Oakland area. The city's Board of Adjustment denied Williamson a permit to build and occupy the site when residents of the area protested that the proposed business "would bring gamblers, taverns and night club revelers, and other persons who would disturb their sleep . . . after their night on the town." Williamson retorted that his use of the property would be "no worse than that to which it was already being put."[115]

Pittsburgh's African Americans who recall postwar integration also lament the decline of local professional and leisure institutions that had served the segregated black community. Emblematic of these changes was the demise of the Musicians Club, where Pittsburgh's black musicians honed their skills. By the late 1940s, jobs in local clubs required evidence of union membership, and the Musicians Club, maintained by the all black Musicians Local 471 of the American Federation of Musicians offered black musicians a place to play at all hours of the day or night. In 1965, Local 471 merged with the all white Local 60, and the Musicians Club closed its doors within the next year. African Americans lost a key venue for perfecting their craft and sustaining a local music culture. Local 60 had a Musicians Club, but it also closed shortly after the merger. Trumpet player Charles Austin later recalled the centrality of the Musicians Club for black artists in Pittsburgh. In an interview with RAP, he said, "When the club was here . . . it was open 24/7, 48 hours a day, I mean it was always open. You'd go by and you'd play, we'd put a band together. You play, you learn, you play new tunes. . . . We were all of one cause, it was just to play music you know." Austin also recalled how local musicians would play with nationally known musicians when they came to town, "and some of the battles that you'd see on horn were just beyond belief." Pittsburgh musicians would repeatedly recall large numbers of local musicians who would become nationally and internationally renowned artists, including jazz musicians Mary Lou Williams, Earl Garner, Joe Brown, Earl Fatha Hines, and Grover Mitchell. According to Austin, the closure of the city's black and white musicians clubs "killed [black musicians] because we come out of this environment and then, whoa, all of a sudden it's bare and the doors are closed, and you can't do this." Other black musicians—drummer Cecil Brooks II, trumpeter Judge Watson, and pianist George Spaulding—all lamented the closing of the black Musicians Club as a blow to the vitality of Pittsburgh's music and cultural scene.[116]

African Americans also rued the demise of the Negro Leagues and a plethora of other leisure time, business, and professional establishments. Even as local blacks celebrated the arrival of Jackie Robinson and other black Major League Baseball players at Forbes Field, they decried the decline of Greenlee Field, the Homestead Grays, and the Pittsburgh Crawfords. In addition to the destruction of black institutions under the impact of urban renewal, the gradual opening of predominantly white restaurants, hotel chains, nightclubs, and diverse places of amusement to black patrons hastened the decline of historic black institutions that provided similar services.[117]

Despite internal fragmentation and social conflict, the modern Civil Rights and Black Power movements had a profound impact on the politics of the city. Although Pittsburgh employed an at-large electoral system, blacks were regularly elected to city council posts during the 1960s. In 1967, when city councilman James Jordan resigned his office, Mayor Barr and the party endorsed, nominated, and elected African American Louis Mason, who served as as council president and remained on city council for ten years. In 1969, the Democratic Party endorsed and nominated George Shields, who won election to the city council from the fifth ward, where his mother served as a Democratic Party leader. He gained reelection until 1973, when, though publicly supported by party leaders, he was defeated. According to Wendell Freeland, the 1973 primary revealed that Shields was "cut" from the slate "by white ward and district figures" and thus received "poor support in the white communities."[118]

Democratic mayor Joseph Barr (1959–1969) served the city of Pittsburgh through the 1960s. Barr ordered police restraint in the riot of 1968; supported the War on Poverty program; and attracted Manpower Development and Training Act funds to Pittsburgh. The Barr regime also expanded the power of the Fair Housing Law; created the first rent withholding program in the state (designed to protect poor families against evictions by landlords as a result of complaints for code violations); and intervened in the Black Construction Coalition's protest at nine city construction sites. By stopping construction during the BCC protests, Barr helped to set the groundwork for an agreement with the UNPC and NAACP.[119]

Despite elements of progress under the Barr administration, African Americans expressed deep dissatisfaction with the slow pace of change and challenged the city's established Democratic machine. In the Hill District, as early 1961–1962, Charles Wilson opposed the regular Democratic organization and ran for the fifth ward alderman's seat as an independent. Wilson decried the low numbers of black teachers in the public schools and the dearth of black policemen. Similarly dissatisfied with the Democratic Party's mistreatment of black voters, Wendell Freeland, president of the Urban League of Pittsburgh, campaigned for the state legislature on the Republican ticket. The *Pittsburgh Courier* and significant numbers of other blacks supported Freeland's run. At the same time, NAACP president Byrd Brown reminded Democrats that African Americans made up the largest single voting bloc in Allegheny County, and could, if not treated with respect, leave the party. On the North Side, in 1967, Rev. Jimmy Joe Robinson joined the insurgent group Allegheny Alliance and challenged the incumbent Democrat for one of the at-large aldermanic seats. Although each of these efforts failed, they nonetheless put the Democratic Party on notice that it could no longer take the black vote for granted.[120]

Partly as a result of the rising challenge posed by the modern black freedom movement and the growing perception among many whites that African Americans were gaining ground at their expense, Mayor Barr decided not to run for office in 1969. Barr and the regular Democratic Party supported Judge Harry Kramer's candidacy for the mayor's office, while African Americans supported independent Pete Flaherty. In his campaign, Flaherty promised to focus attention on neighborhoods rather than continuing preoccupation with Downtown's Central Business District. Flaherty's election symbolized the end of Renaissance I in Pittsburgh's post–World War II history, and observers soon praised Flaherty as the mayor who largely returned city government to neighborhood people.[121]

In the 1973 mayoral race, Flaherty lost African American support, but won by some ten thousand votes on the Democratic ticket and by nearly that much as a write-in candidate on the Republican ticket. Between 1973 and 1977, Flaherty cut social welfare programs and reduced support for the Mayor's Commission on Human Relations. At the same time, when President Richard Nixon disbanded the Office of Economic Opportunity and instituted federal revenue sharing programs, he put the bulk of federal money into the police and fire departments, which continued to resist federal affirmative action mandates and hired few blacks.[122]

African Americans helped to defeat Pete Flaherty in his bid for the U.S. Senate in 1974. Under the leadership of Phil Carter, president of the state's Black Political Assembly, black Pennsylvanians held political conferences, voter registration drives, and campaign training programs designed to defeat Flaherty for the Senate seat. Black Philadelphians like Rev. Leon Sullivan, head of the Opportunities Industrialization Centers, vigorously supported the Republican candidate, Richard Schweiker. In western Pennsylvania, while blacks did not actively support Schweiker, they offered Flaherty little help and enabled the Republican to win the Senate seat. Following the election, Schweiker awarded a large appropriation to Sullivan's OIC, including its Pittsburgh branch which expanded job training activities among the city's black population.[123]

Blacks did not leave the Flaherty era entirely empty-handed. The Flaherty administration claimed the first black to head a city department; first black to be appointed assistant superintendent of police; appointment of nine blacks to the 15-member Commission on Human Relations;

and direct intervention to quell racial conflict in two of the city's high schools. In 1971, the creation of the Home Loan Revolving Fund also represented a key victory for the African American community, as did the Landlord Repair Program, which subsidized home repair loans for low-income homeowners. Flaherty also aided the ongoing African American quest for equal protection under the law (particularly for young offenders) when he insisted on nonpolitical appointees as magistrates and removed justices of the peace from fee for services arrangements over the determined opposition of the Pittsburgh Fraternal Order of Police.[124]

African Americans continued to make political gains as K. Leroy Irvis moved into powerful leadership positions in state government. The Democrats elected Irvis chairman of the state Democratic Party caucus during the early 1960s; majority whip in 1968; and speaker of the house in 1977. In addition to his sponsorship of legislation that strengthened the Pennsylvania Human Relations Commission, he initiated laws that increased opportunities for higher education among poor and working-class blacks and whites across the state and region. The Pennsylvania Higher Education Equal Opportunity Program and the Pennsylvania Higher Education Assistance Agency among other education measures helped to revitalize both the University of Pittsburgh and Temple University by transforming them into state-supported institutions of higher education, and by mandating lower tuition fees that allowed them to attract more working-class and African American students. For initiating fundamental social legislation that cut across the racial divide, the *Pittsburgh Courier* described Irvis as "a citizen of the whole state and a Negro." Although his legislative accomplishments benefited both whites and blacks, they also represented the fruits of the ongoing civil rights and political struggles of black people in Pittsburgh, the state, and the nation.[125]

As some middle- and upper-class blacks expanded their footing into previously all-white occupations, neighborhoods, and schools, the African American struggle for equality took on more daunting race, gender, and class dimensions. Furthermore, the benefits of the modern black freedom movement came at the very moment that the region's old industrial base rapidly declined. A new postindustrial African American community would gradually take shape by the turn of the new century.

4

In the Shadows of Renaissance II

The modern Civil Rights and Black Power movements provided African Americans in Pittsburgh with a broader and more diverse range of neighborhoods, jobs, and schools. At the same time, the material foundation for these changes eroded as the city's manufacturing economy and population continued to shrink. Seeking to stem the tide of job and population losses, the city energized its public-private partnership and launched Renaissance II, which revitalized the Central Business District (CBD) and created new technology-intensive firms. While African Americans remained largely in the shadows of the Pittsburgh renaissance, they gradually gained jobs in the emerging postindustrial economy, moved into new neighborhoods within and outside the city, and developed strategies for bringing about their own urban revival.[1]

By the turn of the twenty-first century, the steel industry had nearly disappeared from the urban landscape of Pittsburgh and western Pennsylvania. U.S. Steel closed its blast furnace and mill complexes at Rankin (1982), Duquesne (1984), Homestead (1986), McKeesport (1987), and, except for a coke plant, Clairton (1984). During the same period, Jones and Laughlin (later LTV Steel) closed its Hazelwood and South Side plants in Pittsburgh along with its Aliquippa Works in Beaver County. Producers of steel in the United States confronted increasing foreign competition, effective alternatives to metal products, and small mini-mills that specialized in the production of steel from scrap metal. Using advanced technology (including continuous casting processes and electric furnaces) to reduce labor costs and to effectively compete with their larger counterparts, mini-mills increased their share of all U.S. steel production from a mere 3 percent in the 1960s to nearly 30 percent by the early 1990s.[2]

Other related industrial firms also drastically downsized their operations. Westinghouse Electric and Westinghouse Airbrake trimmed 15,000 workers from East Pittsburgh in the 1980s before ceasing the manufacture of airbrakes and electric generators in the 1990s. Between 1979 and 1987, Pittsburgh and the surrounding metropolitan area lost 127,500 manufacturing jobs, with 63,100 of these in basic steel.[3] By the end of the century, manufacturing jobs made up less than 15 percent of the Pittsburgh region's workforce; unemployment soared to over twice the national average; and Pittsburgh slipped from third to fourth place among the nation's corporate headquarters. In 1986, when the U.S. Steel Corporation changed its name to USX and acquired two large energy firms, the company acknowledged the passing of the "steel era" in the history of Pittsburgh and western Pennsylvania.[4]

As Pittsburgh's industrial economy declined, a new service economy gradually emerged. In the mayoral election of 1976, Richard S. Caliguiri, the Democratic candidate, gained election on the promise that he would initiate a second Renaissance in the city of Pittsburgh. Caliguiri pledged to develop new high-technology firms and attract lucrative corporate headquarters to the city. Such firms would enable the city to assemble a new highly skilled workforce, and to shed its old image as a "smokestack" metropolis. Following his election, Caliguiri brought together a variety of public and private agencies: four major city departments (planning, housing, economic development, and urban redevelopment); the Allegheny Conference for Community Development (ACCD); and area universities and colleges—Carnegie Mellon, Duquesne, and the University of Pittsburgh—to help reorganize the city's economy.[5]

Over the next decade, the city's public-private partnership constructed a plethora of new office, restaurant, corporate, commercial, convention, hotel, residential, and cultural complexes. The most prominent buildings in the Renaissance II development included One Oxford Centre (forty-six stories of office and retail space); One Mellon Center, a fifty-four-story bank headquarters; and PPG Place, the headquarters of Pittsburgh Plate Glass, which consists of six Gothic-style glass buildings next to Market Square. In 1985, the University of Pittsburgh and Carnegie Mellon University joined city and county governments to develop "Strategy 21: Pittsburgh Allegheny Economic Development Strategy to Begin the 21st Century." A master plan for the new century, Strategy 21 emphasized the development of international marketing and communications systems; diversified light and heavy manufacturing; and "a new mix of large and small businesses marked by a renewed spirit of entrepreneurship and university-linked research and development."[6]

By the turn of the twenty-first century, Pittsburgh had shifted from a predominantly manufacturing center to a new, service-oriented economy. Nearly fifty-five foreign companies opened offices in western Pennsylvania between about 1980 and 1990, and by 2000, Pittsburgh ranked twenty-fifth out of the fifty largest metropolitan regions in the concentration of high-tech industry businesses. The number of jobs in government, services, and finance equaled those in manufacturing.[7] Political and business leaders enthusiastically announced the rise of the new Pittsburgh. In 1988, the Urban Redevelopment Authority (URA) articulated a growing commitment to "Pittsburgh's evolution from a town founded on heavy industry to a city on the cutting edge of innovative research and technology." Carnegie Mellon's president, Richard Cyert, imagined a city that would transform itself into "the software capital of the world." Similarly, the University of Pittsburgh's president, Wesley Posvar, predicted the rise of Pittsburgh as a "biotech valley." Like California's Silicon Valley, Pittsburgh's emerging technology sector was considered to be an "incubator for an exciting new industry" that would "infuse new economic vitality into the area."[8] In 1985, Rand McNally selected Pittsburgh as the nation's "most livable city," and confirmed the city's effort to reinvent itself and change its blue-collar industrial image.[9]

As city and regional elites constructed a new economy and new image, some steelworkers and their unions resisted deindustrialization and the unequal distribution of rewards in the emerging economy. Visiting Pittsburgh, Rev. Jesse Jackson addressed a rally of some five hundred people gathered to protest the closing of "Dorothy Six," the Duquesne Works of U.S. Steel. In zero-degree weather on 18 January 1985, Jackson described the Mon Valley as "the Selma" of the plant shutdown movement.[10] Lynn Williams, president of the United Steel Workers of America (USWA) and Pittsburgh mayor Richard Caliguiri also addressed the group. Amid rising worker activism, the *Pittsburgh Post-Gazette* editorialized that such activism had spurred public officials into "a more active and creative role" in addressing the problems of deindustrialization.[11]

In his study *Can Workers Have a Voice?*, political scientist Dale Hathaway documents the protest activities of three groups: the Denominational Ministry Strategy (DMS), the Tri-State Conference on Steel, and the Mon Valley Unemployed Committee (MVUC). Whereas the first two groups sought to wrest control of deindustrialization from what they called an "elite-dominated decision-making process," the MVUC focused primarily on the day-to-day needs of laid-off workers and supported workers' demands for more unemployment compensation during the most critical moment of plant closures and mounting joblessness in the region.[12]

The ameliorative work of the MVUC and similar organizations were insufficient to offset job losses in steel and other basic industries. Between 1974 and 1995, mining, manufacturing, and construction lost 162,000 above-average wage jobs, while 85 percent of the 181,000 new jobs paid lower than average wages. Moreover, compared to fifteen other U.S. metropolitan regions, the greater Pittsburgh region experienced the slowest growth in service jobs during the closing decades of the twentieth century. Making matters worse, inflation in western Pennsylvania increased by nearly 50 percent between 1974 and 1986, but per capita income rose by only 8 percent during the same time.[13]

Pittsburgh found it increasingly difficult to create new jobs, retain its existing population, and attract new people into the region. The city's population continued to decline from 520,000 in 1970 to under 370,000 in the 1990s. The large exodus of young people from the region unbalanced the city's age profile, making Pittsburgh second (18 percent in Allegheny County) only to Florida in the percentage of retirement-age adults. In many other late-twentieth-century U.S. cities, new waves of Latino and Asian immigrants created greater ethnic, nationality, and racial diversity, but Pittsburgh retained its earlier predominantly south, central, and eastern European ethnic makeup. Thus, as we will see below, the city's late-twentieth-century social history would continue to revolve around black-white rather than multi-ethnic, class, and racial relationships.[14]

Industrial Decline, African Americans, and Economic Inequality

The transformation of the city's economy took a huge toll on Pittsburgh's African American community. The black population dropped from

105,000 in 1970 to just over 94,000 in 2000. In his report on blacks and deindustrialization, journalist Jim McKay observed the rising exodus of blacks out of the city, "It seems everyone knows or is related to young blacks who left Pittsburgh for an education and didn't or couldn't return because of the lack of job opportunities." Ralph Proctor, who served as director of the Kingsley Association youth center in East Liberty, underscored how young blacks left the region because of racism as well as declining job opportunities. "Young black professionals knew there was nothing for them here so they left because of discrimination." In the Cain family, three sisters who could not find jobs in the city moved to Columbus, Boston, and New York City, where they obtained employment as a chemistry teacher, education coordinator for the state parole board, and staffer for the *Wall Street Journal*, respectively. Lois Cain, their mother, lamented that her children "came home, couldn't survive and moved on. . . . In the end, our best is milked off." Eric Webb, an award-winning poet and journalist, explained to reporter Jim McKay that Pittsburgh was "a good place for white families" to raise their children, but for African American families "those opportunities aren't there."[15]

In the spring of 1990, the *Wall Street Journal* carried a front-page story on the "reverse exodus" of middle-class African Americans from northern cities like Pittsburgh to sunbelt cities like Atlanta. Attorney Justin L. Johnson, son of renowned Pennsylvania Superior Court Judge Justin M. Johnson, returned to Pittsburgh after receiving his law degree from Harvard in 1986. Mayor Richard Caliguiri appointed Johnson to the Civil Service Commission and the *Pittsburgh Post-Gazette* soon named him "one of 20" young people "to watch" in 1988. By 1990, however, Johnson had moved to Atlanta, Georgia. In Pittsburgh, Johnson told the *Wall Street Journal*, "I had every advantage . . . but I really feel more comfortable here. . . . In Pittsburgh I was always in a white environment, and I had the feeling of isolation. Down here, you see successful blacks, and you feel a sense of well-being and pride." Over the next decade, Johnson held a variety of high-profile public- and private-sector jobs in Atlanta. In addition to service as assistant city attorney, he worked as counsel for the Turner Broadcasting System; the firm of Alston and Bird; and the Atlanta Life Financial Group. At about the same time that Johnson left the city, Eric Thompson, a twenty-nine-year-old accountant at Mellon Bank's Pittsburgh office, also quit his job and moved to Atlanta, where he took a job at Coca Cola's corporate headquarters. Compared to Mellon, he said Coca-Cola provided blacks more opportunities to work in "revenue

Attorney Justin L. Johnson (center), son of the prominent Pennsylvania Superior Court Judge Justin M. Johnson (right), and nephew of Judge Livingstone Johnson (left).

Source: Justin M. and Florence Johnson, private collection.

generating jobs." In Atlanta, Thompson emphasized, you see more blacks in positions "where they have an effect on the bottom line."[16]

When the manufacturing economy faltered, African Americans again entered the ranks of the unemployed in larger numbers and stayed there longer than their white counterparts. In metal products, textiles, food, and electrical equipment firms, the number of black workers dropped from about 9,400 in 1970 to 6,000 in 1980. Between 1970 and 1990, the number of all gainfully employed black workers sixteen years of age and older dropped from an estimated 31,700 to 28,900 (see tables 24, 25, and 26). By 1990, over 37 percent of black men were unemployed, compared to 13 percent of their white brothers. Sheryl Johnson, one of the few women who gained jobs following the steel industry consent decree, a federal affirmative action agreement, found that her job in the steel industry was short-lived. She worked only about four years between 1979 and 1982, before the Irwin works closed down. Ten years later, as small mini-mills took hold in the region, Johnson hoped to return, without success, to a high-paying job in the dwindling steel industry. She expressed increasing frustration and anger over the repeated rejections of her application by such firms. "I did as well as anyone else in the mill. But now I'm not worthy," she said.[17]

Black men fared even worse than their female counterparts. Although the union provided supplemental unemployment benefits, de-scribed as SUB pay, to unemployed workers, such income often expired before black workers could make the transition to new and better jobs.[18] Veronica Morgan-Lee, director of Carlow College's Hill District campus in 1994, came to Pittsburgh in the mid-1980s. She later recalled seeing huge numbers of unemployed black men on the streets of the city. "I had never in my life seen the number of people, mostly males, just in throngs. . . . What a waste of creative energy. I could not believe that all those folks did not have the potential to be productive citizens. It blew my mind that we could write off that many people because that's what has literally happened. They've been written off."[19] The *Post-Gazette* declared that for each black man living in the Pittsburgh metropolitan region, there was "a better than one-in-three chance you are enduring a depression, one that seemingly never ends. That's how bleak the employment situation is for black males here."[20]

African Americans were not only disproportionately hurt by the de-cline of manufacturing, they traveled a bumpy road toward jobs in the emerging postindustrial economy. During the 1990s, Urban League of Pittsburgh chief executive officer Esther Bush lamented that for too many African Americans, Pittsburgh's "Golden Triangle" was more akin to an "Iron Circle—a never-ending cycle of glass ceilings, revolving doors and broken ladders."[21] The number of complaints filed with the Pennsylvania Human Relations Commission (PHRC) continued to rise through the early 1990s, before peaking at about 4,850 in 1993–1994. Although some blacks preferred to base their complaints on grounds other than the color of their skin, the percentage of race-based complaints nonetheless ranged between 15 and 20 percent of all cases filed with the PHRC during that decade. In 1992, when the Pennsylvania Department of Transportation (PennDOT) passed over Calvin Clinton for promotion to a higher level administrative post, he took his case to the Pennsylvania Civil Service Commission (PCSC). Citing PennDOT for failing to follow proper pro-cedure by posting the position, the Civil Service Commission ruled in Clinton's favor. Following the state's decision, PennDOT posted the job and accepted Clinton's application. Again, however, the agency refused to hire him and again Clinton announced his intention to sue PennDOT for discrimination on the basis of race.[22]

In the service sector, African Americans sometimes complained that they were excluded from better-paying positions in restaurants, hotels, and shops in downtown Pittsburgh, the suburbs, and at the airport. An estimated 20 percent of job seekers cited lack of transportation as a cause for their unemployment. As economist Ralph Bangs showed in a 1991 study, however, the main barrier to black employment was not transportation, but entry-level jobs that paid lower than the so-called "reservation wage," below which workers viewed unemployment as more attractive than working. Between about 1985 and 1995, Alonzo Wilson (who was forty-seven years of age in 1996) worked as a laborer for an electrical supply company. During the entire decade, he had not received a promotion and consistently earned about $17,000 per year. Wilson barely brought home enough to take care of himself and his family, including maintenance of a family car. Urban planning scholar Karen Gibson and her associates highlighted how "overrepresentation of black men and women in low-wage service occupations produced a racial job profile reminiscent of the occupational distribution presumed to have disappeared over the 1960s."[23]

Employment for all workers in the building and construction trades declined dramatically during the last decades of the twentieth century, but African Americans found it especially difficult to work in this sector of the economy. Blacks in Pittsburgh occupied a disproportionately low number of jobs as carpenters, electricians, plumbers, pipefitters, steam-fitters, and machinists (see tables 27 and 28). Some twenty-seven years after the Black Construction Coalition opened up high-paying and skilled building trade union jobs for black workers, African Americans continued to complain that job opportunities eluded them in this field. Jerome Williams, a carpenter who benefited from the inroads of the BCC, declared, "It's worse today. I'll tell anybody that."[24]

African American men and women were nearly totally excluded from the top tier of jobs in finance, marketing, public relations, sales, architecture, and the law. African Americans (especially women) were often occupied as nurses' aides and laboratory and health technicians, but rarely among the higher paid registered nurses. While many African Americans found work as general, file, and data-entry clerks and typists, they were underrepresented as secretaries or front-office receptionists (see tables 29 and 30). In 1996, Felicia Harrison, owner of a job placement service for professional blacks and other minorities, maintained "a drawer full of resumes from college-educated blacks," who could not find jobs in the Pittsburgh region. At the same time, Carla Murray, a licensed practical nurse, spoke for many black workers when she said, "When you apply for a job you go with a negative attitude toward who your competition is going to be . . . you feel someone has put a star or a check on your application."[25]

One black woman saved her many job rejection letters as a reminder of discrimination in Pittsburgh's late-twentieth-century labor force. "I just didn't fit the picture," she said, but it was not just about color, "I wasn't thin. I didn't have long hair. I was unemployed. It had nothing to do with my ability to do a job." In 1996, Darryl Daughtry, a job skills instructor for Job Links, an Oakland-based community organization, declared, "It has a lot to do with networking. . . . And the reality is that the person who has the power to give you the job, the person who has the power to mentor you, is not black."[26] In 1999, public policy analysts Leon Haley and Ralph Bangs concluded that "employment discrimination" partly explained the small number of Pittsburgh blacks in key industries. Some blacks believed that their applications for good jobs were routinely disregarded, or simply "thrown into the trash."[27]

Life was not entirely smooth for black business and professional people at the middle and upper levels of the city's economy. During the late 1970s, Earl Hord, a senior vice president at Dollar Bank (and later head of the Pittsburgh Minority Enterprise Corporation), left the organization following a heated three-way battle to become president. Hord later recalled, "Every step of the way there were racial overtones, although I wasn't always acutely aware of what was driving them. . . . This thing of being different, being treated on a negative basis, is a tremendously heavy load to carry, psychologically and job-security wise."[28] Felicia Harrison, who came to Pittsburgh from New York, painted a similar picture of Pittsburgh's corporate offices. "I worked at least 30 different assignments in [Pittsburgh] corporations, major corporations, where I would be the only black in a department of 20 people or more. . . . It's [a] very uncomfortable feeling. You wake up every morning saying, 'Do I have to go to this job again today?'"[29] In 1999, a report prepared for the Pittsburgh Foundation concluded that racism was limiting economic opportunities for African Americans in Pittsburgh: "Many African Americans we interviewed indicated that racism exists, limiting the opportunities of African American professionals to advance in their chosen fields. Further, the racial climate of Pittsburgh is such that many African Americans feel shut out both politically and socially."[30]

The dearth of procurement contracts with city and county government agencies presented special difficulties for black entrepreneurs. Government contracts represent billions of dollars in annual contracting with local business organizations. Although African Americans made up about 28 percent of all working-age people in the city of Pittsburgh, black-owned businesses received only about 4 percent of municipal spending and procurement contracts. This racial disparity was also apparent when measured against the relative percent of black-owned businesses in the city. In 1998, the University of Pittsburgh's Center for Social and Urban Research reported that African Americans made up about 13 percent of available architecture and engineering firms, but received none of the prime contracts in these areas of business.[31]

Exclusion from entrepreneurial, administrative, and professional opportunities reinforced racial disparities in annual earnings. In 1990, in blue-collar jobs where black men were overrepresented, employees earned a median annual wage of $8,000, compared to $12,000 in jobs where black men were underrepresented. Similarly, for black women in blue-collar jobs, wages in jobs where they were overrepresented reached $6,800 per year, compared to an annual average of $13,800 a year in jobs where they were underrepresented (see tables 29–34). At the same time, the University of Pittsburgh's Center for Social and Urban Research found that only 10.8 percent of blacks ages twenty-five years and over held college degrees, compared to nearly 30 percent for whites in that age group. The earnings return on the same levels of education was also much lower for blacks than for whites in the Pittsburgh metropolitan region.[32]

The African American quest for economic justice in the late twentieth century was compounded by new federal policies. In 1980, Ronald Reagan, Republican governor of California, became president of the United States and helped to nationalize the California-led property tax revolt, and the growing opposition to affirmative action and government-funded social welfare programs. The Reagan administration sharply curtailed federal support for equal employment measures and set off a wave of similar state and local policies across the country. In the presidential election of 1992, William Jefferson Clinton, the Democratic candidate, campaigned on a promise to "End Welfare as We Know It." In 1994, young Republicans came together from across the nation and forged the so-called "Contract with America," and insisted that the Clinton administration uphold its mandate. In 1996, Clinton signed into law the Republican Personal Responsibility and Work Act. This legislation mandated strict time limits on public assistance to able-bodied men and women, and required a rapid transition of recipients from welfare to predominantly low wage-earning jobs.[33]

Late-twentieth-century federal policy helped to demolish the old New Deal social welfare order and expanded the ranks of the low-wage working poor. In the wake of federal budget cuts, the percentage of federal aid to cities dropped from an annual peak of about 17 percent in 1978 to just over 7 percent in 1992. The reduction of federal money to Community Development Block Grants (CBDGs) decreased Pittsburgh's allotment from $26 million in 1980 to $17 million in 1986.[34] In 1982, the Pennsylvania legislature passed Act 75, a measure that removed many needy families (disproportionately blacks) from the state's public assistance rolls. Partly because Republican governor Richard Thornburgh vigorously promoted and signed the bill into law, opponents soon dubbed the measure, "Thornfare."[35]

As federal and state funds declined, the city of Pittsburgh cut social services and curtailed enforcement of affirmative action programs. Mayor Richard Caliguiri rescinded agreements to hire blacks and other minorities in the city's fire and police departments; resisted implementation of a minority business enterprise program; and hampered implementation of affirmative action programs like The Pittsburgh Plan, which had given a generation of black men much-needed training for jobs in the building trades. In a variety of forums—in the courts, on talk radio, and in legislative assemblies—whites expressed increasing fear that they might lose their jobs to a "less qualified black person." In the *Pittsburgh Post-Gazette's* 1996 race relations survey, nearly 80 percent of whites expressed this fear, whereas nearly 60 percent of blacks believed that whites were unlikely to lose out to blacks in affirmative action hiring and promotion. One white man from West Mifflin seemed to speak for many of his counterparts when he said, "Sometimes, white guys don't get a fair shake, and that's happened to a couple of my friends."[36]

In 1999, the U.S. Circuit Court ruled in favor of nine white police officers who filed a racial discrimination suit against the City of Pittsburgh challenging the city's affirmative action efforts on behalf of women and minorities in hiring of new police officers. The anti-affirmative action Washington Legal Foundation celebrated the outcome of the case as a victory for "freedom and justice" on its Web site. Between 1993 and 1996, the American Civil Liberties Union had conducted reviews of over five hundred complaints of police misconduct, mostly African American. The

ACLU concluded, "underlying police misconduct was complete indifference by elected officials and the senior management of the Pittsburgh Police Department." Based mainly on evidence from the ACLU study, the U.S. Justice Department filed a lawsuit against the City of Pittsburgh for civil rights violations by members of Pittsburgh's Bureau of Police. This case represented the first to be tried under the federal Violent Crime Control Act of 1994.

As a result of this suit, the City of Pittsburgh signed a consent decree that placed the police department under the oversight of the U.S. Justice Department. Under the impact of the consent decree, the police department reported significant improvement in relations between the police and the community. The number of complaints from the African American community dropped by nearly 20 percent between October 1997 and October 1999. In October 1998, Amnesty International and a variety of civil rights organizations launched a major investigation of human rights violations by police departments in several selected U.S. cities, including Chicago, Los Angeles, and Pittsburgh. Following public hearings in Pittsburgh on 28 October 1999 at the Community for Reconciliation offices, Amnesty International concluded that the consent decree "is working and is a useful instrument and that the DOJ and the City of Pittsburgh should keep it in place." The local branch of the NAACP hoped to expand the decree's coverage to Port Authority and Housing Authority police.[37]

Resistance to affirmative action and cuts in social programs signaled a decline of African American influence in the city's Democratic Party organization. Black Pittsburghers regularly received the party's endorsement for seats on city council between the 1960s and the mid-1980s. Since the Democrats dominated the city's political process, the party's endorsement usually ensured success. Between 1979 and 1985, for example, all nominees of the Democratic Party won in the general election. In 1985, however, two black candidates, William Russell Robinson and Cathryn L. Irvis, wife of state legislator K. LeRoy Irvis, lost their bids for council seats in the Democratic Party primary. The party advanced an all-white slate in the general election, thereby serving notice that blacks would find it increasingly difficult to maintain representation in city government. For its part, the Republican Party endorsed for council Doris Carson Williams in 1977 and Elmer McClung in 1985. The black Republican candidates polled strongly within the black community, but failed among both white Republican and white Democratic voters.[38]

African Americans responded to this shock by mobilizing a strong grassroots campaign to replace the at-large system of voting for council seats with district elections. When the all-white council took office, 60 to 100 representatives of neighborhood groups massed in the lobby of the City-County Building. They carried signs protesting the absence of an African American councilman and chanted, "Council by district, let the people vote" and "Nine and O! Way to go!" Carl Redwood Jr., a spokesman for the demonstrators and co-convener of the newly formed Coalition for District Elections, expressed the sentiments of the group when he told reporters, ""The new council does not truly represent the people of Pittsburgh. This new council does not represent us."[39]

Even when the party endorsed black candidates before the mid-1980s, racial stereotypes and discrimination persisted among party leaders as well as the rank and file. Attorney Wendell Freeland, whose light skin color allowed him to witness unedited conversation among white party members, stated that he had overheard blacks "referred to as 'niggers' by white political figures, both Democratic and Republicans, in connection with many campaigns." Although councilman William R. Robinson received the party's nomination in 1981, he later recalled limits on his access to the party's networks and resources: "I could not get the other [white] candidates to meet with me, work together with me, raise money, campaign with me, or attend political functions with me as a member of a group. In fact, I stopped getting notices of political functions, and was not invited to appear jointly with the white council of candidates."[40]

Coupled with the curtailment of social programs, deindustrialization, and economic restructuring, the decline of African American representation in city government heightened the spread of poverty and the rise of the so-called "urban underclass" in Pittsburgh's black neighborhoods. The disparity of poverty among the races in Pittsburgh was alarmingly high. By 1989, some 41 percent of blacks in Pittsburgh lived in poverty compared to only 14 percent of their white counterparts. Both Pittsburgh and Allegheny County ranked forty-seventh in the degree of poverty disparity by race among the fifty largest U.S. cities. Ralph Bangs and his colleagues at the University of Pittsburgh concluded, "The high share of whites in the City's and County's population compared to that of many other large cities and counties means that the low poverty rates among whites in the City and County have more impact on overall poverty rates [in metropolitan Pittsburgh] than in most other large cities and counties."[41]

Poverty was disproportionately concentrated in the city's public housing projects. Between 1970 and 1990, African Americans increased from 76 percent of all public housing residents to over 80 percent. Some 36 percent of blacks occupied public housing or subsidized private rental properties, compared to only 13 percent of whites. Predominantly black public housing units—Allequippa Terrace, Broadhead Manor, Arlington Heights, Addison Terrace, Northview Heights, and St. Clair Village— were located in six of Pittsburgh's poorest census tracts. The same was not true for the nearly all-white public housing projects of Carrick, Squirrel Hill, and the South Side. Over half the black public housing population were children under eighteen years of age. In these families, the poverty rate ranged between 88 and 98 percent; referrals for child protective services reached four to six times the overall rate for Allegheny County; and juvenile delinquency (as measured in Juvenile Court dispositions) rose to between three and four times that of the county as a whole. More than two-thirds of the families were on public assistance, and unemployment was three times the jobless rate of the city.[42]

In 1992, the federal government enacted new legislation designed to dismantle the nation's large predominantly black, urban public housing projects. The law, called HOPE VI, called not only for the demolition of old projects, described as "severely distressed housing," but encouraged the relocation of low-income black families to government-subsidized Section 8 housing in the private market. By 2001, the city had demolished Allequippa Terrace, and Bedford Dwellings experienced a similar fate.[43]

Most African American low-income Section 8 families moved into homes in predominantly black residential areas, including the communities of Wilkinsburg, Braddock, Homestead, Duquesne, and North Braddock White Section 8 families occupied the suburbs of Bethel Park, Brentwood, Blawnox, Mt. Lebanon, Ross, Shaler, and South Park, and only one black family lived in Section 8 housing in all of these communities. In 1996, Alroi Milliones, Section 8 application director for Pittsburgh, told the Post-Gazette, "Elderly whites who qualify for Section 8 housing most often pass up units in black communities and wait for years to move to Carrick or Squirrel Hill." In the same year, Regina Morrow, an African American mother of four, moved her family to East Liberty, she said, because, "White people don't want us to come into their areas."[44]

In seven predominantly white eastern suburbs, white residents resisted a court-approved plan to move twenty-three black public housing families into their neighborhoods during the mid-1990s. These protests came on the heels of an eight-year-old federal lawsuit, in which African Americans prevented Allegheny County from demolishing a black low-income high-rise in Braddock and erecting a new one in the same community. Black residents argued that such a move would reinforce racial segregation. When the court ruled in their favor, however, it was almost impossible to find space for low-income black families in predominantly white suburbs. George Arendas, head of the county housing authority, noted that whites agreed that desegregation of public housing should take place, but the "attitude is it needs to be done, but not in my back yard."[45]

Squeezed between low-paying entry level jobs in the service economy, family responsibilities, and the requirements of welfare payments, many poor and working-class black women in the 1980s and 1990s found it difficult to break into the wage-earning sector of the city's economy and still earn enough to adequately care for themselves and their children. In 1994, when Charlet Holley completed a sixteen-week computer program at the Bidwell Training Center on the city's North Side, the forty-two-year-old, widowed mother of three children sought a good-paying job close to her home in Oakland, but entry level pay for Bidwell graduates was $7.00 per hour or lower. Few women with children could expect to make a living on such wages. Thus, city and county social welfare programs figured prominently among black families. These included Medicaid, Earned Tax Income Credit (ETIC), food stamps, Temporary Assistance to Needy Families (TANF, formerly AFDC), general assistance, and public housing.[46]

The challenges that faced young people were closely intertwined with the struggles of single black women. In Pittsburgh, the percentage of women as heads of families below the poverty line increased from 46.6 in the 1970s to over 61 percent by 1990. The percentage of black children living in poverty reached 57 percent in 1989 (the second highest rate in the country behind Milwaukee, Wisconsin), compared to 16 percent for white children. Unemployment for black male youth between sixteen and nineteen years of age reached nearly 50 percent during the 1980s and early 1990s, which was three times the rate of white male youth unemployment at 17 percent. Black female youth unemployment reached about 40 percent compared to only about 11 percent for white female youth. David Young grew up in the Bedford Dwellings housing project during the 1970s and 1980s and later attended the University of Pittsburgh part time. In 1996, he told the *Post-Gazette* that his generation of young black men had few opportunities to make a decent living in Pittsburgh, "There's just not a lot of opportunity for people in my situation. . . . A lot of people I grew up with aren't employed. They've had nickel and dime jobs. But there's nothing that you can do for the rest of your life. There's no careers, no jobs you can support a family on. It's just about hopeless."[47]

The carpenter Jerome Williams participated in the movement to open up construction jobs for blacks during the late 1960s and early 1970s. Nearly thirty years later, he lamented the lack of job opportunities for young blacks as the city approached the new century: "What hurts me are the kids I see on the streets. I know they need a job more than anything." Barbara Hart-Greer, a teacher at the Allegheny Middle School on the North Side, lamented that her students glorified "all the street stuff," and seemed oblivious to the prospect of preparing for a future that included a steady job.[48] Dianna Green, senior vice president at Duquesne Light Company and cochair of Youth Works 96, a job training program, urged the city to match its zeal for combating crime with equal enthusiasm for creating jobs for unemployed black youth.[49] Nate Smith, the civil rights activist, also underscored the importance of creating jobs for young people, especially young black men. In Smith's view, "An 18- or 19-year old kid would rather trade their gun for a job. But if they don't have a job they're going to have a gun, because they want to feel powerful. . . . They want to be able to buy something when they want to buy it, and they're going to rob, steal and murder. But we could put a stop to that. All you do is give them a job."[50]

Fueled by widespread youth unemployment, drugs, and the proliferation of handguns, the number of gangs dramatically increased in Pittsburgh's black neighborhoods during the 1980s and 1990s. Before the mid-1980s, only a handful of highly organized youth gangs, including the Black Mafia Unit, the West Hills Posse, and the Brushton Hilltop Gang, seem to have existed in Pittsburgh's black community. James Dickerson, commander of the city's organized crime unit in the early 1990s, noted how these early groups generally limited their activities to underage drinking, fistfights and low-level drug activities. But the advent of crack cocaine during the mid- to late 1980s ushered in a new, interurban gangs that acted as intermediaries in drug sales, making it more difficult for police to identify the heads of narcotics rings. Jerome Taylor, a University of Pittsburgh professor and codirector of the Institute for the Black Family, explained that gangs "provide a degree of protection, a means of earning money, and a basis for developing friendships."[51]

In 1994, Bert Hathaway, a juvenile probation officer and head of

Allegheny County juvenile court's gang task force in the early 1990s, estimated the number of active gang members in Pittsburgh at between 1,500 and 2,500. These gangs increasingly used graffiti and guns to mark and protect turf. In Brashear High School, rivalries between Hill District and Hazelwood gangs created widespread fear among students and the surrounding community. One gang member explained, "No way you can be in the hood without being involved in some way. If you live there, you're automatically part of the gang. If you're not, you're going to move. You're not going to want to be there if you're not." Movies like *Colors* and *New Jack City*, which showed somewhat glamorized views of gang life, also no doubt gave some of Pittsburgh's black youths ideas about how to create more tightly organized gangs and how to create their own sign language to communicate without words in dangerous situations.[52]

Pittsburgh's inner-city neighborhoods erupted in gang violence in the early 1990s, with Homewood at the epicenter. Many of the community's older residents called it "The Wild West."[53] In Allegheny County, the homicide rate for young black males between fifteen and twenty-four years of age increased from 69 per 100,000 population in 1974 to 130 per 100,000 population in 1996. Although African Americans made up only 11 percent of the county's population, they accounted for the vast majority of homicide victims. These deaths of were closely related to the rise of crack cocaine and related wars over drug turf. In 1993, Allegheny County had a record 118 homicides, of which 46 of the victims were black males between the ages of fifteen and twenty-four, killed mostly by other black males. Reports of drive-by shootings routinely led the evening news, and, over the course of five years, the youth homicide rates quadrupled, and the Allegheny County Health Department identified murder as the leading cause of death among teenagers.[54]

As gang activity and fear of crime in the black community increased between 1981 and 1999, the state built eighteen new prisons. The number of drug offenders committed annually to Pennsylvania state prisons increased from 202 in 1981 to 1,784 in 1997. In the mid-1990s, state sentencing guidelines made selling cocaine more serious than selling marijuana, and people with criminal records received harsher sentences than first-time offenders. These new measures disproportionately affected Pittsburgh's African American communities. Between 1990 and 1997, while the number of white offenders in state prisons increased 54 percent (from 29,600 to 46,300), the number of black drug offenders increased 67 percent (from 79,800 to 133,400).[55]

Allegheny County Courthouse. For a variety of reasons, disproportionately large numbers of Pittsburgh's African American residents found themselves before the city's bar of justice.

Source: Photo by Sue Abramson. Carnegie Museum of Art, photo #2001.35.82344.

African Americans were more likely to be arrested for crimes involving cocaine and heroin, while whites were more likely to be arrested for marijuana-related crimes. Roy Austin, an authority on incarceration patterns in the state, suggested that blacks were more likely to accumulate criminal records because police were more likely to target poor minority communities than predominantly white suburban neighborhoods. A Washington DC Justice Policy Institute study demonstrated that blacks in Pennsylvania were incarcerated at a rate of fourteen times that of whites, the highest disparity rate of any state in the nation. From 1990 to 1994, Pennsylvania minorities were four times as likely as whites to be imprisoned for drug-related offenses. The Pennsylvania State University study reported only 1 in 38 white men (1,690 of 64,875) arrested for drug offenses served time in prison compared to 1 in 9 (7,606 of 69,294) men of other races. By 2001, African Americans constituted 57 percent of the inmates at the Allegheny County Jail. [56]

The precise reasons for the higher rates of incarceration were hotly debated. Richard Garland, executive director of Youth Works, which trains at-risk youth in Allegheny County, reported that many black defendants lacked resources to mount meaningful legal defenses against the charges leveled against them and often settled for overextended public defenders. Garland also noted that many black defendants chose to plea bargain in order to serve less time. These defendants, once released, suffered from the stigma of incarceration as they sought meaningful employment and a second chance. Moreover, under new, tougher laws, many found themselves disenfranchised during their probation periods. Turhan Shabazz, a street poet, storyteller, ex-convict, and former lightweight boxer, explained his experience to a *Post-Gazette* reporter: "For one thing, I've got too many strikes against me. I'm old. I'm black and I'm an ex-convict. . . . Nobody will hire me." At the time of his interview, Shabazz was a man in his fifties, but his experience underscored the employment difficulties that confronted growing numbers of working-age black men who were incarcerated at one time or another. [57]

Turhan Shabazz, storyteller, street poet, and former lightweight boxer, 28 Apr. 1996.

At the turn of the twenty-first century, in addition to higher rates of unemployment, drug use, and incarceration, African Americans struggled against the ravages of unequal health care. In 2000, three times as many black men (between the ages of thirty-three and forty-four) and women (between the ages of forty-four and fifty-four) died of heart disease than whites in Allegheny County. Black infants were twice as likely to die before age one as white infants. African Americans were disproportionately represented among all major diseases, but they were underrepresented among inpatient admissions in the region's major hospitals. In May 2001, the Pittsburgh public schools threatened to expel some 11,200 students, mostly black, because of improper documentation for vaccinations against mumps, measles, and rubella. Largely through the Urban League's education director, Nina Lynch, African Americans mobilized necessary support for an immunization taskforce that resulted in most children receiving immunization by the deadline.[58]

African Americans also received less access to organ transplants. Nationally, between 1996 and 1999, among all "clinically appropriate candidates" for kidney transplants, only 17 percent of blacks received these operations, compared to 52 percent for whites (see tables 35 and 36). During the late 1980s, Pittsburgh's African American community had waged a public campaign on behalf of Tabatha Foster, a poor black child who required an exceedingly expensive series of five transplanted organs to stay alive. In an interview with *Courier* reporter Debran Rowland, NAACP president Harvey Adams declared that the Tabatha Foster case was one of the organization's greatest accomplishments: "She was being denied (organs) because she was poor and black. They were going to let her die." Although Tabatha soon died, she became one of the longest survivors of such radical surgery.[59]

During the 1990s, Stephen Thomas, the Philip Hallen Professor of Community Health and Social Justice at the University of Pittsburgh, spearheaded the development of a vigorous public health campaign on behalf of the city's black community. Thomas told the *Post-Gazette* that racial discrimination in Pittsburgh's healthcare system was often "unintentional." Yet, "in subtle ways," he said, "minorities get substandard care." Thus, rather than sitting at lunch counters, Thomas said, today's black freedom movement should target "the doorsteps of health care facilities." Thomas pledged to help move health care "out of the ivory tower ... into the communities." Under his leadership, the University of Pittsburgh's Center for Minority Health enlisted the aid of some twenty-eight neighborhood barbershops and thirty-three beauty shops in its campaign to transform the health of African Americans in Pittsburgh.[60]

New Inner-City Neighborhoods and Suburbanization

Even as African American neighborhoods saw increases in poverty, black families moved into a rising number of heretofore all white communities in the Pittsburgh metropolitan area. Within the city limits, the most striking growth took place in Garfield, Point Breeze, Highland Park, Stanton Heights, and Perry North and South (see table 37). Other blacks moved into the nearby municipalities of Swissvale, North Braddock, Duquesne, Wilkinsburg, and McKeesport.

In almost every community, white homeowner improvement clubs and civic associations—the Perry North Citizens Council; the Point Breeze Good Neighbor Club; and the Stanton Heights Civic Association, for example—monitored the movement of black residents into their neighborhoods. Sometimes established black residents allied themselves with these efforts. In North Point Breeze in the early 1970s, white and black residents accused the Pittsburgh Board of Realtors (PBR) of blockbusting the McPherson Boulevard area. They argued that the 6900 block had shifted from 95 percent white to 95 percent black within a two-year period, partly because realtors had mounted an aggressive door-to-door campaign, "telling white owners they could get a higher price for their home by selling to blacks . . . and advising white buyers not to buy a home north of Penn Ave."[61]

On the North Side, in 1977, white residents complained that real estate agents discouraged prospective white homeowners from buying in the Perry North and South areas by citing the predominantly black Northview Heights housing project as a "bad racial situation" and steering white buyers away from the neighborhood. Under pressure from white homeowners' organizations, the Equal Opportunity Committee of the Greater Pittsburgh Board of Realtors cautioned its members against "overly active soliciting the community" and forged voluntary agreements to limit sales in areas undergoing racial integration. Compared to earlier periods in the city's history, "panic selling" and precipitous "white flight" dissipated during the 1980s and 1990s.[62]

Along with movement into new city neighborhoods, African Americans increased their numbers in the suburbs. North of Pittsburgh they crossed what some called the "Mason-Dixon line," into such towns as McCandless, Butler, Cranberry, Franklin Park, Marshall, and Pine. In

Monroeville, east of Pittsburgh, the black population rose from 562 in 1970 to over 2,400 in 2000. When Theodore and Janie Clemons moved to Monroeville with their three children in the early 1970s, most white families moved out of their block, but other whites soon moved in. As blacks moved into the municipality's Garden City community, this area became known as "Monroeville's black Mecca."[63] In Penn Hills, also east of Pittsburgh, the white population declined by 10 percent between 1990 and 2000, while the municipality's black population increased from 7,900 to 11,300. A black realtor, Milton Holt, explained to the Eastwood Civic Club that black families moved to Penn Hills in such large numbers because of racial restrictions in other suburban locations. In much the same way that city residents had resisted the influx of African Americans, white and black homeowners in Penn Hills formed the Eastwood Civic Club to discourage white flight and curb the rising number of blacks moving into the community. One white resident recalled that her parents had panicked and moved from Homewood to Penn Hills: "I watched that happen to my parents . . . and I have no intention of letting it happen here to me. If everyone would just sit tight, the races could live together without any problem." Nonetheless, in the Eastwood section of Penn Hills, the white population dropped from nearly 5,900 in 1970 to only 1,100 in 1990. Many white families later recalled selling their property for less than market value in their rush to move out.[64]

When African Americans moved into new, predominantly white neighborhoods within and outside the city of Pittsburgh, the degree of residential segregation along racial lines decreased. The index of dissimilarity for Pittsburgh dropped from 63 percent in 1970 to 56 percent in 1990 based on municipal ward statistics, and from 79 to 74 percent between 1970 and 1990 based on census tract data. Fifty-three of the city's ninety neighborhoods showed an increase in the number of African Americans over the decades of the 1980s and 1990s. In a 1996 *Pittsburgh Post-Gazette* survey of race relations, over 90 percent of whites responded "yes" to the question: "Would you accept a black family moving in next door to you and your family?" After more than twenty-five years of civil rights laws and a reputation as "one of the most segregated cities" in America, journalist Clarke Thomas wrote that blacks were now "moving into white neighborhoods without the white flight that once seemed automatic."[65]

Both within and outside the city, black home ownership gradually increased. By 1990, in high-income suburbs (those with average incomes of 10 percent or more greater than the county's median household income), black mortgage holders stood at nearly 77 percent compared to 64 percent for whites. Doris Carson Williams, president of the African American Chamber of Commerce of Southwestern Pennsylvania, maintained that the growth of the black population in these communities represented people "moving where the opportunities are . . . African-Americans can no longer be considered a monolithic community. We can live wherever our economics allow us to move." Based on U.S. census figures for the region, the number of African-American homeowners grew by 12 percent between 1990 and 2000, compared to only 2 percent for whites. In the city of Pittsburgh, white home ownership actually dropped by 10 percent, while black homeownership increased by 3 percent. In Allegheny County, the five municipalities with the highest percentage of black home-ownership, between 1990 and 2000, were Sewickley, McCandless, Bethel Park, Penn Hills, and Churchill. Black home ownership in Butler County increased by 35 percent compared to 19 percent among whites.[66]

Although many new areas of the metropolitan housing market opened up to African American occupancy, blacks continued to face barriers gaining access to good houses at reasonable prices. African Americans remained concentrated in established, predominantly black communities in the Hill District, Homewood, East Liberty, Manchester, and Beltzhoover. With the exception of East Liberty, however, most of these neighborhoods lost population during the period (see table 37). At the same time, the black population in these areas rose to well over 95 percent of the total. About one-third of

CENSUS2000

Black population in Pittsburgh

The 20 Pittsburgh neigborhoods with the greatest black population and the change since 1990:

Neighborhood	2000 Black	% change
Homewood	8,949	-20%
East Liberty	4,980	7%
Lincoln-Lemington-Belmar	4,924	-15%
Garfield	4,537	-6%
Hill District	4,024	-19%
East Hills	3,706	-13%
Perry South	3,430	8%
Terrace Village	2,509	-50%
Northview Heights	2,427	-8%
Crawford Roberts	2,374	1%
Beltzhoover	2,288	-17%
Larimer	2,287	-31%
Manchester	2,143	-19%
Marshall-Shadeland	2,142	53%
Bedford Dwellings	2,023	-10%
Highland Park	1,991	67%
Hazelwood	1,835	7%
Central Northside	1,778	-14%
Stanton Heights	1,735	52%
Point Breeze North	1,564	-8%

Source: U.S. Census   Post-Gazette

CENSUS2000

Black population in Pittsburgh
Neighborhoods of 1,000 or more and the change in the black population, 1990-2000

Neighborhood	1990 Black	2000 Black	no. change	% change
Sheraden	482	1,277	795	165%
Perry North	612	1,115	503	82%
Golden Triangle	1,142	2,071	929	81%
Highland Park	1,191	1,991	800	67%
Marshall-Shadeland	1,399	2,142	743	53%
Stanton Heights	1,144	1,735	591	52%
Knoxville	1,139	1,481	342	30%
Perry South	3,174	3,430	256	8%
Hazelwood	1,707	1,835	128	7%
East Liberty	4,641	4,980	339	7%
North Oakland	1,009	1,031	22	2%
Crawford Roberts	2,346	2,374	28	1%
Garfield	4,841	4,537	-304	-6%
Northview Heights	2,628	2,427	-201	-8%
West Oakland	1,313	1,208	-105	-8%
Point Breeze North	1,703	1,564	-139	-8%
Bedford Dwellings	2,256	2,023	-233	-10%
Upper Hill	2,187	1,949	-238	-11%
East Hills	4,280	3,706	-574	-13%
Central Northside	2,071	1,778	-293	-14%
Lincoln-Lemington-Belmar	5,789	4,924	-865	-15%
Homewood North	5,199	4,366	-833	-16%
Beltzhoover	2,750	2,288	-462	-17%
Manchester	2,632	2,143	-489	-19%
Homewood West	1,335	1,047	-288	-22%
Homewood South	4,699	3,536	-1,163	-25%
Middle Hill	2,789	2,075	-714	-26%
St. Clair	1,741	1,221	-520	-30%
Larimer	3,338	2,287	-1,051	-31%
Terrace Village	4,986	2,509	-2,477	-50%

Source: U.S. Census   Post-Gazette

black home buyers who purchased property between 1992 and 1994 did so in one of twenty black-dominated areas in Allegheny County. Regardless of their socioeconomic status, African Americans lived in only 15— or about 12 percent—of all 130 independent municipalities in Allegheny County.[67]

Despite years of affirmative action and antidiscrimination laws, fair housing legislation was not systematically enforced. Homeowners, realtors, and bankers developed new and more subtle tactics for limiting

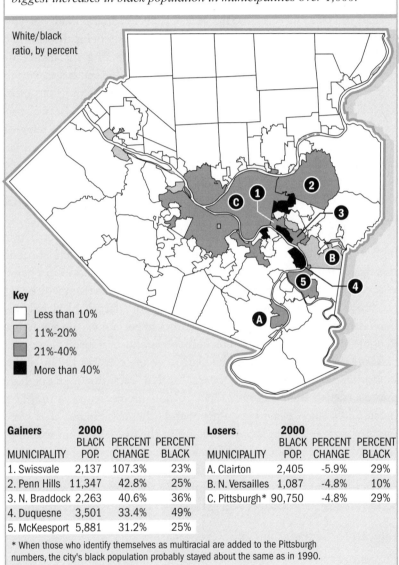

CENSUS2000

Black population: Allegheny County

Areas of Allegheny County according to black population and the biggest increases in black population in municipalities over 1,000:

White/black ratio, by percent

Key
- ☐ Less than 10%
- ☐ 11%-20%
- ☐ 21%-40%
- ■ More than 40%

Gainers MUNICIPALITY	2000 BLACK POP.	PERCENT CHANGE	PERCENT BLACK	Losers MUNICIPALITY	2000 BLACK POP.	PERCENT CHANGE	PERCENT BLACK
1. Swissvale	2,137	107.3%	23%	A. Clairton	2,405	-5.9%	29%
2. Penn Hills	11,347	42.8%	25%	B. N. Versailles	1,087	-4.8%	10%
3. N. Braddock	2,263	40.6%	36%	C. Pittsburgh*	90,750	-4.8%	29%
4. Duquesne	3,501	33.4%	49%				
5. McKeesport	5,881	31.2%	25%				

* When those who identify themselves as multiracial are added to the Pittsburgh numbers, the city's black population probably stayed about the same as in 1990.

Source: U.S. Census Bureau

James Hilston/Post-Gazette

African Americans to certain areas of the city. During the 1980s, John Gabriel, executive director of the PHRC, described the emergence of subtler racial practices in the real estate industry, "More and more there is a sophistication among realtors that was absent ten years ago. No longer do they outright refuse to show you properties or apartments but the effect is still that minorities are unable to obtain certain housing." James Frazier, housing director of the local Urban League, opined, "If you're African American, you stand a 50 percent chance of being discriminated against every time you enter the [Pittsburgh] market for any kind of housing service."[68] Allegheny County accounted for the largest number of state housing discrimination complaints (22 percent, or 53 out of 245) lodged with the PHRC between July 1983 and June 1984. Between 1992 and 1994, the National Apartment Leasing Company coded telephone housing inquiries by race, on the basis of voice quality, and eliminated persons identified as black from consideration for rental units. Later renamed Mozart Management, the firm agreed to out-of-court settlements with black plaintiffs in three discrimination suits, totaling more than $1.3 million.[69]

Lenders continued to turn African Americans down at a much higher rate than their white counterparts. In a 1992 survey, lenders denied mortgage applicants from black neighborhoods (populations 90 percent or more black) three times more often than applicants from white neighborhoods (90 percent or more white). Some poor, largely black neighborhoods such as Homewood and Beltzhoover got almost no home loans in 1991–1992. Prospective white homebuyers also refused to purchase residences owned or occupied by blacks. When Carolyn Dillon and her husband sought to sell their house, Carolyn "took down all the family photos, turned the bindings of her precious books to the wall, hid the music and packed away the sculpture and other art. Finally, after watching prospective [white] buyers drive up to the house, see her working in the yard or in the doorway, and then turn away, Carolyn Dillon and her husband made one final change. Each time a white buyer came by, she and her husband deserted their home." By the 1990s, some residents described the city's pattern of segregation as, "Pittsburgh's apartheid."[70]

Education, Segregation, and Resegregation

Pittsburgh's racially segregated housing market reinforced the color line in the city's public schools. Although African American access to the housing market was restricted in more subtle ways, resistance to the school desegregation movement was explicit. Growing numbers of whites (and some blacks) sent their children to private schools; between 1976 and 1981, the total number of students in the public schools dropped from 59,000 to 43,000. At the same time, the black percentage of all public school enrollments rose from 45 to just over 50 percent. By the turn of the century, blacks made up over 56 percent of the city's public school children.[71]

As white opposition to busing to achieve racial balance in the schools intensified, the Allegheny Conference on Community Development helped to develop a compromise approach. In 1978, the Citizens Advisory Council, chaired by the ACCD's Robert Pease, developed the magnet schools program, a system of voluntary, racially desegregated, special subject schools, which required the limited reassignment and busing of students to achieve racial balance. In order to improve those schools that remained segregated, the ACCD created the Public Information Advisory Committee and the Allegheny Conference Education Fund (ACEF). These two bodies aimed to facilitate communication between the various agencies interested in public education and to provide funding for innovative projects in the poverty area schools. As a result, as John Portz, Lana Stein, and Robin R. Jones have argued, the ACCD crafted a compromise between those who worried about the "quality of education" on one hand and those who emphasized the equal distribution of educational resources on the other.[72]

Mayor Richard Caliguiri called for peaceful implementation of the magnet school plan, though he neither endorsed nor opposed it. The board's Magnet School Advisory Committee submitted its final recommendations in February 1979, and the full school board ratified the plan the following month. As part of the plan, the board designed three types of magnet programs: the magnet school, the add-on magnet, and the school-within-a-school. Magnet schools utilized entire facilities and had district-wide, open enrollment. They included traditional academics, performing and creative arts, open classrooms, and a Montessori program for kindergarten through twelfth grade. In contrast, add-on magnets existed in the regular public schools and offered specialized daily instruction to students in addition to their regular curricula. Many programs were offered with this option including: leadership and language training; business and management; engineering and architecture; science, law and government; and Army ROTC, among many others. Within the same setting, the school-within-a-school program offered a regular academic schedule and a separate magnet program, each with its own distinct student populations. While they might share certain facilities, the two student groups relied on two entirely separate administrative personnel. The board planned school-within-a-school programs to focus on healthcare-related careers, child development, and practical arts.[73]

Whites viewed busing of children for reasons other than desegregation, i.e., to provide access to innovative programs, in highly positive terms. As Ogle Duff observed in 1982, "transportation which is provided, at least in Pennsylvania, for students who travel up to ten miles beyond school district lines is perceived as an enhancement for the educational programs of some school districts."[74]

The Pittsburgh Board of Education inaugurated the magnet schools program at the beginning of the 1979–1980 academic year, but the PHRC ruled that the plan failed to go far enough toward integrating the city's schools. The school board then redesigned its desegregation plan to include not only magnet schools but also redistricting that compelled many students to attend schools outside their neighborhoods. The program went into effect in August 1980. As the *New York Times* noted, "after twelve years of litigation, [Pittsburgh] is scheduled to implement its first busing plan. Under the plan, about 7,000 pupils will be bused in the program. . . . [A] workable desegregation plan was finally put into effect, mixing voluntary and mandatory shifts in student assignment."[75]

Two years later, the Pennsylvania Human Relations Commission ruled that the city's school desegregation plans were in compliance. Although several schools remained all white or all black, between 1979 and 1986, the percentage of students attending integrated schools (as defined by the PHRC) increased from 27 to 61 percent. By 1989, the city of Pittsburgh reported that 83 percent of its middle schools (grades six through eight) had been fully integrated. [76]

The district's magnet program remained intact through the early twenty-first century. In 2004, the district had magnet programs in twenty-five of its eighty-six regular schools, and nearly all had met the PHRC's integration standards. Both blacks and whites applauded the school board's innovative magnet program as an improvement over previous desegregation plans. Richard Payne, the African American activist and spokesperson for the Homewood Community Committee for Direct Action, declared his support for the board's program, noting, "we've been without hope for 11 years. . . . As of today, our children have carried the burden of busing. Statements from the new board have brought a breath of fresh air."[77] White parents praised the magnet schools for their culture, ethnic diversity, and academic reputation. Cindy Goldstein, a white Shadyside parent, sent her three children to Linden International Studies Academy, a magnet elementary school in Point Breeze. "What I have found at Linden" she said, "is there are many different cultural opportunities that are brought to the classroom when you have children of different racial and economic backgrounds. . . . I think the kids benefit from that exposure." Her children, she said, were just as likely to bring home a black friend as a white one. As Helen Faison, a former Pittsburgh school superintendent and administrator, noted, "I think [the magnet schools program] held in the district some families the district would have lost."[78] In its 1996 survey of racial attitudes in the city, the *Post-Gazette* showed that 97 percent of white and 83 percent of black respondents would send their children to a school where "a few" of the students were black. Moreover, 87 percent of whites "completely accepted" someone of the other race teaching their children, while nearly 70 percent of blacks so reported.[79]

Despite ongoing efforts to desegregate the city's schools, the movement toward racial parity in the Pittsburgh public schools was only partially successful. In 1996, in a special *Post Gazette* report on school desegregation efforts, both blacks and whites gave the city "a failing grade." By the turn of the twenty-first century, large numbers of Pittsburghers expressed a "new willingness to separate" black and white students, and to return to an earlier pattern of racial segregation in the school districts of western Pennsylvania. Growing numbers of black children in Pittsburgh could easily spend their entire education in schools that were more than 95 percent black. This was especially true for those who went from Lincoln Elementary to Milliones Middle School to Westinghouse High School.[80]

The Pittsburgh Board of Education played a major role in reestablishing patterns of racial segregation in the schools. In 1994–1995, for example, the Milliones school in the Hill District was 61 percent black. Shortly thereafter, the school board opened two new middle schools in the South Hills—South Hills Middle in 1996 and South Brook in 2001—and students from the South Hills area, who were mostly white, no longer crossed the river to Milliones. As a result, Milliones shifted to 96 percent black, and South Hills and South Brook remained about 14 percent black. In 1996, the Pittsburgh Board of Education proposed to formally "return to neighborhood schools after 15 years of busing to achieve racial balance." In the same year, a new Pennsylvania state law limited the PHRC's power to reassign students to any public school other than the one closest to the student's home, unless there was a "specific violation" of the equal protection clause of the Fourteenth Amendment of the U.S. Constitution.[81]

Although the majority of students in Pittsburgh's public schools were black, most of the teachers remained white. In the six-county Pittsburgh metropolitan area, African Americans made up only 4 percent of the total teaching force, with over 50 percent of the schools reporting a teaching staff of less than 1 percent black. Black students complained that "they were not treated fairly in disciplinary matters." In 1994, the Penn Hills chapter of the NAACP charged the school with expelling a disproportionately large number of black students for infraction of school rules. Although black students accounted for only 30 percent of the student body, they made up nearly 50 percent of all suspensions.[82]

Some teachers and administrators continued to make erroneous racial assumptions about black students in particular and black people in general. Between 1994 and 1996, six teachers were "either fired, suspended or transferred" to other posts for making racist remarks to students in the public schools of Pittsburgh, Penn Hills, Wilkinsburg, Monessen, Woodland Hills, and the Trinity district of Washington County. At one predominantly white high school, the principal invited only black students to attend a black history lecture in the school's cafeteria. In another high school, white students occasionally remarked that a black male student was "the whitest black kid I know" and that certain aspects of behavior represented "a niggerish thing to do." A black female high school student reported that she maintained her closest white friendship partly by ignoring the many times that she heard "the n-word" in the halls of the school.[83]

In another school, white and black students watched a video about homeless children in America during the mid-1990s. When the film highlighted the faces of white children on the screen, white students loudly applauded, while falling silent and even "sneering" when a black face appeared on the screen. The vice president of the junior class and one of the few black students in the school, reported that she "couldn't believe it. . . . I grew up with some of these kids." A white student also recalled saying to himself "over and over again, you shouldn't be doing this. This is wrong." Both black and sympathetic white students said that the teachers "did nothing to stop the outbursts." A *Post-Gazette* reporter confirmed that such incidents were quite widespread throughout the district, "Such incidents aren't uncommon in the region's schools. Racial slights, slurs, graffiti and other evidence of bigotry are part of the everyday school life."[84]

A variety of special honors classes and programs enrolled few or no black students, even in schools where blacks were a majority. At the Reizenstein Middle School, for example, blacks made up over 75 percent of the student body but the school enrolled few black students in honors courses. At the Penn Hills Linton Middle School, blacks made up 30 percent of the student body, though only one black belonged to the school's unique language arts class for gifted seventh graders. Black and white students also experienced growing separation from each other as they advanced beyond elementary to the middle and high school grades. Elizabeth Louik, a white student, confirmed this separation when she told a reporter, "I had black and white friends in elementary school. But in middle school, I started to notice it—the separation. We weren't friends anymore. . . . If I had gone over and sat [with black students] at another table . . . my friends would have thought it was strange."[85]

Such attitudes and continued segregation followed Pittsburgh's African Americans into the twenty-first century. But as in previous moments in the city's history, Pittsburgh's black population would build upon existing forms of resistance to racial and class inequality to address the challenges of the city's postindustrial renaissance.

5

Toward the New Century

FORGING THEIR OWN RENAISSANCE

While many of Pittsburgh's young people responded to hard times and declining economic opportunities by moving elsewhere at the end of the twentieth century, most African Americans stayed and fought for jobs and business opportunities in Pittsburgh's evolving postindustrial economy. In the Hill District, some black workers took eight- to ten-week crash courses that were designed to improve their test scores on qualifying exams for apprenticeships in the building and construction trades. William Garner, who completed apprenticeship training with the International Brotherhood of Electrical Workers, later underscored the heavy commitment of time and work that his program entailed: "You have to commit five years of your life. Nothing is going to be given to you. ... You have to work hard. You have to take the initiative to learn, to show up on time and to be dependable." When she lost her job at the U.S. Steel Corporation in Irwin, Lois Brown returned to school and then entered the field of social work, serving as a counselor for the "economically disadvantaged." Alonzo Wilson, the electrical supply laborer mentioned previously in this book, enrolled in Carlow College's Hill Program for adult students, explaining, "I haven't really established myself in anything. . . . I've chosen school to get around that." Even before deindustrialization took its full toll on black youth, Will Thompkins recalled how his father impressed upon him the value of education. "My father would say, 'Get as much education as you can,' which was his way of saying, 'Don't do the backbreaking work I've done all my life' as a laborer." A 1967 graduate of Oliver High School, Thompkins later became vice president of programs and services for the Urban League of Pittsburgh (ULP).[1]

Despite seemingly insurmountable obstacles in the business world, some former steelworkers created their own ventures to counteract the loss of industrial jobs. When Bobby J. Hunt lost his job at U.S. Steel's Homestead works in 1983, he went into business for himself. He opened a hair care business and trained eighty black hair stylists in the city of Pittsburgh. By the early 1990s, Hunt owned beauty shops in Penn Hills, East Liberty, Downtown, and the city's North Side. "Most young blacks," he said, "don't even feel they are part of society. It's very difficult for them. Some are so energetic and talented, but they need help."[2]

On the city's North Side, Delorese Ambrose, a college professor, created a diversity and employment consulting and training firm. Ambrose described diversity training as preparation for understanding "all aspects of social differences: race, age, gender, education, culture, and lifestyle."[3]

Established black businesses like the *Pittsburgh Courier*, Robert Lavelle's real estate company, and Dwelling House Savings and Loan Association continued to provide employment opportunities and business services to the city's black community. As mainstream news media, real estate firms, and financial institutions gradually opened their doors to black commerce, these well-known black businesses lost some of their customer base. In response to this changing business environment for African American realtors, Gloria Spearman purchased a franchise from Realty World and opened an office in East Liberty in 1988. However, new, highly successful, black-owned enterprises such as Milton Washington's Allegheny Housing Rehabilitation Corporation; Randy Harper's American Micrographics Company; and Ron Davenport's Sheridan Broadcasting Corporation, the nation's largest minority-owned broadcasting company, helped to improve the employment and entrepreneurial climate for blacks in postindustrial Pittsburgh.[4]

Grassroots, direct-action campaigns for equal employment persisted into the late 1970s and 1980s. Under the leadership of Harvey Adams, chief of police for the Pittsburgh Housing Authority, the NAACP re-

Under the leadership of Harvey Adams, president of the Pittsburgh branch of the
NAACP during the 1970s and 1980s, the city's black community continued to mount
direct nonviolent protests for equal rights. From left to right: Carrie Washington,
Mayor Richard Caliguiri, Joseph Rhodes, Roland Hayes, Marion Charles, Nate
Smith, Ewari (Ed) Ellis, Clyde Jackson, and Harvey Adams at ribbon-cutting
ceremony for the Black Solidarity Fair outside Gate 3 of the Civic Arena, May 1972.
Source: New Pittsburgh Courier, 10 Dec. 1988.

established and maintained positive relationships with area churches;
built a strong interracial coalition of social justice organizations; and
demanded jobs for blacks on Renaissance II building and construction
projects. According to Debran Rowland, city editor for the *Pittsburgh
Courier*, the NAACP "took on a new face" during the 1980s. At one
point in negotiations with city officials and contractors, Adams declared,
"should these firms not fulfill their obligations to the black community
and set realistic goals modeled after federal mandates, then this coalition is prepared to picket, seek court injunctions to stop construction
and to essentially close the multi-million dollar Oxford project down."[5]
An "affirmative action" rally at Market Square, a showcase of Renaissance II, attracted some five hundred protesters. Blacks and their white
supporters opposed cutbacks in social welfare spending, the dismantling

of hard-won affirmative action programs, and the exclusion of African Americans from Renaissance building projects.[6]

Faced with the prospect of massive picketing, municipal and corporate elites negotiated affirmative action agreements with civil rights and social justice organizations. The list included the Pittsburgh Plate Glass company (PPG); USX; the Oxford Development Corporation; Kaufmann's Department Store; Duquesne Light; Red Lobster; the Port Authority; Warner Cable Company; Giant Eagle markets, the Vista Hotel, and Volkswagen. In varying degrees, fair share agreements with each of these entities opened up new employment opportunities for the city's black population. Although public sector agreements failed to specify percentages of minority hires, both the city and state soon used a 15 percent minority "set-aside," as an automatic goal to ensure employment diversity on government-funded projects. At about the same time, an independent group, the Affirmative Action Fair Share Strategy 21 Coalition, negotiated land, facilities, jobs, and economic development agreements with the Catholic Church and added to the African American campaign for jobs and economic development. While we found little published evidence on agreements with the Catholic Church, Harvey Adams later praised the success of these efforts: "We applaud them. There is a need for more groups like that, because there is enough work to go around."[7]

Fair share agreements led to increasing African American employment at all levels of the municipal and corporate workforces. During this time, Duquesne Light Company hired Diana L. Green as senior vice president in charge of customer operations, making her the first African American in such a position at a utility company in the city of Pittsburgh. PNC Bank hired Marva Harris as its first African American female senior vice president. In addition to continuing to hire blacks in traditional categories of work as dishwashers, waiters, and waitresses, the Red Lobster restaurant chain opened the door to African Americans in managerial positions as well. In the case of cable television, African American organizations helped to negotiate the terms on which Warner entered the Pittsburgh market in the 1980s. As early as January 1981, the Bidwell training institute enthusiastically reported the graduation of twenty-seven students from its cable television installers' training program. The Warner Cable company funded this program in collaboration with the U.S. government's Comprehensive Employment and Training Act (CETA). The company agreed to immediately hire all recent graduates with a promise to hire more as the Bidwell training program expanded. Moreover, six months later the organization named an African American, James Tripp-Haith, executive producer for its Pittsburgh corporate office. When the company later left Pittsburgh, the black community received a monetary settlement, which helped to underwrite scholarships for some of the city's college-bound young people.[8]

The Volkswagen campaign, Harvey Adams later recalled, was "the most successful" of the 1980s attempts to open up a heretofore closed company to African American employment—but it was also one of the most contentious. Adams recalled, "A black person could not even get an application prior to our intervention," and "We picketed and demonstrated at the site while truck drivers were trying to run over us. There was snow and ice, but the demonstrators held fast." He described Robert Pitts, head of the NAACP's labor and economic committee, as "the lightning rod" of the Volkswagen campaign. Pitts himself later recalled telling corporate leaders, "If you want African American business . . . then hire and promote."[9] At the conclusion of this campaign, the company added about eight hundred black workers to its labor force.

The fight for affirmative action in Pittsburgh became increasingly linked to the struggle against apartheid in South Africa in the 1980s. In 1985, African Americans and their white allies boycotted a Squirrel Hill store carrying the Krugerrand. In the same year, they also increased pressure on the Pittsburgh Board of Education to examine its investment portfolio with an eye for eliminating contracts with firms doing business with South Africa. Reinforcing their commitment to a global struggle against racial inequality, about 250 Pittsburghers attended a large anti-apartheid rally in Washington DC. Matthew Hawkins, a young African American community organizer at the time, explained that he had previously protested "federal cuts in valuable social programs," but now merged his activism with international issues like resistance to the nuclear arms race and the South African apartheid regime.[10]

William Russell Robinson, councilman from the Hill District, became one of Pittsburgh's leading proponents of divestment. When he proposed measures to limit the city's business with companies operating in South Africa, Robinson lost his bid for reelection on the Democratic ticket. As he recalled, his divestment proposals were "strongly opposed" by the mayor and other party leaders: "I was informed that if I did not go along with their views on this issue that I would prompt opposition from white elected officials and party leaders and they would even ensure that black party leaders opposed me as well. Indeed the Chamber of Commerce and City administration coordinated their efforts to defeat my initiatives in this area and planned for my defeat in the 1985 party endorsement and nomination."[11]

The Urban League of Pittsburgh and numerous neighborhood-based social service organizations enabled African Americans to rebuild their community within the context of the new economy and declining government support for poor and working-class people. Despite a reduction in its staff and salary cuts for its employees, under the leadership of chief executive officer Leon A. Haley (1984–1994), the Urban League of Pittsburgh maintained and even intensified its efforts to train blacks for jobs in the wake of steel's decline. As Haley put it, the Urban League recognized from the outset "that the impact of post-industrialization on African Americans was both profound and lasting, we began searching for new responses to the changing demands of the workplace. . . . We looked for ways of training young people to be ready for the high tech and service sector opportunities that we believed would replace the factory and mill jobs of the past." In 1987, the organization offered a state-funded program to help able-bodied men and women (ages 18–45) prepare for the new workforce. The program provided "an intensive mix of basic skills instruction, vocational training, and job search/life skills training, referral, and placement services."[12]

During the 1990s, as the economy improved, the Urban League of Pittsburgh added more staff members and diversified its job training activities within the black community. These efforts unfolded under the energetic leadership of Esther Bush. Born and raised in Pittsburgh, Bush returned to the city in 1994 after heading branches of the Urban League in New York and Connecticut, namely Staten Island, Manhattan, and Hartford. In collaboration with the NAACP and the Allegheny Conference for Community Development (ACCD), the Urban League monitored city and county service contracts to minority firms; published a black leadership directory designed to improve the representation of blacks in managerial and professional jobs; and pushed for more African American appointments to influential government, philanthropic, and corporate decision-making boards. The organization also conducted a Hospitality-Leisure Training Institute, which enabled participants to earn online associate degrees in management through Pennsylvania State University's "World Campus," and a Bonding Placement Program to assist ex-offenders reentering the workforce. In the first year of the

Urban League of Pittsburgh CEO
Esther Bush and Chairman of the
Board Glenn Mahone, during a
meeting of the National Urban
League in Pittsburgh in 2003.
Source: New Pittsburgh Courier, 23 July
2003.

Bonding Placement Program, the Urban League placed all ten of its clients in jobs. The Urban League also administered the Career Advancement Network (CAN, initially known as the "GAPs initiative"), which
helped families, especially women, make the transition from welfare to
work. This program emerged in the wake of the federal mandate to dismantle the welfare state.[13]

While the Urban League and other social service and civil rights
organizations lamented the hardships that the new legislation imposed
on the African American community, they also called attention to the
helpful contributions of programs like CAN in the lives of the city's poor
and working-class blacks. In 1998, Valerie Lauw, a single mother, enrolled
in one of the Urban League's family support programs. Five years later,
Esther Bush, chief executive officer, identified Lauw as a stellar example
of the League's work with low-income families:

> There are many success stories as a result of family support inter-
> vention in the lives of women and children in Allegheny County.
> One is Valerie Lauw, president of the Northview Heights Estates
> parent support group . . . Ms. Lauw, now 40, was a teenage mother
> who came to the Northview Heights Estates housing project in 1998
> after 13 weeks in a homeless shelter. As a parent in transition, she
> voluntarily enrolled in the Urban League Northview Heights Fam-
> ily Support Center program with her two daughters, ages 4 and
> 10. . . . Ms. Lauw is now a transportation specialist for the Urban

League Northview Heights residents, transporting them to appointments for housing, legal assistance, and support programs that will place them on the road to self-sufficiency.[14]

Other late-twentieth-century job training and social service programs reinforced the ULP's work within the African American community. William "Bill" Strickland had, in 1968, established a youth arts program on Pittsburgh's North Side called the Manchester Craftsmen's Guild. In 1972, Strickland was asked to also lead the nearby Bidwell Training Center, an occupational education institution. Spurred by a National Endowment for the Arts grant and local foundation and government support, the combined organization opened a new facility on the North Side in 1987. The new building included vocational training and arts classrooms, workshops, and a 350-seat concert hall. By the mid-1990s, more than 350 high school students from across the city took advantage of the center's afterschool programs. The Manchester Craftsmen's Guild and Bidwell Training Center not only prepared young people for a life in the arts and a vocation for making a living, it also endeavored to "equip and educate leaders to further demonstrate entrepreneurship potential."[15]

As the Reagan, Bush, and Clinton administrations cut spending on social services during the 1980s and 1990s, they simultaneously encouraged federal support for faith-based social welfare initiatives. During the late 1990s alone, United States churches spent almost $20 billion on faith-based social services at the state and local levels. In Pittsburgh, African American and interracial churches developed a plethora of services for poor and working-class blacks. In the East Liberty neighborhood alone, at the turn of the twenty-first century, five churches and three interfaith community-wide social service organizations (including African American Baptist and Pentecostal bodies and a predominantly white Presbyterian church) supported Community Ministry, a coalition of forty-seven congregations, parishes, and religious institutions in the area; the neighborhood-based Community Development Corporation; and the Community Health Care Center. These faith-based organizations provided programs dealing with unemployment, hunger, housing, homelessness, health care, drug abuse, and child care for working mothers. They also provided computer literacy classes for both adult and youth members of the East Liberty community.[16]

Several previously all-white institutions also addressed the needs of a predominantly black clientele by the early twenty-first century. These organizations—originally designed to aid the settlement of European immigrant groups—included most notably the Kingsley Association on the East Side and the Irene Kaufmann Center in the Hill District. Formed in 1893 to serve immigrants in the city's Strip District, the Kingsley Association moved to the Hill in 1900 and to East Liberty in 1923, where it remains to this day. In the wake of increasing black migration to the area in the aftermath of urban renewal and the demolition of the Lower Hill, the organization focused increasingly on the needs of poor and working-class black families in East Liberty, Garfield, Homewood, Lincoln-Lemington, and other communities on the city's East End. Similarly, the Irene Kaufmann Center, a Jewish settlement house, became Hill House and served a predominantly African American population.[17]

Claiming New Living Space, Educational Opportunities, and Cultural Expression

In the midst of the changing economy, African Americans worked hard to improve their access to better housing and education. Following ongoing civil rights protests against discriminatory lending policies, some of the region's largest banks and financial institutions helped to underwrite African American movement into heretofore all-white communities in the Pittsburgh metropolitan area. By the early 1990s, PNC, Integra, Mellon, and Dollar banks had increased lending to low-income and minority groups. They cut rates, lessened insurance and down payment requirements, and altered their advertising with the view of attracting more low-income and black applicants. As a result, Integra and PNC, the first and second biggest lenders in the region, approved white and black applicants for home-purchase loans at roughly equal rates in 1992.[18]

From 1990 to 2000, the Allegheny County Economic Development (ACED) office helped over 2,600 first-time buyers, including African Americans, gain mortgage loans totaling $133.4 million. The Pittsburgh Urban Redevelopment Authority conducted two low-interest mortgage programs: the Pittsburgh Home Ownership Program (PHOP) and the Home Ownership for Less project, a partnership between the Federal Housing Administration (FHA) and Urban Redevelopment Authority (URA). By the late 1990s, the Pittsburgh Partnership Office of the Federal National Mortgage Association reported that housing costs in the six-county Pittsburgh metropolitan area represented "some of the most affordable in the United States," and African Americans' "increasing propensity . . . to save money and the willingness of lenders to offer credit to them contributed to the spike in black home ownership." One new homeowner, Denise Brundage, took advantage of homeownership courses before buying her house. "The courses told me what the mortgage lenders would be looking for. I realized by capitalizing on this that my mortgage rates would be comparable to my rental rates."[19]

Public housing residents also demanded better space for themselves and their families. During the 1990s, according to a study by the Pittsburgh Housing Authority, 70 percent of black public housing residents expressed a desire to move out of the projects. When the city's housing authority proposed to close the Broadhead Manor public housing project and move residents into Section 8 housing, one resident, Gloria Martin, said, "What I want is to get out of Broadhead. . . . Y'all can blow it up, I don't care. I hate when I come home and I see the hooligans out on the corner because the police are too scared to come up here and clean up. I hate it when I have to come home and my ceiling is leaking and my toilet is leaking." Another resident, Carol Moore, remarked, "I got a bullet hole in my door. . . . Why spend all that money remodeling? Why waste it?" Still another Broadhead inhabitant stated simply, "I just want to move. I'm scared to death for my children [ages eleven and four]."[20]

At a public meeting of over two hundred people to discuss the future of Broadhead Manor, however, other residents opposed demolition of the project. They demanded renovations rather than transfers to Section 8 housing. Sharon McDonald, a Broadhead Manor resident who had lived in the project for over twenty years, led the opposition to closing the facility. McDonald declared that Broadhead Manor represented her roots and that the Pittsburgh Housing Authority could not "take my roots from me." Members of the Broadhead Manor Residents Council also criticized housing authority officials for leaving the meeting in frustration and for ignoring the council's plea for the development of alternatives to demolition. One resident complained, "The housing authority . . . wouldn't hear us out, so they just got up and walked out of the meeting." Housing Authority director Stanley Lowe explained that the Housing Authority of the City of Pittsburgh (HACP) had been named a "distressed" agency by the federal government and given a mandate to take action to remove themselves from that status within two years. The agency only collected 70 percent of its rents, maintained a high vacancy rate, and suffered a lack of adequate security, but many Broadhead Manor residents repeatedly affirmed that their community

Pittsburgh's Civil Rights and Black Power movements included public housing activists. This photo shows Frankie Mae Jeter, St. Clair Village public housing and welfare activist, 6 March 1990.

may have been "distressed," but it could be fixed, and they demanded that the city take steps to do so.[21]

When Mayor Tom Murphy proposed to demolish Allequippa Terrace and move residents into better housing, they also rejected his proposal. At a protest meeting in 1994, one public housing resident told housing officials to "Give us jobs. Get us off welfare," but she insisted that residents did not want to move from their homes.[22] In the Hill District, residents of Bedford Dwellings preferred renovation over demolition by a ratio of three to one. In the wake of the federal legislation known as HOPE VI, leaders of Hill District social service organizations formed the Hill District Collaborative to help residents resist unjust public housing and urban redevelopment policies. Under the leadership of Terri Baltimore, head of Hill House, the Hill District Collaborative brought together a variety of organizations to oversee public housing plans in the area. Participants included Eric Hearn of Housing Opportunities Unlimited; Louevella Ellis of the Allequippa Terrace Residents' Council; and Vaughn Stagg and Matilda Theiss of the Child Development Center, to name only a few.[23]

Through a generous grant from the Falk Fund, the Hill District Collaborative brought mental health and urban planning professionals Robert and Mindy Fullilove to Pittsburgh for a yearlong period of planning for equitable redevelopment of public housing in the Hill Dis-

trict. Assisted by the Fullíloves, Hill residents created a new organization called the Coalition for a Healthy Habitat to help public housing
residents shape urban renewal policies in their own interests. According
to Mindy Fullilove, Pittsburgh's urban renewal seemed to be repeating
itself in 1997; under HOPE VI, Pittsburgh planned to demolish both
Allequippa Terrace and Bedford Dwellings and thus displace more people.[24] Anthony Robbins, a postdoctoral fellow at the University of Pittsburgh Center for Minority Health, explained that the center became
involved with this event by "community building" and emphasizing "the
idea that residents must take control of their destiny and the destiny of
their communities."[25] Organizational activities included a series of teach-
ins, a research partnership with the architecture department at Carnegie
Mellon University, and conferences to aid grassroots community organizing around issues of public housing and community development.[26]

As a result of growing community-based activism, the city of Pittsburgh modified plans to destroy existing public housing and spread the
resident population across the city. As historian Laurence Glasco notes,
the city continued its program of converting public housing into mixed-
income neighborhoods of townhouses in Oakland and the Hill, but now
employed a deliberate policy of including public housing residents in the
decision-making process. In the Hill District, planners proposed to dismantle Bedford Dwellings Addition (27 buildings, 460 units); to meet
the needs of the 340 households slated for displacement by the demolition of the Bedford Dwellings, the plan also called for the construction
of 185 new onsite units and 475 offsite units. Area residents insisted upon
and succeeded in a plan that allowed the construction of new units close
by; and, in addition, the city approved a plan for residents to remain in
their homes as the new units were constructed. By 2005, the first phase
of the three-phase building program was complete. Patricia Murphy, a
community organizing and development consultant, concluded a recent
review of the development on a hopeful but cautious note: resident activism produced a less disruptive process of public housing change, but
"residents with little or no income could not be guaranteed permanent
housing. While all residents could return for one year at negligible rent,
they would have to show a source of income in subsequent years."[27]

During the 1990s, a growing number of middle-class blacks returned
to Pittsburgh's Hill District in a residential shift that some observers
called "black regentrification." The Hill received more than $300 million
in government and private money to tear down dilapidated buildings,

rebuild public housing, and provide upscale housing. Crawford Square was a $34 million development spearheaded by Marva Harris, the first African American senior vice president of community development for PNC Bank. Harris directed the bank's lending to low- and moderate-income communities. Working with the Hill Community Development Corporation and other equity investors, Harris sought to revitalize the community just to the east of the Civic Arena, an area that had remained fragmented since the Lower Hill development of the 1950s. With a combination of market-rate and government-subsidized housing, Crawford Square attracted a cross-class residential population of African Americans from within and outside the area. Between 1998 and 2002, the neighborhood attracted more than five hundred new residents, including retirees, low-income families, corporate employees, teachers, artists, and professional athletes—most of them black. Upon returning to the Hill in 2002, Justin Lang, a program officer for a nonprofit organization at the time, believed that African Americans had diluted their strength by moving "to far-out places." "We're black," he said, "we might as well face it and try to rebuild our communities from a position of strength." Another returnee, Steve Radney, a twenty-nine-year-old engineer, remarked, "When I look around here I don't see it as it is. I see it as it could be, because I know what it was." Newcomer to the Hill, Margo Roberson, a flight attendant, and her husband, Erik, purchased a home in Crawford Square, while Taneika Hillman, who was born and raised in the Hill District, occupied a two-bedroom rental unit with her eight-year-old son through a low-income housing assistance program. Hillman remarked on the level of class integration in the development: "We swim in the same pool, use the same fitness room as doctors and lawyers and teachers." As time went on, however, poor and working-class black residents of Crawford Square came to resent the behavior of "stuck-up" newcomers, while middle-class residents openly worried about sending their children to predominantly poor and working-class schools in the area. Many also feared that housing subsidies for low-income families would be phased out and that rising prices would sooner or later force them to move elsewhere. In 2002, for example, one single-family home in Crawford Square sold for over $300,000. When a news reporter approached one young man on the street about the Crawford Square development, he refused to be interviewed, saying, "Ain't none of this got nothing to do with me."[28]

Alongside efforts to improve their work and housing conditions, African Americans continued to seek viable strategies for advancing the education of their children. In the face of rising grassroots white opposition to busing, African Americans sought effective alternatives. Educator Barbara Sizemore, for example, argued that activists made a mistake at the start of Pittsburgh's desegregation efforts: "We accepted the assumption that anything that was all black was all bad. I spent a lot of time in Pittsburgh trying to disprove that theory." Kim Williams, a Hill District parent, sent her daughter to the 99 percent black Lincoln Elementary School in Larimer, explaining that her older child had endured racism in mostly white schools. In her view, Lincoln was one of the best schools in the city. "I believe in good schools," said Williams. "I don't believe in all-black schools or all-white. I believe parents should have a choice to send their child based on how they feel the school is. I don't believe a parent should be made to put their child in a school where they don't want their child."[29]

All black private schools, available to parents who could afford them, promised to equip black children with necessary reading, writing, and math skills; to introduce students to black history and culture; and to save them from daily bus trips to schools in hostile white neighborhoods. Recalling the angry white protests that greeted her and other black children at the city's Taylor Allderdice High School in the mid-1970s, Marjorie Howard resolved to protect her five-year-old son from the same experience. During the 1990s, Howard enrolled her son in kindergarten class at the Sixth Mt. Zion Christian Academy in Larimer. Howard spoke for many when she said: "I didn't want him spending his time fighting black inferiority in a neighborhood where he was called 'nigger.'" Another black family enrolled their child in an all-black private school after the child expressed a desire to have a white rather than black brother or sister. As the girl's father put it, "I'm not pushing for segregation, but at that young age cultural issues are important as far as understanding self and having self-esteem."[30]

The earliest black private schools in the city (those formed before and just after World War I) continued alongside those formed during the late twentieth century. By the late 1990s, African Americans in Pittsburgh maintained nearly a dozen private schools for black children, most of which were faith-based academies that offered classes at the elementary and middle school grades. Protestants operated the Central Baptist Academy in the Hill District, the Temple Christian Academy in Lawrenceville, the Imani Christian Academy in Penn Hills, and the Sixth Mt. Zion Christian Academy and the Ethnan Christian School in the Larimer-Lincoln-Lemington area. Ethnan Christian was one of Pittsburgh's earliest black private schools, formed in 1934. Black Muslims maintained the Sister Clara Muhammad Elementary School in Homewood, and Catholics conducted St. Benedict the Moor in the Hill District (founded in 1907 at St. Richard School), St. Agnes in Oakland, and Holy Rosary in Homewood. Other black private schools included the Manchester Development Center's Day School on the North Side and the Tolatr Academy in Highland Park.[31]

In 1998, the Urban League of Pittsburgh added to the roster of alternative African American schools when it launched the Urban League Charter School of Pittsburgh in East Liberty. Housed in the old B'nai Israel Synagogue building, the school served one hundred students from kindergarten through fourth grade. ULP raised $1.4 million for the effort and had a surplus of $245,000 at the end of its first year. Since demand was so high, the school instituted a lottery system to determine admission. Under the leadership of Janet Bell, chief administrator, and Roman Douardo, director of education, the ULP soon enrolled nearly two hundred students for its charter school. The school also became the second charter school in Pennsylvania to receive accreditation by the Middle States Commission on Elementary Education.[32]

Most of the private black academies covered elementary and middle school training only, enrolled fewer than 150 students, occupied less than optimum physical facilities, and closely followed the curriculum required by the Pittsburgh public schools. Students had to transfer to other schools to gain high school diplomas. While the majority of these students transferred to public schools, others enrolled in predominantly white private schools. Black enrollment at the Ellis School in Shadyside rose from 19 students (4.6 percent) during the mid-1980s to 30 (6.8 percent) by the mid-1990s. During the same time period, African American enrollment in the exclusive Sewickley Academy increased from 20 (3 percent) to 45 (6 percent). African Americans attending schools in the Catholic Diocese of Pittsburgh in those decades rose from 1,200 (3.7 percent) to 1,450 (5.1 percent).[33]

A variety of community-based programs encouraged black youth not only to stay in school but to excel in their studies. Area churches initiated community-based graduation ceremonies and funded scholarships for college-bound black youth. The NAACP initiated a "Back-to-School, Stay in School" program designed to encourage youth from low-income families to continue their education. The ULP celebrated youth who

An African American college graduate shown with the University of Pittsburgh's Cathedral of Learning in the background. This photo symbolized the opening up of the city's predominantly white institutions of higher education to black students.
Source: Carnegie Museum of Art, Charles "Teenie" Harris Collection, photo #2001.35.6344. Photograph © 2009 Carnegie Museum of Art, Pittsburgh.

were "Doing the Right Thing" and inducted teenagers into its Thurgood Marshall Achievers Society. Under the slogan "Achievement Matters," the Urban League's African American achievers program served over six hundred students annually by the turn of the century. The ULP also collaborated with the University of Pittsburgh and published both youth and adult versions of its study, *The State of Black Youth in Pittsburgh*. Under the editorship of Ralph Bangs and Major Mason, this volume called attention to both the promise and plight of Pittsburgh's black youth.[34]

The movement to create a state-of-the-art African American cultural center also underscored the many ways that black people moved out of the shadows of the city's revitalization. In 1996, the Pittsburgh branch of the NAACP, under the leadership of president Tim Stevens, created a proposal entitled "Plans for Progress," which included the establishment of an African American museum. The proposal urged Mayor Tom Murphy to use his authority to provide "strong financial and resource" support for building the facility. Murphy responded by appointing Pittsburgh city council members Valerie McDonald and Sala Udin to head a task force for "making the dream of building an African American cultural center a reality."[35]

Over the next decade, work on the development of the African American Cultural Center (renamed the August Wilson Center for African American Culture in 2006, in honor of the renowned Pittsburgh playwright) moved forward under energetic leadership from a broad cross-section of Pittsburgh's African American community. In addition to Sala Udin, Arthur Edmunds, Tim Stevens, Oliver Byrd, Mulugetta Birru, Ellsworth Brown, Ralph Proctor, and William Strickland Jr., to name a few, African American women took pivotal leadership positions in helping to realize the dream of an African American cultural center. Among others, these included most notably Nancy Washington, an associate professor emerita at the University of Pittsburgh, Doris Carson Williams, president of the African American Chamber of Commerce, Yvonne Cook, president of the Highmark Foundation and vice president of Highmark's community and health programs, and Cecile Springer, a past president of the Westinghouse Foundation. The cultural center also benefited from the service of a diverse group of white Pittsburghers in addition to Mayor Murphy, including Richard Stafford of the Allegheny Conference on Community Development, Carol Brown, president of the Pittsburgh Cultural Trust, and Andrew Masich, CEO and president of the Heinz Regional History Center, and others.[36]

Under the leadership of Neil Barclay, chief executive officer, the August Wilson Center's new building opened in September 2009. Describing itself as "A Center for Dynamic Culture," the August Wilson Center (AWC) builds upon Harlem Renaissance writer Claude McKay's reference to the intersection of Wylie and Fullerton Avenues in the Hill District as the "Crossroads of the World." Inspired by McKay's view of Pittsburgh's early-twentieth-century black community, the AWC advances the broadest possible definition of culture that aims to help bridge social cleavages within the city, while linking Pittsburgh's African American community to African and other people around the globe: "The Center will serve as a hub for people celebrating and experiencing the ongoing contributions of African Americans—in music, theater, dance, science, athletics, business and many other aspects of American life. . . . In particular the Center seeks to emphasize the ways in which its culture has influenced cultural expression on every continent." From its temporary quarters in downtown Pittsburgh to its grand opening in 2009, the AWC had already compiled an impressive record of cultural programming designed to implement its mission.[37]

Development of the August Wilson Center was closely intertwined with efforts to increase representation of blacks in cultural institutions like the Historical Society of Western Pennsylvania (HSWP). In 1989, the HSWP (renamed the Senator John Heinz History Center in 1996) responded to the growing concerns of the city's black population by establishing an African American Collection Project and the African American Advisory Committee (AAAC). Spearheaded by HSWP board of trustees member Cecile Springer, the collection project and AAAC aimed "to identify and collect primary resources essential to original research on the art and culture of the African American Community and their contributions to the history of the region and to the nation." Three years later, in a proposal for its multicultural arts initiative, the HSWP reiterated its intention to "document, preserve, promote, celebrate, and pay tribute to Pittsburgh's black cultural art forms, figures, and places." Over the next decade and a half, the Heinz History Center increased its programming in African American history and culture, and in 2001, hired Samuel Black as curator of African American collections. In addition to various local projects, Black's innovative exhibit on African American Vietnam veterans has received national acclaim.[38]

Challenging New Forms of Disfranchisement

Shortly after the defeat of Cathryn L. Irvis and William Russell Robinson for city council in the 1985 spring primary, a number of organizations came together to advocate reform of the city's electoral system. These included most notably the Coalition for District Elections, the Association of Community Organizations for Reform Now (ACORN), and the Metropolitan Pittsburgh Crusade for Voters (MPVC), among others. For a variety of reasons, including concern about remaining nonpartisan, the Urban League of Pittsburgh, NAACP, and the Black Political Empowerment Project (B-PEP) initially opposed endorsement of the grassroots mobilization to replace at-large election of city councilmen with elections by district. By the spring of 1987, however, under the impact of increasing internal and external pressures, each of these organizations had changed their position and endorsed the movement for district elections.[39]

The emergence of community-wide support for district elections gained potent expression in the creation of a new coordinating organization, the Pittsburgh Alliance for District Elections (PADE). This alliance also represented the successful convergence of legislative and judicial strategies for bringing about electoral change. The Coalition for District Elections pushed for passage of state legislation permitting a public referendum and change of the system by popular vote. The state legislature approved a referendum on the item for the May 1987 election. Tom Murphy, a state representative at the time, accented the color line that continued to divide blacks and whites in the political life of the city as the basis of his decision to support by-district elections. Murphy estimated that 70 percent of all employees of city and county governments were white party ward officers, committee people, and family members who hoped to hold on to their white privileges. Only by moving to by-district elections, Murphy believed, would blacks stand a chance of equitable representation in city government.[40]

A strong legal challenge complemented the push for a referendum. Under the leadership of Rev. Thomas E. Smith, pastor of the Metropolitan Baptist Church in the Hill District, the MPCV invoked the Civil Rights Act of 1965 and initiated a federal lawsuit against the City of Pittsburgh. Voting rights legislation guaranteed the franchise under provisions of the Fourteenth and Fifteenth Amendments to the U.S. Constitution. In *Metropolitan Pittsburgh Crusade for Voters vs. City of Pittsburgh* (1986), the MPCV argued that Pittsburgh retained at-large elections, "for the purpose and with the effect of preserving political white supremacy, and have had the result of minimizing and diluting black voting strength."[41] In publicity announcing the suit, the MPVC vowed to end "political white supremacy" in the city of Pittsburgh. Living in Pittsburgh following the election of 1985, Smith said at a press conference, was "almost like living in South Africa."[42]

The National Lawyers' Committee for Civil Rights Under Law represented African American plaintiffs in the suit, and commented: "Voting rights battles like those waged 10 or 20 years earlier in the South were now being fought out in northern cities like Pittsburgh."[43] The MPCV asked the court to issue an injunction against further elections until the city of Pittsburgh satisfactorily addressed the issue of African American representation. A federal judge refused to issue an injunction but set an early court date of June 1987 for the trial. This move prevented municipal authorities from dragging the legal process out over a long period of time.

The city's own precedent for district elections in the case of the school

Rev. Thomas Smith, pastor of the Monumental Baptist Church in the Hill District, helped to organize the Metropolitan Pittsburgh Crusade for Voters to replace at-large with district elections to ensure African American representation on city council.
Source: New Pittsburgh Courier, 7 Feb. 1987.

board undermined its effort to defend at-large elections. The Pittsburgh Board of Education had adopted district elections in 1976. Following this change, African Americans had consistently elected members of their own group to the board, including Rev. James "Jimmy Joe" Robinson, Ronald Suber, and Jake Milliones, who served as board president until 1983. African Americans and their white supporters believed that the city should use the Board of Education as a model for resolving the issue of disfranchisement of black voters in municipal elections.[44]

In the May 1987 vote on the referendum, African Americans and their white allies achieved a major victory when voters chose district over at-large elections. Shortly thereafter, the city of Pittsburgh and the Metropolitan Pittsburgh Crusade for Voters signed a consent degree placing the reapportionment of the districts under the jurisdiction of the U.S. federal courts. The MPCV agreed to drop its lawsuit but retained the right to review and object to a reapportionment plan that it considered unjust. Under the new system of district voting, beginning in 1989, African Americans soon elected Duane Darkins, Jake Milliones, Valerie McDonald, and Sala Udin to city council from the Homewood-Brushton and Hill District areas.[45]

Black elected officials initiated and supported measures designed to enhance African American access to better housing, education, jobs, and protection under the law, amid other priorities. In her campaign for the ninth district (East End) council seat, Valerie McDonald emphasized

Valerie McDonald, councilwoman from
the city's ninth district, serving the
East Liberty and Homewood-Brushton
communities.

Source: New Pittsburgh Courier, 4 Jan. 1995.

participation in municipal politics as a vehicle for obtaining resources
necessary to effect socioeconomic change within the city's black community. Queried about her reasons for seeking office, she later recalled that
there was "so much disparity in achievements and resources," between
blacks and whites that the creation of more jobs in her district represented "the key" to progress. McDonald had also served as president of
the Pittsburgh Board of Education and believed that she could do more
to improve the education and lives of young people through a seat on
city council. In the sixth district, Sala Udin represented a wide range
of neighborhoods (including the predominantly white Downtown, parts
of Oakland, and the Hill District). He identified several issues of importance to his constituents, but concluded, "At the top of the heap in
importance was the question of the district's economic vitality."[46]

During his tenure in office, Sala Udin introduced legislation designed to improve the employment prospects of minorities and women.
A measure titled "Pittsburgh Works" proposed that city residents receive 35 percent, minorities 25 percent, and women 10 percent of all jobs
on publicly funded projects. When city council rejected the ordinance,
Udin helped to mobilize a grassroots movement to place the issue on the
November 1999 ballot as a referendum item. Following nearly seventeen
weeks of intensive campaigning and marching to get the necessary votes,
Udin and the Pittsburgh Works Support Coalition delivered some 15,000
signatures, nearly double the 7,884 required for approval, to the County

City councilman Sala Udin at the Crawford Square development in the Hill District with downtown skyscrapers in the background, 12 April 1999.

Source: Copyright ©, *Pittsburgh Post-Gazette*, 2009, all rights reserved. Reprinted with permission.

Office Building. In the November election, the legislation passed with 61 percent of voters selecting "yes." Udin considered this an "overwhelming mandate" from citizens of Pittsburgh. For her part, community activist Celeste Taylor McCurdy declared a victory for social activism: "It was a tremendous effort by many groups, organizations and dedicated individuals. Activism sometimes produces results, and this is one time to be an activist." McCurdy concluded that if she could help create "one job" in Pittsburgh, it would be worth the effort.[47]

Alongside jobs, African Americans focused increasing attention on the spread of youth violence, drug use, HIV-AIDS, and police brutality. Black women took the lead in identifying gang conflicts as a key challenge facing the late-twentieth-century black urban community. In 1995, Constance Parker, executive convener of the Black Women's Political Crusade, articulated this mission in a speech before the group: "We've got to work . . . to address all these killings that are going on. We are an organization of women—we're the mothers, we've got to get back to basics. . . . The times are crying out for us to pay attention to this, more so than anything else."[48]

As HIV-AIDS activism slowly gained a footing within Pittsburgh's black community, some black men and women cooperated with Prevention Point Pittsburgh. Formed in May 1995, this interracial coalition helped to raise public awareness about the relationship between drug use and HIV-AIDS. In 2002, the Allegheny County Health Department declared that a public health emergency existed based on the exceedingly high rates of HIV and Hepatitis C infection in injection drug users. As an "emergency" public health measure, the Allegheny County Health Department approved Prevention Point's needle exchange program for drug users. In varying degrees, the health activities of the Urban League of Pittsburgh, Hill House, the Pittsburgh area Vietnam Era Veterans Organization, and many other social service organizations assisted the fight against alcoholism, drug use, and HIV-AIDS.[49]

Black Pittsburghers expressed equal concern over mounting evidence of police brutality. Between 1993 and 1998, about eight young black men died through encounters with local law enforcement officers. The most widely publicized of these events occurred on 12 October 1995, when Brentwood police stopped and killed Jonny Gammage on the basis that he was driving a Jaguar that belonged to his cousin, Pittsburgh Steelers football player Ray Seals. Gammage, who was driving in a predominantly white neighborhood, was unarmed and was not under the influence of alcohol or drugs. This incident struck a raw nerve in the black community's relations with police; being stopped and harassed by law enforcement officers under such circumstances was an experience often described by African Americans with the phrase "Driving While Black" (DWB).[50]

The Jonny Gammage case touched off a wave of grassroots protests in the Pittsburgh region. Following a not-guilty verdict for the officers involved in the killing of Gammage, Michele Robertson of the *Pittsburgh Courier* described the disbelief that "hung in the bone-chilling air," as shocked members of the African American community traveled through the streets of Downtown. Tim Stevens, president of the NAACP, condemned the trial as "littered with injustices," ranging from the selection of Lackawanna County (99.3 percent white) as the venue for the trial to the reduction of the numbers of officers charged from five to three. Under Stevens's leadership, the local chapter of the NAACP used this case to launch a spirited campaign for a police civilian review board, charged with providing more responsible oversight of police and policies governing police behavior.[51] When city council rejected efforts to set up such a civilian review board, Councilman Sala Udin helped to organize a referendum movement that placed the measure on the ballot for popular

Tim Stevens, president of the Pittsburgh NAACP and grassroots community organizer, with councilwoman Valerie McDonald.

Source: New Pittsburgh Courier, 25 Feb. 1995.

vote. In May 1997, voters overwhelmingly approved an amendment to the city charter permitting the establishment of the Pittsburgh Citizen Police Review Board, authorized to receive and act on complaints of police misconduct.[52]

The Gammage case also engendered a lawsuit filed by the American Civil Liberties Union of Greater Pittsburgh, the NAACP, and Parents Against Violence against the Pittsburgh police department. As a result, the U.S. government placed Pittsburgh's police under federal supervision for nearly a five-year period during the late 1990s and the early part of the new century.[53]

The economic situation in Pittsburgh continued to create grave concern for working African Americans. When a fire destroyed the uninsured computer equipment used in his struggling graphic design company, Clarence Williams of East Liberty, who was thirty-four years old at the time, worried about the impact of unemployment on his relationship with his son, a high school senior: "I don't have any advice to give him because there's nothing I have that's stable. He can say: 'Hey dad, you're not working, what are you doing . . .' I can't even buy him a graduating suit. I can't provide. These are the things that make a man angry."[54]

The gang and drug culture intensified generational tensions within Pittsburgh's black community. Lloyd Bell, a clinical psychologist who lived and worked in Wilkinsburg in the late 1990s, explained in 1994, "Many older folks, angry and frustrated, believe that their lives are being constrained by violence . . . while young people, on the other hand, often have little patience, trust or understanding of how older blacks address problems. [. . .] They have a philosophy that older folks have let white folks push them around. The youth have generated an attitude that there are no deities. 'Mama's' not a deity. 'Papa's' not a deity, the police aren't deities, the president isn't a deity. They're not subscribing to deities that will keep them in their place."[55]

Growing numbers of poor young people engaged in violent street battles over drug turf, often in return for a substantial short-term monetary gain. One unemployed black man lamented, "It's hard to tell a young person to stop destroying, stop poisoning our community if he's getting into a Mercedes or a BMW and I'm getting on a PAT bus."[56]

Tensions also increased between African American men and women over economic issues. Good jobs were by no means plentiful for black women compared to their white counterparts, but a disproportionate number of educated black women held higher-paid professional jobs compared to black men. In 1970, African American women made up about 40 percent of the African American workforce. By 1990, they had increased to over 50 percent of the black labor force. Black women also reversed an earlier trend whereby black men uniformly occupied the higher paid, if more arduous and dangerous, jobs. In 1970, four of the top ten occupations among black women in Pittsburgh included cleaning, cooking, and other domestic and personal service work. In 1990, only two of these jobs remained among the top ten occupations among black women. For their part, black men remained disproportionately represented in the hard laboring jobs requiring heavy lifting and transporting (see tables 27–30). Clarence Williams expressed quite explicitly the tensions that this gender division of labor had generated within the black community: "It's really bad for the black male. . . . Black women are able to get pretty decent jobs. The men are just looking, trying to find things and they can't find them."[57]

Black women also increasingly moved from behind the scenes to center stage of key social struggles. Some African American men welcomed this development as a continuation of the historic role of women in the black community, but others believed that black men had neglected their duty as the vanguard of black social struggles and needed to reassert their centrality in movements for social change. Under the national leadership of the Nation of Islam's leader Minister Louis Farrakhan, the "Million Man March" symbolized the growing effort of some black men (and women) to restore black men to leadership on issues affecting the late-twentieth-century black community.[58]

Minister Anthony X, head of Pittsburgh's Muhammad Mosque 22, emerged as the principal spokesperson for the local Million Man March organization. At a meeting in Homewood, he explained the significance of the march, which would call the black man from "the grave of history" and show the world "that black men could take care of their own women, children, and communities." Attendees at the meeting expressed hope that the march would also inspire a new national movement for social change among black people. Accordingly, in October 1995, a broad coalition of Pittsburghers, including the local chapter of the NAACP and area churches of diverse denominations, traveled to Washington DC for the Million Man March. While recognizing the collective responsibility of black men to their families and their communities, the march emphasized personal accountability and called for an end to welfare dependence, teen pregnancy, drug use, and violence within black families and neighborhoods. Tim Stevens, NAACP president, underscored the expectation that black men would "come back to their communities and become involved in the entire process of community functions, providing leadership and setting examples for others." Similarly, as Anthony X put it, "This will be a march to show our support and say to the world that we are willing to do something for ourselves, our families, and our communities. This will be a day of atonement."[59]

Less than two years after the Million Man March, some black women from Pittsburgh traveled to Philadelphia for the Million Woman March. Beatrice "Bea" Mitchell, a benefits specialist at Carnegie Mellon University, later recalled going to Philadelphia with her two sons and husband and several other women from the Pittsburgh region. According to these women, black men and women needed to forge a more democratic and coequal gender movement for social change. In their view, it was inappropriate to organize the contemporary movement for African American liberation around black male leadership alone.[60]

By the turn of the twenty-first century, in Pittsburgh and elsewhere in urban America, efforts to maintain and extend the benefits of the modern Civil Rights and Black Power movements also gained increasing expression in a new reparations movement. Following publication in 2000 *The Debt* by Randall Robinson, African Americans launched a vigorous reparations movement designed to redress centuries of race- and class-based economic and social injustice. As Robinson put it, the appeal for reparations "was not for affirmative action but, rather, for just compensation as an entitlement" for the generations of uncompensated and undercompensated African American labor in the development of the nation. In the wake of the 9/11 attacks, however, the momentum for reparations dissipated as Pittsburgh and the nation turned their attention toward winning the "war on terror."[61]

Eight years later, the war on terror started to ring hollow for growing numbers of Americans of various shades of color. This sentiment not only resulted from the government's mishandling of the war in Iraq, but also from the rapid deterioration of the U.S. economy as the war dragged on for more than five years. The domestic economy nearly collapsed with the fall of key banking and investment institutions during the presidential election of 2008. In Pittsburgh and elsewhere, African Americans and much of the larger U.S. population rallied behind the presidential candidacy of Senator Barack Obama of Illinois, who promised "Change we can believe in" and the "Audacity of hope."[62] African Americans and people from a variety of ethnic and racial backgrounds built a solid "Get out the vote for Obama" campaign, helping to elect Barack Obama the forty-fourth president of the United States.[63]

African Americans in Pittsburgh and elsewhere supported Obama partly for profound symbolic and historical reasons. The prospect of electing the first U.S. president of African descent resonated deeply with a people imbued with a keen sense of history and collective memories of enslavement, Jim Crow, and the recent ravages of deindustrialization and global economic and social change. Equally important, the idea of a black First Lady, Michelle Obama, a community activist and campaigner, also energized the black electorate. Ultimately, however, like many other Americans, African Americans supported Obama because his candidacy offered Pittsburgh, the state, and the nation the best hope for economic, political, and cultural renewal at home and international peace abroad. As this new era began, Pittsburgh's African Americans had created their own, more hopeful, and even more forward-looking black renaissance. While the full outcome of this new community is yet to be determined, it is clear that African Americans in Pittsburgh believe that the election of Barack Obama as president of the United States will enhance their efforts to build a more just and humane social order in this century than the one they recently left behind.[64]

Pittsburgh's African Americans in a Global Twenty-first Century

The changes of the post–World War II years were not unique to Pittsburgh and western Pennsylvania. Between the Great Depression and the 1970s, the second great migration completed the transformation of

As elsewhere across the country, African Americans in Pittsburgh and their white allies helped to elect Senator Barack Obama the first United States president of African descent. This photo shows Barack Obama and his wife Michelle during a campaign rally at the University of Pittsburgh on 21 April 2008.

Source: Photo by Scott Olson/Getty Images News.

African Americans from a predominantly rural, southern people to a national population with significant concentrations in all regions of the country. As in Pittsburgh, new African American neighborhoods, dubbed the "second ghetto" by some analysts, emerged within the existing borders of northern, western, and southern cities, and the interplay of new federal housing policies and grassroots white opposition to "open housing" reinforced the residential segregation of blacks. The rise of the second ghetto unfolded alongside the increasing suburbanization of the nation's black population. In his study of black suburbia, historian Andrew Wiese not only highlights the interrelated themes of migration, residential segregation, and suburbanization, but also suggests that recent African American population trends point to the suburbs as the site of another perhaps third great migration.[65]

Although African Americans in Pittsburgh shared a great deal with their counterparts in other cities across America—the modern black freedom struggle was undoubtedly the most prominent thread unifying the postwar experiences of urban blacks—a variety of factors distinguish

Pittsburgh's post–World War II history from other industrial cities of the Northeast and Midwest. Rather than reliance on a single industry like steel, large northeastern and midwestern cities like Chicago, Philadelphia, and New York entered the postindustrial era from a more diversified economic foundation than Pittsburgh. The manufacturing base of these cities included substantial textile, clothing, food processing, and other durable goods industries as well as heavy metals.[66] In Pittsburgh, because steel making dominated the economic life of the region, when this vital industry collapsed during the 1980s and 1990s, African American job losses and suffering were even more pronounced than elsewhere.[67]

While smaller industrial cities like Detroit, Milwaukee, Cleveland, and Gary, Indiana, resembled Pittsburgh in their reliance on a narrow industrial core, the black populations in these cities were more geographically concentrated in contiguous neighborhoods than black Pittsburghers. The phenomenon known as white flight was also more pronounced in these cities than in Pittsburgh. These circumstances enabled African Americans in other cities to take increasing control of municipal government, including (except for Milwaukee) the election of African American mayors. Most of these cities have also sent their own representatives to the U.S. Congress, while Pittsburgh has yet to elect an African American to a seat in Washington DC.[68]

Finally, while other industrial cities experienced substantial increases in the number of Latino/a, Asian, West Indian, and African immigrants in the wake of changes to U.S. immigration law and the aftermath of U.S. wars in Vietnam and the Middle East, the Pittsburgh region attracted few of these newcomers. A large percentage of Pittsburgh's immigrants in the late twentieth century came from south, central, and eastern Europe.[69] Although newcomers from other parts of the globe were few, they contributed to the transformation of Pittsburgh, like many of the nation's cities, into a new center of international conflict and collaboration. By 2000, immigrants of Asian and Hispanic descent made up 4 percent of Pittsburgh's total population. A small number of immigrants were people of African descent from the continent and especially the Caribbean. Myrven Caines, a physician on the faculty at the University of Pittsburgh, migrated to the city from Trinidad in 1967. Caines estimated that between two thousand and three thousand Afro-Caribbeans lived in Pittsburgh by the mid 1990s. The city's Caribbean community, similar to the indigenous black population, was widely dispersed across Pittsburgh and Allegheny County. This pattern contrasted with places like New York where blacks from the Caribbean concentrated in specific areas within Brooklyn, the Bronx, Long Island, and parts of Queens.[70]

As the twentieth century came to a close, Pittsburgh's black community continued to exhibit distinct characteristics while participating in larger national and global processes that affected the lives of black people in the United States and abroad. As the new century continues to unfold, it is our hope that this book will not only inspire new historical research on myriad dimensions of Pittsburgh's postwar black community, but help to generate more just social policies and movements for social change.

APPENDIX: Tables

TABLE 1: The Region's African American Population, 1910–2000

	Pittsburgh		Allegheny County		Six-county metro area*	
	No.	%	No.	%	No.	%
1910	25,623	4.8	34,217	3.3	51,712	3.0
1920	37,200	6.4	53,517	4.5	74,789	3.6
1930	54,983	8.2	83,326	6.0	117,530	5.1
1940	62,251	9.3	90,060	6.3	122,767	5.1
1950	82,453	12.2	113,643	7.5	145,776	5.8
1960	100,692	16.6	134,122	8.2	170,067	6.3
1970	104,904	20.1	144,545	9.0	176,979	6.5
1980	101,813	24.0	150,077	11.6	182,261	7.0
1990	95,362	25.7	149,550	11.0	179,700	8.1
2000	93,904	28.7	159,000	12.4	190,511	8.0

NOTE: *Six counties: Allegheny, Butler, Fayette, Beaver, Washington, and Westmoreland.
SOURCES: Hollis Lynch, *The Black Urban Condition: A Documentary History, 1866–1971* (New York: Thomas Crowell Co., 1973), appendix A; Ann G. Wilmoth, "Pittsburgh and the Blacks: A Short History 1780–1875" (PhD diss., Pennsylvania State University, 1975), 210; John Bodnar, Roger Simon, and Michael P. Weber, *Lives of Their Own: Blacks, Italians, and Poles in Pittsburgh, 1900–1960* (Urbana: University of Illinois Press, 1982), 30; Dennis C. Dickerson, *Out of the Crucible: Black Steelworkers in Western Pennsylvania, 1875–1980* (Albany: State University of New York Press, 1986), 17; U.S. Bureau of the Census, *Thirteenth Census of U.S.*, vol. 1, *Population, 1910* (Washington DC: Government Printing Office, 1914), 556–609; U.S. Bureau of the Census, *Fourteenth Census of U.S.*, vol. 3, *Population, 1920* (Washington DC: Government Printing Office, 1922), 305–857; U.S. Bureau of the Census, *Fifteenth Census of U.S.*, vol. 3, pt. 2, *1930* (Washington DC: Government Printing Office, 1932), 525–744.

204

TABLE 2: Pittsburgh Occupations by Race, Ethnicity, and Sex, 1910

Industry	Blacks		Foreign-born whites		Foreign-born mixed parentage		American-born parentage		All workers	
	Number	%	Number	%	Number	%	Number	%	Number	%
MALE										
Total, gainful workers	9,940	100	71,158	100	49,746	100	50,902	100	181,959	100
Manufacturing and mechanical	2,859	28.76	38,135	53.59	17,555	35.29	14,943	29.6	73,498	40.39
Transportation	1,232	12.43	4,916	6.91	3,538	7.11	4,567	8.97	14,255	7.83
Trade	814	8.19	8	11.25	7,510	15.1	8,301	16.31	24,657	13.55
Public service	193	1.94	1,441	2.03	1,230	2.47	814	1.6	3,678	2.02
Professional service	134	1.35	771	1.08	1,039	2.098	2,111	4.15	4,055	2.23
Domestic and personal service	3,023	30.41	3,016	4.24	1,550	3.12	1,325	2.6	8,970	4.93
Clerical occupations	224	2.25	1,659	2.33	6,599	13.27	8,556	16.81	17,042	9.37
FEMALE										
Total, gainful workers	4,279	100	12,704	100	18,902	100	15,789	100	51,678	100
Manufacturing and mechanical	255	5.96	1,676	13.19	3,727	19.72	2,378	15.06	8,036	15.55
Transportation	0	0	36	0.28	461	2.44	369	2.34	866	1.68
Trade	49	1.15	1,128	8.88	2,902	15.35	2,104	13.33	6,183	11.96
Professional service	59	1.38	383	3.01	1,391	7.36	1,969	12.47	3,802	7.36
Domestic and personal service	3,779	88.32	8,166	64.28	5,125	27.11	4,074	25.8	19,200	37.15
Clerical occupations	26	0.61	346	2.72	2,761	14.61	3,216	20.37	6,349	12.29

SOURCES: U.S. Bureau of the Census, *Thirteenth Census of U.S.*, vol. 4: *Population, 1910, Occupation Statistics* (Washington DC: Government Printing Office, 1913), 590–91.

TABLE 3: Pittsburgh Occupations by Race, Ethnicity, and Sex, 1920

Industry	Blacks		Foreign-born whites		Foreign-born mixed parentage		American-born parentage		All workers	
	Number	%	Number	%	Number	%	Number	%	Number	%
MALE										
Total, gainful workers	15,071	100	59,414	100	54,701	100	62,532	100	191,989	100
Agriculture, forestry, & animal husbandry	31	0.21	280	0.47	110	0.2	117	0.19	538	0.28
Mining	79	0.52	192	0.32	139	0.25	275	0.44	685	0.36
Manufacturing & mechanical	7,971	52.89	35,446	59.66	25,250	46.16	23,387	37.4	92,063	47.95
Transportation & communication	1,862	12.35	5,726	9.64	6,520	11.92	8,606	13.76	22,715	11.83
Trade	873	5.79	8,843	14.88	8,703	15.91	10,733	17.16	29,249	15.23
Public service	286	1.9	1,520	2.56	2,116	3.87	1,743	2.79	5,666	2.95
Professional service	227	1.51	1,475	2.48	2,303	4.21	4,812	7.7	8,822	4.6
Domestic and personal service	3,343	22.18	4,146	6.98	1,762	3.22	1,786	2.86	11,191	5.83
Clerical occupations	399	2.65	1,786	3.01	7,798	14.26	11,073	17.71	21,060	10.97
FEMALE										
Total, gainful workers	5,195	100	8,862	100	22,069	100	21,629	100	57,759	100
Agriculture, forestry, and fishing	0	0	3	0.3	2	0.01	8	0.04	13	0.02
Manufacturing & mechanical	350	6.74	1,313	14.82	4,091	18.54	2,404	11.11	8,160	14.13
Transportation & mechanical	4	0.08	143	1.61	1,172	5.31	1,111	5.14	2,430	4.21
Trade	73	1.41	1,356	15.3	3,668	16.62	3,182	14.71	8,280	14.34
Professional service	2	0.04	7	0.08	18	0.08	19	0.09	46	0.08
Domestic and personal service	112	2.16	555	6.26	2,092	9.48	3,431	15.86	6,090	10.54
Clerical occupations	4,537	87.33	4,687	52.89	4,440	20.12	3,837	17.74	17,502	30.3

SOURCE: U.S. Bureau of the Census, *Fourteenth Census of U.S.*, vol. 4, *Population, 1920, Occupations* (Washington DC: Government Printing Office, 1923), 1197–99.

TABLE 4: Pittsburgh Occupations by Race, Ethnicity, and Sex, 1930

Occupation	Blacks		Foreign-born whites		Native white		All workers	
	Number	%	Number	%	Number	%	Number	%
MALE								
Total, gainful workers	19,196	100	50,551	100	138,570	100	208,666	100
Agriculture and forestry	63	0.33	491	0.97	377	0.27	932	0.45
Extraction of minerals	208	1.08	259	0.51	407	0.29	874	0.42
Manufacturing and mechanical	8,599	44.8	26,819	53.05	53,303	38.47	88,797	42.55
Transportation and communication	2,811	14.64	4,753	9.4	17,795	12.84	25,382	12.16
Trade	1,340	6.98	9,163	18.13	27,254	19.67	37,800	18.12
Public service	466	2.43	1,549	3.06	4,980	3.59	7,000	3.35
Professional service	427	2.22	1,948	3.85	9,889	7.14	12,276	5.88
Domestic and personal service	4,823	25.13	4,087	8.08	5,046	3.64	14,139	6.78
Clerical occupations	461	2.4	1,482	2.93	19,519	14.09	21,466	10.29
FEMALE								
Total, gainful workers	6,923	100	8,235	100	54,756	100	69,925	100
Agriculture	0	0	2	0.02	7	0.01	9	0.01
Extraction of minerals	2	0.03	2	0.02	0	0	0	0
Manufacturing and mechanical	303	4.38	983	11.94	5,622	10.27	6,908	9.88
Transportation and communication	9	0.13	110	1.34	2,555	4.67	2,674	3.82
Trade	80	1.16	1,105	13.42	8,070	14.74	9,256	13.24
Public service	5	0.07	11	0.13	83	0.15	99	0.14
Professional service	128	1.85	655	7.95	8,489	15.5	9,272	13.26
Domestic and personal service	6,269	90.55	4,600	55.86	12,931	23.62	23,810	34.05
Clerical occupations	129	1.86	769	9.34	16,997	31.04	17,895	25.59

SOURCE: U.S. Bureau of the Census, *Fifteenth Census of U.S.*, vol. 4, *Population, 1930, Occupations* (Washington DC: Government Printing Office, 1933), 1416–18.

TABLE 5: Top Ten Occupations of Black Men, Pittsburgh, 1930

Rank	Occupation	Number	Percentage
	Total	19,196	100.00
1	Laborers, blast furnaces and steel rolling mills	2,070	10.78
2	Laborers and helpers, building construction	1,953	10.17
3	Janitors and sextons	1,598	8.32
4	Chauffeurs	1,272	6.62
5	Servants	784	4.08
6	All other porters (except in stores)	758	3.94
7	General and not specified laborers	718	3.74
8	Other iron and steel, etc. industries	485	2.52
9	Porters, domestic and personal service	445	2.31
10	Laborers, steam railroad	389	2.02

SOURCE: U.S. Bureau of the Census, *Fifteenth Census of U.S.*, vol. 4, *Population, 1930, Occupations* (Washington DC: Government Printing Office, 1933), 1416–18.

TABLE 6: Top Ten Occupations of All Men, Pittsburgh, 1930

Rank	Occupation	Number	Percentage
	Total	208,666	100.00
1	Clerks (except "clerks" in stores)	15,292	7.32
2	Blast furnaces and steel rolling mills	12,745	6.10
3	Salesmen	11,659	5.58
4	Retail dealers	9,495	4.55
5	Chauffeurs and truck and tractor drivers	8,156	3.90
6	Laborers and helpers, building construction	6,631	3.17
7	Other iron and steel, etc., industries	5,007	2.39
8	Operative, other industries	4,003	1.91
9	Carpenters	3,840	1.84
10	Machinists	3,799	1.82

SOURCE: U.S. Bureau of the Census, *Fifteenth Census of U.S.*, vol. 4, *Population, 1930, Occupations* (Government Printing Office, 1933), 1416–18.

TABLE 7: Top Ten Occupations of Black Women, Pittsburgh, 1930

Rank	Occupation	Number	Percentage
	Total	6,923	100.00
1	Servants	4,268	61.64
2	Laundresses (not in laundry)	1,044	15.08
3	Waitresses	195	2.81
4	Laundry operatives	137	1.97
5	Housekeepers and stewardesses	135	1.95
6	Charwomen and cleaners	128	1.84
7	Operatives, clothing, and other industries	121	1.74
8	Barbers, hairdressers, and manicurists	105	1.51
9	Dressmakers and seamstresses (not in factory)	101	1.45
10	Boarding and lodging housekeepers	99	1.43

SOURCE: U.S. Bureau of the Census, *Fifteenth Census of U.S.*, vol. 4, *Population, 1930, Occupations* (Washington DC: Government Printing Office, 1933), 1416–18.

TABLE 8: Top Ten Occupations of All Women, Pittsburgh, 1930

Rank	Occupation	Number	Percentage
	Total	69,925	100.00
1	Servants	12,831	18.34
2	Stenographers and typists	8,199	11.72
3	Clerks (except "clerks" in stores)	6,634	9.48
4	Saleswomen	5,792	8.28
5	Teachers (school)	3,838	5.48
6	Trained nurses	3,227	4.61
7	Bookkeepers and cashiers	2,705	3.86
8	Waitresses	2,425	3.46
9	Telephone operators	2,335	3.33
10	Operative, other industries	2,285	3.26

SOURCE: U.S. Bureau of the Census, *Fifteenth Census of U.S.*, vol. 4: *Population, 1930, Occupations* (Washington DC: Government Printing Office, 1933), 1416–18.

TABLE 9: Pittsburgh, Occupations by Race, 1950

Occupation	Black male No.	%	Total male No.	%	Black female No.	%	Total female No.	%
Total	31,429	100.0	609,507	100.0	11,174	100.0	199,390	100.0
Professional, technical, and kindred workers	627	1.0	47,492	7.7	369	3.3	27,208	13.6
Farmers and farm managers	14	0.0	5,980	0.9	4	0.0	272	0.1
Managers, officials, and proprietors, except farm	642	2.0	52,684	8.6	141	1.2	6,935	3.4
Clerical and kindred workers	1,263	4.0	49,808	8.1	647	5.7	67,423	33.8
Sales workers	368	1.1	35,594	5.8	234	2.0	25,556	12.8
Craftsmen, foremen, and kindred workers	2,614	8.3	136,001	22.3	101	0.9	2,777	1.3
Operatives and kindred workers	8,272	26.3	150,958	24.7	1,409	12.6	22,623	11.3
Private household workers	372	1.1	841	0.1	4,661	41.7	12,479	6.2
Service workers, except private household	5,984	19.0	35,745	5.8	3,162	28.2	28,177	14.1
Farm laborers and foremen	61	0.1	3,923	0.6	7	0.0	579	0.2
Laborers, except farm and mine	10,848	34.5	85,778	14.0	275	2.4	2,884	1.4
Occupation not reported	364	1.1	4,703	0.7	164	0.1	2,477	1.2

SOURCE: U.S. Bureau of the Census, *Seventeenth Decennial Census of the U.S.*, vol. 2, *Pennsylvania: Characteristics of the Population, 1950* (Washington DC: Government Printing Office, 1952), 397–98.

TABLE 10: Pittsburgh, Occupations by Race, 1960

Occupation	Black male No.	%	Total male No.	%	Black female No.	%	Total female No.	%
Total	31,079	100.0	592,335	100.0	16,050	100.00	239,803	100.0
Professional, technical, and kindred workers	868	2.5	64,073	10.8	956	5.9	36,462	15.2
Farmers and farm managers	3	0.0	3,343	0.5	—		313	0.1
Managers, officials, and proprietors, except farm	427	1.3	51,474	8.6	164	1.0	6,753	2.8
Clerical and kindred workers	1,601	5.1	48,590	8.2	1,325	8.2	79,983	33.3
Sales workers	563	1.8	40,564	6.8	368	2.2	27,651	11.5
Craftsmen, foremen, and kindred workers	3,221	10.3	134,709	22.7	101	0.6	2,432	1.0
Operatives and kindred workers	7,240	23.2	125,670	21.2	1,774	11.0	20,245	8.4
Private household workers	213	0.6	517	0.0	5,169	34.2	12,794	5.9
Service workers, except private household	6,058	19.4	35,200	5.9	4,633	28.8	38,149	15.9
Farm laborers and foremen	34	0.1	2,277	0.3	4	0.0	397	0.1
Laborers, except farm and mine	8,186	26.3	64,209	10.8	232	1.4	1,778	0.7
Occupation not reported	2,665	8.5	21,889	3.6	1,324	8.2	12,846	5.3

SOURCE: U.S. Bureau of the Census, *Eighteenth Decennial Census of the U.S.*, vol. 1, pt. 40, *Pennsylvania: Characteristics of the Population, 1960* (Washington DC: Government Printing Office, 1961), 752–54.

TABLE 11: Top Ten Occupations of Black Men, Pittsburgh Region, 1950

Rank	Occupation	Number	Percentage
	Total	31,429	100.00
1	Laborers, primary metal industries	5,070	16.13
2	Janitors, and porters	4,120	13.10
3	Construction	1,928	6.13
4	Operatives, primary metal industries	1,685	5.36
5	Truck drivers and deliverymen	1,348	4.28
6	Mine operatives and laborers	1,339	4.26
7	Railroads and railway express service	714	2.27
8	Other service workers, except private household	680	2.16
9	Furnacemen, smelters, and heaters	568	1.80
10	Wholesale and retail trade	520	1.65

SOURCE: U.S. Bureau of the Census, *Seventeenth Decennial Census of the U.S.*, vol. 2, *Pennsylvania: Characteristics of the Population, 1950* (Washington DC: Government Printing Office, 1952), 397–98.

TABLE 12: Top Ten Occupations of All Men, Pittsburgh Region, 1950

Rank	Occupation	Number	Percentage
	Total	609,507	100.00
1	Laborers—manufacturing	54,867	9.00
2	Operatives and kindred workers—manufacturing	54,165	8.88
3	Salesmen and sales clerks	27,988	4.59
4	Managers, officials, and proprietors—self employed	24,177	3.96
5	Truck drivers and delivery men	22,803	3.74
6	Mine operatives and laborers	21,324	3.49
7	Managers, officials, and proprietors—salaried	20,803	3.41
8	Other mechanics and repair men and loom fixers	17,339	2.84
9	Foremen	15,616	2.56
10	Machinists and job setters	10,774	1.76

SOURCE: U.S. Bureau of the Census, *Seventeenth Decennial Census of the U.S.*, vol. 2, *Pennsylvania: Characteristics of the Population, 1950* (Washington DC: Government Printing Office, 1952), 397–98.

TABLE 13: Top Ten Occupations of Black Women, Pittsburgh Region, 1950

Rank	Occupation	Number	Percentage
	Total	11,174	100.00
1	Other service workers, except private household	1,198	10.72
2	Laundry and dry cleaning operatives	741	6.63
3	Charwomen, janitors and porters	514	4.59
4	Waitresses, bartenders, and counter workers	494	4.42
5	Other clerical and kindred workers	363	3.24
6	Attendants, hospital, and other institutions	288	2.57
7	Barbers, beauticians, and manicurists	285	2.55
8	Cooks, except private household	258	2.30
9	Stenographers, typists, and secretaries	210	1.87
10	Salesmen and sales clerks, exc. retail trade	186	1.66

SOURCE: U.S. Bureau of the Census, *Seventeenth Decennial Census of the U.S.*, vol. 2, *Pennsylvania: Characteristics of the Population, 1950* (Washington DC: Government Printing Office, 1952), 397–98.

TABLE 14: Top Ten Occupations of All Women, Pittsburgh Region, 1950

Rank	Occupation	Number	Percentage
	Total	199,390	100.00
1	Stenographers, typists, and secretaries	24,592	12.33
2	Salesmen and sales clerks—retail trade	23,745	11.90
3	Operatives and kindred workers—manufacturing	13,917	6.97
4	Teachers	11,037	5.53
5	Waitresses, bartenders, and counter workers	9,436	4.73
6	Private household workers—living out	9,406	4.71
7	Nurses—professional	6,084	3.05
8	Telephone operators	6,056	3.03
9	Charwomen, janitors, and porters	3,653	1.83
10	Laundry and dry cleaning operatives	3,444	1.72

SOURCE: U.S. Bureau of the Census, *Seventeenth Decennial Census of the U.S.*, vol. 2, *Pennsylvania: Characteristics of the Population, 1950* (Washington DC: Government Printing Office, 1952), 397–98.

TABLE 15: Top Ten Occupations of Black Men, Pittsburgh, 1960

Rank	Occupation	Number	Percentage
	Total	31,079	100.00
1	Laborers, primary metal industries	4,015	12.91
2	Janitors and porters	3,617	11.63
3	Truck drivers and deliverymen	1,530	4.92
4	Operatives, primary metal industries	1,407	4.52
5	Other service workers, except private households	1,354	4.35
6	Construction	1,085	3.49
7	Furnacemen, smelters, and heaters	659	2.12
8	Other specified laborers	620	1.99
9	Community, utility, and sanitary service	471	1.51
10	Wholesale and retail trade	415	1.33

SOURCE: U.S. Bureau of the Census, *Eighteenth Decennial Census of the U.S.*, vol. 1, pt. 40, *Pennsylvania: Characteristics of the Population, 1960* (Washington DC: Government Printing Office, 1961), 752–54.

TABLE 16: Top Ten Occupations of All Men, Pittsburgh, 1960

Rank	Occupation	Number	Percentage
	Total	592,335	100.00
1	Operatives and kindred workers—manufacturing	43,500	7.34
2	Laborers—manufacturing	38,661	6.52
3	Salesmen and salesclerks	30,188	5.09
4	Managers, officers, and proprietors—salaried	26,668	4.50
5	Truckdrivers and deliverymen	23,675	3.99
6	Foremen	18,246	3.08
7	Managers, officers, and proprietors—self-employed	16,153	2.72
8	Other craftsmen and kindred workers	13,698	2.31
9	Charmen, janitors, and porters	9,954	1.68
10	Machinists and job setters	8,959	1.51

SOURCE: U.S. Bureau of the Census, *Eighteenth Decennial Census of the U.S.*, vol. 1, pt. 40, *Pennsylvania: Characteristics of the Population, 1960* (Washington DC: Government Printing Office, 1961), 752–54.

TABLE 17: Top Ten Occupations of Black Women, Pittsburgh, 1960

Rank	Occupation	Number	Percentage
	Total	16,050	100.00
1	Private household workers—living out	4,811	29.97
2	Other service workers except private households	1,431	8.91
3	Laundry and dry cleaning operatives	1,075	6.69
4	Attendants, hospitals, and other institutions	1,013	6.31
5	Other clerical and kindred workers	694	4.32
6	Charwomen, janitors, and porters	548	3.41
7	Practical nurses and midwives	462	2.87
8	Waiters, bartenders, and counter workers	424	2.64
9	Operatives and kindred workers	363	2.26
10	Private household workers—live in	358	2.23

SOURCE: U.S. Bureau of the Census, *Eighteenth Decennial Census of the U.S.*, vol. 1, pt. 40, *Pennsylvania: Characteristics of the Population, 1960* (Washington DC: Government Printing Office, 1961), 752–54.

TABLE 18: Top Ten Occupations of All Women, Pittsburgh 1960

Rank	Occupation	Number	Percentage
	Total	239,803	100.00
1	Saleswomen and sales clerks—retail trade	24,196	10.08
2	Secretaries	19,307	8.05
3	Waiters, bartenders, and counter workers	11,114	4.63
4	Private household workers—living out	10,882	4.53
5	Teachers	9,874	4.11
6	Nurses, professional	8,495	3.54
7	Bookkeepers	7,088	2.95
8	Operatives and kindred workers—manufacturing	6,948	2.89
9	Stenographers	5,720	2.38
10	Typists	4,850	2.02

SOURCE: U.S. Bureau of the Census, *Eighteenth Decennial Census of the U.S.*, vol. 1, pt. 40, *Pennsylvania: Characteristics of the Population, 1960* (Washington DC: Government Printing Office, 1961), 752–54.

TABLE 19: Employment of African Americans at Sears Stores, Pittsburgh Region, 1969–1970

Location	No. of Blacks	Total
East Liberty	59	599
Penn Center	12	469
51st Street Control Service Unit	9	307
Baden	13	408
Greensburg	5	393
North Side	64	693
South Hills	19	599
West Mifflin	16	444

SOURCES: "Sears Stores Here Facing Black Boycott," *New Pittsburgh Courier*, 8 Nov. 1969; "Massive 'Black Monday' Protest Set Against Sears," *New Pittsburgh Courier*, 15 Nov. 1969.

TABLE 20: Project Sites and BCC Demonstrations, August 25, 1969

Project site	Cost (in millions)
Bell Telephone building	$8.5
College Hall, Duquesne University	$3.5
Corran Hall, Carlow College	$1.6
Dormitory complex, Duquesne University	$10.0
Pittsburgh National Bank	$20.0
School of Engineering building, Univ. of Pittsburgh	$14.5
Three Rivers Stadium	$31.9
University Health Centers & Blood Bank	$2.0
U.S. Steel building on Grant Street	$100.0
Westinghouse building	$20.0
WQED-WQEX building, CMU campus	$2.1
Total cost	$214.1

SOURCES: Edward Verlich and Roger Stuart, newsclipping, *Pittsburgh Press*, 25 August 1969; "Traffic Snarls Add to Furor in Job Protest," *Pittsburgh Press*, 26 August 1969.

TABLE 21: Developments by the Housing Authority of the City of Pittsburgh (7011 total dwellings)

Black residents (%)	Year
46.7	1944
43.7	1948
41.7	1955
42.7	1956
45.3	1957
46.8	1958
47.5	1960
70.9	1969
76.2	1970

SOURCES: Bureau of Social Research, Federation of Social Agencies of Pittsburgh and Allegheny County, "The Population of Public Housing" (Pittsburgh: Federation of Social Agencies of Pittsburgh and Allegheny County, ca. 1944). 10; "Pittsburgh. Housing. Public, 1958," vertical file, Carnegie Library of Pittsburgh, main branch; Housing Authority of the City of Pittsburgh, "A Report to the People: Public Housing in Pittsburgh, 1938–1953" (Pittsburgh: HACP, ca. 1954); Roy Lubove, *Twentieth-Century Pittsburgh*, (Pittsburgh: University of Pittsburgh Press, 1969), 1:85–86; Barbara W. Scott, "The Status of Housing of Negroes in Pittsburgh" (Pittsburgh: Commission on Human Relations, 1962), 22; "1969 HACP Annual Summary," 10, Box 5, Folder 1969, Annual Summary, Matson Papers, Archives of Industrial Society, University of Pittsburgh.

TABLE 22: Pittsburgh Middle Schools' Percentage of Black Students, 1976

Greater than 66%	%	Less than 32%	%	Within PHRC guidelines	%
1 = Baxter	100	5 = Knoxville	31.9	7 = Arsenal	56.5
2 = Gladstone	68.2	6 = Prospect	20	8 = Columbus	53.4
3 = Herron Hill	98.8			9 = Greenway	39.8
4 = McNaugher	74.7			10 = Latimer	39.1
				11 = Reizenstein	56.5

SOURCE: Marcella DeMarco, "Magnet Programs in the Pittsburgh Schools: Development to Implementation 1977 through 1982" (PhD diss., University of Pittsburgh, 1983), 55.

TABLE 23: Pittsburgh High Schools' Percentage of Black Students, 1976

Greater than 66%	%	Less than 32%	%	Within PHRC guidelines	%
1 = Schenley	84.9	3 = Alderdice	16	8 = Allegheny	46.5
2 = Westinghouse	99.9	4 = Carrick	13.1	9 = Brashear	41.0
		5 = Langley	17.9	10 = Oliver	35.8
		6 = South	19.1	11 = Peabody	43.8
		7 = South Hills	23.9	12 = Perry	56.3

SOURCE: Marcella DeMarco, "Magnet Programs in the Pittsburgh Schools: Development to Implementation 1977 through 1982" (PhD diss., University of Pittsburgh, 1983), 53.

TABLE 24: Pittsburgh Occupations by Race, 1970

Occupations by race	Black	%	Total population	%
Total employed	31,702	100.00	192,565	100.00
White-collar workers				
Professionals	2,760	8.71	29,799	15.47
Managers and administrators, except farm	762	2.4	11,601	6.02
Sales, clerical, and kindred workers	6,531	20.6	65,160	33.84
Blue-collar workers				
Craft and kindred workers	2,448	7.72	22,766	11.82
Operatives, including transport	5,332	16.79	27.283	14.17
Laborers, except farm	3,013	9.5	11,279	5.86
Farm workers				
Farmers and farm managers	39	0.12	93	0.05
Farm laborers and supervisors	64	0.2	163	0.08
Service workers				
Private households	1,944	6.13	2,974	1.54
Other	8,810	27.79	31,447	16.33
Occupations not reported	3,119	9.85	13,374	6.03

SOURCE: U.S. Bureau of the Census, *1970 Census of Population: Characteristics of the Population, Pa., Section 1* (Washington DC: Government Printing Office, 1973), 40.451–40.468.

TABLE 25: Pittsburgh Occupations by Race, 1980

Occupations by race, both sexes	Black	%	Total population	%
Total—over 16 yrs. old	31,042	100.00	170,591	100.00
Managerial and professional	4,713	15.18	38,874	22.79
Technical, sales, and administrative support	9,443	30.42	56,774	33.28
Farming, forestry, and fishing	66	0.21	701	0.41
Precision production, craft, and repair	2,037	6.56	16,144	9.46
Operators, fabricators, and laborers	5,955	19.18	26,224	15.37
Domestic service	458	1.48	890	0.52
Protection service	993	3.2	5,056	2.96
Other service	7,377	23.76	25,919	15.19
Males (by calculation)				
Total—over 16 yrs. old	15,179	100.00	92,301	100.00
Managerial and professional	2,001	13.18	21,361	23.14
Technical, sales, and administrative support	2,637	17.37	19,086	20.68
Farming, forestry, and fishing	66	0.43	593	0.64
Precision lroduction, craft, and repair	1,857	12.23	14,982	16.23
Operators, fabricators, and laborers	4,809	31.68	21,941	23.77
Domestic service	29	0.19	42	0.05
Protection service	784	5.17	4,267	4.62
Other service	2,996	19.74	10,020	10.86

SOURCE: U.S. Bureau of the Census, *1980 Census of Population: General Social and Economic Characteristics, Pennsylvania* (Washington DC: Government Printing Office, 1983), 40.405–40.409.

TABLE 26: Pittsburgh Occupations by Race, 1990

Occupations by race, both sexes	Black	%	Total population	%
Total—over 16 yrs. old	28,882	100.00	122,067	100.00
Managerial and professional	5,415	18.75	36,811	30.16
Technical, sales, and administrative support	9,862	34.15	43,229	35.41
Farming, forestry, and fishing	98	0.34	644	0.53
Precision production, craft, and repair	1,471	5.09	9,784	8.02
Operators, fabricators, and laborers	3,871	13.4	11,834	9.69
Domestic service	270	0.93	329	0.27
Protection service	1,049	3.63	3,326	2.72
Other service	6,846	23.7	16,110	13.2
Males (by calculation)				
Total—over 16 yrs. old	12,757	100.00	63,428	100.00
Managerial and professional	2,098	16.45	18,504	29.17
Technical, sales, and administrative support	2,646	20.74	15,624	24.63
Farming, forestry, and fishing	94	0.74	559	0.88
Precision production, craft, and repair	1,296	10.16	9,083	14.32
Operators, fabricators, and laborers	2,832	22.2	9,792	15.44
Domestic service	6	0.05	23	0.04
Protection service	794	6.22	2,800	4.41
Other service	2,991	23.45	7,043	11.1

SOURCE: U. S. Bureau of the Census, *1990 Census of Population: Social and Economic Characteristics, Pennsylvania* (Washington DC: Government Printing Office, 1993), 1055–56.

TABLE 27: Top Ten Occupations of Black Males, Pittsburgh, 1970

Rank	Occupation	Number	% of total
	Total	17,764	100.00
1	Laborers, except farm	2,997	16.87
2	Craftsmen, foremen, and kindred workers	2,306	12.98
3	Cleaning service workers	2,123	11.95
4	Clerical and kindred workers	1,847	10.39
5	Operatives, durable goods manufacturing	1,489	8.38
6	Transport equipment operatives	1,466	8.25
7	Professional, technical, and kindred workers	1,204	6.77
8	Food service workers	986	5.55
9	Operatives, nonmanufacturing industries	886	4.98
10	Managers and administrators, except farm	547	3.07

SOURCE: U.S. Bureau of the Census, 1970 Census of Population: Characteristics of the Population, Pa. Section 1 (Washington DC: Government Printing Office, 1973), 40.451–40.468.

TABLE 28: Top Ten Occupations of Black Females, Pittsburgh 1970

Rank	Occupation	Number	% of total
	Total	13,938	100.00
1	Clerical and kindred workers	3,540	25.39
2	Private household workers	1,880	13.48
3	Health service workers	1,555	11.15
4	Professional, technical, and kindred workers	1,556	11.16
5	Cleaning service workers	1,051	7.54
6	Food service workers	986	7.07
7	Operatives, nonmanufacturing industries	669	4.79
8	Sales workers	635	4.55
9	Personal service workers	505	3.62
10	Operatives, nondurable goods manufacturing	355	2.54

SOURCE: U.S. Bureau of the Census, 1970 Census of Population: Characteristics of the Population, Pa. Section 1 (Washington DC: Government Printing Office, 1973), 40.451–40.468.

TABLE 29: Top Ten Occupations of Black Males, Pittsburgh, 1990

Rank	Occupation	Number	% of total
	Total	12,757	100.00
1	Operators, fabricators, and laborers	2,832	22.19
2	Managerial and professional specialty occupations	1,453	11.38
3	Precision production, craft, and repair occupations	1,296	10.15
4	Professional specialty occupations	1,115	8.74
5	Food services occupations	1,105	8.66
6	Handlers, equipment cleaners, helpers, and laborers	1,004	7.87
7	Executive, administrative, and managerial occupations	983	7.70
8	Transportation occupations	877	6.87
9	Protective service occupations	794	6.22
10	Sales occupations	647	5.07
11	Other	651	5.10

SOURCE: U.S. Bureau of the Census, *1990 Census of Population: Social and Economic Characteristics, Pennsylvania* (Washington DC: Government Printing Office, 1993), 1055–56.

TABLE 30: Top Ten Occupations of Black Females, Pittsburgh, 1990

Rank	Occupation	Number	% of total
	Total	18,285	100.00
1	Professional specialty occupations	2,216	12.11
2	Secretaries, stenographers, and typists	1,352	7.39
3	Sales occupations	1,303	7.12
4	Executive, administrative, and managerial occupations	1,101	6.02
5	Operators, fabricators, and laborers	1,039	5.68
6	Cleaning and building service occupations	906	4.95
7	Food service occupations	673	3.68
8	Health technologists and technicians	602	3.29
9	Financial record processing occupations	399	2.18
10	Mail and message distributing occupations	299	1.63

SOURCE: U. S. Bureau of the Census, *1990 Census of Population: Social and Economic Characteristics, Pennsylvania* (Washington DC: Government Printing Office, 1993), 1055–56.

TABLE 31: Black Male Representation in Blue-collar Occupations, Allegheny County, 1990

Underrepresented	Evenly represented	Overrepresented
Median wage = $12,000	Median wage = $14,700	Median wage = $8,000
Waiters and waitresses	Punch/stamp press	Misc. food preparation
Auto mechanics	machine operators	Printing press operators
Carpenters	Truck drivers	Machine operators
Electricians	Nursing aides, orderlies,	Construction laborers
Plumbers, pipefitters, and	and attendants	Laborers, except
steamfitters		construction
Machinists		Cooks
Butchers and meat cutters		Maids and housemen
Early childhood teaching		Janitors and cleaners
assistants		Assemblers
Pressing machine operators		Bus drivers

SOURCE: Karen J. Gibson, William A. Darity, and Samuel L. Meyers, "Revisiting Occupational Crowding in the U.S.: A Preliminary Study," *Feminist Economics* 4, no. 3 (1998): 81.

TABLE 32: Black Female Representation in Blue-collar Occupations, Allegheny County, 1990

Underrepresented	Evenly represented	Overrepresented
Median wage = $13,800	Median wage = $0	Median wage = $6,800
Waiters and waitresses		Cooks
Misc. food preparation		Nursing aides, orderlies,
Auto mechanics		and attendants
Carpenters		Maids and housemen
Electricians		Janitors and cleaners
Plumbers, pipefitters, and		Early childhood teaching
steamfitters		assistants
Machinists		Pressing machine operators
Butchers and meat cutters		Assemblers
Punch/stamp press		Bus drivers
machine operators		
Printing press operators		
Machine operators, not		
specified		
Truck drivers		
Construction laborers		
Laborers, except		
construction		

SOURCE: Karen J. Gibson, William A. Darity, and Samuel L. Meyers, "Revisiting Occupational Crowding in the U.S.: A Preliminary Study," *Feminist Economics* 4, no. 3 (1998): 82.

TABLE 33: Black Male Representation in White-collar Occupations, Allegheny County, 1990

Underrepresented	Evenly represented	Overrepresented
Median wage = $20,900	Median wage = $19,500	Median wage = $22,800
*Financial managers *Purchasing managers *Managers, marketing, advertising, and public relations *Mgrs., medicine and health *Funeral directors *Mgrs. and administrators Administrators, protective services Architects Physicians Lawyers Accountants Registered nurses Computer programmers Sales—supervisors and proprietors Sales workers, other Secretaries Receptionists Clinical laboratory technicians Licenses practical nurses Health technicians Cashiers Typists File clerks General office clerks Administrative support	Managers, service organizations Data-entry	Chief executives and general administrators, public administration Personnel and labor relations managers Managers, food serving and lodging establishments Managers, properties and real estate Technicians Administrators and officials, public administrators Computer operators Administrators, education and related fields Postal clerks, excluding mail carriers

NOTE: *Subgroup median wage = $30,500
SOURCE: Karen J. Gibson, William A. Darity, and Samuel L. Meyers, "Revisiting Occupational Crowding in the U.S.: A Preliminary Study," *Feminist Economics* 4, no. 3 (1998): 85.

TABLE 34: Black Female Representation in White-collar Occupations, Allegheny County, 1990

Underrepresented	Evenly represented	Overrepresented
Median wage = $26,400	Median wage = $19,400	Median wage = $16,000
Chief executives and general administrators, public administration	Administrators and officials, public administrators	Administrators, education and related fields
Administrators, protective services	Computer operators	Managers, service organizations
Financial managers		Accountants
Personnel and labor relations managers		Clinical laboratory technicians
Purchasing managers		Licensed practical nurses
Managers, marketing, advertising, and public relations		Health technicians
Managers, medicine and health		Cashiers
Managers, food serving and lodging establishments		Typists
Managers, properties and real estate		File clerks
Funeral directors		Postal clerks, excluding mail carriers
Managers and administrators		General office clerks
Architects		Data-entry
Physicians		Administrative support
Registered nurses		
Lawyers		
Computer programmers		
Technicians		
Sales—supervisors and proprietors		
Sales representatives— mining, manufacturing, and wholesale		
Sales workers, other		
Secretaries		
Receptionists		
File clerks		
General office clerks		
Administrative support		

SOURCE: Karen J. Gibson, William A. Darity, and Samuel L. Meyers, "Revisiting Occupational Crowding in the U.S.: A Preliminary Study," *Feminist Economics* 4, no. 3 (1998): 87.

TABLE 35: Percent of Kidney Transplant Dialysis Patients Age 18–54, by Race, U.S., 1996–1999

Among clinically appropriate candidates for transplantation		Among clinically inappropriate candidates for transplantation		Patients who desired a transplant and were placed on a waiting list or received a transplant	
Referred for evaluation %	Received transplant %	Referred for evaluation %	Received transplant %	Referred for evaluation %	Received transplant %
White	Black	White	Black	White	Black	White	Black	White	Black	White	Black
98	90	52	17	58	38	10	2	69	40	68	41

SOURCE: Anita Strikameswaran, "Minorities Lag in Receiving Transplants and Heart Surgeries," *Pittsburgh Post-Gazette*, 23 July 2002.

TABLE 36: Percent of Patients with Coronary Artery Disease, by Severity Prior to Procedure, by Race, U.S., 1984–1992

Underwent angioplasty				Underwent heart bypass surgery				Underwent either procedure			
Mild %		Severe %		Mild %		Severe %		Mild %		Severe %	
White	Black	White	Black	White	Black	White	Black	White	Black	White	Black
26	23	24	25	35	25	45	31	61	48	70	56

SOURCE: Anita Strikameswaran, "Minorities Lag in Receiving Transplants and Heart Surgeries," *Pittsburgh Post-Gazette*, 23 July 2002.

TABLE 37: African American Neighborhoods in Pittsburgh, 1970–1990

	The Hill District									East Liberty		
	Lower Hill/Crawford-Roberts			Middle			Upper					
	1970	1980	1990	1970	1980	1990	1970	1980	1990	1970	1980	1990
Population	5,504	3,398	2,349	7,620	4,221	2,997	3,682	2,272	2,224	1,833	4,255	4,848
% of total	92.7	95.5	95.5	99.2	99.0	98.9	87.9	86.9	85.9	21.2	48.7	60.8
Number of all housing units	3,218	1,856	1,332	3,465	2,262	1,541	1,599	1,351	1,225	4,147	4,660	4,718
% change	-15.2	-42.3	-28.2	-14.1	-34.7	-31.9	-5.5	-15.5	-9.3	-14.0	12.4	1.2
Owner occupied/blacks	395	332	298	844	696	581	732	688	618	62	270	253
% of all units	16.7	22.9	26.5	27.4	37.1	46.7	56.4	61.9	67.8	9.4	13.1	10.3
% white owner-occupied	37.9	4.9	36.4	40.9	42.9	41.2	70.2	78.5	77.0	21.3	20.6	24.3

	Homewood									Larimer		
	North			South			West					
	1970	1980	1990	1970	1980	1990	1970	1980	1990	1970	1980	1990
Population	8,379	6,960	5,252	8,502	6,094	4,724	2,530	1,763	1,349	4,927	4,201	3,410
% of total	96.9	98.6	98.5	95.8	97.9	98.2	92.2	94.1	98.5	66.6	83.3	85.4
Number of all housing units	3,080	2,657	2,317	3,438	2,641	2,250	1,013	794	658	2.942	2,256	1,862
% change	-15.2	-13.7	-12.8	-2.1	-23.2	-14.8	-15.2	-21.6	-17.1	-0.1	-23.3	-17.5
Owner occupied/blacks	1,407	1,294	1,146	904	803	707	739	289	265	572	583	505
% of all units	51.7	55.1	56.9	32.4	35.0	35.8	41.8	43.4	48.8	31.6	39.5	36.4
% white owner-occupied	76.4	67.4	78.1	52.1	62.0	69.7	59.8	65.5	85.7	36.7	39.7	40.1

	Lincoln-Lemington-Belmar			Beltzhoover			Manchester			East Hills		
	1970	1980	1990	1970	1980	1990	1970	1980	1990	1970	1980	1990
Population	6,176	6,580	5,848	4,114	3,349	2,783	3,413	2,391	2,675	3,976	5,301	4,316
% of total	65.2	81.6	88.0	69.6	79.6	83.4	71.4	85.0	86.9	75.0	94.1	95.8
Number of all housing units	2,636	2,547	2,426	1,926	1,661	1,428	2,012	1,476	1,500	1,764	1,985	1,981
% change	-0.3	-3.4	-4.8	-10.1	-13.8	-14.0	-27.3	-26.6	1.6	51.5	12.5	-0.2
Owner occupied/blacks	1,265	1,484	1,395	747	773	722	318	380	384	611	816	743
% of all units	73.0	68.7	68.1	66.3	68.9	69.8	32.1	37.7	35.5	52.7	46.8	44.9
% white owner-occupied	67.9	77.3	81.8	68.9	69.5	78.1	43.2	65.8	46.8			

	Perry	Point Breeze	Garfield
	North	South	Point Breeze North
	1970	1980	1990
Population	184	333	647
% of total	2.4	5.7	13.1
Number of all housing units	2,761	2,367	2,099
% change	3.3	-14.3	-11.3
Owner occupied/blacks	38	57	93

continued

TABLE 37: African American Neighborhoods in Pittsburgh, 1970–1990, continued

	Stanton Heights			Northview Heights			Highland Park		
	1970	1980	1990	1970	1980	1990	1970	1980	1990
Population	194	816	1,159	3,319	3,016	2,653	287	610	1,351
% of total	2.5	13.1	22.8	72.8	93.8	93.7	3.1	7.6	19.2
Number of all housing units	2,418	2,376	2,110	1,158	1,099	966	3,628	3,732	3,403
% change	2.9	-1.7	-11.2	661.8	-5.1	-12.1	5.5	2.9	-8.8
Owner occupied/blacks	43.	227	343	10	22	15	37	67	163
% of all units	78.5	84.9	84.1	1.5	2.7	1.8	40.7	25.4	30.8
% white owner occupied	83.5	84.4	92.0	17.5	14.6	28.8	49.5	46.7	55.1

SOURCE: Department of City Planning, 1990 Census of Population and Housing Reports: Report No. 3, Whole City, A-Z: Population, Social, Economic and Housing Data by Neighborhood, 1940 to 1990 (Pittsburgh: City of Pittsburgh, 1990).

NOTES

Acknowledgments

1. Other interviewees include Harvey Adams, Charles "Chuck" Austin, Lloyd Bell, Victor Bell, Akeia F. Blue, John Brewer, Cecil Brooks II, Regis Bubonis Sr., Karen Butler, Ruth Byrd-Smith, Kingsley L. Carey, Martha Conley, James Cunningham, Stan Denton, Arthur J. Edmunds, David E. Ellis, Michael Flournoy, John L. Ford, Brenda L. Frazier, James T. G. Frazier, Albert French, Jillian C. Giles, Robert W. Goode, Leon Haley, Marion S. Harper, Nelson Harrison, Chelsie L. Hart, Kermit Hawthorne, Cathryn L. Irvis, Alan James, Erika D. Johnson, James Johnson, Anne Jones, Rufus Jordan, Robert Lavelle, Kristen L. Lewis, Vernell Lillie, Fred Logan, Thelma Lovette-Morris, Beatrice M. Mahaffey, Loran Mann, George McClomb, Donald W. McIlvane, Herman Mitchell, John Moon, Chris Moore, Gregory Morris, Paul Mulbah Jr., Robert L. Pitts, Lorraine Poindexter, Herman L. Reid Jr., Ruth Richardson, Valerie MacDonald-Roberts, George Spaulding, Beverly Smith, Margaret Washington Smith, Eric Springer, Milton Washington, and Joseph F. Zunic.

Introduction

1. For an assessment of this scholarship, see Kenneth L. Kusmer and Joe W. Trotter, eds., *African American Urban History Since World War II* (Chicago: University of Chicago Press, 2009); Joe W. Trotter, Earl Lewis, and Tera W. Hunter, eds., *The African American Urban Experience: Perspectives from the Colonial Era to the Present* (New York: Palgrave Publishing Company, 2004); Arvarh E. Strickland and Robert Weems, eds., *The African American Experience: An Historiographical and Bibliographical Guide* (Westport, CT: Greenwood Press, 2001), chapters 1 and 2; Kenneth Goings and Raymond A. Mohl, eds., *The New African American Urban History* (Thousand Oaks, CA: Sage Publications, 1996); Robin D. G. Kelley, *Race Rebels: Culture, Politics, and the Black Working Class* (New York: The Free Press, 1994).

2. Kenneth Love, *One Shot: The Life and Work of Teenie Harris*, film (California Newsreel, 2001); Carolyn S. Blount, "Having Our Say: Black Press Documentary Highlights Nearly Forgotten," *About Time Magazine* (Jan.–Feb. 1999); *The Black Press: Soldiers without Swords*, film (PBS Television, premiere, 8 Feb. 1999).

3. Wilson's Pittsburgh Cycle includes *Ma Rainey's Black Bottom* (New York: Pen-

guin, 1985); *Jitney* (Woodstock, NY: Overlook Press, Peter Mayer, 2003); *Joe Turner's Come and Gone* (New York: Penguin 1988); *Fences* (New York: Penguin, 1986); *The Piano Lesson* (New York: Penguin, 1990); *Two Trains Running* (New York: Penguin, 1993); *Seven Guitars* (New York: Penguin, 1997); *King Hedley II* (New York: Theatre Communications Group, 2005); *Gem of the Ocean* (New York: Theatre Communications Group, 2003); and *Radio Golf* (New York: Theatre Communications Group, 2007). Also see Sandra G. Shannon, *The Dramatic Vision of August Wilson* (Washington DC: Howard University Press, 1995); Dana Williams and Sandra Shannon, eds., *August Wilson and Black Aesthetics* (New York: Palgrave MacMillan, 2004).

4. Mindy Thompson Fullilove, *Root Shock: How Tearing Up City Neighborhoods Hurts America, And What We Can Do About It* (New York: Ballantine Books, One World, 2005), 29.

5. For assessments of this literature, see Goings and Mohl, *New African American Urban History*; Strickland and Weems, *African American Experience*; Trotter, Lewis, and Hunter, *African American Urban Experience*; and Darlene Clark Hine, ed., *The State of Afro-American History: Past, Present, and Future* (Baton Rouge: Louisiana State University Press, 1986).

6. See Jacquelyn Jones, "The Long Civil Rights Movement and the Political Uses of the Past," *Journal of American History*, 91, no. 4 (March 2005): 1233–63; Robert Korstad and Alex Lichtenstein, "Opportunities Found and Lost: Labor, Radicals and the Early Civil Rights Movement," *Journal of American History* 75, no. 3 (Dec. 1988): 786–811; Richard M. Dalfiume, "The 'Forgotten Years' of the Negro Revolution," *Journal of American History*, 55, no. 1 (June 1968): 90–106; Jack Dougherty, "African Americans, Civil Rights, and Race-Making in Milwaukee," March on Milwaukee Symposium (University of Wisconsin-Milwaukee, 29 Sept. 2007, copy in authors' possession).

7. On the second Great Migration, see James Gregory, "The Second Great Migration: An Historical Overview," in Kusmer and Trotter, *African American Urban History Since World War II*, chapter 1; James N. Gregory, *The Southern Diaspora: How the Great Migrations of Black and White Southerners Transformed America* (Chapel Hill, NC: The University of North Carolina Press, 2005); Peter Gottlieb, "Rethinking the Great Migration," in Joe William Trotter Jr., *The Great Migration in Historical Perspective: New Dimensions of Race, Class, & Gender* (Bloomington: Indiana University Press, 1991), 68–82.

8. For the notion of a Second Ghetto, see Arnold R. Hirsch, *Making the Second Ghetto: Race and Housing in Chicago 1940–1960* (Chicago: The University of Chicago Press, 1983); Timothy J. Gilfoyle, guest editor, "Special Section: Urban History, Arnold Hirsch, and the Second Ghetto Thesis," *Journal of Urban History* 29, no. 3 (March 2003), 243–56.

9. Jeanne F. Theoharis and Komozi Woodard, *Freedom North: Black Freedom Struggles Outside the South, 1940–1980* (New York: Palgrave Macmillan, 2003).

10. For postwar studies of other cities, see Matthew Countryman, *Up South: Civil Rights and Black Power in Philadelphia* (Philadelphia: University of Pennsylvania Press, 2006); Martha Biondi, *To Stand and Fight: The Struggle for Civil Rights in Postwar New York City* (Cambridge, MA: Harvard University Press, 2003); Wendell Pritchett, *Brownsville, Brooklyn: Blacks, Jews, and the Changing Face of the Ghetto*

(Chicago: The University of Chicago Press, 2002); Robert O. Self, *American Babylon: Race and the Struggle for Postwar Oakland* (Princeton: Princeton University Press, 2003); Rhonda Williams, *The Politics of Public Housing: Black Women's Struggles Against Urban Inequality* (New York: Oxford University Press, 2004); and Matthew Whitaker, *Race Work: The Rise of Civil Rights in the Urban West* (Lincoln: University of Nebraska Press, 2005).

11. William J. Wilson, *The Truly Disadvantaged: The Inner City, the Underclass, and Public Policy* (Chicago: University of Chicago Press, 1987) and *When Work Disappears: The World of the New Urban Poor* (New York: Knopf, 1996); Nicholas Lemann, *The Promised Land: The Great Black Migration and How It Changed America* (New York: Alfred A. Knopf, 1991); Thomas J. Sugrue, *The Origins of the Urban Crisis: Race and Inequality in Postwar Detroit* (Princeton: Princeton University Press, 1996); Heather Thompson, *Whose Detroit: Politics, Labor and Race in a Modern American City* (Ithaca: Cornell University Press, 2001); Elijah Anderson, *Street Wise: Race, Class, and Change in an Urban Community* (Chicago: The University of Chicago Press, 1990).

12. See, for example, Williams, *Politics of Public Housing*; Whitaker, *Race Work*; Pritchett, *Brownsville*; Steven Gregory, *Black Corona: Race and the Politics of Place in an Urban Community* (Princeton: Princeton University Press, 1998); Andrew Wiese, *Places of Their Own: African American Suburbanization in the Twentieth Century* (Chicago: The University of Chicago Press, 2004); Countryman, *Up South*; and Biondi, *To Stand and Fight*. Also see essays in Kusmer and Trotter, *African American Urban History since World War II*.

Chapter 1: War, Politics, and the Creation of the Black Community

1. Research on other cities of the interwar years include, but is not limited to (see other titles in the bibliography of this volume): Kimberly L. Phillips, *Alabama North: African-American Migrants, Community, and Working-Class Activism in Cleveland, 1915–45* (Chicago: University of Illinois Press, 1999); Lillian Serece Williams, *Strangers in the Land of Paradise: The Creation of an African American Community, Buffalo, New York, 1900–1940* (Bloomington: Indiana University Press, 1999); Richard W. Thomas, *Life for Us Is What We Make It: Building Black Community in Detroit, 1915–1945* (Bloomington: Indiana University Press, 1992); and Cheryl Lynn Greenberg, *Or Does It Explode? Black Harlem in the Great Depression* (New York: Oxford University Press, 1991).

2. For "Pittsburgh's Wall Street," see Edward K. Muller, "Metropolis and Region: A Framework for Enquiry into Western Pennsylvania," in *City at the Point: Essays on the Social History of Pittsburgh*, ed. Samuel P. Hays (Pittsburgh: University of Pittsburgh Press, 1989), 193. For more background on Pittsburgh's industrial history, see, for example, Francis G. Couvares, *The Remaking of Pittsburgh: Class and Culture in an Industrializing City, 1877–1919* (Albany: State University of New York Press, 1984), 9–30, 80–95; David B. Houston, "A Brief History of the Process of Capital Accumulation in Pittsburgh: A Marxist Interpretation," in *Pittsburgh-Sheffield, Sister Cities*, ed. Joel Tarr (Pittsburgh: Carnegie Mellon University Press, 1986), 29–69; and Kenneth Warren, *The American Steel Industry, 1850–1970: A Geographical Interpretation* (Oxford: Clarendan Press, 1973), 124–44.

3. John Bodnar, Roger Simon, and Michael P. Weber, *Lives of Their Own: Blacks,*

Italians, and Poles in Pittsburgh, 1900–1960 (Urbana: University of Illinois Press, 1982), 13–54 (quote, 59). Nora Faires, "Immigrants and Industry," in Hays, *City at the Point*, 3–31.

4. Faires, "Immigrants and Industry," 3–31; Bodnar, Simon, and Weber, *Lives of Their Own*, 13–54. Information about "Pittsburgh's Ellis Island" is drawn from a personal conversation with historian Laurence Glasco, Department of History, University of Pittsburgh, Spring 2006.

5. Faires, "Immigrants and Industry," 3–31; Bodnar, Simon, and Weber, *Lives of Their Own*, 20, 30; Dennis C. Dickerson, *Out of the Crucible: Black Steelworkers in Western Pennsylvania, 1875–1980* (Albany: State University of New York Press, 1986), 22.

6. Chandler, *Visible Hand*, 265–67; Richard Oestreicher, "Working-Class Formation, Development, and Consciousness in Pittsburgh, 1790–1960," in Hays, *City at the Point*, 111–50 (quote on "Railroad War," 126); Warren, *American Steel Industry*, 109–44; Houston, "Brief History"; Temin, *Iron and Steel*, 164–65; David Brody, *Steelworkers in America: The Non-Union Era* (1960; repr., New York: Russell and Russell, 1970), 1–49.

7. Oestreicher, "Working-Class Formation," 126–34; Brody, *Steelworkers in America*; 50–79; Paul Krause, *The Battle for Homestead 1880–1892: Politics, Culture, and Steel* (Pittsburgh: University of Pittsburgh Press, 1992), 177–201, 329–62; S. J. Klienberg, *The Shadow of the Mills: Working-Class Families in Pittsburgh, 1820–1907* (Pittsburgh: University of Pittsburgh, 1989), 3–40.

8. Dickerson, *Out of the Crucible*, 15 (quote). See also R. R. Wright, *The Negro in Pennsylvania: A Study in Economic History* (1912; repr., New York: Arno Press, 1969), 94–100; Sterling D. Spero and Abraham L. Harris, *The Black Worker: The Negro and the Labor Movement* (New York: Atheneum, 1968), 246–55; and William Harris, *The Harder We Run: Black Workers Since the Civil War* (New York: Oxford University Press, 1982), 7–50.

9. Rina C. Youngner, *Industry in Art: Pittsburgh, 1812 to 1920* (Pittsburgh: University of Pittsburgh Press, 2006), 82–84, includes reprints of images of black steelworkers from *Harper's Magazine*.

10. *Iron Age* quoted in Dickerson, *Out of the Crucible*, 17; Spero and Harris, *Black Worker*, 250, 257; Warren C. Whatley, "African American Strikebreaking from the Civil War to the New Deal," *Social Science History* 17, no. 4 (Winter 1993): 525–58; Youngner, *Industry in Art*, 82–84; The Commission of Inquiry, the Interchurch World Movement, *Report of the Steel Strike of 1919* (New York: Harcourt, Brace and World, 1920), 177–78; Joe W. Trotter, "Reflections on the Great Migration to Western Pennsylvania," *Pittsburgh History* (Winter 1995–96): 156.

11. Laurence A. Glasco, ed., *The WPA History of the Negro in Pittsburgh* (Pittsburgh: University of Pittsburgh Press, 2004), 218–19 (quote); Spero and Harris, *Black Worker*, 250–57; Dickerson, *Out of the Crucible*, 8–9, 15–17; Whatley, "African American Strikebreaking," 82–84; Peter Gottlieb, *Making their Own Way: Southern Blacks' Migration to Pittsburgh, 1916–30* (Urbana: University of Illinois Press, 1987), 90–98.

12. Oliver G. Waters, "Smoky City: Part I," *Colored American Magazine* 3, no. 6 (Oct. 1901): 419. The authors are indebted to historian Patricia Mitchell for bringing this series of essays to our attention.

13. Dickerson, *Out of the Crucible*, 11–13; Philip S. Foner, *Organized Labor and the Black Worker, 1619–1973* (New York: Praeger Publishers, 1974), 64.

14. Spero and Harris, *Black Worker*, 47 (quote).

15. Robert L. Vann quoted in Andrew Buni, *Robert L. Vann of The Pittsburgh Courier* (Pittsburgh: University of Pittsburgh Press, 1974), 68. On pro-union sentiment among other black journalists during the period, see Emma Lou Thornbrough's study of the editor of the *New York Age*, titled *T. Thomas Fortune Militant Journalist* (Chicago: University of Chicago Press, 1972), 42–43, 81–82.

16. Spero and Harris, *Black Worker*, 246–57; Whatley, "African American Strikebreaking," 525–58; Youngner, *Industry in Art*, 82–84; Waters, "Smoky City: Part I," 419–21, and Oliver G. Waters, "Smoky City: Part II," *Colored American Magazine* 3, no. 7 (Nov. 1901), 15–17; Commission of Inquiry, *Report of the Steel Strike of 1919*, 177–78; Trotter, "Reflections on the Great Migration," 156; Dickerson, *Out of the Crucible*, 17–21 (Wright remembrance, 20); Glasco, *WPA History*, 218–19.

17. Mattie Rucker Braxton quoted in Bettie Cole, *Their Story: The History of Blacks/African Americans in Sewickley and Edgeworth* (Pittsburgh: Signal Graphics Printing, 2000), 51; Charles Franklin Lee, "Carnival of Blood? African American Workers and the Building of the Pittsburgh, Bessemer, and Lake Erie Railroad, 1897–1912," (PhD diss., Carnegie Mellon University, 2006), 37–54. For other illustrations of pre–World War I domestic and personal service work, see Gottlieb, *Making Their Own Way*, 104–10; Glasco, *WPA History*, 217–18; Bodnar, Simon, and Weber, *Lives of Their Own*, 98–101, 213; Klienberg, *Shadow of the Mills*, 24–25, 163–64; Maurine Weiner Greenwald, "Women and Class in Pittsburgh, 1850–1920," in Hays, *City at the Point*, 39–40, 54–56.

18. See Thomas S. Ewell, "The Smoky City, Part III: Social and Business Life," *Colored American Magazine* 4, no. 2 (Dec. 1901), 133–48; Laurence A. Glasco, "Taking Care of Business: The Black Entrepreneurial Elite in Turn-of-the-Century Pittsburgh," *Pittsburgh History* 78, no. 4 (Winter 1995–96): 177–82.

19. Ewell, "Smoky City, Part III," 133–48; Glasco, "Taking Care of Business," 179–82.

20. Commission of Inquiry, the Interchurch World Movement, *Report of the Steel Strike*, 177–78 (quotes); *Out of the Crucible*, 85–100; Foner, *Organized Labor*, 144–47; John Hinshaw, *Steel and Steelworkers: Race and Class Struggle in Twentieth-Century Pittsburgh* (Albany: State University of New York Press, 2002), 36–38; Gottlieb, *Making Their Own Way*, 147–64; 172–76.

21. Glasco, *WPA History*, 222–23; Laurence A. Glasco, "Double Burden: The Black Experience in Pittsburgh," in Hays, *City at the Point*, 75–88; Peter Gottlieb, "Rethinking the Great Migration," in *The Great Migration in Historical Perspective: New Dimensions of Race, Class, and Gender*, ed. Joe William Trotter Jr. (Bloomington: Indiana University Press, 1991), 68–82; Joe W. Trotter and Earl Lewis, eds., *African Americans in the Industrial Age: A Documentary History, 1915–1945* (Boston: Northeastern University Press, 1996), 1–5, 105–11; Trotter, "Reflections," 153–57; Dickerson, *Out of the Crucible*, 27–53, 119–20, 121–81; Gottlieb, *Making Their Own Way*, 108; Hinshaw, *Steel and Steelworkers*, 1–64.

22. Gottlieb, *Making Their Own Way*, 108 (quote); Dickerson, *Out of the Crucible*,

18–19, 49–50; Foner, *Organized Labor,* 133–34; Spero and Harris, *Black Worker,* 169–81, 337–38.

23. Trotter, "Reflections," 153–57 (quote, 155). For additional insight into black women migrants to Pittsburgh, see Carolyn Leonard Carson, "And the Results Showed Promise . . . Physicians, Childbirth, and Southern Black Migrant Women, 1916–1930: Pittsburgh as a Case Study," in *African Americans in Pennsylvania: Shifting Historical Perspectives,* ed. Joe William Trotter Jr. and Eric Ledell Smith, 330–62 (University Park: The Pennsylvania State University Press, 1997).

24. Trotter, "Reflections," 153–57 (quote, 154). Also see Trotter and Lewis, *African Americans in the Industrial Age,* 33–45.

25. J. Trent Alexander, "The Great Migration in Comparative Perspective: Interpreting the Urban Origins of Southern Black Migrants to Depression-Era Pittsburgh," *Social Science History* 22, no. 3 (Autumn 1998): 330–76 (quote, 367); Gottlieb, "Rethinking the Great Migration," 68–82; Glasco, *WPA History* 222–29; and cf. Darlene Clark Hine, "Black Migration to the Urban Midwest: The Gender Dimension, 1915–1945," in Trotter, *Great Migration,* 127–46.

26. Gottlieb, *Making Their Own Way,* 74–75 (quote, 122); Glasco, *WPA History,* 347 (quote).

27. Dickerson, *Out of the Crucible,* 61–62; Gottlieb, *Making Their Own Way,* 99–100.

28. Dickerson, *Out of the Crucible,* 61–62; Gottlieb, *Making Their Own Way,* 99–100.

29. For an excellent discussion of black teachers, see Ralph Proctor, "Racial Discrimination against Black Teachers and Black Professionals in the Pittsburgh Public School System 1834–1973" (PhD diss., University of Pittsburgh, 1979), especially chapters 2 and 3.

30. Trotter and Lewis, *African Americans in the Industrial Age,* 19 (quote).

31. Pittsburgh Urban League quoted in Gottlieb, *Making Their Own Way,* 103–4; Dickerson, *Out of the Crucible,* 119–20; Bruce M. Stave, *The New Deal and the Last Hurrah: Pittsburgh and Machine Politics* (Pittsburgh: University of Pittsburgh Press, 1970), 33–34; Joe Turner Darden, "The Spatial Dynamics of Residential Segregation of Afro-Americans in Pittsburgh" (PhD diss., University of Pittsburgh, 1972), 16–34.

32. Joe Turner Darden, "The Effect of World War I on Black Occupational and Residential Segregation: The Case of Pittsburgh," *Journal of Black Studies* 18, no. 3 (Mar. 1988): 297–312 (quote, 309); Gottlieb, *Making Their Own Way,* 69; Darden, "Spatial Dynamics," 16–34.

33. Margaret Spratt, "Unity within Diversity: The Issue of Race in the Pittsburgh YWCA, 1918–1946" (Pittsburgh: 1990, research paper, in authors' possession), 4; Abraham Epstein, *The Negro Migrant in Pittsburgh* (Pittsburgh: University of Pittsburgh Press, 1918), 16.

34. Bodnar, Simon, and Weber, *Lives of Their Own,* 256; Joseph H. Bunzel, "Negro Housing Needs in Pittsburgh and Allegheny County" (Pittsburgh: Pittsburgh Housing Association, 1946), 12–17; Gottlieb, *Making Their Own Way,* 66–69; Dickerson, *Out of the Crucible,* 57–58; Darden, "Effect of World War I," 309; Spratt, "Unity Within Diversity," 4; Anne Lloyd, "Pittsburgh's 1923 Zoning Ordinance," *Western Pennsylvania Historical Magazine* 57, no. 3 (July 1974): 289–305; Janet R. Daly,

"Zoning: Its Historical Context and Importance in the Development of Pittsburgh," *Western Pennsylvania Historical Magazine* 71, no. 2 (Apr. 1988): 99–125.

35. N. R. Criss quoted in P. L. Prattis, "Profiles," *Pittsburgh Courier*, 12 Jan. 1963; Proctor, "Racial Discrimination," 28–39, 45; Buni, *Robert L. Vann*, 67; Ancella Livers, "Defining Ourselves: Gender Construction and the Creation of a Black Community in Pittsburgh, 1925–55" (PhD diss., Carnegie Mellon University, 1998), 49, 119.

36. Frank Bolden quoted in Livers, "Defining Ourselves,"119.

37. Kenneth Jackson, *The Ku Klux Klan in the City, 1915–1930* (New York: Oxford University Press, 1967), 170–73; Sala Udin, interview by staff of the Center for Africanamerican Urban Studies and the Economy (CAUSE), Remembering Africanamerican Pittsburgh Oral History Project (RAP), 13 June 2007, Department of History, Carnegie Mellon University, Pittsburgh; Dickerson, *Out of the Crucible*, 63; Knights of the Ku Klux Klan Realm of Pennsylvania, Province No. 1: Official Bulletin No. 5, in Ku Klux Klan Papers, General Files, 1923–1940, Boxes 3–4, Pennsylvania State Archives, Harrisburg.

38. *Duquesne Times* quoted in Dickerson, *Out of the Crucible*, 63; Udin, interview, CAUSE, RAP.

39. Livers, "Defining Ourselves" 32–33 (quote); Dickerson, *Out of the Crucible*, 63.

40. Glasco, *WPA History*, 209–10.

41. Glasco, *WPA History*, 337 (quote); Udin, interview, CAUSE, RAP.

42. Glasco, *WPA History*, 210; Maurice Moss, executive secretary, Urban League of Pittsburgh, to the ULP's local advisory council, 18 Mar. 1937, Part I: D, Series 4, Box 34, National Urban League Papers, Library of Congress, Washington DC (hereinafter, NUL Papers refers to this part, series, and box number within the National Urban League collection).

43. All quotes in this paragraph: Doug Bolin, Christopher Moore, and Nancy Levin, *Wylie Avenue Days: Pittsburgh's Hill District* (Pittsburgh: QED Communications, Inc., 1991), film. On notion of segregation and congregation, see Lewis, *In Their Own Interests*, 89–109.

44. Dennis C. Dickerson, "The Black Church in Industrializing Western Pennsylvania, 1870–1950" in Trotter and Smith, *African Americans in Pennsylvania*, 388–402; Glasco, *WPA History*, 277; for information on Pittsburgh's Storefront Church of God in Christ, see Livers, "Defining Ourselves," 123.

45. Sylviane A. Diouf, *Servants of Allah: African Americans Enslaved in the Americas* (New York: New York University Press 1998), 205–7; Aminah Beverly McCloud, *African American Islam* (New York: Routledge, 1995), 10–18; Laurence Glasco, "The Muslim Community of Pittsburgh," *Pittsburgh History* (Winter 1995–1996), 183–85.

46. Ira DeAugustine Reid quoted in Glasco, *WPA History*, 277; Dickerson, *Out of the Crucible*, 126–28; Bodnar, Simon, and Weber, *Lives of Their Own*, 217; Glasco, "Double Burden," 82; Dickerson, "Black Church in Industrializing Western Pennsylvania," 197–205; Gottlieb, *Making Their Own Way*, 197–205; Livers, "Defining Ourselves," 54.

47. Glasco, *WPA History*, 230–50, 276–79, 280–92, (quote, 277); Joe William Trotter Jr., *River Jordan: African American Urban Life in the Ohio Valley* (Lexington: University Press of Kentucky, 1998), 80–92; Gottlieb, *Making Their Own Way*, 183–215.

48. Glasco, *WPA History*, 248–49 (quote); Buni, *Robert L. Vann*, 42–43; Walker Daniel, *Black Journals of the United States* (Westport, CT: Greenwood Press, 1982), 42–54; Roland E. Wolseley, *The Black Press U.S.A.* (Ames: The Iowa State University Press, 1990), 68–69, 104–5.

49. Livers, "Defining Ourselves," 55–57, 70.

50. Harold C. Tinker Sr. quoted in Livers, "Defining Ourselves," 48–49; Robert Lewis Ruck, *Sandlot Seasons: Sport in Black Pittsburgh* (Urbana: University of Illinois Press, 1993), 4–5, and chaps. 4 and 5; Dickerson, *Out of the Crucible*, 74–75.

51. Quotes in Bolin, Moore, and Levin, *Wylie Avenue Days*; Ruck, *Sandlot Seasons* 4–5, and chaps. 4 and 5; Dickerson, *Out of the Crucible*, 74–75.

52. Judge Warren Watson quoted in Jennifer I. Schuitema, "African American Musician and the Pittsburgh Music Scene, 1940–1960" (seminar paper, CAUSE Oral History Project, Department of History, Carnegie Mellon University, Spring 2006), 56; Bolin, Moore, and Levin, *Wylie Avenue Days*; Judge Warren Watson, interview by Jennifer I. Schuitema for CAUSE, RAP, 6 May 2007.

53. Gottlieb, *Making Their Own Way*, 52–53, 107, 192–97; Dickerson, *Out of the Crucible*, 43–48, 101–18; and Glasco, *WPA History*, 411–24; Buni, *Robert L. Vann*, 92–93.

54. Buni, *Robert L. Vann*, 127–28. See also Stave, *New Deal*, 42–52, 59–83, 89–90; affidavit of Rollo Turner, 1–12, and affidavit of C. B. "Knowledge" Clark, 1–13, in *Metropolitan Pittsburgh Crusade for Voters vs. City of Pittsburgh, et al.*, case no. 86–173, U.S. District Court for the Western District of Pennsylvania, 1986, Group V, Box 2215, Folder 3, NAACP Papers, Library of Congress, Washington DC.

55. Dickerson, *Out of the Crucible*, 76–79 (quote, 78); Henry A. Schooley, "A Case Study of the Pittsburgh Branch of the National Association for the Advancement of Colored People" (master's thesis, University of Pittsburgh, 1952), 7–15, Group II, Box 2, Folder 4, NAACP Papers, Library of Congress, Washington DC; "Pittsburgh Branch, Pittsburgh, Pennsylvania Branch, Organized 1914," Group II, Box C-171, Folder 2, NAACP Papers, Library of Congress, Washington DC.

56. Dickerson, 104–5, 115–17, 190–97; Ruth L. Stevenson, "The Pittsburgh Urban League" (master's thesis, University of Pittsburgh, 1936); Antoinette H. Westmoreland, "A Study of Requests for Specialized Services Directed to the Urban League of Pittsburgh" (master's thesis, University of Pittsburgh, 1938); Edmunds and Bush, *Daybreakers*, 56–79; "The Fifteenth Year, 1918–1932: Annual Report of the Urban League of Pittsburgh," Part I: N, Series 13, Box 22, National Urban League Papers, Library of Congress, Washington DC.

57. Edna McKenzie, "Pittsburgh's Daisy Lampkin: A Life of Love and Service," *Pennsylvania Heritage* 9, no. 3 (Summer 1983): 9–12 (quote, 10); Livers, "Defining Ourselves," 127–28.

58. Gottlieb, *Making Their Own Way*, 187–210.

59. Gottlieb, *Making Their Own Way*, 200–3; Livers, "Defining Ourselves," 50.

60. Steve Nelson, Jame R. Barrett, and Rob Ruck, Steve Nelson, *American Radical* (Pittsburgh: University of Pittsburgh Press, 1981), 25–26, 87, 126–27; "Communist Candidate Here 28th: William Z. Foster to Speak in Labor Lyceum on Miller Street," *Pittsburgh Courier*, 27 Oct. 1928.

61. "UNIA meeting in Pittsburgh," *Negro World*, 26 Sept. 1919, and "Pittsburgh's

Great Enthusiasm," *Negro World*, 3 July 1920, both reprinted in *The Marcus Garvey and Universal Negro Improvement Papers*, vol. II, ed. Robert Hill (Berkeley: University of California Press, 1983), 27–29, 397–98.

62. Dickerson, *Out of the Crucible*, 79–83 (quote, 83); Hill, *Marcus Garvey*, 27–29, 397–98, 399–402; Tony Martin, *Race First: The Ideological and Organizational Struggles of Marcus Garvey and the Universal Negro Improvement Association* (Dover, MA: Majority Press, 1976), 22–40; Judith Stein, *The World of Marcus Garvey: Race and Class in Modern Society* (Baton Rouge: Louisiana State University Press, 1986), 24–37.

63. Randall K. Burkett, *Black Redemption: Churchmen Speak for the Garvey Movement* (Philadelphia: Temple University Press, 1978), 113–20 (quote, 117).

64. Dickerson, *Out of the Crucible*, 80–81 (quote); Federal Bureau of Investigation Reports, Pittsburgh, 28 June 1920, in Hill, *Marcus Garvey*, 399–403.

65. Gottlieb, *Making Their Own Way*, 193–95; Arthur J. Edmunds and Esther Bush, *Daybreakers: The Story of the Urban League of Pittsburgh, The First Sixty-Five Years* (Urban League of Pittsburgh, 1983), 13–55; Gottlieb, *Lives of Their Own*, 52, 107, 194–95; "Wylie Avenue," *Pittsburgh Courier*, 17 June 1933.

66. Livers, "Defining Ourselves," 65–67, 129–30.

67. Foner, *Organized Labor*, 142; Report of the Industrial Relations Department, Urban League of Pittsburgh (ULP), Winter 1933, NUL Papers.

68. Maurice Moss, "The Negro in Pittsburgh's Industries," *Opportunity—Journal of Negro Life* 13, no. 2 (Feb. 1935): 40–42, 59; Edmunds and Bush, *Daybreakers*, 87–94; Gottlieb, *Making Their Own Way*, 103–6; Spratt, "Unity within Diversity," 8; Livers, "Defining Ourselves," 85–86, 100; Dickerson, *Out of the Crucible*, 119–24; Stave, *New Deal*, 33–34.

69. E. Maurice Moss, executive secretary, Urban League of Pittsburgh, to T. Arnold Hill at the National Urban League, 1 Mar. 1939, NUL Papers; E. Maurice Moss executive secretary, Urban League of Pittsburgh, to National Urban League Advisory Council Members, 18 Mar 1937, NUL Papers; Thelma Lovette Sr., interview by staff of CAUSE, RAP, 2 July 2007. See also Celeste Williams, interview by staff of CAUSE, RAP, Summer 2007.

70. Leon Keyserling quoted in Leslie H. Fishel, "The Negro in the New Deal," in *The Negro in Depression and War: Prelude to Revolution, 1930–1945*, ed. Bernard Sternsher (Chicago: Quadrangle Books, 1969), 7–28; Trotter, *River Jordan*, 122–41 (quote, 127); Buni, *Robert L. Vann*, 174–202, 264–324; Harvard Sitkoff, *A New Deal for Blacks: The Emergence of Civil Rights as a National Issue: The Depression Decade* (New York: Oxford University Press, 1978), 52, 54–55; Raymond Wolters, *Negroes and the Great Depression: The Problem of Economic Recovery* (Westport, CT: Greenwood Publishing Company, 1970), 83–213.

71. Reginald A. Johnson, secretary, Industrial Relations Department, ULP, to T. Arnold Hill, NUL, 20 Oct. 1938, NUL Papers; Report of the Department of Industrial Relations, Jan. and Feb. 1933, NUL Papers.

72. "Phil Murray Urges Negro Workers to Join Great Steel Industry Union," *Pittsburgh Courier*, 13 Feb. 1937. Organized by Ben Careathers, the North Side conference included representatives from the Urban League of Pittsburgh, the *Pittsburgh Courier*, the National Association of Colored Women, and Baptist and AME churches.

73. Steve Nelson quoted in Steve Nelson, James R. Barrett, and Rob Ruck, *Steve Nelson, American Radical* (Pittsburgh: University of Pittsburgh Press, 1992), 25; Philip Bonosky, "The Story of Ben Careathers," *Masses and Mainstream*, 6 July 1953, 34–44, reprinted in *The Black Worker: From the Founding of the CIO to the AFL-CIO Merger 1936–1955*, vol. II, ed. Philip S. Foner and Ronald L. Lewis (Philadelphia: Temple University Press, 1983), 46–48; Horace R. Cayton and George S. Mitchell, *Black Workers and the New Unions* (Chapel Hill: The University of North Carolina Press, 1939), 111–22, 190–224; Dickerson, *Out of the Crucible*, 131, 139–49; Foner, *Organized Labor*, 219–37; Wolters, *Negroes and the Great Depression*, 83–229; Peter Gottlieb, "Black Miners and the 1925–28 Bituminous Coal Strike: The Colored Committee of Non-Union Miners, Montour Mine No. 1, Pittsburgh," *Labor History* 28, no. 2 (Spring 1987): 233–41.

74. "Careathers Tells Why He Became Communist Voice," *Pittsburgh Courier*, 23 May 1953.

75. Constance A. Cunningham, "Homer S. Brown: First Black Political Leader in Pittsburgh," *Journal of Negro History* 66, no. 4 (Winter 1981–82), 304–17; John Baxter Streater Jr., "The National Negro Congress, 1936–1947" (PhD diss., University of Cincinnati, 1981); Adam Lapin, "Negro America Acts to Build Steel Unions," *Daily Worker*, 8 Feb. 1937, reprinted in Foner and Lewis, *Black Worker*, 46–48; "Communist Candidate Here 28th: William Z. Foster to Speak in Labor Lyceum on Miller Street," *Pittsburgh Courier*, 27 Oct. 1928; Trotter, *River Jordan*, 134–39, 146.

76. Buni, *Robert L. Vann*, 193–94 (quote), 356–57n75; affidavit of Rollo Turner," *Metropolitan Pittsburgh Crusade*, 1–12 (quote, 8).

77. "Two Local Organizations Announce Platforms," *Pittsburgh Courier*, 1 Aug. 1931.

78. Buni, *Robert L. Vann*, 125–27; Glasco, *WPA History*, 85; Editorial, *Pittsburgh Courier*, 11 Sept. 1932; Cunningham, "Homer S. Brown," 304–17; Livers, "Defining Ourselves," 114–22.

79. Glasco, *WPA History*, 211–12 (quotes); Schooley, "Case Study," 11–12.

80. Questioning of Marcus Aaron, president of the Pittsburgh Board of Education, by Representative Homer S. Brown—1 May 1937, in P. L. Prattis, "Profiles etc.," *Pittsburgh Courier*, 12 Jan. 1963; Questioning of Marcus Aaron by Representative Alfred E. Tronzo, in P. L. Prattis. "Profiles etc.," *Pittsburgh Courier*, 19 Jan. 1963.

81. On NEA Resolution, see E. Maurice Moss, executive secretary, Urban League of Pittsburgh, to National Urban League Advisory Council Members, 18 Mar 1937, NUL Papers; "School Board Guilty of Flagrant Discrimination," *Pittsburgh Courier*, 5 June 1937; Cunningham, "Homer S. Brown," 304–17; Livers, "Defining Ourselves," 98, 114–22; Proctor, "Racial Discrimination," 53–62 (quote, 62); on exclusion of black teachers from Pittsburgh schools some thirty years earlier, see P. L. Prattis, "Profiles etc.: For Teachers' Scrapbooks," *Pittsburgh Courier*, 22 Dec. 1962. The Prattis article also provides an excellent account of Richard F. Jones's questioning of N. R. Criss, school solicitor, about the exclusion of black teachers.

82. Livers, "Defining Ourselves," 132–33; Paul D. Moreno, *From Direct Action to Affirmative Action: Fair Employment Law and Policy in America, 1933–1972* (Baton Rouge: Louisiana State University Press, 1997), 4–5, 30–54; Naison, *Communists in Harlem*, 50–51, 100; Report of the Department of Industrial Relations, NUL Papers.

83. Cunningham, "Homer S. Brown," 304–17; Livers, "Defining Ourselves," 98, 114–22; Stave, *New Deal*, 59–61; Buni, *Robert L. Vann*, 174–205, 206–7, 208–21, 264–98; John B. Kirby, *Black Americans in the Roosevelt Era: Liberalism and Race* (Knoxville: University of Tennessee Press, 1980), 106–51; Sitkoff, *New Deal*, 77–79; "Diversified Jobs Given Negroes in Housing Program," *Pittsburgh Courier*, 21 Sept. 1940.

84. Richard M. Dalfiume, "The Forgotten Years of the Negro Revolution," in Sternsher, *Negro in Depression*, 298–316; Herbert Garfinkel, *When Negroes March: The March on Washington Movement in the Organizational Politics for FEPC* (Glencoe, IL: Free Press, 1959), 37–60; Andrew E. Kersten, *Race, Jobs, and the War: The FEPC in the Midwest, 1941–1946* (Urbana: University of Illinois Press, 2000), 126–40; Buni, *Robert L. Vann*, 325.

85. "Case History of Fight for Negro Street Car Operators," *Pittsburgh Courier*, 7 Apr. 1945. This article provides a digest of the struggle for black streetcar conductors between November 1941 and February 1945.

86. Veteran quoted in Ray Henderson and Tony Buba, *Struggles in Steel: The Fight for Equal Opportunity* (San Francisco: California Newsreel, 1996), film; "They Fight for Democracy" (editorial), *Homestead Daily Messenger*, 28 Feb. 1944; Letter to the editor, *Homestead Daily Messenger*, 8 Mar. 1944; Trotter and Lewis, *African Americans in the Industrial Age*, 290–95.

87. Proprietors quoted in Glasco, *WPA History*, 212; Buni, *Robert L. Vann*, 325; Dalfiume, "Forgotten Years," 298–316; Martha E. Foy, "The Negro in the Courts: A Study in Race Relations" (PhD diss., University of Pittsburgh, 1953), 166–67.

88. Glasco, *WPA History*, 212–14, 353.

89. Bodnar, Simon, and Weber, *Lives of Their Own*, 225–27.

90. Lori Cole, "Voices and Choices: Race, Class, and Identity, Homestead, Pennsylvania, 1941–1945" (PhD diss., Carnegie Mellon University, 1994), 46–76.

91. Percentage of African Americans in federally funded housing is based on data from Bureau of Social Research, *Mobility of Public Housing Residents* (Pittsburgh: Federation of Social Agencies of Pittsburgh and Allegheny County, 1946), 7; see also Livers, "Defining Ourselves," chap. 2.

92. Proctor, "Racial Discrimination," 57–58, 81–82 (quotes); Commonwealth of Pennsylvania, *Final Report of the Pennsylvania State Temporary Commission on the Conditions of the Urban Colored Population*, 408–9.

93. Gerald Fox, interview by Kevin Brown for CAUSE, RAP, 5 July 2007.

94. Commonwealth of Pennsylvania, *Final Report of the Pennsylvania State Temporary Commission on the Conditions of the Urban Colored Population* (Harrisburg: The Pennsylvania General Assembly, Jan. 1943), 467–544; Dolores Allen, typist and filing clerk, Pennsylvania Bell Telephone Company, Case #3-BR-1973; Werner L. Johnson, machine operator trainee, Westinghouse Air Brake Company, Case #3-BR-1990; Mrs. Martha Tate, laborer in the machine shop, Case #3-BR-1955, all in case records of the Committee on Fair Employment Practice, Record Group #228, Region III, National Archives and Records Administration, Philadelphia (hereinafter, FEPC Papers refers to this record group and region number in FEPC records).

95. Pittsburgh Urban League quoted in Dickerson, *Out of the Crucible*, 159–60;

Merl E. Reed, *Seedtime for the Modern Civil Rights Movement: The President's Committee on Fair Employment Practice, 1941–1946* (Baton Rouge: Louisiana State University Press, 1991), 117–204, 219–20; Foner, *Organized Labor*, 242–43.

96. Charles A. Taylor, complaint against the United Bronze Castings Company, 16 May 1945, FEPC Papers; Dickerson, *Out of the Crucible*, 172.

97. "Case History of Fight," *Pittsburgh Courier*, 7 Apr. 1945.

98. Letter from Mrs. William J. Scott to Franklin Delano Roosevelt, 22 Apr. 1944, quoted in Dickerson, *Out of the Crucible*, 161–62.

99. Letter from George E. Denmar, secretary of the Urban League of Pittsburgh, to P. T. Fagan, 27 Oct. 1942, in FEPC Papers, reprinted in Trotter and Lewis, *African Americans in the Industrial Age*, 260–63.

100. Employment Petition to the American Bridge Company, signed by forty-one black men, 3 May 1943, in American Bridge Company file, FEPC Papers; Trotter and Lewis, *African Americans in the Industrial Age*, 261–62. Black women who later gained jobs with the company also complained of unequal treatment, including bathroom breaks: "On several occasions, I was the only Negro in a crew of white girls—I was checked very closely as to my trips away from the job on such occasions and yet many of them [white women] left the job oftener and stayed longer than I." See Elizabeth Davis, complaint against the American Bridge Company, 10 Oct. 1944, Case #3-BR-827, FEPC Papers.

101. Sitkoff, *New Deal*, 314–15 (quotes); Jervis Anderson, *A Philip Randolph: A Biographical Portrait* (1972; repr., Berkeley: University of California Press, 1986); 229–73; William H. Harris, *Keeping the Faith: A Philip Randolph, Milton P. Webster, and the Brotherhood of Sleeping Car Porters, 1925–37* (Urbana: University of Illinois Press, 1977), 217–28; Merl E. Reed, "Black Workers, Defense Industries, and Federal Agencies in Pennsylvania, 1941–1945," *Labor History* 27, no. 3 (Summer 1986): 356–84, reprinted in Trotter and Smith, *African Americans in Pennsylvania*, 1–17; Foner, *Organized Labor*, 239–42; Garfinkel, *When Negroes March*, 37–60.

102. The *Black Worker* quoted in A. Philip Randolph, "March for a Fair Share: The March on Washington Movement, 1941," reprinted in *Afro-American History: Primary Sources*, ed. Thomas R. Frazier (Chicago: The Dorsey Press, 1988), 291–98 (quote, 294); Harris, *Keeping the Faith*, 40, 121–22, and 217–28; A. Philip Randolph, "Why Should We March," *Survey Graphic* 31 (Nov. 1942), reprinted in Foner and Lewis, *Black Worker*, 251–52.

103. Anderson, *A. Philip Randolph*, 256–58.

104. Dickerson, *Out of the Crucible*, 146, 154–56; "FEPC Opens Office Here," *Pittsburgh Courier*, 3 Feb. 1945; "Seeking Permanent Anti-Bias Law," *Pittsburgh Courier*, 20 Jan. 1945; FEPC examiner to James Fleming, 13 Mar. 1944; "President's Committee on Fair Employment Practice: Final Disposition Report," 1 Aug. 1945, both in FEPC Papers.

105. Foner, *Organized Labor* (quotes, 256–57); Harris, *Harder We Run*, 113–22; Foner and Lewis, *Black Worker*, 251–300.

106. Edward D. Porter, Pittsburgh Interracial Action Council, to Ella J. Baker, 2 Apr. 1945, Group II, Box C-171, Folder 2, NAACP Papers, Library of Congress, Washington DC; "Local Race Areas Would Be Targets for Hostile Armies: Defense Council Appeals for Race Co-Operation Here," *Pittsburgh Courier*, 13 Dec. 1941.

107. John L. Clark, "Political Power at Stake in Tuesday's Primary Election," *Pittsburgh Courier*, 16 June 1945 (quotes); Weber, *Don't Call Me Boss*, 278–82. Cf. "Interracial Plan Submitted to Detroit Mayor: 'Live Together in Peace,' Slogan for Detroit Club Plan," *Pittsburgh Courier*, 10 July 1943.

108. "Budget Cut Kills FEPC Here; Closes 5 Offices; Drops 66 Workers," *Pittsburgh Courier*, 4 Aug. 1945; "Fear New Wave of Job Bias Here: Powerless USES and Lack of FEPC 'Protects' Firms," *Pittsburgh Courier*, 15 Sept. 1945; "Local FEPC Law Urged," *Pittsburgh Courier*, 24 Nov. 1945.

109. Sophia B. Nelson, member, Pittsburgh NAACP, to Donald Jones, national headquarters, 29 Mar. 1945, Group II, Box C-171, Folder 2, NAACP Papers, Library of Congress, Washington DC; Edward D. Porter to Ella J. Baker, 2 Apr. 1945, Group II, Box C-171, Folder 2, NAACP Papers, Library of Congress, Washington DC.

110. Herbert Hill, *Black Labor and the American Legal System: Race, Work, and the Law* (Madison: University of Wisconsin, 1985), 379–80; Harris, *Harder We Run*, 123–46; Foner, *Organized Labor*, 274–331; Nelson, *Steve Nelson*, 298–340; Garfinkel, *When Negroes March*, 15–96; Reed, "Black Workers," 356–84; Kersten, *Race, Jobs*, 126–40.

Chapter 2: New Migrations, Renaissance I, and the Challenge to Jim Crow

1. On postwar African American urban life elsewhere in the urban North and West, see Clarence Lange, *Grassroots at the Gateway: Class Politics and Black Freedom Struggle in St. Louis, 1936–75* (Ann Arbor: University of Michigan Press, 2009); Thomas Sugrue, *Sweetland of Liberty: The Forgotten Struggle for Civil Rights in the North* (New York: Random House, 2008); Matthew Countryman, *Up South: Civil Rights and Black Power in Philadelphia* (Philadelphia: University of Pennsylvania Press, 2006); Rhonda Williams, *The Politics of Public Housing: Black Women's Struggles against Urban Inequality* (New York: Oxford University Press, 2004); Wendell Pritchett, *Brownsville, Brooklyn: Blacks, Jews, and the Changing Face of the Ghetto* (Chicago: The University of Chicago Press, 2002); Robert O. Self, *American Babylon: Race and the Struggle for Postwar Oakland* (Princeton: Princeton University Press, 2003); Joshua Sides, *L.A. City Limits: African American Los Angeles from the Great Depression to the Present* (Berkeley: University of California Press, 2003); and Matthew Whitaker, *Race Work: The Rise of Civil Rights in the Urban West* (Lincoln: University of Nebraska Press, 2005). On the post–World War II urban South, see Laurie B. Green, *Battling the Plantation Mentality: Memphis and the Black Freedom Struggle* (Chapel Hill: University of North Carolina Press, 2007).

2. John Hoerr, *And the Wolf Finally Came: The Decline of the American Steel Industry* (Pittsburgh: University of Pittsburgh Press, 1988), 93–101; John Hinshaw, *Steel and Steelworkers: Race and Class Struggle in Twentieth-Century Pittsburgh* (Albany: State University of New York Press, 2002), 108–20, 173–82; Roy Lubove, *Twentieth-Century Pittsburgh: Government, Business, and Environmental Change*, vol. 1 (Pittsburgh: University of Pittsburgh Press, 1969), 107–76, 179–278; Roy Lubove, ed., *Pittsburgh: Documentary History* (New York: Franklin Watts/New Viewpoints, 1976), 177–278; Samuel Hays, ed., *City at the Point: Essay on the Social History of Pittsburgh* (Pitts-

burgh: University of Pittsburgh Press, 1989), especially essays by Nora Faires, Richard Oestricher, Edward Muller, and Joel Tarr, respectively, 17–24, 139–43, 204–6, 249–53.

3. Judith Modell and Charlie Brodsky, ed., *A Town Without Steel: Envisioning Homestead* (Pittsburgh: University of Pittsburgh Press, 1998); John Hinshaw and Judith Modell, "Perceiving Racism: Homestead from Depression to Deindustrialization," *Pennsylvania History* 63, no. 1 (Winter 1996): 17–52; Action Housing, "Urban Renewal Impact Study" (Pittsburgh, 1963), quoted in "Fight for Urban Survival," *Pittsburgh Press*, 24 June 1963, section 2.

4. For insight into these processes, see Bennett Harrison, *The Deindustrialization of America: Plant Closings, Community Abandonment, and the Dismantling of Basic Industry* (New York: Basic Books, 1982), 42–46, 141–47; Bennett Harrison and Barry Bluestone, *The Great U-Turn: Corporate Restructuring and the Polarizing of America* (New York: Basic Books, Inc., 1988), 7–11; Judith Stein, *Running Steel, Running America: Race, Economic Policy, and the Decline of Liberalism* (Chapel Hill: University of North Carolina Press, 1998), 18–22, 24–25; Kenneth Warren, *The American Steel Industry, 1850–1970: A Geographical Interpretation* (Oxford: Clarendon Press, 1973), 254–55; 285–91; David B. Houston, "A Brief History of the Process of Capital Accumulation in Pittsburgh: A Marxist Interpretation," in *Pittsburgh-Sheffield: Sister Cities*, ed. Joel Tarr (Pittsburgh: Carnegie Mellon University Press, 1986), 29–69.

5. Harrison, *Deindustrialization*, 3–34; Harrison and Bluestone, *Great U-Turn*, 3–27; Hoerr, *Wolf*, 93–101; Hinshaw, *Steel and Steelworkers*, 108–20, 173–82; Kurtiak, "Urban Restructuring," 23; Houston, "Brief History," 29–69; Warren, *American Steel Industry*, 249–300.

6. John Bauman and Edward K. Muller, *Before Renaissance: Planning in Pittsburgh, 1889–1943* (Pittsburgh: University of Pittsburgh Press, 2006), 227–77; Urban Redevelopment Authority, "Urban Renewal in Pittsburgh" (Pittsburgh, 1962); Urban Redevelopment Authority, "A Changing City" (Pittsburgh, 1965); Lubove, *Twentieth-Century Pittsburgh*, 1:106–76, especially, 130–32, 163–65, 171–76 (use of term "Golden Triangle," 103, 119); Lubove, *Twentieth Century-Pittsburgh*, 2:vii–x, 2:1–23.

7. Department of City Planning, "Census of Population and Housing Report no. 3, Whole City . . ." in *Population, Social, Economic and Housing Data by Neighborhood, 1940 to 1990* (Pittsburgh, 1990). For the notion of a "Second Great Migration," see James N. Gregory, "The Second Great Migration: A Historical Overview," in *African American Urban History Since World War*, ed. Kenneth L. Kusmer and Joe W. Trotter (Chicago: University of Chicago Press, 2009), 19–38; and Wallace D. Best, *Passionately Human, No Less Divine: Religion and Culture in Black Chicago, 1915–1952* (Princeton: Princeton University Press, 2005).

8. Ervin Dyer, "Revisiting the Great Migration: Senior Citizens Remember the Mass Exodus of Southern Blacks to Northern Cities in the Early to Mid-Twentieth Century," *Pittsburgh Post-Gazette*, 25 Feb. 2001.

9. Betty J. Tillman, interview by Shawn Alfonso Wells for Center for African American Urban Studies and the Economy (CAUSE), Remembering Africanamerican Pittsburgh Oral History Project (RAP), 23 Aug. 2007, Department of History, Carnegie Mellon University, Pittsburgh.

10. Senator John Heinz History Center, *An Interview with Nate Smith: The Tran-*

scription of an Oral History (Pittsburgh: Historical Society of Western Pennsylvania Oral History Service, published by Mechling Bookbindery, Chicora, PA, ca. 2002), 17.

11. Dennis C. Dickerson, *Out of the Crucible: Black Steelworkers in Western Pennsylvania, 1875–1980* (New York: State University of New York Press, 1986), 194–98 (quote, 194).

12. Quotes from Ray Henderson and Tony Buba, *Struggles in Steel: The Fight for Equal Opportunity* (San Francisco: California Newsreel, 1996), film; and Doug Bolin, Christopher Moore, and Nancy Levin, *Wylie Avenue Days: Pittsburgh's Hill District* (Pittsburgh: QED Communications, Inc. 1991), film. See also Hinshaw, *Steel and Steelworkers*, 200–203; John Bodnar, Roger Simon, and Michael Weber, *Lives of Their Own: Blacks, Italians, and Poles in Pittsburgh, 1900–1960* (Urbana: University of Illinois Press, 1982), 225. For statistics on African American occupations, see this volume's appendix, tables 9–18.

13. Dickerson, *Out of the Crucible*, 179–80, 186–88; Hinshaw, *Steel and Steelworkers*, 200–203.

14. Dickerson, *Out of the Crucible*, 177, 216–17, 241–42, 245; Hinshaw, *Steel and Steelworkers*, 134–39, 200–29; Bodnar, Simon, and Weber, *Lives of Their Own*, 247–54; Laurence Glasco, "Double Burden: The Black Experience in Pittsburgh," in *City at the Point: Essays on the Social History of Pittsburgh*, ed. Samuel P. Hays (Pittsburgh: University of Pittsburgh Press, 1989), 88–97; Joe Turner Darden, "The Spatial Dynamics of Residential Segregation of Afro-Americans in Pittsburgh" (PhD diss., University of Pittsburgh, 1972), 22–41; Henderson and Buba, *Struggles in Steel*; Bolin, Moore, and Levin, *Wylie Avenue Days*.

15. Henderson and Buba, *Struggles in Steel*.

16. Dickerson, *Out of the Crucible*, 208–11.

17. Henderson and Buba, *Struggles in Steel*; Dickerson, *Out of the Crucible*, 121.

18. William Wayte quoted in Bolin, Moore, and Levin, *Wylie Avenue Days*; Ernestine Holt, "Status of Steelworkers Presents Sorry Picture: Negroes Refused Supervisory Jobs," *Pittsburgh Courier*, 24 Aug. 1946; Dickerson, *Out of the Crucible*, 179–80; Hinshaw, *Steel and Steelworkers*, 201–2; Henderson and Buba, *Struggles in Steel*.

19. "Room service" quote from Henderson and Buba, *Struggles in Steel*.

20. Hinshaw, *Steel and Steelworkers*, 126–30, 200–203; Dickerson, *Out of the Crucible*, 179–80, 186–88, 230–31; Herbert Hill, "Race and the Steelworkers Union: White Privilege and Black Struggle," *New Politics* 8, no. 4 (Winter 2002): 1–58.

21. Dickerson, *Out of the Crucible* (quotes, 191, 193–94, 209, 231); Holt, "Status of Steelworkers Presents Sorry Picture."

22. F. Ray Marshall and Vernon M. Briggs Jr., *The Negro and Apprenticeship* (Baltimore: The Johns Hopkins University Press, 1967), 113–20; Irwin Dubinsky, *Reform in Trade Union Discrimination in the Construction Industry: Operation Dig and Its Legacy* (New York: Praeger Books, 1973), 3–50.

23. Democratic chairman of the twelfth ward quoted in George E. Barbour. "City, Union 'Pass Buck' on Negro Electrician," *Pittsburgh Courier*, 25 Nov. 1961; Marshall and Briggs, *Negro and Apprenticeship*, 124–25; Dubinsky, *Reform in Trade Union Discrimination in the Construction Industry*, 3–50; Heinz History Center, *Interview with Nate Smith*, 10.

24. Arthur J. Edmunds and Esther Bush, *Daybreakers: The Story of the Urban League of Pittsburgh* (1983; reprt. and rev., Pittsburgh: Urban League of Pittsburgh, 1999), 113–27, 138–51; Holland F. Kelley, "Spur Dept. Store Fight," *Pittsburgh Courier*, 9 Nov. 1946; "Store Heads Still Dodge Race Issue," *Pittsburgh Courier*, 16 Nov. 1946.

25. Quotes from Dorothy Anderson, "Ban Race Nurses: Montefiore Says 'No' to Local Girl," *Pittsburgh Courier*, 1 June 1946. See also "Nurses Pledge Cooperation in Hospital Fight," *Pittsburgh Courier*, 1 June 1946; "Montefiore May Change Policy," *Pittsburgh Courier*, 8 June 1946; "Nurses Pledge Cooperation in Hospital Fight," *Pittsburgh Courier* 1 June 1946; "No Jim Crow for Pitt's New Nurses School," *Pittsburgh Courier*, 29 Nov. 1945.

26. Dan Fitzpatrick, "Rate of Pittsburgh Women Working Evens Up: Region Had Long Trailed Nation," *Pittsburgh Post-Gazette*, 12 Aug. 2003; for national labor force participation rates, see Phyllis A. Wallace, *Black Women in the Labor Force* (Cambridge, MA: MIT Press, 1980), 1–9; for Pittsburgh levels, see Maurine Greenwald, "Women and Class in Pittsburgh, 1850–1920," in Hays, *City at the Point*, 36–37.

27. David E. Ellis, interview by Shawn Alfonso Wells for CAUSE, RAP, 16 Aug. 2007.

28. Bodnar, Simon, and Weber, *Lives of Their Own*, 206–61 (quote, 254); Ralph Brem, "More Negro Leaders Needed to Equalize Housing and Jobs" *Pittsburgh Press*, 24 June 1963; Dickerson, *Out of the* Crucible, 177–78.

29. Lubove, *Twentieth-Century Pittsburgh*, 1:106–41 (for use of the term "reverse welfare state," see 1:106, 1:139).

30. Urban Redevelopment Authority, "Urban Renewal in Pittsburgh" (Pittsburgh: Urban Redevelopment Authority, 1 May 1962); Urban Redevelopment Authority, "The Changing City" (Pittsburgh: Urban Redevelopment Authority, 1969); Urban Redevelopment Authority, "A Changing City" (Pittsburgh: Urban Redevelopment Authority, 1965), all located at Hillman Library, University of Pittsburgh.

31. Lubove, *Twentieth-Century Pittsburgh*, 1:128–29; Kent M. James, "Public Policy and the Postwar Suburbanization of Pittsburgh, 1945–1990" (PhD diss., Carnegie Mellon University, 2005), 697–780; Bodnar, Simon, and Weber, *Lives of Their Own*, 251–52.

32. *Pittsburgh Courier*, 26 Jan. 1946, quoted in Dickerson, *Out of the Crucible*, 177–78.

33. Dickerson, *Out of the Crucible*, 202 (quote); Hinshaw, *Steel and Steelworkers*, 144.

34. Dickerson, *Out of the Crucible*, 179.

35. "Cause Seen for Concern at J&L," *Pittsburgh Courier*, 3 Aug. 1946.

36. Philip S. Foner, *Organized Labor and the Black Worker, 1619–1973* (New York: Praeger, 1974), 296–301.

37. "Jury Finds Communist Defendants Guilty!" *Pittsburgh Courier*, 22 Aug. 1953; "'Pigeon' Cvetic Names Careathers and Wright," *Pittsburgh Courier*, 25 Feb. 1950; "Jury Selection Under Fire at Red Trial," *Pittsburgh Courier*, 21 Mar. 1953; Edna Chappell, "Seeking Permanent Anti-Bias Job Law," *Pittsburgh Courier*, 20 Jan. 1945; Ted Princiotto, "Alex Wright Reveals Secret Cabal of Local Red Plotters," *Pittsburgh Courier*, 24 Dec. 1955; Nelson, Barrett, and Ruck, *Steve Nelson, American Radical*, 298–379.

38. Lubove, *Twentieth-Century Pittsburgh*, 1:165–67; Pittsburgh City Planning Department. "The City Moves Forward: A Progress Report on Urban Renewal and Redevelopment Areas." Pittsburgh: Pittsburgh City Planning Department, n.d., 4, 7; Health and Welfare Association of Allegheny County (HWAAC), "Staff Proposal on the Study of a Selected Social Problem for the Community Renewal Program" (Pittsburgh: HWAAC, Feb. 1964); Pittsburgh City Planning Department, "A Report on Social Problems in Urban Renewal" (Pittsburgh: Community Renewal Program, 1965); Herbert A. Auerbach, "The Status of Housing of Negroes in Pittsburgh" (Pittsburgh: City of Pittsburgh Commission on Human Relations, Nov. 1958), 1–26; Drexler, "Political Economy," 97–99; Housing Authority of the City of Pittsburgh (HACP), "A Report to the People: Public Housing in Pittsburgh, 1938–1953" (Pittsburgh: HACP, 1953), 8–12.

39. "*Courier*, NAACP, NALC Mass Protest Wins: Arena to Improve Job-Hiring Policy," *Pittsburgh Courier*, 16 Sept. 1961 (quote); "NALC Bristles," *Pittsburgh Courier*, 8 Sept. 1962.

40. "'Hire More Negroes at Arena!'—NAACP," *Pittsburgh Courier*, 7 Oct 1961 (quote); "*Courier*, NAACP, NALC Mass Protest Wins"; "NALC Bristles"; "Negroes to Stage Mass Protest at Civic Arena: NAACP, NALC Spark Move," *Pittsburgh Courier*, 21 Oct. 1961; "Arena Improves Hiring Policy: *Courier*, NAACP, NALC Protests Bring Results," *Pittsburgh Courier* 28 Oct. 1961.

41. Dickerson, *Out of the Crucible*, 190–91 (quote, 180–81); Hinshaw, *Steel and Steelworkers*, 139–42.

42. "Powerful Groups Back Department Store Fight: Hand Bills Swamp Downtown District," *Pittsburgh Courier*, 7 Dec. 1946 (quote); Holland F. Kelley, "Plans to 'Work On' Department Stores: Interracial Council," *Pittsburgh Courier*, 3 Feb. 1945; "Store Fight Spurred: 10 Seek Positions," *Pittsburgh Courier*, 9 Nov. 1946; "Store Pickets Will Not Quit," *Pittsburgh Courier*, 14 Dec. 1946; "Break Job Barriers in Pittsburgh Department Stores: Intensive Citizens' Campaign Brings New Opportunities," *Pittsburgh Courier*, 8 Feb. 1947; "Store Heads 'Mum' About Race Issue," *Pittsburgh Courier*, 24 Oct. 1947.

43. "Store Pickets Will Not Quit: Talks with Mayor Called Fruitless," *Pittsburgh Courier*, 14 Dec. 1946 (quote); "Mayor Calls for New Dep't Store Meeting: Parlay Set for New Year's Eve," *Pittsburgh Courier*, 21 Dec. 1946; "Community Action Council Continues Store Picketing," *Pittsburgh Courier*, 21 Dec. 1946.

44. "Catholics Support Dep't Store Fight," *Pittsburgh Courier*, 14 Dec. 1946.

45. Kelley, "Powerful Groups Back Department Store Fight," *Pittsburgh Courier*, 7 Dec. 1946; Daisy Lampkin, chair, and Jeanne S. Scott, secretary, Pittsburgh NAACP, "Social Policy Committee Report," 14 Jan 1946, Group II, Box C-171, Folder 2, NAACP Papers, Library of Congress, Washington DC; Michael S. Snow, "Dreams Realized and Dreams Deferred: Social Movements and Public Policy in Pittsburgh, 1960–1980" (PhD diss. University of Pittsburgh, 2004), 19–22.

46. Reference to "Battle for Democracy" in Lampkin and Scott, "Social Policy Committee Report"; Jeanne Scott to Ella Baker, director of branches, NYC headquarters, 12 Apr. 1946; and Ella Baker to Jeanne S. Scott, 7 Feb. 1948, Group II, Box C-171, Folder 2, NAACP Papers, Library of Congress, Washington DC.

47. "Caravan of Pittsburghers Ready for FEPC Hearings," *Pittsburgh Courier*, 24

Mar. 1945 (quote); John L. Clark, "Brown's Bill Wins 'First Round' . . . 2,000 at Hearing in State Capital," *Pittsburgh Courier,* 31 Mar. 1945; "Hold Meeting to Spur Passage of Brown Bill," *Pittsburgh Courier,* 21 Apr. 1945; Constance Cunningham, "Homer Brown: First Black Political Leader in Pittsburgh," *Journal of Negro History* 66, no. 4 (Winter 1981–1982): 304–17.

48. Anthony S. Chen, "The Passage of State Fair Employment Legislation, 1945–1964: An Event History Analysis with Time-Varying and Time-Constant Covariates," Working Paper Series, Institute for Research on Labor and Employment (University of California-Berkeley, 2001), 6–9 (quote, 7), http://ideas.repec.org/p/cdl/indrel/1016.html (accessed 1 December 2008); Thomas J. Sugrue, "Affirmative Action from Below: Civil Rights, the Building Trades, and the Politics of Racial Equality in the Urban North, 1945–1969," *Journal of American History* 91, no. 1 (June 2004): 148–51.

49. Urban League of Pittsburgh, "State FEPC," in "31st Annual Report of the ULP, 1955," Part I: N, Series 13, Box 22, National Urban League Papers, Library of Congress, Washington DC; Richard F. Jones, "Annual Address by the President to the Pittsburgh Branch of the NAACP," 3 Dec. 1953, Group II, Box 2, Folder 4, NAACP Papers, Library of Congress, Washington DC.

50. "Local FEPC Fight On: Leaders' Views Differ: Homer Brown, Mon Lead Opposition Against Job Law," *Pittsburgh Courier,* 8 Dec. 1945 (quote); "Urban League Opposes Local FEPC Campaign," *Pittsburgh Courier,* 22 Dec. 1945; "A. M. E. Woman's Missionary Society Spurs Campaign for Permanent FEPC," *Pittsburgh Courier* 19 Jan. 1946; Elizabeth C. Marshall, "Deltas Will Promote Improved Social Laws: Back Drive for FEPC PA, Better Housing," *Pittsburgh Courier,* 4 May 1946.

51. Urban League of Pittsburgh, "State FEPC"; Jones, "Annual Address."

52. Pittsburgh: President's Committee on Equal Opportunity, in "Appendix: Interviews," in Marshall and Briggs, *Negro and Apprenticeship,* 267; Edmunds and Bush, *Daybreakers,* 114–16; Pittsburgh Commission on Human Relations, "Time Is Running Out: 1967 Annual Report" (Pittsburgh, 1967), 16–21; Dickerson, *Out of the Crucible,* 176–77, 211–12; John J. Clark, "Political Picture," 29 Dec. 1945; "Editorial," *Pittsburgh Courier,* 14 Sept. 1946; Kent Jackson, "FEPCC Killed by GOP in City, State," *Pittsburgh Courier,* 11 May 1946; "Mayor Fears City FEPC Court Test," *Pittsburgh Courier,* 20 Sept. 1952.

53. Sugrue, "Afirmative Action from Below," 148–51.

54. Bodnar, Simon, and Weber, *Lives of Their Own,* 239–54 (quote, 241).

55. Archie Dennis Jr. (with Robert Paul Lamb), *The Garbage Man's Son* (Monroeville: Crusades International, 2000), 42.

56. Harold L. Keith, "Who's Who in Labor: Independent Refuse Haulers in Debut," *Pittsburgh Courier,* 22 Apr. 1950.

57. Urban League of Pittsburgh, cited in Marshall and Briggs, *Negro Apprenticeship,* 267.

58. Thelma Lovette Sr., interview by staff of CAUSE, RAP, 2 July 2007.

59. Otto Davis and Norman Johnson, "The Jitneys: A Study of Grassroots Capitalism," *Journal of Contemporary Studies* 7, no. 1 (Winter 1984): 81–102; Sandra G. Shannon, *The Dramatic Vision of August Wilson* (Washington DC: Howard University Press, 1995), 56–57; Mindy Thompson Fullilove, *Root Shock: How Tearing Up City*

Neighborhoods Hurts America, And What We Can Do About It (New York: Ballantine Books, One World, 2005), 32–33; "Cabbie Bias Bared Here: Jitneys Under Fire Too," *Pittsburgh Courier*, 29 Jan. 1966.

60. Heinz History Center, *Interview with Nate Smith*, 9–10.

61. Henderson Thomas quoted in Henderson and Buba, *Struggles in Steel*.

62. Marion S. Harper, interview by Shawn Alfonso Wells for CAUSE, RAP, 25 Aug. 2007; and Lorraine Poindexter, interview by Shawn Alfonso Wells for CAUSE, RAP, 14 June 2007; Ellis; interview, CAUSE, RAP; Bodnar, Simon, and Weber, *Lives of Their Own*, 241–42; Lovette, interview, CAUSE, RAP.

63. Dickerson, *Out of the Crucible*, 207; Edmunds and Bush, *Daybreakers*, 138–44; Hinshaw, *Steel and Steelworkers*, 138–39; Pittsburgh Branch NAACP, Annual Reports of the President and Executive Secretary, 18 July 1952, 11 Mar. 1958, and 10 Dec. 1959, Group II, Box 2, Folder 4, NAACP papers; Henry Arthur Schooley, "A Case Study of the Pittsburgh Branch of the NAACP" (MA thesis, University of Pittsburgh, 1952).

64. Edmunds and Bush, *Daybreakers*, 138–69; Dickerson, *Out of the Crucible*, 189–213; Hinshaw, *Steel and Steelworkers*, 138–39; "31st Annual Report of the ULP, 1955."

65. George Evans quoted in George E. Evans, "Here Is a Postwar Job for Pittsburgh . . . Transforming The Hill District," *Greater Pittsburgh* (July–August 1943), reprinted in Anthony Robins, *Hillscapes: A Scrapbook, Envisioning a Healthy Urban Habitat*, 2nd ed. (Pittsburgh: University of Pittsburgh Center for Minority Health, July 1999), 3. See also Pittsburgh City Planning Commission (PCPC), "Pittsburgh, Groundwork and Inventory for the Master Plan" (Pittsburgh: Department of City Planning, 1945), 54, 64; Darden, "Spatial Dynamics," 19–20; "Pittsburgh Album: A Hill Comes Tumbling Down," *Pittsburgh Press*, 17 Feb. 1957, magazine section, 6; Joseph H. Brunzel, "Negro Housing Needs in Pittsburgh, Allegheny County" (Pittsburgh: Pittsburgh Housing Association, 1946); Robert K. Brown, *Public Housing in Action: The Record of Pittsburgh* (Ann Arbor: Edwards Brothers, Inc., 1959), 15, 21; Auerbach, "Status of Housing"; ACTION-Housing, "The Black Population and Its Housing: A Social and Economic Profile of the Black Community in the Pittsburgh Metropolitan Area" (Pittsburgh: ACTION-Housing, Inc., May 1969).

66. Michelle Scott, "Hill District Once a Beacon of Culture," *Pitt News*, 20 Oct. 2004.

67. Pittsburgh Housing Association (PHA), "Housing in Pittsburgh, 1947–1951" (Pittsburgh: Pittsburgh Housing Association, 1951) (quotes); Brunzel, "Negro Housing Needs in Pittsburgh, Allegheny County"; Brown, *Public Housing in Action*, 15, 21; Pittsburgh City Planning Commission (PCPC), "Pittsburgh, Groundwork and Inventory for the Master Plan," 54, 64; Darden, "Spatial Dynamics," 2, 19–20, 173; "Pittsburgh Album" 6; Evans, "Here Is a Postwar Job for Pittsburgh," 3; Bryn J. Hovde, "Report on Population Movements and Housing Trends" (Pittsburgh: Civic Unity Council, 1950), 12.

68. Darden, "Spatial Dynamics," 2, 19–20, 58–63, 71–73; ACTION-Housing, "The Black Population and Its Housing," (Pittsburgh, May 1969), 26–27. On the notion of color tax, see Harold M. Rose, "Milwaukee's Black Community: Can It Survive the Transition to Post-Industrialism Unscathed?" (ms., ca. 1993, in authors' possession),

1–13. Urban League Survey quoted in "Survey Shows Negroes Paying More for Less," *Pittsburgh Courier*, 15 Jan. 1966.

69. Pittsburgh Housing Association, "Housing in Pittsburgh, 1947–1951."

70. Classifieds from the *Pittsburgh Sun Telegraph*, 7 June 1959, and *Pittsburgh Press*, 2 June 1959, both quoted in Darden, "Spatial Dynamics," 71, 77–80.

71. Ruth Reidbord quoted in Laura Pace, "Mt. Lebanon's Past of Not Selling to Minorities Is Highlighted," *Pittsburgh Post-Gazette*, February 21, 2001; Kent James, "Public Policy and the Postwar Suburbanization of Pittsburgh, 1945–1990" (PhD diss., Pittsburgh, Carnegie Mellon University, 2005), 721–61; Darden, "Spatial Dynamics," 71, 77–80.

72. Joe T. Darden, *Afro-Americans in Pittsburgh: The Residential Segregation of a People* (Lexington, KY: D.C. Heath and Company, 1973), 43–62; Darden, "Spatial Dynamics," 65–89; Snow, "Dreams Realized," 114–15; "Multi-List Meeting with Negro Realtor: Lavelle to Try for Membership Again," *Pittsburgh Post-Gazette*, 24 June 1966.

73. Darden, "Spatial Dynamics," 71.

74. EEM quoted in Darden, "Spatial Dynamics," 76–77; "Anti-Trust Suit Hits Pgh. Multi-list," *Pittsburgh Courier*, 8 Apr. 1967; "Multi-list Meeting with Negro Realtor," *Pittsburgh Post-Gazette*, 24 June 1966 and Ervin Dyer, *Pittsburgh Post-Gazette*, "The Sweet Life for Black Pittsburgh: Sugar Top," 17 July 2005. Robert Lavelle reported narrowly escaping bodily harm in his effort to sell homes to blacks in one predominantly white area. See Robert R. Lavelle, interview by Jared Day for CAUSE, RAP, 15 Aug. 2007.

75. National Real Estate Board's "1965 Statement of Policy" quoted in Darden, *Afro-Americans in Pittsburgh*, 46–47.

76. Darden, "Spatial Dynamics," 69, 71, 74, 86, 89; Naavah Deutsch and Eric Monti, "Residential Segregation: The City of Pittsburgh in Comparative Historical Perspective, 1940–2000," Carnegie Mellon University, Department of Statistics, for CAUSE, Spring 2005, 1–7.

77. Pittsburgh City Planning Department (PCPD), "The City Moves Forward: A Progress Report on Urban Renewal and Redevelopment Areas" (Pittsburgh, n.d.), 4–7; Pittsburgh City Planning Department, "Citizen Participation Report: Relationship to Urban Renewal and Planning" (Pittsburgh, 1964), 7; Action Housing, "Urban Renewal Impact Study." For a perspective on the national story, see Amanda I. Seligman, *Block by Block: Neighborhood Policy on Chicago's West Side* (Chicago: University of Chicago Press, 2005); Lawrence J. Vale, *Reclaiming Public Housing: A Half Century of Struggle in Three Public Neighborhoods* (Cambridge, MA: Harvard University Press, 2002); and J. Mitchell, ed., *Federal Housing Policy and Programs: Past and Present* (New Brunswick: Rutgers University Press, 1985).

78. Joseph James Drexler, "The Political Economy of Neighborhood Revitalization: A Case Study of Pittsburgh's North Side Neighborhoods" (PhD diss., University of Pittsburgh, 1981), 96–98; James V. Cunningham, et al., "Neighborhood Shock: Study of Pittsburgh's East Street Expressway and Citizen Participation, 1952–1976" (Pittsburgh: University of Pittsburgh School of Social Work, 1976), 1–30.

79. Lubove, *Twentieth-Century Pittsburgh*, 1:130–32.

80. Urban Redevelopment Authority, "The Changing City" (1969), 8; Evans, "Here Is a Postwar Job"; "Pittsburgh Album," 6; Paul S. Korol, "A Brief History of the Hill,"

Pittsburgh Senior News, 4 Feb. 2002, http://freepages.geneology.rootsweb.com/nnjm1/hillhist.html; Lubove, *Twentieth-Century Pittsburgh*, 1:130–32; Scott, "Hill District Once a Beacon"; Auerbach, "Status of Housing," 1–26; Fullilove, *Root Shock*, 29–36, 59–70; "Lower Hill District (The Future Home of the Civic Arena)," from Photograph Collection, 1957, Library and Archives, Senator John Heinz History Center, Pittsburgh; Pittsburgh Neighborhood Alliance, *Pittsburgh Neighborhood Atlas: The Hill* (Pittsburgh: Pittsburgh Neighborhood Alliance, 1977), 2; Franklin Toker, *Pittsburgh: An Urban Portrait* (University Park: Pennsylvania State University Press, 1986), 234; Bolin, Moore, and Levin, *Wylie Avenue Days*; Roland Sawyer, "A Home to Go to," *Pittsburgh Quote: The Magazine, Its People and Its Institutions*, June 1955.

81. Jacqueline Welch Wolfe, "The Changing Pattern of Residence of the Negro in Pittsburgh, with Emphasis on the Period, 1930–1960" (MA thesis, University of Pittsburgh, 1964), 53–54, 76–84; C. E. De'Ath, "Patterns of Participation and Exclusion: A Poor Italian and Black Urban Community and Its Response to a Federal Poverty Program" (PhD diss., University of Pittsburgh, 1970), 102–7; Darden, "Spatial Dynamics," 3, 38.

82. Ruth McIntyre, "The Organizational Nature of an Urban Residential Neighborhood in Transition: Homewood-Brushton of Pittsburgh" (PhD diss., University of Pittsburgh, 1963), 84, 127, 175–77; Steven W. Sapolsky and Bartholomew Roselli, *Homewood-Brushton: A Century of Community-Making* (Pittsburgh: The Historical Society of Western Pennsylvania, 1987); 17–19, 31–37; Rodney A. Pelton, "The Value System of a Large Voluntary Negro Civic Organization within a Poverty Area: The Homewood-Brushton Community Improvement Association" (PhD diss., University of Pittsburgh, 1968), 64.

83. Clifford C. Ham Jr., "The Neighborhood Church in Urban Extension: A Report for ACTION-Housing, Inc." (Pittsburgh: ACTION-Housing, Aug. 1964), 9 (quote); Auerbach, "Status of Housing of Negroes," 24; Wolfe, 53–54, 76–84; Fullilove, *Root Shock*, 29–36, 59–70; Scott, "Hill District Once a Beacon of Culture"; Bolin, Moore, and Levin, *Wylie Avenue Days*.

84. Lubove, *Twentieth-Century Pittsburgh*, 1:130–32; De'Ath, "Patterns," 28–49; McIntyre, "Organizational Nature," 84, 127, 175–77; Ham, "Neighborhood Church," 2–9; Mayor's Commission on Human Relations, "Status of Intergroup Relations in Pittsburgh" (Pittsburgh: Mayor's Commission on Human Relations, 1965); Sapolsky and Roselli, *Homewood-Brushton*, 17–19, 31–37; Pelton, "Value System," 59–63.

85. Lubove, *Twentieth-Century Pittsburgh*, 1:130–32; M. A. Weiss, "The Origins and Legacy of Urban Renewal," in *Federal Housing Policy and Programs: Past and Present*, ed. J. P. Mitchell (New Brunswick: Rutgers University Press, 1985), 253–76; De'Ath, "Patterns," 28–49; Toker, *Pittsburgh*, 234; Sawyer, "A Home to Go To"; "Lower Hill District"; McIntyre, "Organizational Nature," 84, 127, 175–77; Ham, "Neighborhood Church," 2–9; Mayor's Commission on Human Relations, "Status of Intergroup Relations in Pittsburgh"; Sapolsky and Roselli, *Homewood-Brushton*, 17–19, 31–37; Pelton, "Value System," 59–63.

86. Drexler, "Political Economy," 86–124; Cunningham, et al., "Neighborhood Shock," 1–30, especially 11–17; Darden, "Spatial Dynamics," 3, 38, 69; Sawyer, "Home to Go to"; Pittsburgh Neighborhood Alliance, *Pittsburgh Neighborhood Atlas*; Deutsch and Monti, "Residential Segregation," 1–7; Glasco, "Double Burden," 424–33;

Pittsburgh City Planning Department, "City Moves Forward," 4, 7; Health and Welfare Association of Allegheny County, "Staff Proposal"; Pittsburgh City Planning Department, "A Report on Social Problems in Urban Renewal" (Pittsburgh: Community Renewal Program, 1965).

87. In addition to sources in previous note, please see: Glasco, "Double Burden," 88–97; Urban Redevelopment Authority, "The Changing City" (1969), 8; Lubove, *Twentieth-Century Pittsburgh*, 1:130–32; Auerbach, "Status of Housing," 1–4; Fullilove, *Root Shock*, 29–36, 59–70; Bodnar, Simon, and Weber, 222–23.

88. McIntyre, "Organizational Nature," 84, 127, 175–77; Ham, "Neighborhood Church," 2–9 (quote, 9); Mayor's Commission on Human Relations, "Status of Intergroup Relations in Pittsburgh"; Sapolsky and Roselli, *Homewood-Brushton*, 17–19, 31–37; Pelton, "The Value System of a Large Voluntary Negro Civic Organization within a Poverty Area," 64; quote in "Part of Frankstown Avenue Seen as Homewood Slums," *Pittsburgh Courier*, 10 August 1957.

89. ACTION-Housing, "A Report on the Pilot Program, Neighborhood Urban Extension Homewood-Brushton, 1960–1963" (Pittsburgh: ACTION-Housing, Inc., 1964), 10–11; Ham, "Neighborhood Church," 2, 10, 12,14; Mayor's Commission on Human Relations, "Status of Intergroup Relations"; Sapolsky and Roselli, *Homewood-Brushton*, 17–19, 31–37; Lubove, *Twentieth-Century Pittsburgh*, 1:165–67; Darden, "Spatial Dynamics," 83; McIntyre, "Organizational Nature," 84, 127.

90. Ham, "Neighborhood Church," 2, 9, 8–10; ACTION-Housing, "Report on the Pilot Program," 10–11.

91. McIntyre, "Organizational Nature," 127 (quote, 83–84).

92. Toki Schalk Johnson, "Pittsburgh Neighborhood Units Coping with Urban Renewal Migrations," *Pittsburgh Courier*, 29 Nov. 1958. See also Phyl Garland. "City's Redevelopers Admit Shortcomings," *Pittsburgh Courier*, 23 Dec. 1961; "People Assured Voice in Homewood Renewal Plan," *Pittsburgh Courier*, 6 Jan. 1962; "Homewood Renewal Unit Launches War for Work," *Pittsburgh Courier*, 26 Oct. 1963; "Has Homewood Become a Pgh. Vice Center?" *Pittsburgh Courier*, 16 Nov. 1963.

93. "HCIA Prexy Says Neighborhood Burdened with Taverns, No Police and Youth Mobs," *Pittsburgh Courier*, 19 Oct. 1957.

94. Bureau of Social Research, Federation of Social Agencies of Pittsburgh and Allegheny County, "The Population of Public Housing" (Pittsburgh: Federation of Social Agencies of Pittsburgh and Allegheny County, ca. 1944), 10; Housing Authority of the City of Pittsburgh (HACP), "Annual Summaries, 1958" (Pittsburgh: HACP, ca. 1959), 14-A, 16; HACP, "A Report to the People: Public Housing in Pittsburgh, 1938–1953" (Pittsburgh: HACP, 1953); Lubove, *Twentieth-Century Pittsburgh*, 1:85–86; Barbara W. Scott, "The Status of Housing of Negroes in Pittsburgh" (Pittsburgh: Commission on Human Relations, 1962); HACP, "A Statistical Picture of the 2969 Elderly Families who Make the Pittsburgh Housing Authority Developments Their Home" (Pittsburgh: HACP, 1971), 7; Fidel Campet, "Grassroots Activism and Housing Reform in Pittsburgh, 1965–1973" (Pittsburgh: Carnegie Mellon University, Research Seminar, fall 2006), 6–7; HACP, "Manual for Tenant Selection and Renting" (Pittsburgh: 1941), 101; Brown, *Public Housing*, 81, 91.

95. Housing Authority of the City of Pittsburgh (HACP), "The First Seven Years" (Pittsburgh, HACP: 1944), 3, 20 (quote); James Terry Gardiner Frazier, "Administra-

tion of the Housing Authority of the City of Pittsburgh: Some Political and Legislative Considerations" (MA thesis, University of Pittsburgh, 1966); Zapinski, "Public Housing in Pittsburgh," draft paper (in authors' possession), 9–10.

96. Frazier, "Administration of the Housing Authority," 79–82; "Harrison Moves 2 1/4 Million Yards of Earth for Housing Site," *Construction Magazine*, 1 May 1959, cited in Ken Zapinski, "Housed But Hopeless," *Pittsburgh Post-Gazette*, 11 July 1993.

97. Alfred Tronzo, interview by Dodie Carpenter for the Pittsburgh Renaissance Project, 9 Aug. 1974, Archives of Industrial Society, University of Pittsburgh.

98. Tronzo, interview, CAUSE, RAP.

99. Campet, "Grassroots Activism and Housing Reform in Pittsburgh, 1965–1973," 6–7 (quotes); see also HACP, "Manual for Tenant Selection," 10.

100. Richard Hessler, "Perceived Stress and Physical, Emotional and Social Health Status of a Large Municipal Public Housing Project" (PhD diss., University of Pittsburgh, 1969), 71–72.

101. Joel A. Tarr, *Growth, Stability, and Decline in an Urban Area: One Hundred Years of Hazelwood* (Pittsburgh, Carnegie Mellon University, 1976); Hessler, "Perceived Stress," 7, 221–22, 227.

102. Hessler, "Perceived Stress," 7, 241.

103. Gail Austin, interview by Shawn Alfonso Wells for CAUSE, RAP, 16 Aug. 2007; Sala Udin, interview by staff for CAUSE, RAP, 7 June 2007; Poindexter, interview, CAUSE, RAP; Alan James, interview by Jared Day for CAUSE, RAP, 14 Aug. 2007; James Frazier, interview by Fidel Campet for CAUSE, RAP, 7 Mar. 2007.

104. For quotes by Peterson and Howze, see Fullilove, *Root Shock*, 4, 12–13 (photo, "Hill-o-Phobia," 13), 165, 174; Udin, interview, CAUSE, RAP; Scott, "Hill District," 61.

105. Fullilove, *Root Shock*, 4.

106. Melvin Williams, "Childhood in an Urban Black Ghetto: Two Life Histories," *UMOJA*, 2, no. 3 (Fall 1978), 168–82 (quote, 173). Also see Melvin Williams, *On the Street Where I Lived* (New York: Holt, Rinehart, and Winston, 1981).

107. "Mayor Criticized for No Fair Housing Laws," *Pittsburgh Courier*, 9 Nov. 1957 (quote); "Mayor Proud of Racial Amity Here," *Pittsburgh Courier*, 14 Feb. 1959; "City's Fair-Housing Law to Be Explained," *Pittsburgh Courier*, 4 Apr. 1959; "Citizens Plan 'March' for Fair Housing Bill," *Pittsburgh Courier*, 10 Oct. 1959; "Begin Drive in State for Fair Housing," *Pittsburgh Courier*, 9 Mar. 1957.

108. Darden, "Spatial Dynamics," 68–98; Debrah Elliott and Barbara F. Gluckman, "The Impact of the Pittsburgh Fair Housing Ordinance: A Pilot Study," *Journal of Intergroup Relations* 5, no. 1 (Autumn 1966): 75–85.

109. *Stanton Land Company vs. City of Pittsburgh*: Brief of Amici Curia, no. 1741, Apr. Team, 1963-A, in Group V, Box 2220, folder 7-A, NAACP Papers, Library of Congress, Washington DC.

110. Darden, "Spatial Dynamics," 68–98; Elliott and Gluckman, "Impact," 75–85.

111. Ralph Proctor, "Racial Discrimination, Against Black Teachers and Black Professionals in the Pittsburgh Public School System, 1834–1973" (PhD diss., University of Pittsburgh, 1979), 69–148; Pittsburgh Board of Education (PBE), "The Quest for Racial Equality in the Pittsburgh Public Schools" (Pittsburgh, PBE: Sept. 1965), 7; Jack L. Palmer, "A Case Study in School-Community Conflict over Desegregation"

(PhD diss., University of Pittsburgh, 1974), 53–56; Tracey A. Reed, "The Politics of School Desegregation: The Case of Pittsburgh Public Schools, 1965–1980" (PhD diss. University of Virginia, 1997), 162–69; Richard David Gutkind, "Desegregation of Pittsburgh Public Schools, 1968–1980: A Study of the Superintendent and Educational Policy Dynamics" (PhD diss., University of Pittsburgh, 1983), 27–46; Yvonne H. Davis, "The Concerns of Black Women for Their Children and Schools" (MA thesis, University of Pittsburgh, 1962), 29–45.

112. PBE, "Quest for Racial Equality," 7–13 and 40–45; Bodnar, Simon, and Weber, *Lives of Their Own*, 220–25; Proctor, "Racial Discrimination," 95; Louis H. Mackey, "The Pennsylvania Human Relations Commission and Desegregation in the Public Schools of Pennsylvania 1961–1978" (PhD diss., University of Pittsburgh, 1978), 79–82.

113. PBE, "Quest for Racial Equality," 7–13, 40–45; Bodnar, Simon, and Weber, *Lives of Their Own*, 220–25; Proctor, "Racial Discrimination," 95, 104, 108, 112–13, 115–16; Louis H. Mackey, "The Pennsylvania Human Relations Commission and Desegregation in the Public Schools of Pennsylvania, 1961–1978" (PhD diss., University of Pittsburgh, 1978), 79–82; Alvin Rosensweet, "Race Pressure in City Called 'Rough' on Kids: Discrimination from Birth Is Lot of Non-Whites Here, Says President of NAACP," *Pittsburgh Post-Gazette*, 10 Sept. 1963; Marcella DeMarco, "Magnet Programs in the Pittsburgh Schools: Development to Implementation 1977 through 1982" (PhD diss., University of Pittsburgh, 1983), 53; Reed, "Politics of School Desegregation," 163.

114. PBE, "Quest for Racial Equality," 7–20; Reed, "Politics of School Desegregation," 163–64.

115. Alice Bernice Wade cited in Proctor, "Racial Discrimination," 110–11; Austin, interview, CAUSE, RAP; Lovette, interview, CAUSE, RAP; Harper, interview, CAUSE, RAP; Poindexter, interview, CAUSE, RAP.

116. Proctor, "Racial Discrimination," 151.

117. Austin, interview, CAUSE, RAP (quote); Lovette, interview, CAUSE, RAP; Harper, interview, CAUSE, RAP; Poindexter, interview, CAUSE, RAP.

118. Proctor, "Racial Discrimination," 90–116 (quotes, 92, 107); Reed, "Politics of School Desegregation," 165–66; "Appoint Two More Negro Teachers Here," *Pittsburgh Courier*, 31 Aug. 1946; Esther Mellon-Vann, Alma Thompson-Han, "Background on Braddock School Fight," *Pittsburgh Courier*, 15 Oct. 1955.

119. Dickerson, *Out of the Crucible*, 207; Proctor, "Racial Discrimination," 101, 151, 154, 167; PBE, "Quest for Racial Equality," 40–45.

120. PBE, "Quest for Racial Equality," 37–38; Kevin Brown, "'Where Is the Public Servants Entrance?': Democracy, the Law, and the Pittsburgh Federation of Teachers Strike of 1968" (Carnegie Mellon University, Department of History, seminar paper, December 2007); Reed, "Politics of School Desegregation," 176, 182–83; Daisy Lampkin, chair, and Jeanne S. Scott, secretary, Pittsburgh NAACP, "Social Policy Committee Report," 14 Jan 1946, Group II, Box C-171, Folder 2, NAACP papers, Library of Congress, Washington DC.

121. Thomas A. Hennessy, "Urban League Hits Doctor 'Inequality': Local Committee Regrets Lack of Integration in All Hospitals," *Pittsburgh Post-Gazette*, 10 July 196 (quote); Henry W. Pierce, "Negro MD Plight 1 More Problem: Varied Aspects of

Discrimination Bring Wide List of Observations," *Pittsburgh Post-Gazette*, 11 July 1963; "Four Area Hospitals Charged with Bias," *Pittsburgh Post-Gazette*, 7 Aug. 1964.

122. K. Leroy Irvis quoted in Snow, "Dreams Realized," 19–20; Laurence Glasco, "Two Politicians: Different Generations, Same Story," *Pittsburgh Post-Gazette*, 13 Jan. 2008; Michael Weber, *Don't Call Me Boss: David L. Lawrence, Pittsburgh's Renaissance Mayor* (Pittsburgh: University of Pittsburgh Press, 1988), 278–81.

123. Snow, "Dreams Realized," 25, 26, 29–30.

124. Affidavit of C. B. "Knowledge" Clark, 1–13 (quote, 4), and affidavit of Wendell Freeland, 1–8, *Metropolitan Pittsburgh Crusade for Voters vs. City of Pittsburgh, et al.*, case no. 86–173, U.S. District Court for the Western District of Pennsylvania (1986), in Group V, Box 2215, Folder 3, NAACP Papers, Library of Congress, Washington DC.

125. Glasco, "Two Politicians"; Glasco, "Civil Rights Movement in Pittsburgh," 5–6; Snow, "Dreams Realized," 102–59; "K. Leroy Irvis: The Speaker," Commonwealth of Pennsylvania, Memorial Ceremony, House of Representatives, 25 Apr. 2006.

126. "Honoring Robert E. 'Pappy' Williams: The 2007 Spirit of King Award Ceremony," Pittsburgh, 11 Jan. 2007, program in authors' possession; Ralph L. Hill, "A View of the Hill: A Study of Experiences and Attitudes in the Hill District of Pittsburgh, Pennsylvania from 1900 to 1973 (PhD diss., University of Pittsburgh, 1973), 27–28.

127. George E. Barbour, "Pittsburgh: 1900–2000," *New Pittsburgh Courier*, 15 Feb. 2000; Rosensweet, "Race Pressure in City"; Snow, "Dreams Realized," 25–30; Lisa Johnson, "On Race and Place: The Struggle to Desegregate the Highland Park Pool, Pittsburgh, Pennsylvania, 1948–1952" (seminar paper, Department of History, Carnegie Mellon University, Pittsburgh, 14 May 2002); "Annual Report of ULP, 1951," Part I: N, Series 13, Box 22; "31st Annual Report of the ULP, 1955," Part I: N, Series 13, Box 22; "Quarter of a Century of Exclusion at Highland Park Pool," digest of struggle, 1927, 1952, all from National Urban League Papers, Library of Congress, Washington DC; Jeanne S. Scott, secretary, Pittsburgh branch, to NAACP National Headquarters, 12 April 1946, Group II, Box 2, Folder 4, NAACP Papers, Library of Congress, Washington DC; Paul L. Jones, "Housing Upheavals; How to Meet Them?" *Pittsburgh Courier*, 13 May 1950; "Court Battle Blocks Housing; Aids Slums; North Side 'Pioneers' Create New Hazards for Redevelopment," *Pittsburgh Courier*, 29 Aug. 1953; Frank E. Bolden, "People in Ghettos," *Pittsburgh Courier*, 26 May 1951; "New Homewood Property Improvement Group to Meet," *Pittsburgh Courier*, 17 Sept. 1955; "Property Upkeep Group Plans Mass Meeting in Homewood," *Pittsburgh Courier*, 8 Oct. 1955.

128. Affidavit of Rollo Turner, *Metropolitan Pittsburgh Crusade*, 1–12.

129. "Annual Report of ULP, 1951"; "31st Annual Report of the ULP, 1955"; "Quarter of a Century of Exclusion at Highland Park Pool"; Jeanne S. Scott, to NAACP National Headquarters, 12 April 1946; Johnson, "On Race and Place"; Rosensweet, "Race Pressure in City Called 'Rough on Kids'"; Snow, "Dreams Realized," 25–30; George E. Barbour, "Pittsburgh: 1900–2000," *New Pittsburgh Courier*, 15 Feb. 2000.

130. Judge Livingstone Johnson quoted in Rosensweet, "Race Pressure in City."

Chapter 3: Pittsburgh's Modern Black Freedom Movement

1. For recent critiques of scholarship on the black freedom struggle, see Sundiata Keita Cha-Jua and Clarence Lang, "The 'Long Movement' as Vampire: Temporal and Spatial Fallacies in Recent Black Freedom Studies," *Journal of African American History* 92, no. 2 (Spring 2007): 265–88; Peniel E. Joseph, "Introduction: Towards a Historiography of the Black Power Movement," in *The Black Power Movement: Rethinking the Civil Rights-Black Power Era*, ed. Peniel E. Joseph (New York: Routledge, 2006); Jacquelyn Dowd Hall, "The Long Civil Rights Movement and the Political Uses of the Past," *Journal of American History* 91, no. 4 (March 2005): 1233–63; Jeanne F. Theoharis and Komozi Woodard, *Freedom North: Black Freedom Struggles Outside the South, 1940–1980* (New York: Palgrave Macmillan, 2003); Steven F. Lawson and Charles Payne, *Debating the Civil Rights Movement, 1945–1968* (New York: Roman & Littlefield Publishers, Inc., 1998); Charles M. Payne, *I've Got the Light of Freedom: The Organizing Tradition and the Mississippi Freedom Struggle* (Berkeley: University of California Press, 1995), 1–6.

2. Laurence Glasco, "The Civil Rights Movement in Pittsburgh: To Make This City 'Some Place Special'," Freedom Corner. http://www.freedomcorner.org/downloads/glasco.pdf (accessed 5 October 2009); Arthur J. Edmunds and Esther Bush, *Daybreakers: The Story of the Urban League of Pittsburgh* (1983; reprt. and rev., Pittsburgh: Urban League of Pittsburgh, 1999), 141–59; Bernard L. Ritter, "NAACP Working at Achieving 'The Dream,'" *New Pittsburgh Courier*, 10 Dec. 1988; George E. Barbour, "Pittsburgh: 1900–2000," *New Pittsburgh Courier*, 5 Feb. 2000; A. Vivienne Robinson, "Reflections of a Former NAACP President," *New Pittsburgh Courier*, 10 Dec. 1988; Debran Rowland, "Harvey Adams Jr. . . . The Voice of the NAACP Speaks to the Community," *New Pittsburgh Courier*, 10 Dec. 1988.

3. Dennis C. Dickerson, *Out of the Crucible: Black Steelworkers in Western Pennsylvania, 1875–1980* (Albany: State University of New York Press, 1986), 221–22; "NAACP Campaign Closes July 28, Center City Leads," *New Pittsburgh Courier*, 15 Jul. 1967; Barbour, "Pittsburgh: 1900–2000"; Debran Rowland, "Committee Investigates Area Hiring Practices," *New Pittsburgh Courier*, 10 Dec. 1988; Robinson, "Reflections"; Rowland, "Harvey Adams Jr."; "UNPC Making Headway on Jobs in Dairy Industry," *New Pittsburgh Courier*, 29 Jan. 1966; Marylynne Pitz, "Lawyer Byrd Brown Dies: Giant in Civil Rights Struggle," *Pittsburgh Post-Gazette*, 4 May 2001.

4. "UNPC to Meet with Murphy's A&P on Jobs," *New Pittsburgh Courier*, 12 Aug. 1967; "Isaly's Promises Negro Manager by Sept. 15," *New Pittsburgh Courier*, 24 June 1967; "Black Capitalism Gets a Test in Pittsburgh," *Business Week*, 5 Oct. 1968; "Bell Says 'No' to UNPC: Telephone Co. Refuses to Sign Job Agreement," *New Pittsburgh Courier*, 26 Aug. 1967. For the UNPC and NAACP's boycott of the Pittsburgh Brewing Company in order to increase African American employment, see Mayor's Commission on Human Relations, "Bread of Bitterness" (Pittsburgh: Mayor's Commission on Human Relations, 1968), 10.

5. "Duquesne Light Picketed by 300 in Racial Case," *Pittsburgh Post-Gazette*, 13 Aug. 1963; Edward Jensen, "Police Defied by Duquesne Light Pickets: 3 Race Leaders Arrested," *Pittsburgh Post-Gazette*, 14 Aug. 1963; "Duquesne Light Agrees to Hire 350

Negroes," *New Pittsburgh Courier,* 28 Oct. 1967; "Gas Co. To Hire 100 Negroes . . . Lerner's May Face Boycott," *New Pittsburgh Courier,* 15 Jul. 1967.

6. Jensen, "Police Defied" (quote); "Duquesne Light Picketed"; Dickerson, *Out of the Crucible,* 223–24, 230; John Hinshaw, *Steel and Steelworkers: Race and Class Struggle in Twentieth-Century Pittsburgh* (Albany: State University of New York Press, 2002), 208–9; Joe William Trotter Jr., *River Jordan: African American Urban Life in the Ohio Valley* (Lexington: University Press of Kentucky, 1998), 159–60.

7. Roger Stuart, "The Life and Thoughts of James Mc Coy, Jr.," *Pittsburgh Press,* 20 March 1969 (quote); Thomas Snyder, "Negroes Charge County With Job Discrimination," *Pittsburgh Post-Gazette,* 26 June 1963; "Oppose Hiring Police," n.d. in authors' possession, newsclipping file, Carnegie Library of Pittsburgh, main branch.

8. On the notion of a "Marching Season," see Michael S. Snow, "Dreams Realized and Dreams Deferred: Social Movements and Public Policy in Pittsburgh, 1960–1980" (PhD diss. University of Pittsburgh, 2004), 94–99. A. Philip Randolph quoted in Jervis Anderson, *A. Philip Randolph: A Biographical Portrait* (Berkeley: University of California Press, 1986), 328. See also Cynthia Taylor, *A. Philip Randolph: The Religious Journey of an African American Labor Leader* (New York: New York University Press, 2006).

9. Carl Morris, "The Black Mood in Pittsburgh," *New Pittsburgh Courier,* series, 2–16 Mar. 1968; "Reflections on Bouie Haden," *New Pittsburgh Courier,* 3 August 1974; "Homewood Merchants Face Boycotts: Group Demand Managers, Issue Ultimatum," *New Pittsburgh Courier,* 27 May 1967; "Homewood Boycott On: Pickett Homewood Avenue Merchants," *New Pittsburgh Courier,* 3 June 1967; Carl Morris, "Comment," *New Pittsburgh Courier,* 8 July 1967; "Fear of Black Militancy Terror: Threatens to Close H-B Stores," *New Pittsburgh Courier,* 9 Dec. 1967.

10. F. Ray Marshall and Vernon M. Briggs Jr., *The Negro and Apprenticeship* (Baltimore: The Johns Hopkins Press, 1967), 275 (quote); Senator John Heinz History Center, *An Interview with Nate Smith: The Transcription of an Oral History* (Pittsburgh: Historical Society of Western Pennsylvania Oral History Service, published by Mechling Bookbindery, Chicora, PA, ca. 2002), 34–46; Irwin Dubinsky, *Reform in Trade Union Discrimination in the Construction Industry: Operation Dig and Its Legacy* (New York: Praeger Books, 1973), 44–84.

11. David Epperson, interview by Jared Day for the Center for Africanamerican Urban Studies and the Economy (CAUSE), Remembering Africanamerican Pittsburgh Oral History Project (RAP), Department of History, Carnegie Mellon University, Pittsburgh, 19 July 2007; Morton Coleman, interview by Jared Day for CAUSE, RAP, 24 July 2007.

12. Epperson, interview, CAUSE, RAP; Coleman, interview, CAUSE, RAP.

13. Theoharis and Woodard, *Freedom North,* 1–15; Lawson and Payne, *Debating,* 3–42; Carol A. Horton, *Race and the Making of American Liberalism* (New York: Oxford University Press, 2005); 3–14; John Higham, ed., *Civil Rights and Social Wrongs: Black-White Relations Since World War II* (University Park: The Pennsylvania State University Press, 1997), 3–30; Marshall and Briggs, *Negro and Apprenticeship,* 113–20; Paul Boyer, ed., *The Oxford Companion to United States History* (New York: Oxford Press, 2001), 220–321.

14. Mayor's Committee on Human Resources, "The War on Poverty: A 1966 Progress Report to Pittsburghers" (Pittsburgh: Mayor's Committee on Human Resources, 1966), 1–37 (quote, 37). The Mayor's Committee on Human Resources was a distinct entity from Pittsburgh's Mayor's Commission on Human Relations. Formed in 1963, the Committee on Human Resources focused directly on the issue of poverty and economic deprivation, whereas the Commission on Human Relations focused mainly on eradicating forms of discrimination based religion, nationality, and color.

15. Mayor's Committee on Human Resources, "War on Poverty," 28–31; Snow, "Dreams Realized," 75–79.

16. Marshall and Briggs, *Negro and Apprenticeship*, 113–20.

17. Marshall and Briggs, *Negro and Apprenticeship*, 113–20, (quote, 116–17); Epperson, interview, CAUSE, RAP. See also Coleman, interview, CAUSE, RAP.

18. "NAACP Will Continue School Board Pickets," *Pittsburgh Post-Gazette*, 24 Aug. 1965 (quote); Tracey A. Reed, "The Politics of School Desegregation: The Case of Pittsburgh Public Schools, 1965–1980" (PhD diss., University of Virginia, 1997), 180–82; Richard David Gutkind, "Desegregation of Pittsburgh Public Schools, 1968–1980: A Study of the Superintendent and Educational Policy Dynamics" (Pittsburgh: University of Pittsburgh, 1983), 31; Ralph Proctor, "Racial Discrimination Against Black Teachers and Black Professionals in the Pittsburgh Public School System 1834–1973" (PhD diss., University of Pittsburgh, 1979), 121–48.

19. "School Busing Plan Case Reset," *New Pittsburgh Courier*, 28 Oct. 1967; Proctor, "Racial Discrimination," 121–22; Louis H. Mackey, "The Pennsylvania Human Relations Commission and Desegregation in the Public Schools of Pennsylvania 1961–1978" (PhD diss., University of Pittsburgh, 1978), 78–107; "School Board Picketing to Continue," *Pittsburgh Post-Gazette*, 24 Aug. 1965, 1; Pittsburgh Board of Education (PBE), "The Quest for Racial Equality in the Pittsburgh Public Schools" (Pittsburgh: PBE, Sept. 1965), 1–52; Edward William Schuerle, "A Study of the Administrative Decentralization in the Pittsburgh Public Schools" (PhD diss., University of Pittsburgh, 1973), 24–26; Mayor's Commission on Human Relations, "Time Is Running Out" (Pittsburgh: Mayor's Commission on Human Relations, 1967), 8–9; Mayor's Commission on Human Relations, "Warning to City Clear on All Sides: Time Running Out for Racial Action" (Pittsburgh: Mayor's Commission on Human Relations, 1968.)

20. Hugh Brock Springer, "The Dynamics of Policy Formation in Urban Schools: Pittsburgh's Education Park/Great High Schools Concept" (PhD diss., University of Pittsburgh, 1974), 68–84, 85–101, 167–74 (quote, 178n52); PBE, "Quest for Racial Equality" 41–43 (quote); Nicholas Wheeler Robinson, "Marland's 'Magnificent' Gamble: Pittsburgh's Great High Schools," *Urban Review*, Nov. 1968, 28–34; Jack L. Palmer, "A Case Study in School-Community Conflict Over Desegregation" (PhD diss., University of Pittsburgh, 1974), 61–74; Mackey, "Pennsylvania Human Relations Commission," 81–82; Reed, "Politics of School Desegregation," 172–80; Marilyn Fredericka Barnett, "Superintendents, Desegregation and the Politics of Compliance: Wilkinsburg, Pennsylvania: 1968–1986" (PhD diss., University of Pittsburgh, 1990), 60–119.

21. PBE, "Quest for Racial Equality," 44, 46; Springer, "Dynamics," 167–75; "Community Applauds School Hiring Policy," *Pittsburgh Courier*, 7 Mar. 1964.

22. Reed, "The Politics of School Desegregation," 178–87 (quote, 178); Mackey, "Pennsylvania Human Relations Commission," 44–61, 78–107; Palmer, "Case Study," 61–70; PBE, "Quest for Racial Equality," 7; Rufus Jordan, interview by Kevin Brown for CAUSE, RAP, 1 Aug. 2007; Marva and Gene Harris, interview by Jared Day for CAUSE, RAP, 15 Aug. 2007.

23. PBE, "Quest for Racial Equality," 5, 44.

24. PBE, "Quest for Racial Equality," Proctor, "Racial Discrimination," 166–68. Cf. Bart Landry, *The New Black Middle Class* (Berkeley: University of California Press, 1987).

25. "Dick Jones New School Bd. Veep," *New Pittsburgh Courier*, 19 Nov. 1966, "Gladys McNairy First Black School Board Head," *New Pittsburgh Courier*, 13 Nov. 1971; Mackey, "Pennsylvania Human Relations Commission," 90–91; Springer, "Dynamics," 195–206; Reed, "Politics of School Desegregation," 182–84, 191; Gutkind, "Desegregation," 66–67.

26. Glasco, "Double Burden," 91–92; PBE, "Quest for Racial Equality," 40; Proctor, 154–64.

27. PBE, "Quest for Racial Equality," 31–55.

28. Deborah M. Elliott and Barbara Felman Gluckman. "The Impact of the Pittsburgh Fair Housing Ordinance: A Pilot Study," *Journal of Intergroup Relations* 5, no. 1 (Autumn 1966): 75–85; Woodrow Taylor, "State, Realtors Reach Anti-Bias Housing Pact," *New Pittsburgh Courier*, 27 Jul. 1974; Darden, "Spatial Dynamics," 65–104; James N. Crutchfield, "Housing Issue: Black vs. White," *Pittsburgh Press*, ca. June 1970; James Terry Gardiner Frazier, "Administration of the Housing Authority of the City of Pittsburgh: Some Political and Legislative Considerations" (PhD diss., University of Pittsburgh, 1966; John Golightly, "City Housing Probe Resumes Today," *Pittsburgh Post-Gazette*, 16 May 1974; Richard M. Hessler, "Perceived Stress and Physical, Emotional and Social Health Status of a Large Municipal Public Housing Project" (PhD diss., University of Pittsburgh, 1969); David Mackey, "City Housing Entry Rules Hit," *Pittsburgh Press*, 7 Oct. 1971.

29. Darden, "Spatial Dynamics," 90–112 (quotes, 78, 86); "Anti-Trust Suit Hits Pgh. Multilist," *Pittsburgh Courier*, 8 Apr. 1967; Ervin Dyer, "The Sweet Life for Black Pittsburgh's Sugar Top," *Pittsburgh Post-Gazette*, 17 July 2005; Robert Lavelle, interview by Jared Day for CAUSE, RAP, 15 Aug. 2007.

30. Fidel Campet, "Grassroots Activism and Housing Reform in Pittsburgh, 1965–1973" (seminar paper, Department of History, Carnegie Mellon University, Pittsburgh, fall 2006); Donald W. McIlvane, interview by Fidel Campet for CAUSE, RAP, 19 Mar. 2007.

31. Marshall and Briggs, *Negro and Apprenticeship*, 275 (quotes); Irwin Dubinsky, *Reform in Trade Union Discrimination in the Construction Industry*, chap. 2; Heinz History Center, *Interview with Nate Smith*, 42–43; Pittsburgh Building and Construction Industry, "The Pittsburgh Plan," Pittsburgh: Pittsburgh Building and Construction Industry, n.d., in authors' possession; Mayor's Commission on Human Relations, "Choice and Challenges: 1966 Annual Report" (Pittsburgh: Mayor's Commission on Human Relations, 1966), 2–3.

32. Carl Morris, "The Black Mood in Pittsburgh," *New Pittsburgh Courier*, 2–16 Mar. 1968 (for quote, see section titled "Renaissance or Riots").

33. Morris, "Black Mood" (for quote, see section titled "Black Is Beautiful Honky"); Kevin Mumford, "Harvesting the Crisis: The Newark Uprising, The Kerner Commission, and Writings on Riots," in Kusmer and Trotter, ed., *African American Urban History Since World War II*, 203–18.

34. Snow, "Dreams Realized," 324n104; "Reverend Jimmy Joe Robinson," Civil Rights Digital Library, University of Georgia, http://crdl.usg.edu/people/r/robinson_jimmy_joe/ (accessed 3 Dec. 2009); Whitney M. Young Jr., "Racism and the Future of American Cities," speech at the Pittsburgh Plate Glass Foundation, 18 May 1964, Part II: E, Series 5, Box 43, National Urban League Papers, Library of Congress, Washington DC.

35. Morris, "Black Mood in Pittsburgh"; Alyssa Ribeiro, "'A Period of Turmoil'— Pittsburgh's April 1968 Riots and their Aftermath" (MA seminar paper, University of Pittsburgh, 2006); Epperson, interview, CAUSE, RAP; Valerie McDonald, interview by Kevin Brown for CAUSE, RAP, 21 June 2007.

36. Robert Lavelle quoted in Jane Blotzer, "King is Missed: Frustration, Loss of Hope Still is Felt," *Pittsburgh Post-Gazette*, 4 Apr. 1988. Lavelle Realty had experienced vandalism and robbery before; see "Glass Bandits Hit Crew Offices of Hill Realty," *Pittsburgh Courier*, 1 Apr. 1967.

37. Blotzer, "King is Missed" (quotes). Copters flew over Homewood and the Hill District in 1969; see "Copters Over Hill Open New Horizon," *Pittsburgh Press*, 14 Apr. 1969; "Additional Troops Called in by Shaffer," *Pittsburgh Post-Gazette*, 9 Apr. 1968.

38. Blotzer, "King is Missed."

39. "Craig Credits Police 5-Year Plan with Keeping Riots Here Bloodless: Tactical Platoons Modeled in 1963," *Pittsburgh Press*, 14 Apr. 1969 (quotes); Laurence Glasco, "Two Politicians: Different Generations, Same Story," *Pittsburgh Post-Gazette*, 13 Jan. 2008.

40. "Blacks Beat Asst. Supt. Kelley," *Pittsburgh Post-Gazette*, 23 Aug. 1968; "Four Men Indicted for Kelley Assault," *Pittsburgh Post-Gazette*, 21 Sept. 1968.

41. Mayor's Commission on Human Relations, "Warning to City Clear"; Kenneth J. Heineman, "Model City: The War on Poverty, Race Relations, and Catholic Social Activism in 1960s Pittsburgh," *Historian* 65 (2003): 867–900; "City Escapes Planned Riot: Informer Tells Cops of Plan," *New Pittsburgh Courier*, 12 Aug. 1967; "'Coy' Gov. Shafer Sends 'Feeler' He Would Like Talks with City's Miffed Rights Leaders," *New Pittsburgh Courier*, 12 Aug. 1967; "Red-Vested Black Militants Volunteer to Help 'Cool It,'" *New Pittsburgh Courier*, 13 Apr. 1968; "Blacks Quit Barr's Riot 'Task Force,'" 20 Apr. 1968, *New Pittsburgh Courier*.

42. Ribeiro, "'Period of Turmoil'" (quote); Morris, "Black Mood"; Epperson, interview, CAUSE, RAP; McDonald interview, CAUSE, RAP; Vince Gagetta, "Hill's Businessmen Demand Payments for Riots' Losses," *Post-Gazette*, 17 Apr. 1968.

43. "Red Vested Black Militants Volunteer to Help 'Cool It,'" *New Pittsburgh Courier*, 13 Apr. 1968 (includes an excellent photo of Haden confronting Slusser).

44. Campet, "Grassroots Activism"; McIlvane, interview, CAUSE, RAP.

45. Aminah B. McCloud, *African American Islam* (New York: Routledge, 1995), 24–58; Sylvaine A. Diouf, *Servants of Allah: African Muslims Enslaved in the Americas* (New York: New York University Press, 1998), 128–210; Jameela A. Hakim, "History of the First Muslim Mosque of Pittsburgh, Pennsylvania," in *Islam in North America:*

A Sourcebook, ed. Michael A. Köszegi and J. Gordon Melton (New York: Garland Publishing, Inc., 1992), 153–63.

46. "Derrick Bell Says Conditions Make Muslims: NAACP Leader Decries Hate, But Believes Muslims and Others Thrive on Injustice" *Pittsburgh Courier*, 5 Sept. 1959 (quotes); "'We're Not Subversive': Malcolm X" *Pittsburgh Courier*, 1 Sept. 1960; Haroon Al-Qahtani, *An Oral History of Islam in Pittsburgh* (Pittsburgh: Pittsburgh Muslim Media, 2007), film, http://ia331333.us.archive.org/1/items/An_Oral_History_of_Islam_in_Pittsburgh/an_oral_history_of_islam_in_pittsburgh-hi.mp4 (accessed 9 Dec. 2008).

47. Morris, "Black Mood"; Austin, interview, CAUSE, RAP.

48. Samuel W. Black, "'As I Recall': From the Hill and Homewood to the War in Vietnam," in *Soul Soldiers: African Americans and the Vietnam Era* (Pittsburgh: Senator John Heinz History Center, 2006), 132.

49. Black, "'As I Recall,'" 128–46.

50. Black, "'As I Recall,'" 130, 142, 146 (Michael Flournoy quote, 138); Wallace Terry, *Bloods: An Oral History of the Vietnam War* (New York: Random House, 1984), quoted in Black, "'As I Recall,'" 142.

51. "Massive 'Black Monday' Protest Set Against Sears" *New Pittsburgh Courier*, 15 Nov. 1969 (quote); "Sears Stores Here Facing Black Boycott," *New Pittsburgh Courier*, 8 Nov. 1969; "Sears Now Ready for Negotiations," *New Pittsburgh Courier*, 13 Dec. 1969; "List of Demands to Sears," *New Pittsburgh Courier*, 20 Dec. 1969; "UBPC, Sears Set Meeting," *New Pittsburgh Courier*, 10 Jan. 1970; Ralph Koger, "Sears Boycott Ends, HRC Plays Key Role," *New Pittsburgh Courier*, 28 Mar. 1970; "UNPC Schedules More Job Talks," *New Pittsburgh Courier*, 19 July 1969.

52. Diane Perry, "Golden Triangle is Hit with COP Brutality, Mass Arrests: Thousands See Blacks Clubbed," *Pittsburgh Courier*, 30 Aug. 1969; "Court Limits, OKs Stadium Pickets; Big March Vowed," *Pittsburgh Post-Gazette*, 16 Aug. 1969; "Still Few Blacks in Unions," *Pittsburgh Post-Gazette*, 15 Aug. 1969; "Blacks Uniting in Fight to Get Building Jobs," *Pittsburgh Press*, 17 Aug. 1969; "White 'Establishment' Secretly Rooting for Blacks on Jobs," *Pittsburgh Press*, 20 Aug. 1969; "Vow More Protests on Jobs," *Pittsburgh Press*, 20 Aug. 1969; "Picketing Stops Work at 3 Homewood Sites," *Pittsburgh Press*, 23 Aug. 1969; "Traffic Snarls Add to Furor in Job Protest," *Pittsburgh Press*, 26 Aug. 1969; "Confrontation and Change," *Pittsburgh Press*, 17 Oct. 1982.

53. Perry, "Golden Triangle is Hit" (quote); "Confrontation and Change"; "Court Limits, OKs Stadium Pickets"; "Still Few Blacks in Unions"; "Blacks Uniting in Fight"; "White 'Establishment' Secretly Rooting," and "Vow More Protests on Jobs."

54. Perry, "Golden Triangle is Hit" (quote); "Confrontation and Change"; Snow, "Dreams Realized," 114–15.

55. Perry, "Golden Triangle is Hit" (quotes); Snow, "Dreams Realized," 110–15; Wendell Freeland, interview by Benjamin Houston for CAUSE, RAP, 24 July 2007.

56. Perry, "Golden Triangle is Hit" (quotes); Snow, "Dreams Realized," 110–15; Freeland, interview, CAUSE, RAP; Perry, "Golden Triangle"; "Confrontation and Change"; "Court Limits, OKs Stadium Pickets"; "Still Few Blacks in Unions"; "Blacks Uniting in Fight"; "White 'Establishment' Secretly Rooting," and "Vow More Protests on Jobs."

57. Diane Perry, "Black Panther Party Opens H'Wood Office," *New Pittsburgh*

Courier, 18 Apr. 1970 (quote); "Panther Unit Scores Negro Moderates," *New Pittsburgh Courier,* 25 Apr. 1970; "Pittsburgh Panther Posters," *New Pittsburgh Courier,* 2 May 1970.

58. Perry, "Black Panther Party."

59. "'Panthers No Threat': Says U.S. Atty.-Gen," *New Pittsburgh Courier,* 23 May 1970; "Housing, Jobs, Representation: Basic Issues in Outgoing 1970," *New Pittsburgh Courier,* 2 Jan. 1971.

60. Snow, "Dreams Realized," 102–59; Blotzer, "King is Missed"; Urban Redevelopment Authority, "The Changing City" (Pittsburgh: Urban Redevelopment Authority, 1969), 1–22; "Black Capitalism Gets a Test in Pittsburgh," *Business Week,* 5 Oct. 1968; biographical sketch of Clyde Jackson, Civil Rights Digital Library, University of Georgia, http://crdl.usg.edu/people/j/jackson_clyde/?Welcome (accessed 5 Dec. 2009).

61. Dickerson, *Out of the Crucible,* 183–86; Tim Stevens, interview by staff for CAUSE, RAP, 18 July 2007; Alan James, interview by Jared Day for CAUSE, RAP, 14 Aug. 2007.

62. Dickerson, *Out of the Crucible,* 219.

63. Schuerle, "Administrative Decentralization," 24–31; Springer, "Dynamics," 91–92n47; Reed, "Politics of School Desegregation," 162–200.

64. Byrd Brown quoted in Schuerle, "Administrative Decentralization," 24–25.

65. Proctor, "Racial Discrimination," 94n51; PBE, "Quest for Racial Equality," addendum, 27–28.

66. Frankie Pace quoted in Springer, "Dynamics," 154–55.

67. Norman Johnson quoted in Springer, "Dynamics," 157.

68. Laurence Glasco, "Double Burden," in *City at the Point: Essay on the Social History of Pittsburgh. Pittsburgh,* ed. Samuel P. Hays (University of Pittsburgh Press, 1989), 92–93.

69. Carnegie Mellon University, "Report of the Commission on the Status of Underrepresented Minorities at Carnegie Mellon University," 4 Dec. 1995, 9–13.

70. Robert Wideman quoted in John Edgar Wideman, *Brothers and Keepers* (New York: Penguin Books, 1984), 113–20; see also Proctor, "Racial Discrimination," 116–17; Campet, "Urban League."

71. Wideman, *Brothers and Keepers,* 116–17

72. Wideman, *Brothers and Keepers,* 117.

73. Diane Perry, "The Coming Crisis in Pittsburgh Schools," *New Pittsburgh Courier,* 29 Aug. 1970.

74. "UNPC Calls for Resignations at Housing Auth.," *New Pittsburgh Courier,* 25 Nov. 1967 (quote); Civil Rights Group List Demands for Housing," *New Pittsburgh Courier,* 15 July 1967; Greg Mims, "McIlvane Charges 'End Run' Behind Backs of Citizens," *New Pittsburgh Courier,* 20 Oct. 1973; "PHA Board Members Get Wide Support," *New Pittsburgh Courier,* 7 Feb. 1970; David Mackey, "City Housing Entry Rules Hit," *Pittsburgh Press,* 7 Oct. 1971; "Resident Named to Housing Board," *Pittsburgh Post-Gazette,* 7 Aug. 1970.

75. Mackey, "City Housing."

76. "Activism/Rent Strike: PHA Threatened by Rent Strike," *Pittsburgh Post-Gazette,* 19 Feb. 1971; "Northview School Mothers March on Board of Education,"

New Pittsburgh Courier, 28 Oct. 1967; "Housing Authority, Tenants Reach Agreement on Five Crucial Issues," *New Pittsburgh Courier*, 13 Mar. 1971; and "Many Changes in the Offing for Housing Authority," *New Pittsburgh Courier*, 28 Apr. 1973; "Blacks Increase Share of Public Housing" *Pittsburgh Press*, 26 Apr. 1970; Jerry Sharpe, "Northview Tenants Seek Housing Project Control," *Pittsburgh Press*, 23 Sept. 1974.

77. Greg Mims, "Community Slighted in Kohlman Issue," *New Pittsburgh Courier*, 22 Sept. 1973; Greg Mims, "Kohlman Answers Latest Accusations," *New Pittsburgh Courier*, 10 Nov. 1973; "C. Kohlman Clears the Air," *New Pittsburgh Courier*, 26 May 1973; Ulish Carter, "News Media Draws Wrath of Angry Black Leaders Who Support Kohlman," *New Pittsburgh Courier*, 12 Jan. 1974; Mims, "McIlvane Charges."

78. Al Donalson, "Fear Part of the Bargain at Housing Projects," *Pittsburgh Press*, 21 Sept. 1973 (quotes); Beth Dunlop, "To Residents, Housing Patrol Means Cop When You Need One," *Pittsburgh Press*, 13 May 1973; "Tronzo and Janitor Issue Resurrected," *Pittsburgh Press*, 9 Nov. 1971.

79. "City Housing Agency Plans Security Hike," *Pittsburgh Press*, 21 Jan. 1972; Dunlop, "To Residents, Housing Patrol Means Cop When You Need One"; Thomas Benic, "Perils and the Project Housing Authority Aim's Security," *Pittsburgh Post-Gazette*, 1 Dec. 1975; Stephen Franklin, "Housing Authority's Security Force OKd," *Pittsburgh Post-Gazette*, 30 Sept. 1972; "Housing Board Votes to Dismiss Tronzo," *Pittsburgh Post-Gazette*, 27 Feb. 1970.

80. "Many Changes in the Offing" (quote).

81. "City Housing Agency Plans Security Hike."

82. Dunlop, "To Residents, Housing Patrol Means Cop."

83. Darden, "Spatial Dynamics," 6, 10, 11, 46, 79, 83, 94, 96; Ed Wintermantel and Al Schriner, "From Slaves to Statesmen: A History of Blacks in Pittsburgh," *Pittsburgh Press*, 17 Oct. 1982.

84. Darden, "Spatial Dynamics," 90–99 (quote, 94n1).

85. Darden, "Spatial Dynamics," 106–12.

86. Gene Reid, "Local Group Formed to Fight Brutality," *New Pittsburgh Courier*, 20 July 1974 (quote); Harvey Adams, interview by Jared Day for CAUSE, RAP, 6 July 2007; Al Donalson, "Group Vows Police Watch: Seeks to Prevent Alleged Abuse," *Pittsburgh Press*, ca. 20 July 1974, newsclippings file, Carnegie Library of Pittsburgh; "Black Leaders Hit Alleged Cop Brutality," *Pittsburgh Post-Gazette*, 4 May 1971; "Youth, Mistaken for Fugitive, Killed by Local Policeman," *New Pittsburgh Courier*, 23 June 1971.

87. Thomas M. Hritz, "Blue Flue: Flaherty to Delay Police Transfers," *Pittsburgh Post-Gazette*, 23 Apr. 1970 (quote); Richard Scaglion, "Data Report to the Police Community Relations Project" (Pittsburgh Police Community Relations Project, Sept. 1972–July 1972), 133–35, Hillman Library, University of Pittsburgh; "Police Strike Unjustifiable," editorial, *Pittsburgh Post-Gazette*, Apr. 1970.

88. Eileen Coliani, "Pittsburgh: Who Polices the Police," *Pittsburgh Magazine*, Mar. 1976, 27–51 (quote, 51).

89. Coliani, "Pittsburgh," 27. Within the context of rising black resistance to police brutality, some white officers reported that they had themselves become the victims of citizen abuse by the early 1970s. See the comprehensive report on citizen attitudes towards the police: Scaglion, "Data Report," 27–51.

90. For intervention of Lieutenant Moore, see "Cops Force Calm at Gladstone; Cmdr. Bill Moore Cools Militant Students," *New Pittsburgh Courier*, 22 Feb. 1969; see also "Local Group Formed to Fight Police Brutality," *New Pittsburgh Courier*, 20 July 1974; "White Officers Patrol Troubled Oliver·High," *New Pittsburgh Courier*, 22 Feb. 1969; "White Students, Cop Arrested in Gladstone School Crisis, Hill Constables Make Arrests," *New Pittsburgh Courier*, 1 Mar. 1969.

91. Chuck Staresinic, "Send Freedom House," *Pitt Med* (Feb. 2004): 32–34; Phil Hallen interview by Johanna Fernandez for CAUSE, RAP, 19 July 2007; Betty Tillman, interview by Shawn Wells for CAUSE, RAP, 23 Aug. 2007.

92. Quote from Hallen, interview, CAUSE, RAP; Staresinic, "Send Freedom House!"; Tillman, interview, CAUSE, RAP.

93. Staresinic, "Send Freedom House!" 34.

94. Ben Fischer, "The Steel Consent Decree: A Civil Rights Milestone," Pittsburgh: Carnegie Mellon University Center for Labor Studies, 1997 (quote); Dickerson, *Out of the Crucible*, 244–45; Ray Henderson and Tony Buba, *Struggles in Steel: The Fight for Equal Opportunity* (San Francisco: California Newsreel, 1996), film; Hinshaw, *Steel and Steelworkers*, 207–8, 211–17. In 1974, the U.S. Department of Housing and Urban Development (HUD) denied the city of Pittsburgh additional funds, citing the failure of Pittsburgh to develop appropriate proposals for dealing with the spread of poverty within the city's poor and working-class neighborhoods.

95. Fischer, "Steel Consent Decree"; Dickerson, *Out of the Crucible*, 244–45; Hinshaw, *Steel and Steelworkers*, 211–17; Henderson and Buba, *Struggles in Steel*.

96. Palmer, "Case Study," 60–61; Reed, "Politics of School Desegregation," 205–16; Mackey, "Pennsylvania Human Relations Commission," 78–107.

97. Palmer, "Case Study," 70–102.

98. Wideman, *Brothers and Keepers*, 116–17.

99. Gutkind, "Desegregation," 81.

100. Gutkind, "Desegregation," 69, 81, 83.

101. Snow, "Dreams Realized," 163–82; Carl Morris, "The Circus Comes to Homewood," *New Pittsburgh Courier*, 23 Dec. 1967.

102. Ron Suber, "Homewood Parents Rally to Boycott Baxter School," *New Pittsburgh Courier*, 30 Aug. 1975.

103. "For Blacks and Whites in Our Region, School Desegregation Gets a Failing Grade," *Pittsburgh Post-Gazette*, 21 Apr. 1996; Carmen Lee, "Survey to Study Student Decline," *Pittsburgh Post-Gazette*, 10 Apr. 1995, cited in *City Schools and City Politics: Institutions and Leadership in Pittsburgh, Boston, and St. Louis*, ed. John Portz, Lana Stein, and Robin R. Jones (Lawrence: University Press of Kansas, 1999), 74.

104. Eleanor Chute, "Walking in Circles: 50 Years Later, Many Children Still Go to Schools That Are Nearly All White or All Black," *Pittsburgh Post-Gazette*, 16 May 2004.

105. Laura Pace, "Mt. Lebanon's Past of Not Selling to Minorities is Highlighted," *Pittsburgh Post-Gazette*, 21 Feb. 2001.

106. "Highlights of Council's Housing Authority Inquiry," *New Pittsburgh Courier*, 24 May 1974; Mims, "Kohlman Answers"; David Warner, "Housing Pete's Pawn, Tronzo Says," *Pittsburgh Press*, 18 May 1974; Roger Stuart and Jack Grochot, "Hiring Under Kohlman Authority 'All in the Family,'" *Pittsburgh Press*, 16 Dec. 1973; Mims,

"McIlvane Charges"; Mims, "Community Slighted"; Taylor, "Housing Authority Borders on Chaos in Land of Plenty," *Pittsburgh Courier*, 6 Oct. 1973; Tom Stokes, "Blacks Rally for Support, Kohlman to Stay—for Now," *New Pittsburgh Courier*, 18 Aug. 1973; "Kohlman's Exit: Pete's Opening," *Pittsburgh Post-Gazette*, 22 Aug. 1973.

107. "Kohlman Quitting Housing Post," *Pittsburgh Press*, 13 Aug. 1973; Stokes, "Blacks Rally"; Ulish Carter, "News Media Draws Wrath of Angry Black Leaders Who Support Kohlman," *Pittsburgh Courier*, 12 Jan. 1974; Woodrow Taylor, "Housing Authority Borders on Chaos in Land of Plenty," *Pittsburgh Courier*, 6 Oct. 1973.

108. Jerry Sharpe, "Northview Tenants Seek Housing Project Control," *Pittsburgh Press*, 23 Sept. 1974.

109. "H-B Med. Center Approved," *New Pittsburgh Courier*, 8 Apr. 1967; "Getting to Know Alma Illery Medical Center/Primary Care Health Services," *Networks: Caring for the Whole Person* (Nov. 2001), http://www.coordinatedcarenetwork.org/CCN/newsletters/November.pdf (accessed 23 Jan. 2010); George E. McClomb, interview by Jared Day for CAUSE, RAP, 20 Aug. 2007.

110. Simone M. Caron, "Birth Control and the Black Community in the 1960s: Genocide or Power Politics?" *Journal of Social History* 31, no. 3 (Spring 1998): 545–69.

111. Haden quoted in Caron, "Birth Control," 555–56. See also "Ouster of Bouie Haden is Hailed by Many Whites in Area," *New Pittsburgh Courier*, 12 July 1969; "Bouie Haden's Family Cherishes His Memory," *New Pittsburgh Courier*, 18 February 1978; Greg Mims, "Black Populace Gathers for Haden's Final Rites," *New Pittsburgh Courier*, 10 August 1974.

112. Caron, "Birth Control," 559–60.

113. PBE, "Quest for Racial Equality" (quote); Springer, "Dynamics," 85–101; Gutkind, "Desegregation," 27–35.

114. "West End Resident Fight Public Housing," *New Pittsburgh Courier*, 14 Oct. 1967; "Negro Homeowners Fight for Stiff Zoning Ordinance," *New Pittsburgh Courier*, 1 Apr. 1967.

115. "R. Williamson Can't Move to Davenport St.," *Pittsburgh Courier*, 9 Nov. 1957.

116. Jennifer I. Schuitema, "African American Musicians and the Pittsburgh Music Scene, 1940–1960" (oral history project paper, Center for Africanamerican Urban Studies and the Economy, Department of History, Carnegie Mellon University, Pittsburgh, spring 2007), 57–59.

117. Rob Ruck, *Sandlot Seasons: Sport in Black Pittsburgh* (Urbana: University of Illinois Press, 1987), 170–210.

118. Glasco, "Double Burden," 90; Laurence Glasco, *A Legacy of Bricks and Mortar: African American Landmarks in Allegheny County* (Pittsburgh: Pittsburgh History and Landmark Foundation, 1995), 29; affidavit of Wendell Freeland, 1–8, in *Metropolitan Pittsburgh Crusade for Voters vs. City of Pittsburgh, et al.*, case no. 86–173, U.S. District Court for the Western District of Pennsylvania (1986), Group V, Box 2215, Folder 3, NAACP Papers Library of Congress, Washington DC.

119. Snow, "Dreams Realized," 19–20, 63–92; "Blacks Quit Barr's Riot Task Force: NAACP Head Raps City's Civil Disorder Probe, Mayor Faces Negro Revolt in City Hall," *Pittsburgh Courier*, 20 Apr. 1968; Laurence Glasco, "Two Politicians: Different Generations, Same Story," *Pittsburgh Post-Gazette*, 13 Jan. 2008; Lawrence Walsh, "Barr Years: This Family's Influence on the City . . ." *Pittsburgh Press*, 28 Dec. 1969;

Mayor's Committee on Human Resources, "The War on Poverty: A 1966 Progress Report to Pittsburghers" (Pittsburgh: Mayor's Committee on Human Resources, 1966); Stefan Lorant, *Pete: The Life of Peter F. Flaherty* (Authors Edition, Inc., 1978), 81–84; Bob McCarthy, *Malice Toward None: Remembering Mayor Joe Barr* (Pittsburgh: Dorrance Publishing Company, 2002), 1–29.

120. Snow, "Dreams Realized," 73–160.

121. Lorant, *Pete*, 81–84; McCarthy, *Malice Toward None*, 81–82; Walsh, "Barr Years," 9–12; Snow, "Dreams Realized," 73–160.

122. Snow, "Dreams Realized," 102–60; Lorant, *Pete*, 81–84; Mayor's Committee on Human Resources, "War on Poverty," 9–28.

123. Snow, "Dreams Realized," 151.

124. Snow, "Dreams Realized," 148–59; Lorant, *Pete*; Mayor's Committee on Human Resources, "War on Poverty, 9–28.

125. Glasco, "Two Politicians"; Glasco, "Civil Rights Movement," 5–6; Snow, "Dreams Realized," 102–59; "K. Leroy Irvis: The Speaker," Commonwealth of Pennsylvania, Memorial Ceremony, House of Representatives, 25 Apr. 2006.

Chapter 4: In the Shadows of Renaissance II

1. On the national level, these developments paralleled debates over what some scholars have called the "urban crisis" and the growth of a new "underclass" in the wake of the modern black freedom struggle. Sociologist William J. Wilson largely established the parameters of this debate in a series of studies on Chicago's late twentieth-century African American community. For recent historical critiques of this scholarship, see, among others: Kenneth L. Kusmer and Joe W. Trotter, eds., *African American Urban History since World War II: The Dynamics of Race, Class, and Gender* (University of Chicago Press, 2009); Thomas J. Sugrue, *The Origins of the Urban Crisis: Race and Inequality in Postwar Detroit* (Princeton: Princeton University Press, 1996); Rhonda Williams, *The Politics of Public Housing: Black Women's Struggles against Urban Inequality* (New York: Oxford University Press, 2004); Matthew Countryman, *Up South: Civil Rights and Black Power in Philadelphia* (Philadelphia: University of Pennsylvania Press, 2006).

2. John P. Hoerr, *And the Wolf Finally Came: The Decline of the American Steel Industry* (Pittsburgh: University of Pittsburgh Press, 1988), 89–101; John Hinshaw, *Steel and Steelworkers: Race and Class Struggle in Twentieth-Century Pittsburgh* (Albany: State University of New York Press, 2002), 231–46; Bennett Harrison, *The Deindustrialization of America: Plant Closings, Community Abandonment, and the Dismantling of Basic Industry* (New York: Basic Books, 1982), 36–37, 54.

3. Bennett Harrison and Barry Bluestone, *The Great U-Turn: Corporate Restructuring and the Polarizing of America* (New York: Basic Books, Inc., 1988), 36–37, 85–86; Judith Stein, *Running Steel, Running America: Race, Economic Policy, and the Decline of Liberalism* (Chapel Hill: University of North Carolina Press, 1998), 197–228; Judith Modell and Charlee Brodsky, *A Town Without Steel: Envisioning Homestead* (Pittsburgh: University of Pittsburgh Press, 1998), 1–89; Kenneth Warren, *The American Steel Industry, 1850–1970: A Geographical Interpretation* (Oxford: Clarendon Press, 1973), 285–89; Roy Lubove, *Twentieth-Century Pittsburgh: The Post-Steel Era*, vol. II (Pittsburgh: University of Pittsburgh Press, 1996), 3–40; Dale A. Hathaway, *Can*

Workers Have a Voice?: The Politics of Deindustrialization in Pittsburgh (University
Park: Pennsylvania State University Press, 1993), 20–23, 132–60.

4. Hoerr, *And the Wolf*, 520–21; Hathaway, *Can Workers*, 37–38; Lubove, *Twentieth-
Century Pittsburgh*, 2:7.

5. Lubove, *Twentieth-Century Pittsburgh*, 2:57–85; Robert E. Gleeson, *Cash Cows
and Glass Towers: Business and Metropolitan Development in Twentieth-Century
Pittsburgh* (Pittsburgh: University of Pittsburgh Press, forthcoming), chaps. 7 and
8; Hathaway, *Can Workers*, 39–48; Robert E. Gleeson, "Toward a Shared Economic
Vision for Pittsburgh and Southwestern Pennsylvania: A White Paper Update"
(Pittsburgh: Center for Economic Development, H. John Heinz III School of Public
Policy and Management, Carnegie Mellon University, 1994), 12–16.

6. Lubove, *Twentieth-Century Pittsburgh*, 2:50–85 (quote, 50).

7. Hoerr, *And the Wolf*, 591; Lubove, *Twentieth-Century Pittsburgh*, 2:57–85; Richard Florida, "Pittsburgh's Prosperity Depends on Diversity," *Pittsburgh Post-Gazette*,
15 Oct. 2000.

8. Lubove, *Twentieth-Century Pittsburgh*, 2:53.

9. Rand McNally, *Places Rated Almanac: Your Guide to Finding the Best Places to
Live in America* (Chicago: Rand McNally & Company, 2007); see also Dan Majors,
"Pittsburgh Rated 'Most Livable City' Once Again," *Pittsburgh Post-Gazette*, 26 Apr.
2007.

10. "Reindustrialization from Below: The Steel Valley Authority," *Labor Research
Review* 5, no. 2 (1986): 9–34 (quote by Rev. Jesse Jackson, 25).

11. Stout, "Reindustrialization from Below," 31.

12. Hathaway, *Can Workers*, 20–23, 132–60.

13. Ralph L. Bangs, "Economic Benchmarks: Indices for the City of Pittsburgh and
Allegheny County" (University of Pittsburgh, University Center for Social and Urban
Research, 1994), 1; Ralph Bangs, "Black and White Economic Conditions in the City
of Pittsburgh: A Benchmarks Special Report" (University of Pittsburgh, Center
for Social and Urban Research, 1995), 5–7, 36–38; Hathaway, *Can Workers*, 20–23,
132–60; Andrew Martinez, "On the Brink? City's Economic Decline May Be Tough
to Stop," *Pittsburgh Post-Gazette*, 15 Feb. 1995.

14. Bangs, "Economic Benchmarks," 49; David B. Houston, "A Brief History of
the Process of Capital Accumulation in Pittsburgh: A Marxist Interpretation," in
Pittsburgh-Sheffield: Sister Cities, ed. Joel Tarr (Pittsburgh: Carnegie Mellon University
Press, 1986), 29–69; "Jobs First, Immigrants Second," *Pittsburgh Post-Gazette*, 10 June
2001; Martinez, "On the Brink?"; Steve Levin, "Census Shows Changing Racial
Makeup of County," *Pittsburgh Post-Gazette*, 13 Mar. 2001; Ralph Reiland, "Pittsburgh:
First in Shrinkage," *New Pittsburgh Courier*, 28 Oct. 1998.

15. Quotes by Jim McKay, Ralph Proctor, Lois Cain, and Eric Webb all drawn
from Jim McKay, "Blacks Lost Jobs and a Generation with Manufacturing's Demise,"
Pittsburgh Post-Gazette, 15 Nov. 1994.

16. James S. Hirsch and Suzanne Alexander, "Reverse Exodus: Middle Class
Blacks Quit Northern Cities and Settle in the South," *Wall Street Journal*, 22 May
1990; "Obituary: Justin L. Johnson: Prominent Attorney and Son of Superior Court
Judge," *Pittsburgh Post-Gazette*, 25 Aug. 2004.

17. Sheryl Johnson quoted in McKay, "Blacks Lost Jobs"; Rob Ruck, "Perspectives

on Pittsburgh: African American History and Contemporary Social Inequality" (lecture, Center for Africanamerican Urban Studies and the Economy, Department of History, Carnegie Mellon University, Pittsburgh, 10 Apr. 1997), 1–23.

18. Hathaway, *Can Workers*, 131–60; Ralph L. Bangs, "Linking the Unemployed to Growth Centers in Allegheny County: Final Report" (University of Pittsburgh, University Center for Social and Urban Research, 1991), 5–6; Dennis C. Dickerson, "From the Periphery to Poverty: Black Steelworkers and Their Descendants" (lecture, Center for Africanamerican Urban Studies and the Economy, Department of History, Carnegie Mellon University, Pittsburgh, 3 Apr. 1997), 15–16; Rob Ruck and Christopher Fletcher, "Unequal Opportunity," *Pittsburgh Magazine*, Sept. 1995, 80.

19. Veronica Morgan-Lee quoted in McKay, "Blacks Lost Jobs."

20. Jim McKay, "Unequal Payback: For Blacks and Whites in Our Region," *Pittsburgh Post-Gazette*, 28 Apr. 1996; Jim McKay, "An Economic Crisis of Shocking Proportions for Region's Black Males," *Pittsburgh Post-Gazette*, 28 Apr. 1996.

21. Esther L. Bush, "The State of Black Pittsburgh" (Urban League of Pittsburgh, 28 Oct. 1999), 6.

22. Tawanda Williams, "Both Races Feel Victimized," *Pittsburgh Post-Gazette*, 28 Apr. 1996.

23. Karen J. Gibson, William A. Darity, and Samuel L. Meyers, "Revisiting Occupational Crowding in the U.S.: A Preliminary Study," *Feminist Economics* 4, no. 3 (1998): 73–95 (quote, 81); Ralph Bangs, "Linking the Unemployed," 6; McKay, "Unequal Payback"; "Education, Role Models Are Key to Progress," *Pittsburgh Post-Gazette*, 28 Apr. 1996.

24. Jerome Williams quoted in Jim McKay, "Backslide: Jobs, Programs Haven't Fulfilled Promises for Blacks," *Pittsburgh Post-Gazette*, 28 Apr. 1996. See also Gibson, Darity, and Meyers, "Revisiting Occupational Crowding," 73–95; Karen J. Gibson, "Race, Class, and Space: An Examination of Underclass Notions in the Steel and Motor Cities" (paper, Center for Africanamerican Urban Studies and the Economy, Department of History, Carnegie Mellon University, Pittsburgh, 3 Mar. 1998, 1–22.

25. Felicia Harrison quoted in McKay, "Blacks Lost Jobs"; Carla Murray quoted in McKay, "Economic Crisis." Also see Carolyn Shropshire, "New Industry Old Story: Like Other Industries, High-Tech Sector Lacks African American Managers, Workers," *Pittsburgh Post-Gazette*, 22 Feb. 2001.

26. Darryl Daughtry quoted in McKay, "Economic Crisis"; see also McKay, "Education, Role Models."

27. Leon Haley and Ralph Bangs, "Policies to Improve African American Economic Conditions in Pittsburgh and Allegheny County," in *The State of the Region: Economic, Demographic, and Social Conditions and Trends in Southwestern Pennsylvania*, ed. Ralph Bangs (Pittsburgh: University of Pittsburgh Center for Social and Urban Research, Sept. 1999), 141–50.

28. Earl Hord quoted in McKay, "Economic Crisis."

29. Felicia Harrison quoted in McKay, "Blacks Lost Jobs."

30. Susan McElroy, Leon Andrews, and Sheila Washington, *African Americans Choosing Allegheny County: Factors That Influence Their Decisions* (report to the Pittsburgh Foundation, Oct. 1999), quoted in Esther L. Bush, "The State of Black Pittsburgh" (Urban League of Pittsburgh, 23 Oct. 2000), 3.

31. Ralph Bangs, "Current Social Conditions of African Americans in the Pittsburgh Region" (University of Pittsburgh, University Center for Social and Urban Research, 23 Oct. 2000), 1–2; "Disparity Study for the City of Pittsburgh and Its Authorities," 27 July 2000, Mason Tillman Associates.

32. Darity and Meyers, "Revisiting Occupational Crowding," 73–95; Gibson, "Income, Race, and Space," 22–23; Sonya Toler, "Bush: State of Black Pittsburgh 'Dismal,'" *New Pittsburgh Courier*, 28 Oct. 2000; Center for Urban and Social Research, "Black and White Economic Conditions" (Pittsburgh: University of Pittsburgh, June 1995); Bangs, "Economic Benchmarks," 20.

33. Esther L. Bush, "State of Black Pittsburgh" (28 Oct. 1999), 6–8; Trotter, *African American Experience*, 611–14; The Republican National Committee, *Contract with America* (New York: Random House/Times Books/The Republican National Committee, 1994); Donald G. Nieman, *Promises to Keep: African Americans and the Constitutional Order, 1776 to the Present* (New York: Oxford University Press, 1991), especially chaps. 6 and 7; Manning Marable, *Race, Reform, and Rebellion: The Second Reconstruction in Black America, 1945–1990* (Jackson: University Press of Mississippi, 1991), chaps. 7 and 8.

34. Gregory J. Crowley, *The Politics of Place: Contentious Urban Development in Pittsburgh* (Pittsburgh: University of Pittsburgh Press, 2005), 94–97, 101–2.

35. Arthur J. Edmunds and Esther L. Bush, *Daybreakers: The Story of the Urban League of Pittsburgh* (1983; reprt. and rev., Pittsburgh: Urban League of Pittsburgh, 1999), 182–83; Crowley, *Politics of Place*, 96–97, 101–2.

36. Quote and survey information from Williams, "Both Races Feel Victimized"; George E. Barbour, "Pittsburgh: 1900–2000," *New Pittsburgh Courier*, 5 Feb. 2000; Debran Rowland, "Early NAACP Efforts Set Stage for Future Successes," 10 Dec. 1988; Bernard L. Ritter, "NAACP Working at Achieving 'The Dream,'" *New Pittsburgh Courier*, 10 Dec. 1988.

37. Washington Legal Foundation, commentary on *Michael Hopp, et al. v. City of Pittsburgh*. U.S. Court of Appeals for the Third Circuit, 1999, case nos. 98–3411, 98–3427, http://openjurist.org/194/f3d/434/michael-hopp (accessed January 2009); Kwame Dixon and Patricia E. Allard, "Amnesty International USA: Police Brutality and International Human Rights in the United States: The Report on Hearings Held in Los Angeles, California, Chicago, Illinois, and Pittsburgh, Pennsylvania, Fall, 1999" (New York: Amnesty International, 2000), 28.

38. Affidavits of William Russell Robinson, 1–15, Thomas J. Murphy, 1–12, and Wendell Freeland, 1–8, *Metropolitan Pittsburgh Crusade for Voters vs. City of Pittsburgh, et al.*, case no. 86–173, U.S. District Court for the Western District of Pennsylvania (1986), in Group V, Box 2215, Folder 3, NAACP Papers, Library of Congress, Washington DC; Jan Ackerman, "Black Leaders Suit Challenges at-Large Voting," *Post-Gazette*, 23 Jan. 1986; "Districts and Dissenters," *Post-Gazette*, 5 Feb. 1987.

39. Marty Willis, "All-White Council Ceremony Draws Protest," *New Pittsburgh Courier*, 18 Jan. 1986 (quote); "Jan. 6 Demonstration To Greet All-White City Council," *New Pittsburgh Courier*, 11 Jan. 1986; B-PEP, Black Political Empowerment Project, http://www.b-ep.net/police_accountability.htm (accessed December 2008); Landmark Education Program, "Tim Stevens: Black Political Empowerment

Project, Community Action Builds African-American Voter Impact," http://www.
landmarkeducation.com/display_content.htm (accessed December 2008).

40. Affidavits by Freeland, 1–8, and Robinson, 1–15, *Metropolitan Pittsburgh Crusade.*

41. Bangs, "Economic Benchmarks," 25–26; Andres Martinez, "On the Brink: City's Economic Decline May Be Tough to Stop," *Pittsburgh Post-Gazette*, 15 Feb. 1995.

42. John M. R. Bull, "Patterns of Racial Division: Pittsburgh's Housing Projects among Nation's Most Segregated," *Pittsburgh Post-Gazette*, 14 Apr. 1996; Douglas Heuck, "Surviving St. Clair Village," *Pittsburgh Post-Gazette*, 4 Mar. 1990.

43. Mindy Thompson Fullilove, *Root Shock: How Tearing Up City Neighborhoods Hurts America, And What We Can Do about It* (New York: Ballantine Books, One World, 2005), 68, 147, 176–78, 188.

44. Bull, "Patterns of Racial Division."

45. Bull, "Patterns of Racial Division."

46. McKay, "Blacks Lost Jobs."

47. David Young quoted in McKay, "Economic Crisis"; Bangs, "Economic Benchmarks," 26; Bangs, "Benchmarks," 20–21, 24.

48. Jerome Williams quoted in McKay, "Backslide"; Barbara Hart-Greer quoted in Diana Nelson Jones, "Surviving Oliver High's Racial Divide," *Pittsburgh Post-Gazette*, 28 Apr. 1996.

49. Jim McKay and Tawanda Williams, "What Can Be Done?" *Pittsburgh Post-Gazette*, 28 Apr. 1996.

50. McKay, "Backslide."

51. Jerome Taylor quoted in Jean Bryant, "Fearful Mothers Rely on Faith, Communication," *Pittsburgh Post-Gazette*, 29 June 1994; Bill Moushey, "Gangs Are All They Have," *Pittsburgh Post-Gazette*, 26 June 1994; LaMont Jones Jr., "City Should Have Read the Gang Signs Years Ago," *Pittsburgh Post-Gazette*, 27 June 1994.

52. Moushey, "Gangs" (quote); Jones, "City Should Have Read."

53. Moushey, "Gangs"; Jones, "City Should Have Read."

54. Ralph L. Bangs, "Demographic, Social, and Economic Conditions of African American Youth in Pittsburgh and Allegheny County," in *The State of Black Youth in Pittsburgh: Perspectives on Young African Americans in the City of Pittsburgh and Allegheny County*, ed. Major Albert Mason III and Ralph L. Bangs (Pittsburgh: Urban League of Pittsburgh, 1999), 64–/25; Ernest D. Preate Jr., "The 'De Facto' Racism that Cannot Be Ignored," also in Mason and Bangs, *State of Black Youth*, 99–123 (particularly 105–7); Bryant, "Fearful Mothers"; Edmunds and Bush, *Daybreakers*, 184; Jones, "City Should Have Read."

55. Preate, "'De Facto' Racism that Cannot Be Ignored," 96–107.

56. Roy L. Austin and Mark D. Allen, "Racial Disparity in Arrest Rates as an Explanation of Racial Disparity in Commitment to Pennsylvania's Prisons," *Journal of Research in Crime and Delinquency* 37, no. 2 (May 2000): 200–20; Justice Policy Institute Study, cited in Charles N. Brown, "Pennsylvania Tops Prison Disparity," *New Pittsburgh Courier*, 18 Aug. 2001; Tim Molloy, "Study Says PA Minorities Four Times as Likely to Be Imprisoned for Drugs," Associated Press and Local Wire, 5 Aug. 2000.

57. Turhan Shabazz quoted in McKay, "Unequal Payback"; Brown, "Pennsylvania

Tops Prison Disparity"; "Keeping African American Males in High School Should Be a Top Priority," editorial, *New Pittsburgh Courier,* 13 Oct. 1993.

58. Marla Perlman, "It Is Income, Not Race, That Is the Marker of Infant Mortality," *Post-Gazette,* 5 Dec. 1993; Clarke Thomas, "As Different as Black and White: Why Don't Minorities Get the Same Benefit from Pittsburgh's Health-Care System?" *Post-Gazette,* 7 Apr. 2004; Haslyn Hunte, Ralph Bangs, and Ken Thompson, "The Health Status of African Americans in Allegheny County: A Black Paper for the Urban League of Pittsburgh," Black Papers on African American Health in Allegheny County (Pittsburgh: University Center for Social and Urban Research, University of Pittsburgh/Urban League of Pittsburgh, 2002); Urban League of Pittsburgh, "Blacks in White" (Pittsburgh: Urban League of Pittsburgh, 1982), 5–6.

59. Harvey Adams quoted in Debran Rowland, "Harvey Adams, Jr.: The Voice of the NAACP Speaks to the Community," *New Pittsburgh Courier,* 10 Dec. 1988; Anita Strikameswaran, "Minorities Lag in Receiving Transplants and Heart Surgeries," *Pittsburgh Post-Gazette,*" 23 July 2002; Ritter, "NAACP Working at Achieving" *Pittsburgh Courier,* 10 Dec. 1988; "Transplant Recipient Nears One-Month Mark," *New York Times,* 27 Nov. 1987.

60. Strikameswaran, "Minorities Lag in Receiving Transplants and Heart Surgeries."

61. Kent M. James, "Public Policy and the Postwar Suburbanization of Pittsburgh, 1945–1990" (PhD diss., Pittsburgh: Carnegie Mellon University, 2005), 757 (quote); Steve Levin, "Census Shows Changing Racial Makeup of County," *Pittsburgh Post-Gazette,* 13 Mar. 2001; Brian Lyman, "Growing Diversity: More Minorities Call Northern Towns Home, But Their Numbers Are Still Small," *Pittsburgh Post-Gazette,* 28 Jan. 2001.

62. James, "Public Policy," 757 (quotes); Jean Bryant, "Discrimination Limits Blacks' Housing Choices," part of series, "It's Still a House Divided for Blacks and Whites in the Region," *Pittsburgh Post-Gazette,* 14 Apr. 1996; Levin, "Census Shows."

63. James, "Public Policy," 756–57, 761; Brian Lyman, "Growing Diversity: More Minorities Call Northern Towns Home, But Their Numbers Are Still Small," *Pittsburgh Post-Gazette,* 28 Jan. 2001; Bryant, "Discrimination Limits."

64. James, "Public Policy," 750–61 (quote, 158); Jeffrey Alan Hinkelman, "Penn Hills: The Development of a Suburban Community" (senior honors program paper, Humanities and Social Sciences, Carnegie Mellon University, Pittsburgh, 25 Apr. 1991), 11–14.

65. James, "Public Policy," 721, 724; Clarke Thomas, "Neighborhood City: Tending the Pieces that Make Up Pittsburgh's Still Key," *Pittsburgh Post-Gazette,* 3 Apr. 1996.

66. Steve Levin, "Census Shows Changing Racial Makeup of County," *Pittsburgh Post-Gazette,* 13 Mar. 2001 (quote); Steve Levin, "Region Sees More Blacks Buying Their Own Homes," *Pittsburgh Post-Gazette,* 26 Aug. 200.

67. Bryant, "Discrimination Limits."

68. John Gabriel and James Frazier quoted in James, "Public Policy," 751; David Michelmore, "The Color of Money: Loan Statistics Continue to Indicate Discrimination Against Blacks," *Pittsburgh Post-Gazette,* 12 May 1994; "Mortgaging Inequality— Blacks Still Have Less Chance of Getting a Home Loan," *Pittsburgh Post-Gazette,* 13 May 1994.

69. Community Housing Resource Board, "The Greater Pittsburgh Community Housing Resource Board: Needs, Assessment, Fair Housing and Law Compliance (Pittsburgh: Community Housing Resource Board, ca. 1983); Bush, "State of Black Pittsburgh" (1999), 8–9; (2000), 12–13; and (2004), 8–9; Bryant, "Discrimination Limits."

70. Quote about Carolyn Dillon from "It's Still a House Divided." For "Pittsburgh's apartheid," see Bull, "Patterns of Racial Division." See also Center on Race and Social Problems, *Pittsburgh's Racial Demographics: Differences and Disparities* (Pittsburgh: School of Social Work, University of Pittsburgh, June 2007), 53–62.

71. "For Blacks and Whites in Our Region, School Desegregation Gets a Failing Grade," *Pittsburgh Post-Gazette*, 21 Apr. 1996; Carmen Lee, "Survey to Study Student Decline," *Pittsburgh Post-Gazette*, 10 Apr. 1995.

72. John Portz, Lana Stein, and Robin R. Jones, *City Schools and City Politics: Institutions and Leadership in Pittsburgh, Boston, and St. Louis* (Lawrence: University Press of Kansas, 1999), 60–61. For an examination of the antecedents to Pittsburgh's magnet schools programs, see Marcella DeMarco, "Magnet Programs in the Pittsburgh Schools: Development to Implementation, 1977–1982" (PhD diss., University of Pittsburgh, 1983), 22–23.

73. Pittsburgh Board of Education (PBE), "The Pittsburgh Desegregation Plan" (Pittsburgh: PBE, 1979), 8–11, cited in Richard D. Gutkind, "Desegregation of Pittsburgh Public Schools, 1968–1980" (PhD diss., University of Pittsburgh, 1983), 103–6.

74. Ogle B. Duff, "The Pros and Cons of Busing in Pennsylvania" (Pittsburgh: University of Pittsburgh Race Desegregation Assistance Center, 1982).

75. Robert Lindsey, "School Integration Looks More Than Ever Like a Lost Horizon," *New York Times*, 24 Aug. 1980 (quote); Gene I. Maeroff, "Magnet Schools Used as Tool for Equity," *New York Times*, 31 Jan. 1984; Tracey A. Reed, "The Politics of School Desegregation: The Case of Pittsburgh Public Schools, 1965–1980" (PhD diss., University of Virginia, 1997), 256–57; "For Blacks and Whites in Our Region, School Desegregation."

76. Reed, "Politics of School Desegregation," 256–57; Maeroff, "Magnet Schools Used"; Lindsey, "School Integration"; "For Blacks and Whites in Our Region, School Desegregation."

77. Karen DeWitt, "Pittsburgh Moves to Integrate Schools," *New York Times*, 13 Dec. 1979.

78. Eleanor Chute, "Walking in Circles: 50 Years Later, Many Children Still Go to Schools that are Nearly All White or All Black," *Pittsburgh Post-Gazette*, 16 May 2004.

79. Bill Schackner, "Forced Integration Hasn't Balanced Schools' Makeup," *Pittsburgh Post-Gazette*, 21 Apr. 1996.

80. "For Blacks and Whites in Our Region, School Desegregation"; Chute, "Walking in Circles."

81. Chute, "Walking in Circles."

82. Eleanor Chute, "A Look at Linton: Racially Mixed School a Study in Successes, Problems," *Pittsburgh Post-Gazette*, 21 Apr. 1996.

83. Jane Zemel, "Finding Her Way in the World," *Pittsburgh Post-Gazette*, 21 Apr. 1996; Jane Zemel, "Upper St. Clair Teen Takes on Role as a Representative of His Race," *Pittsburgh Post-Gazette*, 21 Apr. 1996; Jane Zemel, "Words That Hurt: Blatant

or Subtle, Racist Comments and Actions Can Be Damaging," *Pittsburgh Post-Gazette*, 21 Apr. 1996.

84. Zemel, "Words That Hurt."

85. Schackner, "Forced Integration."

Chapter 5: Toward the New Century

1. Jim McKay, "Blacks Lost Jobs and a Generation with Manufacturing's Demise," *Pittsburgh Post-Gazette*, 15 Nov. 1994.

2. McKay, "Blacks Lost Jobs."

3. Jim McKay and Tawanda Williams, "What Can Be Done?" *Pittsburgh Post-Gazette*, 28 Apr. 1996.

4. Laurence Glasco, "The Civil Rights Movement in Pittsburgh: To Make This City 'Some Place Special,'" Freedom Corner, http://www.freedomcorner.org/downloads/glasco.pdf, 12–13 (accessed 29 September 2009); Ervin Dyer, "The Sweet Life for Black Pittsburghers: Sugar Top," *Pittsburgh Post-Gazette*, 17 July 2005; Pamela Foster, "Gloria Spearman: Destined Businesswoman," *New Pittsburgh Courier*, 3 Mar. 1990.

5. For the NAACP "took on a new face," see Debran Rowland, "Early NAACP Efforts Set Stage For Future Successes," *New Pittsburgh Courier*, 10 Dec. 1988. For quote by Harvey Adams, see Debran Rowland, "Harvey Adams Jr. . . . The Voice of the NAACP Speaks to the Community," *New Pittsburgh Courier*, 10 Dec. 1988.

6. Bernard L. Ritter, "NAACP Working at Achieving 'The Dream,'" *New Pittsburgh Courier*, 10 Dec. 1988.

7. Harvey Adams quoted in Rowland, "Harvey Adams Jr."; Ritter, "NAACP Working"; A. Vivienne Robinson, "Adams Meets NAACP Challenges with Commitment, Compassion," *New Pittsburgh Courier*, 10 Dec. 1988.

8. Sonya M. Haynes, "A Tragic Loss," *New Pittsburgh Courier*, 17 May 1997; "Bidwell Graduates First Cable Class," *New Pittsburgh Courier*, 3 Jan. 1981; "Pittsburgher Named Top Executive for Warner," *New Pittsburgh Courier*, 27 June 1981; Marva Harris and Gene Harris, interview by Jared Day for the Center for Africanamerican Urban Studies and the Economy (CAUSE), Remembering Africanamerican Pittsburgh Oral History Project (RAP), Department of History, Carnegie Mellon University, Pittsburgh, 15 Aug. 2007.

9. Quote from Robert Pitts, interview by Jared Day for CAUSE, RAP, 7 Aug. 2007. See also Robinson, "Adams Meets"; Roland, "Harvey Adams Jr."

10. Matthew Hawkins quoted in Marty Willis, "D.C. Rally Hits New Issues," *Pittsburgh Courier*, 17 Apr. 1985; "NAACP Demonstration Targets Weitz," *New Pittsburgh Courier*, 19 Jan. 1985; Marty Willis, "School Board Links to South Africa," *New Pittsburgh Courier*, 12 Jan. 1985; Rowland, "Harvey Adams Jr."

11. See affidavit of William Russell Robinson, *Metropolitan Pittsburgh Crusade for Voters vs. City of Pittsburgh, et al.*, case no. 86–173, U.S. District Court for the Western District of Pennsylvania (1986), in Group V, Box 2215, Folder 3, NAACP Papers, Library of Congress, Washington DC.

12. Leon L. Haley, "The Post-Industrial Era," in *Daybreakers: The Story of the Urban League of Pittsburgh*, Arthur J. Edmunds and Esther Bush (1983; reprt. and rev., Pittsburgh: Urban League of Pittsburgh, 1999), 179–94 (quotes, 180, 182).

13. Esther L. Bush, "The State of Black Pittsburgh," keynote addresses delivered annually, 1990–2004 for the Urban League of Pittsburgh, Pittsburgh.

14. Bush, "State of Black Pittsburgh" (2001), 22.

15. Manchester Craftsmen's Guild, "MCG History," http://www.manchesterguild.org/MCG_History.htm (accessed 2 October 2009).

16. Damon T. Bethea, "Faith-Based Organizing and Partnership in a Pittsburgh Neighborhood: A Look at East Liberty" (MA thesis, Duquesne University, Apr. 2004), 1–2, 10–29.

17. The Kingsley Association, "Who We Are," http://kingsleyassociation.org/who_we_are.html (accessed 2 October 2009); Hill House Association, "Mission and Purpose," http://www.hillhouse.org/aboutus (accessed 2 October 2009).

18. David Michelmore, "The Color of Money: Loan Statistics Continue to Indicate Discrimination Against Blacks," *Pittsburgh Post-Gazette*, 12 May 1994; "Mortgaging Inequality—Blacks Still Have Less Chance of Getting a Home Loan," *Pittsburgh Post-Gazette*, 12 May 1994; Steve Levin, "Census Shows Changing Racial Makeup of County," *Pittsburgh Post-Gazette*, 13 Mar. 2001; "It's Still a House Divided for Blacks and Whites in the Region," *Pittsburgh Post-Gazette*, 14 Apr. 1996.

19. On the two low-interest loan programs (including quote), see Joyce Gannon, "A Tough Goal on Home Ownership," *Pittsburgh Post-Gazette*, 4 Aug. 1996. Denise Brundage quoted in Steve Levin, "Region Sees More Blacks Buying Their Own Homes," *Pittsburgh Post-Gazette*, 26 Aug. 2001.

20. Quotes from public housing residents in Nathaniel Wilkes, "Angry Confrontation at Broadhead Manor," *New Pittsburgh Courier*, 17 Aug. 1996; John M. R. Bull, "Patterns of Racial Division: Pittsburgh's Housing Projects among Nation's Most Segregated," *Pittsburgh Post-Gazette*, 14 Apr. 1996; Tom Barnes, "Broadhead Manor Residents Tangle," *Pittsburgh Post-Gazette*, 6 Sept. 1996; Gary Rotstein, "Broadhead Manor Residents Rally," *Pittsburgh Post-Gazette*, 2 Aug. 1996. Compare Douglas Heuck, "Surviving St. Clair Village," *Pittsburgh Post-Gazette*, 4 Mar. 1990.

21. Sharon McDonald quoted in Wilkes, "Angry Confrontation"; Broadhead Manor resident quoted in Barnes, "Broadhead Manor Residents Tangle." See also Rotstein, "Broadhead Manor Residents Rally."

22. Sonya M. Haynes, "Fireworks on the Terrace," *New Pittsburgh Courier*, 16 July 1994 (quote); Sandy Hamm, "Residents Can't Get Straight Answers to Honest Questions," *New Pittsburgh Courier*, 16 July 1994; "Residents Protests Kill Murphy Plan," *Pittsburgh Post-Gazette*, 8 Jan. 1995.

23. Terri Baltimore, "Grappling with Displacement," in Anthony Robbins, *Hillscapes: A Scrapbook Envisioning a Healthy Urban Habitat*, 2nd. ed. (Pittsburgh: University of Pittsburgh Center for Minority Health, July 1999), 11–13.

24. Mindy Thompson Fullilove, *Root Shock: How Tearing Up City Neighborhoods Hurts America, And What We Can Do About It* (New York: Ballantine Books, One World, 2005), 188–91, 236; Mindy Fullilove, associate professor of psychiatry and public health, to Sala Udin, Pittsburgh city councilman, 30 July 1997, in Robbins, *Hillscapes*, 16–17.

25. Robbins, "Asking the Question," in Robbins, *Hillscapes*, 7–9; Memorandum from Phil Hallen, CEO Falk Fund, to Center for Minority Health, 12 Jan. 1998

(announcing funding for program to support minority health fellows), in Robbins, *Hillscapes*, 18.

26. Terri Baltimore, "Grappling with Displacement," in Robbins, *Hillscapes*, 1–18; David Lewis, "The Hill Rebuilds Itself," in Robbins, *Hillscapes*, 65–66; Robert Fullilove, "Teach-Ins and Community Organizing," in Robbins, *Hillscapes*, 20–21; Mindy Fullilove, "Is My Community Dead?" in Robbins, *Hillscapes*, 23.

27. Patricia Murphy, "The Housing That Community Built," National Housing Institute's *Shelter Force* 138 (Nov.–Dec. 2004), http://www.nhi.org/online/issues/138/bedford.html (accessed on 10 Dec. 2009); Mindy Fullilove, "Comments on Urban Design," in Robbins, *Hillscapes*, 19; Glasco, "Civil Rights Movement," 13. For the spread of these changes to other public housing projects, see "St. Clair Village's Last Public Housing Units to Be Demolished," *Pittsburgh Tribune-Review*, 24 July 2009.

28. Lynette Clemetson, "Revival for a Black Enclave," *New York Times*, 9 Aug. 2002; Harris and Harris, interview, CAUSE, RAP.

29. Eleanor Chute, "Walking in Circles: 50 Years Later, Many Children Still Go to Schools That Are Nearly All White or All Black," *Pittsburgh Post-Gazette*, 16 May 2004.

30. Carmen J. Lee, "Trying for the Best of Both Worlds: Area's Black Private Schools Offer Safe Environment, Cultural Focus," *Pittsburgh Post-Gazette*, 21 Apr. 1996.

31. Chute, "Walking in Circles"; Lee, "Trying for the Best."

32. Bush, "State of Black Pittsburgh" (2001), 19–20; Bush, "State of Black Pittsburgh" (2004), 7.

33. Lee, "Trying for the Best."

34. Debran Rowland, "Committees Keep in Touch with Community," *New Pittsburgh Courier*, 10 Dec. 1988; Edmunds and Bush, *Daybreakers*, 213; Bush, "State of Black Pittsburgh" (1999), 10–13; Bush, "State of Black Pittsburgh" (2001), 20; Bush, "State of Black Pittsburgh" (2003), 6; Major Albert Mason III and Ralph L. Bangs, eds. *The State of Black Youth in Pittsburgh: Perspectives on Young African Americans in the City of Pittsburgh and Allegheny County*. Pittsburgh: Urban League of Pittsburgh, 1999.

35. August Wilson Center, "Brief History," http://www.augustwilsoncenter.org/about/history.php (accessed on 10 Dec. 2009); African American Cultural Center of Greater Pittsburgh, "A Center for Dynamic Culture" (Pittsburgh: African American Cultural Center of Greater Pittsburgh, 2003), 1–5; African American Cultural Center of Greater Pittsburgh, "Charette Summary," (Pittsburgh: African American Cultural Center of Greater Pittsburgh, Oct. 2000), 2–17; August Wilson Center, "Our History: A Vision of the Future" (Pittsburgh: August Wilson Center, Fall 2008).

36. African American Cultural Center of Greater Pittsburgh, "Center for Dynamic Culture," 1–5; African American Cultural Center of Greater Pittsburgh, "Charette Summary," 2–17; August Wilson Center, "Our History."

37. African American Cultural Center of Greater Pittsburgh, "Center for Dynamic Culture," 5 (quote); August Wilson Center, "Brief History"; African American Cultural Center of Greater Pittsburgh, "Charette Summary," 2–17; August Wilson Center, "Our History"; Glasco, "Double Burden," 76.

38. "African American Collection Project: Multi-Cultural Arts Initiative Proposal" (Historical Society of Western Pennsylvania [Heinz History Center], 18 May 1992), 1–7 (quotes, 1, 3); Samuel W. Black, ed., *Soul Soldiers: African Americans and the Vietnam Era* (Pittsburgh: The Senator John Heinz History Center, 2006); Samuel Black, "Soul Soldiers: Tour Schedule," correspondence to Soul Soldiers Ad Hoc Committee, 24 Jan. 2009, correspondence, in authors' possession.

39. See series of articles by Marty Willis, "All-White Council Ceremony Draws Protest," 18 Jan. 1986; "Jan. 6 Demonstration to Greet All-White City Council," 11 Jan. 1986; and "Electoral Reform Public Forum," 4 Jan. 1986, all in *New Pittsburgh Courier*.

40. Marty Willis, "Black Groups Unify Around District Elections Effort," *New Pittsburgh Courier*, 11 Apr. 1987; Marty Willis, "B-PEP Endorses District Council Elections," *New Pittsburgh Courier*, 11 Apr. 1987; B-PEP, "Black Political Empowerment Project," http://www.b-ep.net/police_accountability.htm (accessed December 2008); Landmark Education Program, "Tim Stevens: Black Political Empowerment Project, Community Action Builds African-American Voter Impact," http://www.landmarkeducation.com/display_content.htm (accessed December 2008).

41. Jan Ackerman, "Black Leaders' Suit Challenges At-Large Voting," *Post-Gazette*, 23 Jan. 1986; William L. Robinson, director Lawyers' Committee for Civil Rights Under Law, to Benjamin M. Hooks, executive director NAACP, National Office, 19 Feb. 1987; Civil Action No. 86–173, in *Metropolitan Pittsburgh Crusade for Voters vs. City of Pittsburgh, et al.*, case no. 86–173, U.S. District Court for the Western District of Pennsylvania, 1986, Group V, Box 2215, Folder 3, NAACP Papers, Library of Congress, Washington DC. For insight into ongoing internal conflict over district versus at-large-elections, see "Districts and Dissenters," editorial, *Pittsburgh Post-Gazette*, 5 Feb. 1987, and articles by Philip Shropshire, "NAACP's Stance Key Factor in Lawsuit," 21 Mar. 1987; and "City Uses NAACP Vote to Bolster Position in Suit Against Crusade," 14 Mar. 1987, both in *New Pittsburgh Courier*.

42. Rev. T. E. Smith quoted in Ackerman, "Black Leaders' Suit."

43. Ackerman, "Black Leaders' Suit."

44. Affidavits of Thomas J. Murphy, Rev. James "Jimmy Joe" Robinson, Jake Milliones, and Ronald Suber, *Metropolitan Pittsburgh Crusade*.

45. Philip Shropshire, "City Crusade Agree to Consent Decree: District Election Reapportionment Under Federal Court Control," *New Pittsburgh Courier*, 6 June 1987; "Judge Denies Injunction: Grants Earlier Trial Date," *New Pittsburgh Courier*, 28 Feb. 1987; Laurence Glasco, "Double Burden," in Hays, *City at the Point*, 90; Laurence Glasco, *A Legacy of Bricks and Mortar: African American Landmarks in Allegheny County* (Pittsburgh: Pittsburgh History and Landmark Foundation, 1995), 29.

46. Sala Udin quoted in Sandy Hamm, "Sala Udin Emerges as the 6th District Front Runner," *New Pittsburgh Courier*, 15 Feb. 1995; Sandy Hamm, "History Made in Pittsburgh: Former School Board President Becomes 1st Afro-American [Woman] on City Council," *New Pittsburgh Courier*, 26 Nov. 1994; Valerie McDonald Roberts, interview by Kevin Brown for CAUSE, RAP, 21 June 2007.

47. Celeste Taylor McCurdy quoted in "15,000 Sign Udin's Pittsburgh Works Petition," *New Pittsburgh Courier*, 21 Aug. 1999; "Pittsburgh Works! Gets Mixed Reaction," *New Pittsburgh Courier*, 3 Mar. 1999; "March for Jobs," *New Pittsburgh Courier*,

3 July 1999; N. Charles, "Udin's Pittsburgh Works Gets Council's Preliminary OK," *New Pittsburgh Courier*, 21 Apr. 2001; "Udin's Pittsburgh Works Supporters Jam Council Hearing," *New Pittsburgh Courier*, 13 Feb. 1999; "Pittsburgh Works Referendum," *New Pittsburgh Courier*, 7 June 2000; "Pittsburgh Works! Passes, Still Faces Challenges," *New Pittsburgh Courier*, 6 Nov. 1999.

48. Jean S. Farrish, "Women's Political Crusade Expands Focus," *New Pittsburgh Courier*, 25 Feb. 1995 (quote); Bush, "State of Black Pittsburgh" (2001), 26–27; Bush and Edmunds, *Daybreakers*, 184–86.

49. Bruce W. Dixon, director, Allegheny County Health Department, to Alice Bell, Prevention Point coordinator, 16 Jan. 2002, www.pppgh.org/pppghletter.pdf (accessed 8 Feb. 2010); Caroline Acker, associate professor of history, Carnegie Mellon University, personal communication to Joe W. Trotter and Jared Day, 17 Apr. 2008; Black, *Soul Soldiers*, 129–46, particularly 144; Bush, "State of Black Pittsburgh" (2003), 10–11.

50. Sonya M. Haynes, "Stevens: Trial Littered with Injustices," *New Pittsburgh Courier*, 16 Nov. 1996; Sonya M. Haynes, "Gammage Case Brings National NAACP to City," *New Pittsburgh Courier*, 23 Nov. 1996; "For Blacks and Whites in the Region, the Issue Is . . . The Color of the Law," *Pittsburgh Post-Gazette*, 5 May 1996; Edmunds and Bush, *Daybreakers*, 198–201.

51. Michele D. Robertson, "Blacks Shocked, Express Disbelief," *New Pittsburgh Courier*, 16 Nov. 1996; Tim Stevens quoted in Haynes, "Stevens." Also see Doug Heuck, Cindi Lash, Bill Schackner, Bill Hetzel, and Tom Barnes, "Justice Delay Brings Letdown," *Pittsburgh Post-Gazette*, 20 Oct. 1996; Jan Ackerman and Jan Schmitz, "Verdict Ends First of 2 Criminal Prosecutions in Traffic Stop Death," *Pittsburgh Post-Gazette*, 14 Nov. 1996; and Dennis Roddy, "The Gammage Case: Brentwood Waits, Prepares for Trouble," *Pittsburgh Post-Gazette*, 14 Nov. 1996.

52. Deepak Karamcheti, "'Journey for Justice' Marchers Seek Federal Intervention in Gammage Case," *New Pittsburgh Courier*, 19 Feb. 1997; Michele D. Robertson, "Youth on the March," *New Pittsburgh Courier*, 27 Nov. 1996; "Justice Probe Requested by National NAACP," *New Pittsburgh Courier*, 14 Dec. 1996.

53. Kwame Dixon and Patricia E. Allard, "Police Brutality and International Human Rights in the United States: Report on Hearings Held in Los Angeles, California, Chicago, Illinois, and Pittsburgh, Pennsylvania, Fall 1999" (New York: Amnesty International USA, Feb. 2000), 28–36; Pittsburgh City Council, "Proclamation: The Citizens Police Review Board," http://profile.myspace.com-citizenpolicereviewboard/htm (accessed January 2008).

54. Jim McKay, "Unequal Payback: For Blacks and Whites in Our Region," *Pittsburgh Post-Gazette*, 28 Apr. 1996.

55. Mark S. Warnick, "Gangs Triggering Fear in their Neighborhoods," *Pittsburgh Post-Gazette*, June 30, 1994.

56. McKay, "Unequal Payback."

57. McKay, "Unequal Payback."

58. Robin D. G. Kelley, "Into the Fire: 1970 to the Present," in *To Make Our World Anew: A History of African Americans*, ed. Robin D. G. Kelley and Earl Lewis (New York: Oxford University Press, 2000), 597–98.

59. Rahmon Hart, "Million Man March: It's Time for the Black Man to Do His Part," *New Pittsburgh Courier*, 18 Jan. 1995; Aubrey Bruce, "March Organizers Say Event Will Resurrect Black Pride," *New Pittsburgh Courier*, 7 Oct. 1995.

60. Beatrice "Bea" Mitchell, email correspondence to Joe W. Trotter, Carnegie Mellon University, 25 Jan. 2008.

61. Randall Robinson, *The Debt: What America Owes to Blacks* (New York,: Penguin Putnam Inc., 2000), 246 (quote).

62. See Barack Obama, *Change We Can Believe In: Barack Obama's Plan to Renew America's Promise* (New York: Three Rivers Press, 2008); Barack Obama, *Dreams from My Father: A Story of Race and Inheritance* (New York: Times Book, 1995); Barack Obama, *The Audacity of Hope: Thoughts on Reclaiming the American Dream* (New York: Crown Publishers, 2006).

63. David Espo, associated press special correspondent, "Obama Wins . . . Elected Nation's 44th President: Landslide Victory a Triumph Over Racial Barriers," *New Pittsburgh Courier*, 4 Nov. 2008; C. Denise Johnson, "Obama Makes Pittsburgh Debut as Candidate," *New Pittsburgh Courier*, 27 June 2007; Jesse Washington, "Obama's Color: Is He Black, White . . . or Neither? Racial Categories Are Falling Apart," *New Pittsburgh Courier*, 31 Dec. 2008.

64. James O'Toole, "Historic Wave Sweeps Obama to Victory," *Pittsburgh Post-Gazette*, 5 Nov. 2008; James O'Toole, "A Torch Is Passed, a Barrier Broken: Barack Obama Is Sworn in as 44th President" *Pittsburgh Post-Gazette*, 21 Jan. 2009; Monica Haynes and Deborah M. Todd, "African American Pittsburghers Celebrate Historic Presidential Vote," *Pittsburgh Post-Gazette*, 5 Nov. 2008; Peter Wallsten, *Pittsburgh Post-Gazette*, "Analysis: Whites Boost Obama Victory," 6 Nov. 2008.

65. Kenneth L. Kusmer and Joe W. Trotter, ed., *African Americans Urban History Since World War II* (Chicago: University of Chicago Press, 2009); James N. Gregory, *The Southern Diaspora: How the Great Migrations of Black and White Southerners Transformed America* (Chapel Hill: The University of North Carolina Press, 2005); Arnold Hirsch, *Making the Second Ghetto: Race and Housing in Chicago 1940–1960* (1983; reprt., Chicago: The University of Chicago Press, 1998); Joe W. Trotter, Earl Lewis, Earl, and Tera W. Hunter, ed., *The African American Urban Experience: From the Colonial Era to the Present* (New York: Palgrave Publishing Company, 2004); Andrew Wiese, *Places of Their Own: African American Suburbanization in the Twentieth Century* (Chicago: University of Illinois Press, 2004).

66. Matthew Countryman, *Up South: Civil Rights and Black Power in Philadelphia* (Philadelphia,: University of Pennsylvania Press, 2006); Wendell Pritchett, *Brownsville, Brooklyn: Blacks, Jews, and the Changing Face of the Ghetto* (Chicago: The University of Chicago Press, 2002); Steven Gregory, *Black Corona: Race and the Politics of Place in an Urban Community* (Princeton: Princeton University Press, 1998); William J. Wilson, *The Truly Disadvantaged: The Inner City, the Underclass, and Public Policy* (Chicago: The University of Chicago Press, 1987); Alan H. Spear, *Black Chicago: The Making of a Negro Ghetto 1890–1920* (Chicago: The University of Chicago Press, 1967); Gilbert Osofsky, *Harlem: The Making of a Ghetto: Negro New York, 1890–1930* (Chicago: Elephant Paperback, 1966); W. E. B. DuBois, *The Philadelphia Negro: A Social Study* (1899; reprt. Philadelphia: University of Pennsylvania Press, 1996); St. Clair

Drake and Horace A. Cayton, *Black Metropolis: A Study of Negro Life in a Northern City* (1945; reprt., Chicago: The University of Chicago Press, 1993).

67. Ralph Bangs, "Economic Benchmarks: Indices for the City of Pittsburgh and Allegheny County," University of Pittsburgh, University Center for Social and Urban Research, 1994, 12–13.

68. Thomas J. Sugrue, *The Origins of the Urban Crisis: Race and Inequality in Postwar Detroit* (Princeton: Princeton University Press, 1996); Kenneth L. Kusmer, *A Ghetto Takes Shape: Black Cleveland, 1870–1930* (Urbana: University of Illinois Press, 1976); Joe William Trotter Jr., *Black Milwaukee: The Making of an Industrial Proletariat, 1915–45* (Urbana: University of Illinois Press, 1985); Douglas S. Massey and Nancy A. Denton, *American Apartheid: Segregation and the Making of the Underclass* (Cambridge, MA: Harvard University Press, 1993); Kimberley L. Phillips, *Alabama North: African-American Migrants, Community, and Working-Class Activism in Cleveland, 1915–45* (Urbana: University of Illinois Press, 1999); Andrew Hurley, *Environmental Inequalities: Class, Race, and Industrial Pollution in Gary, Indiana, 1945–1980* (Chapel Hill: The University of North Carolina Press, 1995); Alice O'Connor, Chris Tilly, Lawrence D. Bobo, eds., *Urban Inequality: Evidence from Four Cities* (New York: Russell Sage Foundation, 2001); Richard W. Thomas, *Life for Us Is What We Make It: Building Black Community in Detroit, 1915–1945* (Bloomington: Indiana University Press, 1992); Kenneth L. Kusmer, ed., *Progress versus Poverty: 1970 to the Present* (New York: Garland Publishing, Inc., 1991).

69. Nancy Foner and George M. Fredrickson, eds., *Not Just Black and White: Historical and Contemporary Perspectives on Immigration, Race, and Ethnicity in the United States* (New York: Russell Sage Foundation, 2004); Charles Hirschman, Philip Kasinitz, and Josh DeWind, eds., *The Handbook of International Migration: The American Experience* (New York: Russell Sage Foundation, 1999).

70. Joe W. Trotter, with H. LaRue Trotter, "The Caribbean Experience in Pittsburgh: An Interview with Myrven Caines, M.D.," *Pittsburgh History: A Magazine of the City and Its Region* (Winter 1995/96), 193–96; Center on Race and Social Problems, *Pittsburgh's Racial Demographics: Differences and Disparities* (Pittsburgh: University of Pittsburgh School of Social Work, 2007).

BIBLIOGRAPHY

Manuscript Collections

FEPC (Committee on Fair Employment Practice) Papers, Record Group #228. National Archives and Records Administration, Region III, Philadelphia.

> Davis, Elizabeth. Complaint against the American Bridge Company, 10 Oct. 1944, Case #3-BR-827.
>
> Denmar, George E., secretary of the Urban League of Pittsburgh, to P. T. Fagan, 27 Oct. 1942.
>
> Employment Petition to the American Bridge Company, 3 May 1943, American Bridge Company file (no case number included).
>
> Examiner to James Fleming, 13 Mar. 1944, Case #3-BR-1821.
>
> Johnson, Werner L. machine operator trainee, Westinghouse Air Brake Company, Case #3-BR-1990.
>
> "President's Committee on Fair Employment Practice: Final Disposition Report." 1 Aug. 1945, Case #3-BR-1821I.
>
> Tate, Mrs. Martha (laborer in the machine shop), Case #3-BR-1955.
>
> Taylor, Charles A. Complaint against the United Bronze Castings Company, 16 May 1945, Case #3-BR-1981.

Library and Archives, Senator John Heinz History Center, Pittsburgh.

> "Lower Hill District (The Future Home of the Civic Arena)." Photograph Collection, 1957,

NAACP Papers, Library of Congress, Washington DC.

> Baker, Ella (director of branches, NYC headquarters), to Jeanne S. Scott (secretary, Pittsburgh branch). 7 Feb. 1948. Group II, Box C-171, Folder 2.
>
> Jones, Richard F. "Annual Address by the President to the Pittsburgh Branch of the NAACP." 3 Dec. 1953, Group II, Box 2, Folder 4.
>
> Lampkin, Daisy E. (chair, Pittsburgh branch), and Jeanne S. Scott (secretary, Pittsburgh branch). "Social Policy Committee Report." 14 Jan. 1946. Group II, Box C-171, Folder 2.

Metropolitan Pittsburgh Crusade for Voters vs. City of Pittsburgh, et al., case no. 86–173, U. S. District Court for the Western District of Pennsylvania. 1986. Group V, Box 2215, Folder 3. Includes affidavits (all for the plaintiff) of: C. B. "Knowledge" Clark, Wendell Freeland, Jake Milliones, Thomas J. Murphy, Rev. James "Jimmy Joe" Robinson, William Russell Robinson, Ronald Suber, and Rollo Turner.

Nelson, Sophia B. (member, Pittsburgh NAACP), to Donald Jones (N.Y. national headquarters). 29 Mar. 1945. Group II, Box C-171, Folder 2.

Pittsburgh NAACP. Annual Reports of the President and Executive Secretary. 18 July 1952, 11 Mar. 1958, and 10 Dec. 1959, Group II, Box 2, Folder 4.

Pittsburgh NAACP. "Pittsburgh, Pennsylvania Branch, Organized 1914." Group II, Box C-171, Folder 2.

Porter, Edward D. (Inter-racial Action Council), to Ella J. Baker, 2 Apr. 1945, Group II, Box C-171, Folder 2.

Robinson, William L. (director, Lawyers' Committee for Civil Rights Under Law), to Benjamin M. Hooks (executive director NAACP, national office), 19 Feb. 1987, Group V, Box 2215, Folder 3.

Scott, Jeanne S. (secretary, Pittsburgh branch), to Ella J. Baker (director of branches, NYC headquarters). 12 April 1946, Group V, Box 2215, Folder 3.

Schooley, Henry A. "A Case Study of the Pittsburgh Branch of the National Association for the Advancement of Colored People." MA thesis, University of Pittsburgh, 1952, Group II, Box 2, Folder 4.

"Stanton Land Company vs. City of Pittsburgh: Brief of Amici Curia." No. 1741, Apr. Team, 1963-A, in Group V, Box 2220, folder 7-A.

National Urban League (NUL) Papers, Library of Congress, Washington DC.

"Annual Report of ULP, 1951." Part 1: N, Series 13, Box 22.

"The Fifteenth Year, 1918–1932: Annual Report of the Urban League of Pittsburgh." Part 1: N, Series 13, Box 22.

"31st Annual Report of the ULP, 1955." Part 1: N, Series 13, Box 22.

Johnson, Reginald A. secretary, Industrial Relations Department, ULP, to T. Arnold Hill, 20 Oct. 1938. Part 1: D, Series 4, Box 34.

Moss, E. Maurice, executive secretary Urban League of Pittsburgh, to T. Arnold Hill, National Urban League, 1 Mar. 1939. Part 1: D, Series 4, Box 34.

Moss, E. Maurice, executive secretary, Urban League of Pittsburgh, to National Urban League Advisory Council Members, 18 Mar 1937. Part 1: D, Series 4, Box 34.

"Quarter of a Century of Exclusion at Highland Park Pool." Digest of struggle, 1927, 1952.

Report of the Department of Industrial Relations, Jan. and Feb. 1933. Part 1: D, Series 4, Box 34.

Young, Whitney M., Jr. "Racism and the future of American Cities." Speech at the Pittsburgh Plate Glass Foundation, 18 May 1964, in Part 2: E, Series 5, Box 43.

Interviews, Personal Communications, Speeches

Acker, Caroline, associate professor of history, Carnegie Mellon University, letter to Joe W. Trotter and Jared Day, 17 Apr. 2008.

Black, Samuel W. "Soul Soldiers: Tour Schedule." Correspondence to Soul Soldiers Ad Hoc Committee, 24 Jan. 2009. In personal collection of Joe W. Trotter.

Bush, Esther L. "The State of Black Pittsburgh." Keynote addresses delivered annually, 1990–2004 for the Urban League of Pittsburgh, Pittsburgh.

Center for African American Urban Studies and the Economy (CAUSE), Remembering Africanamerican Pittsburgh Oral History Project (RAP). Department of History, Carnegie Mellon University, Pittsburgh.

    Adams, Harvey. Interview by Jared Day, 6 July 2007.

    Bell, Lloyd. Interview by Jared Day, 17 Aug. 2007.

    Coleman, Morton. Interview by Jared Day, 24 July 2007.

    Epperson, David. Interview by Jared Day, 19 July 2007.

    Fox, Gerald. Interveiw by Kevin Brown, 5 July 2007.

    Frazier, James. Interview by Fidel Campet, 7 Mar. 2007.

    Hallen, Phil. Interview by Johanna Fernandez, 19 July 2007.

    Harris, Marva, and Gene Harris. Interview by Jared Day, 15 Aug. 2007.

    James, Alan. Interview by Jared Day, 14 Aug. 2007.

    Lavelle, Robert R. Interview by Jared Day, 15 Aug. 2007.

    Lovette, Thelma, Sr. Interview by staff, 2 July 2007.

    McClomb, George E. Interview by Jared Day, 20 Aug. 2007.

    McDonald Roberts, Valerie. Interview by Kevin Brown, 21 June 2007.

    McIlvane, Robert. Interview by Fidel Campet, 19 Mar. 2007.

    Morris, Gregory. Interview by staff, 7 Aug. 2007.

    Pitts, Robert. Interview by Jared Day, 7 Aug. 2007.

    Stevens, Tim. Interview by staff, 18 July 2007.

    Tillman, Betty J. Interview by Shawn Alfonso Wells, 23 Aug. 2007.

    Udin, Sala. Interview by staff, 13 June 2007.

    Watson, Warren. Interview by Jennifer I. Schuitema, 6 May 2007.

    Williams, Celeste. Interview by staff, Summer 2007.

Dixon, Bruce W. Director, Allegheny County Health Department. Letter to Alice Bell, Prevention Point Coordinator, 16 Jan. 2002, www.pppgh.org/pppghletter.pdf (accessed 8 Feb. 2010).

"Honoring Robert E. 'Pappy' Williams: The 2007 Spirit of King Award Ceremony." Pittsburgh, PA, 11 Jan. 2007.

"K. Leroy Irvis: The Speaker." Commonwealth of Pennsylvania, Memorial Ceremony, House of Representatives, 25 Apr. 2006.

Mitchell, Beatrice "Bea." email correspondence to Joe W. Trotter, Carnegie Mellon University, 25 Jan. 2008.

Senator John Heinz History Center. *An Interview with Nate Smith: The Transcription of an Oral History.* Pittsburgh: Historical Society of Western Pennsylvania Oral History Service, published by Mechling Bookbindery, Chicora, PA, ca. 2002.

Tronzo, Alfred. Interview by Dodie Carpenter for the Pittsburgh Renaissance Project. 19 Aug. 1974. Archives of Industrial Society, University of Pittsburgh.

Organization and Government Reports, Dissertations, Seminar Papers

ACTION-Housing. "The Black Population and Its Housing: A Social and Economic Profile of The Black Community in the Pittsburgh Metropolitan Area." Pittsburgh: ACTION-Housing, Inc., May 1969.
———. "A Report on the Pilot Program, Neighborhood Urban Extension Homewood-Brushton, 1960–1963." Pittsburgh: ACTION-Housing, Inc., 1964.
———. "Urban Renewal Impact Study." Pittsburgh: ACTION-Housing, Inc., 1963.
African American Cultural Center of Greater Pittsburgh. "A Center for Dynamic Culture." Mission statement. Pittsburgh, 2003.
———. "Charette Summary." Pittsburgh: African American Cultural Center of Greater Pittsburgh, Oct. 2000.
Auerbach, Herbert A. "The Status of Housing of Negroes in Pittsburgh." Pittsburgh: City of Pittsburgh Commission on Human Relations, Nov. 1958.
August Wilson Center. "Our History: A Vision of the Future." Pittsburgh: August Wilson Center, Fall 2008.
Bangs, Ralph. "Black and White Economic Conditions in the City of Pittsburgh: A Benchmarks Special Report." University of Pittsburgh, Center for Social and Urban Research, 1995.
———. "Current Social Conditions of African Americans in the Pittsburgh Region." University of Pittsburgh, University Center for Social and Urban Research, 23 Oct. 2000.
———. "Economic Benchmarks: Indices for the City of Pittsburgh and Allegheny County." University of Pittsburgh, University Center for Social and Urban Research, 1994.
———. "Linking the Unemployed to Growth Centers in Allegheny County: Final Report." University of Pittsburgh, University Center for Social and Urban Research, 1991.
Barnett, Marilyn Fredericka. "Superintendents, Desegregation and the Politics of Compliance: Wilkinsburg, Pennsylvania: 1968–1986." PhD diss., University of Pittsburgh, 1990.
Bethea, Damon T. "Faith-Based Organizing and Partnership in a Pittsburgh Neighborhood: A Look at East Liberty." MA thesis, Duquesne University, 2004.
Bunzel, Joseph H. "Negro Housing Needs in Pittsburgh and Allegheny County." Pittsburgh: Pittsburgh Housing Association, 1946.
Bureau of Social Research, Federation of Social Agencies of Pittsburgh and Allegheny County. "Mobility of Public Housing Residents." Pittsburgh: Federation of Social Agencies of Pittsburgh and Allegheny County, 1946.
———. "The Population of Public Housing." Pittsburgh: Federation of Social Agencies of Pittsburgh and Allegheny County, ca. 1944.
Campet, Fidel. "Urban League of Pittsburgh, 1964–1973." Pittsburgh: Carnegie Mellon University, Department of History, CAUSE Oral History Research Project Paper, 12 May 2007.

Center for Urban and Social Research. "Black and White Economic Conditions." Research report. University of Pittsburgh, June 1995.

———. "Economic Benchmarks." Research report. University of Pittsburgh, Oct. 1994.

Center on Race and Social Problems. "Pittsburgh's Racial Demographics: Differences and Disparities." Pittsburgh: University of Pittsburgh School of Social Work, 2007.

Cole, Lori. "Voices and Choices: Race, Class, and Identity, Homestead, Pennsylvania, 1941–1945." PhD diss., Carnegie Mellon University, 1994.

Commission of Inquiry, the Interchurch World Movement. *Report of the Steel Strike of 1919.* New York: Harcourt, Brace and World, 1920.

Commonwealth of Pennsylvania. *Final Report of the Pennsylvania State Temporary Commission on the Conditions of the Urban Colored Population.* Harrisburg: The Pennsylvania General Assembly, Jan. 1943.

Community Housing Resource Board. "The Greater Pittsburgh Community Housing Resource Board: Needs, Assessment, Fair Housing and Law Compliance." Pittsburgh: Community Housing Resource Board, ca. 1983.

Darden, Joe T. "The Spatial Dynamics of Residential Segregation of Afro-Americans in Pittsburgh." PhD diss., University of Pittsburgh, 1972.

Davis, Yvonne H. "The Concerns of Black Women for Their Children and Schools." MS thesis, University of Pittsburgh, 1962.

De'Ath, C. E. "Patterns of Participation and Exclusion: A Poor Italian and Black Urban Community and Its Response to a Federal Poverty Program." PhD diss., University of Pittsburgh, 1970.

DeMarco, Marcella. "Magnet Programs in the Pittsburgh Schools: Development to Implementation 1977 through 1982." PhD diss., University of Pittsburgh, 1983.

Department of City Planning. "Census of Population and Housing Report No. 3, Whole City," in *Population, Social, Economic and Housing Data by Neighborhood, 1940 to 1990.* Pittsburgh, 1990.

Deutsch, Naavah, and Eric Monti. "Residential Segregation: The City of Pittsburgh in Comparative Historical Perspective, 1940–2000." Carnegie Mellon University, Department of Statistics, for CAUSE, Spring 2005, pp. 1–7.

Dickerson, Dennis C. "From the Periphery to Poverty: Black Steelworkers and Their Descendants." Carnegie Mellon University, lecture, CAUSE, 3 Apr. 1997.

"Disparity Study for the City of Pittsburgh and Its Authorities." 27 July 2000, Mason Tillman Associates.

Dixon, Kwame, and Patricia E. Allard. "Amnesty International USA: Police Brutality and International Human Rights in the United States: The Report on Hearings Held in Los Angeles, California, Chicago, Illinois, and Pittsburgh, Pennsylvania, Fall, 1999." New York: Amnesty International, 2000.

Drexler, Joseph James. "The Political Economy of Neighborhood Revitalization: A Case Study of Pittsburgh's North Side Neighborhoods." PhD diss., University of Pittsburgh, 1981.

Duff, Ogle B. "The Pros and Cons of Busing in Pennsylvania." Pittsburgh University of Pittsburgh Race Desegregation Assistance Center, 1982.

Foy, Martha E. "The Negro in the Courts: A Study in Race Relations." PhD diss., University of Pittsburgh, 1953.

Frazier, James Terry Gardiner. "Administration of the Housing Authority of the City of Pittsburgh: Some Political and Legislative Considerations." MA thesis, University of Pittsburgh, 1966.

Gibson, Karen J. "Income, Race, and Space: A Comparative Analysis of the Effects of Poverty Concentration on White and Black Neighborhoods in the Detroit and Pittsburgh Metropolitan Areas." PhD diss., University of California, Berkeley, 1996.

———. "Race, Class, and Space: An Examination of Underclass Notions in the Steel and Motor Cities. Center for Africanamerican Urban Studies and the Economy, Department of History, research paper, Carnegie Mellon University, Pittsburgh, 3 Mar. 1998.

Gleeson, Robert E. "Toward a Shared Economic Vision for Pittsburgh and South-western Pennsylvania: A White Paper Update." Pittsburgh Center for Economic Development, H. John Heinz III School of Public Policy and Management, Carnegie Mellon University, 1994.

Ham, Clifford C., Jr. "The Neighborhood Church in Urban Extension: A Report for ACTION-Housing, Inc." Pittsburgh: ACTION-Housing, Aug. 1964.

Historical Society of Western Pennsylvania. "African American Collection Project: Multi-Cultural Arts Initiative Proposal." Historical Society of Western Pennsylvania [Senator John Heinz History Center], 18 May 1992.

Housing Authority of the City of Pittsburgh (HACP)."1958 Annual Summaries." ca. 1959. Located in vertical file "Pittsburgh. Housing. Public, 1958." Carnegie Library of Pittsburgh, main branch.

———. "The First Seven Years." Pittsburgh: HACP, 1944.

———. "Manual for Tenant Selection and Renting." Pittsburgh: HACP, 1941.

———. "A Report to the People: Public Housing in Pittsburgh 1938–1953." Pittsburgh: HACP, 1953.

———. "A Statistical Picture of the 2969 Elderly Families Who Make the Pittsburgh Housing Authority Developments Their Home." Pittsburgh: HACP, 1971.

Hunte, Haslyn, Ralph Bangs, and Ken Thompson. "The Health Status of African Americans in Allegheny County: A Black Paper for the Urban League of Pittsburgh." Black Papers on African American Health in Allegheny County. Pittsburgh: University Center for Social & Urban Research, University of Pittsburgh/ Urban League of Pittsburgh, 2002.

Lee, Charles Franklin. "Carnival of Blood? African American Workers and the Building of the Pittsburgh, Bessemer, and Lake Erie Railroad, 1897–1912." PhD diss., Carnegie Mellon University, 2006.

Livers, Ancella. "Defining Ourselves: Gender Construction and the Creation of a Black Community in Pittsburgh, 1925–55." PhD diss., Carnegie Mellon University, 1998.

Mackey, Lewis H. "The Pennsylvania Human Relations Commission and Desegregation in the Public Schools of Pennsylvania, 1961–1978." PhD diss., University of Pittsburgh, 1978.

Mayor's Commission on Human Relations. "Bread of Bitterness." Pittsburgh: Mayor's Commission on Human Relations, 1968.

———. "Choice and Challenge: 1966 Annual Report." Pittsburgh: Pittsburgh Commission on Human Relations. 1966.

———. "Status of Intergroup Relations in Pittsburgh." Pittsburgh: Mayor's Commission on Human Relations, 1965.

———. "Time Is Running Out." Pittsburgh: Mayor's Commission on Human Relations, 1967.

———. "Warning to City Clear on All Sides: Time Running Out for Racial Action." Pittsburgh: Mayor's Commission on Human Relations, 1968.

———. "The War on Poverty: A 1966 Progress Report to Pittsburghers." Pittsburgh: Mayor's Committee on Human Resources, 1966

McIntyre, Ruth. "The Organizational Nature of an Urban Residential Neighborhood in Transition: Homewood-Brushton of Pittsburgh." PhD diss., University of Pittsburgh, 1963.

Pennsylvania Human Relations Commission (PHRC). "Warning to City Clear on All Sides: Time Running Out for Racial Action." Annual Report. Harrisburg: PHRC, 20 June 1968.

Pittsburgh Board of Education (PBE). "The Pittsburgh Desegregation Plan." Pittsburgh: Pittsburgh Board of Education, 1979.

———. "The Quest for Racial Equality in the Pittsburgh Public Schools." Pittsburgh: PBE, Sept. 1965.

Pittsburgh Building and Construction Industry. "The Pittsburgh Plan." Pittsburgh: Pittsburgh Building and Construction Industry, n.d., in authors' posession.

Pittsburgh City Council. "Proclamation: The Citizens Police Review Board." http://profile.myspace.com-citizenpolicereviewboard/htm (accessed January 2008).

Pittsburgh City Planning Commission. "Pittsburgh, Groundwork and Inventory for the Master Plan." Pittsburgh, Pittsburgh City Planning Commission, 1945.

Pittsburgh City Planning Department. "Citizen Participation Report: Relationship to Urban Renewal and Planning." Pittsburgh: Pittsburgh City Planning Department, 1964.

———. "The City Moves Forward: A Progress Report on Urban Renewal and Redevelopment Areas." Pittsburgh: Pittsburgh City Planning Department, n.d.

———. "A Report on Social Problems in Urban Renewal." Pittsburgh: Community Renewal Program, 1965.

Pittsburgh Housing Association. "Housing in Pittsburgh, 1947–1951." Pittsburgh: Pittsburgh Housing Association, 1951.

Reed, Tracey A. "The Politics of School Desegregation: The Case of Pittsburgh Public Schools, 1965–1980." PhD diss., University of Virginia, 1997.

Ribeiro, Alyssa. "'A Period of Turmoil'—Pittsburgh's April 1968 Riots and Their Aftermath." MA seminar paper, Department of History, University of Pittsburgh, 2006.

Rose, Harold M. "Milwaukee's Black Community: Can It Survive the Transition to Post-Industrialism Unscathed?" unpublished ms., ca. 1993, in authors' possession.

Ruck, Rob. "Perspectives on Pittsburgh: African American History and Contemporary Social Inequality." Seminar paper, Center for Africanamerican Urban Studies and the Economy, Department of History, Carnegie Mellon University, 10 Apr. 1997.

Scaglion, Richard. "Data Report to the Police Community Relations Project." Pittsburgh Police Community Relations Project, Sept. 1972–July 1972. Hillman Library, University of Pittsburgh.

Schuerle, Edward William. "A Study of the Administrative Decentralization in the Pittsburgh Public Schools." PhD diss., University of Pittsburgh, 1973.

Schuitema, Jennifer I. "African American Musicians and the Pittsburgh Music Scene, 1940–1960." Seminar paper, CAUSE Oral History Project, Carnegie Mellon University, spring 2007.

Scott, Barbara W. "The Status of Housing of Negroes in Pittsburgh." Pittsburgh: Pittsburgh Commission on Human Relations, 1962.

Snow, Michael S. "Dreams Realized and Dreams Deferred: Social Movements and Public Policy in Pittsburgh, 1960–1980." PhD diss. University of Pittsburgh, 2004.

Spratt, Margaret. "Unity within Diversity: The Issue of Race in the Pittsburgh YWCA, 1918–1946." Pittsburgh: 1990, research paper, manuscript in authors' possession.

Springer, Hugh Brock. "The Dynamics of Policy Formation in Urban Schools: Pittsburgh's Education Park/Great High Schools Concept." PhD diss., University of Pittsburgh, 1974.

Stevenson, Ruth L. "The Pittsburgh Urban League." MA thesis, University of Pittsburgh, 1936.

U.S. Census Bureau. *1950 Census of Population*. Washington, D.C.: Government Printing Office, 1953.

———. *Fifteenth Census of U.S.* Vol. 4: *Population, 1930*. Washington, D.C.: Government Printing Office, 1933.

University Center for Social and Urban Research. "Economic Benchmarks: Indices for the City of Pittsburgh and Allegheny County." University of Pittsburgh, Oct. 1994, pp. 12–13.

Urban League of Pittsburgh. "Blacks in White." Pittsburgh: Urban League of Pittsburgh, 1982.

Urban Redevelopment Authority. "A Changing City." Pittsburgh: Urban Redevelopment Authority, 1965.

———. "The Changing City." Pittsburgh: Urban Redevelopment Authority, 1969.

———. "Urban Renewal in Pittsburgh." Pittsburgh: Urban Redevelopment Authority, 1962.

Westmoreland, Antoinette H. "A Study of Requests for Specialized Services Directed to the Urban League of Pittsburgh." MA thesis, University of Pittsburgh, 1938.

Wolfe, Jacqueline Welch. "The Changing Pattern of Residence of the Negro in Pittsburgh, with Emphasis on the Period, 1930–1960." MA thesis, University of Pittsburgh, 1964.

Zapinski, Ken. "Public Housing in Pittsburgh." Unpublished draft paper, in authors' possession.

Books, Journals, Magazines

Alexander, J. Trent. "The Great Migration in Comparative Perspective: Interpreting the Urban Origins of Southern Black Migrants to Depression-Era Pittsburgh." *Social Science History* 22, no. 3 (Autumn 1998): 330–76.

Anderson, Elijah. *Street Wise: Race, Class, and Change in an Urban Community.* Chicago: The University of Chicago Press, 1990.

Anderson, Jervis. *A Philip Randolph: A Biographical Portrait.* 1972. Reprint, Berkeley: University of California Press, 1986.

Austin, Roy L., and Mark D. Allen. "Racial Disparity in Arrest Rates as an Explanation of Racial Disparity in Commitment to Pennsylvania's Prisons." *Journal of Research in Crime and Delinquency* 37, no. 2 (May 2000): 200–220.

Baltimore, Terri. "Grappling with Displacement." In Robbins, *Hillscapes,* 1–18.

Bangs, Ralph. "Demographic, Social, and Economic Conditions of African American Youth in Pittsburgh and Allegheny County." In Mason and Bangs, *State of Black Youth,* 64–65.

Bauman, John, and Edward K. Muller. *Before Renaissance: Planning in Pittsburgh, 1889–1943.* Pittsburgh: University of Pittsburgh Press, 2006.

Best, Wallace D. *Passionately Human, No Less Divine: Religion and Culture in Black Chicago, 1915–1952.* Princeton: Princeton University Press, 2005.

Biondi, Martha. *To Stand and Fight: The Struggle for Civil Rights in Postwar New York City.* Cambridge, MA: Harvard University Press, 2003.

Black, Samuel W. ed., *Soul Soldiers: African Americans and the Vietnam Era.* Pittsburgh: Senator John Heinz History Center, 2006.

"Black Capitalism Gets a Test in Pittsburgh." *Business Week,* Oct. 5, 1968.

Blount, Carolyn S. "Having Our Say: Black Press Documentary Highlights Nearly Forgotten." *About Time Magazine,* Jan.–Feb. 1999.

Bodnar, John, Roger Simon, and Michael P. Weber. *Lives of Their Own: Blacks, Italians, and Poles in Pittsburgh, 1900–1960.* Urbana: University of Illinois Press, 1982.

Bonosky, Philip. "The Story of Ben Careathers." *Masses and Mainstream,* 6 July 1953, 34–44.

Boyer, Paul, ed., *The Oxford Companion to United States History.* New York: Oxford University Press, 2001.

Brody, David. *Steelworkers in America: The Non-Union Era.* 1960. Reprint, New York: Russell and Russell, 1970.

Broussard, Albert S. *Black San Francisco: The Struggle for Racial Equality in the West, 1900–1954.* Kansas: University of Kansas Press, 1993.

Brown, Kevin. "'Where Is the Public Servants Entrance?': Democracy, the Law, and the Pittsburgh Federation of Teachers Strike of 1968." Seminar paper, Department of History, Carnegie Mellon University, December 2007.

Brown, Robert K. *Public Housing in Action: The Record of Pittsburgh.* Ann Arbor: Edwards Brothers, Inc., 1959.

Brunzel, Joseph H. "Negro Housing Needs in Pittsburgh, Allegheny County." Pittsburgh: Pittsburgh Housing Association, 1946.

Buni, Andrew. *Robert L. Vann of the* Pittsburgh Courier. Pittsburgh: University of Pittsburgh Press, 1974.

Burkett, Randall K. *Black Redemption: Churchmen Speak for the Garvey Movement.* Philadelphia: Temple University Press, 1978.

Bush, Rod. *We Are Not What We Seem: Black Nationalism and Class Struggle in the American Century.* New York: New York University Press, 1999.

Campet, Fidel. "Grassroots Activism and Housing Reform in Pittsburgh, 1965–1973." Seminar paper, Department of History, Carnegie Mellon University, fall 2006.

———. "Urban League of Pittsburgh, 1964–1973." Oral history project paper, Center for Africanamerican Urban Studies and the Economy, Department of History, Carnegie Mellon University, Pittsburgh, 12 May 2007.

Cannadine, David. *Mellon: An American Life.* New York: Alfred A. Knopf, 2006.

Caron, Simone M. "Birth Control and the Black Community in the 1960s: Genocide or Power Politics?" *Journal of Social History* (Spring 1998): 545–69.

Carson, Carolyn Leonard. "And the Results Showed Promise . . . Physicians, Childbirth, and Southern Black Migrant Women, 1916–1930: Pittsburgh as a Case Study." In *African Americans in Pennsylvania: Shifting Historical Perspectives*, edited by Joe William Trotter Jr. and Eric Ledell Smith, 330–62. University Park: The Pennsylvania State University Press, 1997.

Cayton, Horace R., and George S. Mitchell. *Black Workers and the New Unions.* Chapel Hill: The University of North Carolina Press, 1939.

Cha-Jua, Sundiata Keita, and Clarence Lang. "The 'Long Movement' as Vampire: Temporal and Spatial Fallacies in Recent Black Freedom Studies." *Journal of African American History* 92, no. 2 (Spring 2007): 265–88.

Chandler, Alfred D., Jr., *The Visible Hand: The Managerial Revolution in American Business.* Cambridge, MA: The Belknap Press of Harvard University Press, 1977.

Chen, Anthony S. "The Passage of State Fair Employment Legislation, 1945–1964: An Event History Analysis with Time-Varying and Time-Constant Covariates." Working Paper Series, Institute for Research on Labor and Employment. University of California-Berkeley, 2001.

Cole, Bettie. *Their Story: The History of Blacks/African Americans in Sewickley and Edgeworth.* Pittsburgh: Signal Graphics Printing, 2000.

Coliani, Eileen. "Pittsburgh: Who Polices the Police." *Pittsburgh Magazine*, Mar. 1976, 27–51.

Countryman, Matthew. *Up South: Civil Rights and Black Power in Philadelphia.* Philadelphia: University of Pennsylvania Press, 2006.

Couvares, Francis G. *The Remaking of Pittsburgh: Class and Culture in an Industrializing City, 1877–1919.* Albany: State University of New York Press, 1984.

Crowley, Gregory J. *The Politics of Place: Contentious Urban Development in Pittsburgh.* Pittsburgh: University of Pittsburgh Press, 2005.

Cunningham, Constance. "Homer Brown: First Black Political Leader in Pittsburgh." *Journal of Negro History* 66, no. 4 (Winter 1981–82): 304–17.

Cunningham, James V. et al. "Neighborhood Shock: Study of Pittsburgh's East Street Expressway and Citizen Participation, 1952–1976." Pittsburgh: University of Pittsburgh School of Social Work, 1976.

Dalfiume, Richard M. "The 'Forgotten Years' of the Negro Revolution." *Journal of American History* 55, no. 1 (June 1968): 90–106.

Daly, Janet R. "Zoning: Its Historical Context and Importance in the Development of Pittsburgh." *Western Pennsylvania Historical Magazine* 71, no. 2 (Apr. 1988): 99–125.

Daniel, Walker. *Black Journals of the United States.* Westport, CT: Greenwood Press, 1982.

Darden, Joe T. *Afro-Americans in Pittsburgh: The Residential Segregation of a People.* Lexington, KY: D. C. Heath and Company, 1973.

———. "The Effect of World War I on Black Occupational and Residential Segregation: The Case of Pittsburgh." *Journal of Black Studies* 18, no. 3 (Mar. 1988): 297–312.

Davis, Otto, and Norman Johnson. "The Jitneys: A Study of Grassroots Capitalism." *Journal of Contemporary Studies* 7, no. 1 (Winter 1984): 81–102.

Dennis, Archie, Jr., with Robert Paul Lamb. *The Garbage Man's Son.* Monroeville, PA: Crusades International, 2000.

Dickerson, Dennis C. "The Black Church in Industrializing Western Pennsylvania, 1870–1950." In Trotter and Smith, *African Americans in Pennsylvania,* 388–402.

———. *Out of the Crucible: Black Steelworkers in Western Pennsylvania, 1875–1980.* Albany: State University of New York Press, 1986.

Diouf, Sylviane A. *Servants of Allah: African Americans Enslaved in the Americas.* New York: New York University Press, 1998.

Dougherty, Jack. "African Americans, Civil Rights, and Race-Making in Milwaukee." March on Milwaukee Symposium. University of Wisconsin-Milwaukee, Sept. 29, 2007, copy in authors' possession.

Drake, St. Clair, and Horace A. Cayton. *Black Metropolis: A Study of Negro Life in a Northern City.* New York: Harcourt Brace, 1945.

Dubinsky, Irwin. *Reform in Trade Union Discrimination in the Construction Industry: Operation Dig and Its Legacy.* New York: Praeger Books, 1973.

DuBois, W. E. B. *The Philadelphia Negro: A Social Study.* 1899. Reprint, Philadelphia: University of Pennsylvania Press, 1996.

Edmunds, Arthur J., and Esther Bush. *Daybreakers: The Story of the Urban League of Pittsburgh.* 1983. Reprint with revisions, Pittsburgh: Urban League of Pittsburgh, 1999.

Elliott, Debrah M., and Barbara Felman Gluckman. "The Impact of the Pittsburgh Fair Housing Ordinance: A Pilot Study." *Journal of Intergroup Relations* 5, no. 1 (Autumn 1966): 75–85.

Epstein, Abraham. *The Negro Migrant in Pittsburgh.* Pittsburgh: University of Pittsburgh Press, 1918.

Evans, George E. "Here Is a Postwar Job for Pittsburgh . . . Transforming The Hill District." *Greater Pittsburgh* (July–August 1943). In Robbins, *Hillscapes,* 3–5.

Ewell, Thomas S. "The Smoky City, Part III: Social and Business Life." *Colored American Magazine* 3, no. 9 (Dec. 1901): 133–48.

Faires, Nora. "Immigrants and Industry." In Hays, *City at the Point,* 3–31.

Fischer, Ben. "The Steel Consent Decree: A Civil Rights Milestone." Research paper, Carnegie Mellon University Center for Labor Studies, Pittsburgh, 1997.

Fishel, Leslie H. "The Negro in the New Deal." In *The Negro in Depression and War:*

Prelude to Revolution, 1930–1945, ed. Bernard Sternsher, 7–28. Chicago: Quadrangle Books, 1969.

Foner, Nancy, and George M. Fredrickson, ed. *Not Just Black and White: Historical and Contemporary Perspectives on Immigration, Race, and Ethnicity in the United States.* New York: Russell Sage Foundation, 2004.

Foner, Philip S. *Organized Labor and the Black Worker, 1619–1973.* New York: Praeger Publishers, 1974.

Foner, Philip S., and Ronald L. Lewis, eds. *The Black Worker: From the Founding of the CIO to the AFL-CIO Merger 1936–1955.* Vol. II. Philadelphia: Temple University Press, 1983.

Frazier, Thomas R., ed. *Afro-American History: Primary Sources.* Chicago: The Dorsey Press, 1988.

Fullilove, Mindy Thompson. "Comments on Urban Design." In Robbins, *Hillscapes,* 19.

———. "Introduction." In Robbins, *Hillscapes,* vii.

———. *Root Shock: How Tearing Up City Neighborhoods Hurts America, And What We Can Do about It.* New York: Ballantine Books, One World, 2005.

Fullilove, Robert. "Comments on the Self-Sufficiency and Community Building Work Plan." In Robbins, *Hillscapes,* 20.

———. "Teach-Ins and Community Organizing." In Robbins, *Hillscapes,* 21–22.

Garfinkel, Herbert. *When Negroes March: The March on Washington Movement in the Organizational Politics for FEPC.* Glencoe, IL: Free Press, 1959.

Gibson, Karen J., William A. Darity, and Samuel L. Meyers. "Revisiting Occupational Crowding in the U.S.: A Preliminary Study." *Feminist Economics* 4, no. 3. (1998): 73–95.

Gilfoyle, Timothy J., guest editor. "Special Section: Urban History, Arnold Hirsch, and the Second Ghetto Thesis." *Journal of Urban History* 29, no. 3. (March 2003): 243–56.

Glasco, Laurence A. "Double Burden: The Black Experience in Pittsburgh." In Hays, *City at the Point,* 69–109.

———. *A Legacy of Bricks and Mortar: African American Landmarks in Allegheny County.* Pittsburgh: Pittsburgh History and Landmark Foundation, 1995.

———. "The Muslim Community of Pittsburgh." *Pittsburgh History* (Winter 1995/1996): 183–85.

———. "Pittsburgh, Pennsylvania." In *Encyclopedia of the Great Migration.* Edited by Steven A. Reich. Vol. 2, M–Z. Westport, CT: Greenwood Press, 2006.

———. "Taking Care of Business: The Black Entrepreneurial Elite in Turn-of-the-Century Pittsburgh." *Pittsburgh History* 78, no. 4 (Winter 1995–96): 177–82.

———, ed. *The WPA History of the Negro in Pittsburgh.* Pittsburgh: University of Pittsburgh Press, 2004.

Gleeson, Robert E. *Cash Cows and Glass Towers: Business and Metropolitan Development in Twentieth-Century Pittsburgh.* Pittsburgh: University of Pittsburgh Press, forthcoming.

Goings, Kenneth, and Raymond A. Mohl, eds. *The New African American Urban History.* Thousand Oaks, CA: Sage Publications, 1996.

Gottlieb, Peter. "Black Miners and the 1925–28 Bituminous Coal Strike: The Colored

Committee of Non-Union Miners, Montour Mine No. 1, Pittsburgh." *Labor History* 28, no. 2 (Spring 1987): 233–41.

———. *Making Their Own Way: Southern Blacks' Migration to Pittsburgh, 1916–30.* Urbana: University of Illinois Press, 1987.

———. "Rethinking the Great Migration." In Trotter, *Great Migration,* 68–82.

Greenberg, Cheryl Lynn. *Or Does It Explode? Black Harlem in the Great Depression.* New York: Oxford University Press, 1991.

Greenwald, Maurine Weiner. "Women and Class in Pittsburgh, 1850–1920." In Hays, *City at the Point,* 33–68.

Gregory, James N. *The Southern Diaspora: How the Great Migrations of Black and White Southerners Transformed America.* Chapel Hill, NC: The University of North Carolina Press, 2005.

Gregory, James. "The Second Great Migration: A Historical Overview." In Kusmer and Trotter, *African American Urban History,* 19–39.

Gregory, Steven. *Black Corona: Race and the Politics of Place in an Urban Community.* Princeton: Princeton University Press, 1998.

Gutkind, Richard David. "Desegregation of Pittsburgh Public Schools, 1968–1980: A Study of the Superintendent and Educational Policy Dynamics." PhD diss., University of Pittsburgh, 1983.

Hakim, Jameela A. "History of the First Muslim Mosque of Pittsburgh, Pennsylvania." In *Islam in North America: A Sourcebook,* edited by Michael A. Kōszegi and J. Gordon Melton, 153–63. New York: Garland Publishing, Inc., 1992.

Haley, Leon. "The Post-Industrial Era." In Edmunds and Bush, *Daybreakers,* 179–94.

Haley, Leon, and Ralph Bangs. "Policies to Improve African American Economic Conditions in Pittsburgh and Allegheny County." In *The State of the Region: Economic, Demographic, and Social Conditions and Trends in Southwestern Pennsylvania,* edited by Ralph Bangs, 141–50. Pittsburgh: University of Pittsburgh Center for Social and Urban Research, Sept. 1999.

Hallen, Phil. "CEO Falk Fund, to Center for Minority Health." Memorandum announcing funding for program to support minority health fellows, 12 Jan. 1998. In Robbins, *Hillscapes,* i–ii.

Harris, William. *The Harder We Run: Black Workers Since the Civil War.* New York: Oxford University Press, 1982.

———. *Keeping the Faith: A Philip Randolph, Milton P. Webster, and the Brotherhood of Sleeping Car Porters, 1925–37.* Urbana: University of Illinois Press, 1977.

Harrison, Bennett. *The Deindustrialization of America: Plant Closings, Community Abandonment, and the Dismantling of Basic Industry.* New York: Basic Books, 1982.

Harrison, Bennett, and Barry Bluestone. *The Great U-Turn: Corporate Restructuring and the Polarizing of America.* New York: Basic Books, Inc., 1988.

"Harrison Moves 2 1/4 Million Yards of Earth for Housing Site." *Construction Magazine,* 1 May 1, 1959.

Hathaway, Dale A. *Can Workers Have a Voice?: The Politics of Deindustrialization in Pittsburgh.* University Park: Pennsylvania State University Press, 1993.

Haynes, Monica, and Deborah M. Todd. "African American Pittsburghers Celebrate Historic Presidential Vote," 5 Nov. 2008.

Hays, Samuel P., ed. *City at the Point: Essays on the Social History of Pittsburgh.* Pittsburgh: University of Pittsburgh Press, 1989.

Health and Welfare Association of Allegheny County (HWAAC). "Staff Proposal on the Study of a Selected Social Problem for the Community Renewal Program." Pittsburgh: HWAAC, Feb. 1964.

Heineman, Kenneth J. "Model City: The War on Poverty, Race Relations, and Catholic Social Activism in 1960s Pittsburgh." *Historian* 65 (2003): 867–900

Hessler, Richard M. "Perceived Stress and Physical, Emotional and Social Health Status of a Large Municipal Public Housing Project." PhD diss., University of Pittsburgh, 1969.

Higham, John, ed. *Civil Rights and Social Wrongs: Black-White Relations Since World War II.* University Park: The Pennsylvania State University Press, 1997.

Hill House Association. "Mission and Purpose." http://www.hilhouse.org/aboutus. (accessed 5 October 2009).

Hill, Herbert. *Black Labor and the American Legal System: Race, Work, and the Law.* Madison: University of Wisconsin Press, 1985.

———. "Race and the Steelworkers Union: White Privilege and Black Struggle." *New Politics* 8, no. 4 (Winter 2002): 1–58.

Hill, Ralph L. "A View of the Hill: A Study of Experiences and Attitudes in the Hill District of Pittsburgh, Pennsylvania from 1900 to 1973. PhD diss., University of Pittsburgh, 1973.

Hill, Robert A. ed. *The Marcus Garvey and Universal Negro Improvement Papers.* Berkeley: University of California, 1983–1986.

Hine, Darlene Clark. "Black Migration to the Urban Midwest: The Gender Dimension, 1915–1945." In Trotter, *Great Migration*, 127–46.

———, ed. *The State of Afro-American History: Past, Present, and Future.* Baton Rouge: Louisiana State University Press, 1986.

Hinkelman, Jeffrey Alan. "Penn Hills: The Development of a Suburban Community." Senior honor program paper, Humanities and Social Sciences, Carnegie Mellon University, Pittsburgh, 25 Apr. 1991.

Hinshaw, John. *Steel and Steelworkers: Race and Class Struggle in Twentieth-Century Pittsburgh.* Albany: State University of New York Press, 2002.

Hinshaw, John, and Judith Modell. "Perceiving Racism: Homestead from Depression to Deindustrialization." *Pennsylvania History* 63, no. 1 (Winter 1996): 17–52.

Hirsch, Arnold. *Making the Second Ghetto: Race and Housing in Chicago 1940–1960.* 1983. Reprint, Chicago: The University of Chicago Press, 1998.

Hirsch, James S., and Suzanne Alexander. "Reverse Exodus: Middle Class Blacks Quit Northern Cities and Settle in the South." *Wall Street Journal*, 22 May 1990.

Hirschman, Charles, Philip Kasinitz, and Josh DeWind, eds. *The Handbook of International Migration: The American Experience.* New York: Russell Sage Foundation, 1999.

Hoerr, John P. *And the Wolf Finally Came: The Decline of the American Steel Industry.* Pittsburgh: University of Pittsburgh Press, 1988.

Honey, Michael K. *Southern Labor and Black Civil Rights: Organizing Memphis Workers.* Chicago: University of Illinois, 1993.

Horton, Carol A. *Race and the Making of American Liberalism*. New York: Oxford University Press, 2005.

Houston, David B. "A Brief History of the Process of Capital Accumulation in Pittsburgh: A Marxist Interpretation." In *Pittsburgh-Sheffield, Sister Cities*, ed. Joel A. Tarr, 29–69. Pittsburgh: Carnegie Mellon University Press, 1986.

Hovde, Bryn J. "Report on Population Movements and Housing Trends." Pittsburgh: Civic Unity Council, 1950., p. 12.

Hurley, Andrew. *Environmental Inequalities: Class, Race, and Industrial Pollution in Gary, Indiana, 1945–1980*. Chapel Hill: The University of North Carolina Press, 1995.

Jackson, Kenneth. *The Ku Klux Klan in the City, 1915–1930*. New York: Oxford University Press, 1967.

James, Kent. "Public Policy and the Postwar Suburbanization of Pittsburgh, 1945–1990." PhD diss., Pittsburgh, Carnegie Mellon University, 2005.

Jensen, Edward. "Police Defied by Duquesne Light Pickets: 3 Race Leaders Arrested," 14 Aug. 1967.

Johnson, Lisa. "On Race and Place: The Struggle to Desegregate the Highland Park Pool, Pittsburgh, Pennsylvania, 1948–1952." Seminar paper, Department of History, Carnegie Mellon University, Pittsburgh, 14 May 2002.

Jones, Jacquelyn. "The Long Civil Rights Movement and the Political Uses of the Past." *Journal of American History* 91, no. 4 (March 2005): 1233–63.

Joseph, Peniel E. "Introduction: Towards a Historiography of the Black Power Movement." In *The Black Power Movement: Rethinking the Civil Rights-Black Power Era*, edited by Peniel E. Joseph, New York: Routledge, 2006, 1–25.

Kelley, Robin D. G. *Hammer and Hoe: Alabama Communists During the Great Depression*. Chapel Hill: The University of North Carolina Press, 1990.

———. *Race Rebels: Culture, Politics, and the Black Working Class*. New York: The Free Press, 1994.

Kersten, Andrew E. *Race. Jobs, and the War: The FEPC in the Midwest, 1941–1946*. Urbana: University of Illinois Press, 2000.

Kirby, John B. *Black Americans in the Roosevelt Era: Liberalism and Race*. Knoxville: University of Tennessee Press, 1980.

Klienberg, S. J. *The Shadow of the Mills: Working-Class Families in Pittsburgh, 1820–1907*. Pittsburgh: University of Pittsburgh, 1989.

Knights of the Ku Klux Klan Realm of Pennsylvania, Province No. 1: Official Bulletin No. 5, in Ku Klux Klan Papers, General Files, 1923–1940, Boxes 3–4. Harrisburg, Pa. Pennsylvania State Archives.

Korstad, Robert, and Alex Lichtenstein. "Opportunities Found and Lost: Labor, Radicals and the Early Civil Rights Movement." *Journal of American History* 75, no. 3. (Dec. 1988): 786–811.

Krause, Paul. *The Battle for Homestead 1880–1892: Politics, Culture, and Steel*. Pittsburgh: University of Pittsburgh Press, 1992.

Kurtiak, Raymond J. "Urban Restructuring and Socio-Economic Polarization: An Analysis of Income Levels in Pittsburgh, PA 1950–1990." PhD diss., West Virginia University, 1994.

Kusmer, Kenneth L. *A Ghetto Takes Shape: Black Cleveland, 1870–1930*. Urbana: University of Illinois Press, 1976.

———, ed. *Progress versus Poverty: 1970 to the Present*. New York: Garland Publishing, Inc. 1991.

Kusmer, Kenneth L., and Joe W. Trotter, eds. *African American Urban History Since World War II*. Chicago: University of Chicago Press, 2009.

Landry, Bart. *The New Black Middle Class*. Berkeley: University of California Press, 1987.

Lawson, Steven F., and Charles Payne. *Debating the Civil Rights Movement, 1945–1968*. New York: Roman & Littlefield Publishers, Inc., 1998.

Lemann, Nicholas. *The Promised Land: The Great Black Migration and How It Changed America*. New York: Alfred A. Knopf, 1991.

Lewis, Earl. *In Their Own Interests: Race, Class, and Power in Twentieth-Century Norfolk, Virigina*. Los Angeles: University of California Press, 1991.

Lloyd, Anne. "Pittsburgh's 1923 Zoning Ordinance." *Western Pennsylvania Historical Magazine* 57, no. 3 (July 1974): 289–305.

Lorant, Stefan. *Pete: The Life of Peter F. Flaherty*. Authors Edition, Inc.

Lubove, Roy, ed. *Pittsburgh: Documentary History*. New York: Franklin Watts/New Viewpoints, 1976.

———. *Twentieth-Century Pittsburgh*. 2 vols. Pittsburgh: University of Pittsburgh Press, 1969–1996.

Marable, Manning. *Race, Reform, and Rebellion: The Second Reconstruction in Black America, 1945–1990*. Jackson: University Press of Mississippi, 1991.

Marable, Manning, and Leith Mullings, eds. *Let Nobody Turn Us Around: Voices of Resistance, Reform, and Renewal*. New York: Roman & Littlefield Publishers, Inc., 2000.

Marshall, F. Ray, and Vernon M. Briggs Jr. *The Negro and Apprenticeship*. Baltimore: The Johns Hopkins Press, 1967.

Martin, Tony. *Race First: The Ideological and Organizational Struggles of Marcus Garvey and the Universal Negro Improvement Association*. Dover, MA: Majority Press, 1976.

Mason, Major Albert III, and Ralph L. Bangs, eds. *The State of Black Youth in Pittsburgh: Perspectives on Young African Americans in the City of Pittsburgh and Allegheny County*. Pittsburgh: Urban League of Pittsburgh, 1999.

Massey, Douglas S., and Nancy A. Denton. *American Apartheid: Segregation and the Making of the Underclass*. Cambridge, MA: Harvard University Press, 1993.

McCarthy, Bob. *Malice Toward None: Remembering Mayor Joe Barr*. Pittsburgh: Dorrance Publishing Company, 2002.

McCloud, Aminah Beverly. *African American Islam*. New York: Routledge, 1995.

McKenzie, Edna. "Pittsburgh's Daisy Lampkin: A Life of Love and Service." *Pennsylvania Heritage* 9, no. 3 (Summer 1983): 9–12.

Mitchell, J. P., ed. *Federal Housing Policy and Programs: Past and Present*. New Brunswick: Rutgers University Press, 1985.

Modell, Judith, and Charlee Brodsky. *A Town Without Steel: Envisioning Homestead*. Pittsburgh: University of Pittsburgh Press, 1998.

Moreno, Paul D. *From Direct Action to Affirmative Action: Fair Employment Law and Policy in America, 1933–1972.* Baton Rouge: Louisiana State University Press, 1997.

Moss, R. Maurice. "The Negro in Pittsburgh's Industries." *Opportunity—Journal of Negro Life* 13, no. 2 (Feb. 1935): 40–42, 59.

Mumford, Kevin. "Harvesting the Crisis: The Newark Uprising, The Kerner Commission, and Writings on Riots." In Kusmer and Trotter, *African American Urban History,* 203–18.

Murphy, Patricia. "The Housing That Community Built." National Housing Institute's *Shelter Force* 138 (Nov.–Dec. 2004), http://www.nhi.org/online/issues/138/bedford.html (accessed 10 Dec. 2009).

Naison, Mark. *Communists in Harlem during the Depression.* Chicago: University of Illinois Press, 1983.

Nelson, Steve, James R. Barrett, and Rob Ruck. *Steve Nelson: American Radical.* Pittsburgh: University of Pittsburgh Press, 1992.

Nieman, Donald G. *Promises to Keep: African Americans and the Constitutional Order, 1776 to the Present.* New York: Oxford University Press, 1991.

Obama, Barack. *The Audacity of Hope: Thoughts on Reclaiming the American Dream.* New York: Crown Publishers, 2006.

———. *Change We Can Believe In: Barack Obama's Plan to Renew America's Promise.* New York: Three Rivers Press, 2008.

———. *Dreams from My Father: A Story of Race and Inheritance.* New York: Times Book, 1995.

O'Connor, Alice. Chris Tilly, Lawrence D. Bobo, eds. *Urban Inequality: Evidence from Four Cities.* New York: Russell Sage Foundation, 2001.

Oestreicher, Richard. "Working-Class Formation, Development, and Consciousness in Pittsburgh, 1790–1960." In Hays, *City at the Point,* 111–50.

Osofsky, Gilbert. *Harlem: The Making of a Ghetto: Negro New York, 1890–1930.* Chicago: Elephant Paperback, 1966.

Palmer, Jack L. "A Case Study in School-Community Conflict Over Desegregation." PhD diss., University of Pittsburgh, 1974.

Payne, Charles M. *I've Got the Light of Freedom: The Organizing Tradition and the Mississippi Freedom Struggle.* Berkeley: University of California Press, 1995.

Pelton, Rodney A. "The Value System of a Large Voluntary Negro Civic Organization within a Poverty Area: The Homewood-Brushton Community Improvement Association." PhD diss., University of Pittsburgh, 1968.

Phillips, Kimberly L. *Alabama North: African-American Migrants, Community, and Working-Class Activism in Cleveland, 1915–45.* Chicago: University of Illinois Press, 1999.

Pittsburgh Neighborhood Alliance. *Pittsburgh Neighborhood Atlas: The Hill.* Pittsburgh: Pittsburgh Neighborhood Alliance, 1977.

Portz, John, Lana Stein, and Robin R. Jones. *City Schools and City Politics: Institutions and Leadership in Pittsburgh, Boston, and St. Louis.* Lawrence: University Press of Kansas, 1999.

Preate, Ernest D., Jr. "The 'De Facto' Racism that Cannot Be Ignored." In Mason and Bangs, *State of Black Youth,* 96–107.

Pritchett, Wendell. *Brownsville, Brooklyn: Blacks, Jews, and the Changing Face of the Ghetto*. Chicago: The University of Chicago Press, 2002.

Proctor, Ralph. "Racial Discrimination Against Black Teachers and Black Professionals in the Pittsburgh Public School System, 1834–1973." PhD diss., University of Pittsburgh, 1979.

Rand McNally. *Places Rated Almanac: Your Guide to Finding the Best Places to Live in America*. Chicago: Rand McNally & Company, 2007.

Randolph, A. Philip. "March for a Fair Share: The March on Washington Movement." *Black Worker*, May 1941.

———. "Why Should We March." *Survey Graphic*, Nov. 1942.

Reed, Merl E. "Black Workers, Defense Industries, and Federal Agencies in Pennsylvania, 1941–1945." *Labor History* 27, no. 3 (Summer 1986): 356–84.

———. *Seedtime for the Modern Civil Rights Movement: The President's Committee on Fair Employment Practice, 1941–1946*. Baton Rouge: Louisiana State University Press, 1991.

Republican National Committee. *Contract with America: The Bold Plan by Rep. Newt Gingrich, Rep. Dick Armey, and the House Republicans to Change the Nation*. New York: Random House/Times Books/The Republican National Committee, 1994.

Robbins, Anthony. *Hillscapes: A Scrapbook Envisioning a Healthy Urban Habitat*, 2nd. ed. Pittsburgh: University of Pittsburgh Center for Minority Health, July 1999.

Robinson, Nicholas Wheeler. "Marland's 'Magnificent' Gamble: Pittsburgh's Great High Schools." *Urban Review*, Nov. 1968, 28–34.

Robinson, Randall. *The Debt: What America Owes to Blacks*. New York: Penguin Putnam Inc., 2000.

Ruck, Rob. *Sandlot Seasons: Sport in Black Pittsburgh*. Urbana: University of Illinois Press, 1987.

Ruck, Rob, and Christopher Fletcher. "Unequal Opportunity." *Pittsburgh Magazine*, Sept. 1995, 87–89.

Rusk, David. *Cities Without Suburbs*. Woodrow Wilson Center Press: Baltimore, 2003.

Sapolsky, Steven W., and Bartholomew Roselli. *Homewood-Brushton: A Century of Community-Making*. Pittsburgh: The Historical Society of Western Pennsylvania, 1987.

Sawyer, Roland. "A Home to Go to." *Pittsburgh Quote: The Magazine, Its People and Its Institutions*, June 1955.

Self, Robert O. *American Babylon: Race and the Struggle for Postwar Oakland*. Princeton: Princeton University Press, 2003.

Seligman, Amanda I. *Block by Block: Neighborhood Policy on Chicago's West Side*. Chicago: University of Chicago Press, 2005.

Shannon, Sandra G. The *Dramatic Vision of August Wilson*. Washington DC: Howard University Press, 1995.

Sitkoff, Harvard. *A New Deal for Blacks: The Emergence of Civil Rights as a National Issue: The Depression Decade*. New York: Oxford University Press, 1978.

Spear, Alan H. *Black Chicago: The Making of a Negro Ghetto 1890–1920*. Chicago: The University of Chicago Press, 1967.

Spero, Sterling D., and Abraham L. Harris. *The Black Worker: The Negro and the Labor Movement*. New York: Atheneum, 1968.

Staresinic, Chuck. "Send Freedom House." *Pitt Med*, Feb. 2004, 32–34.

Stave, Bruce M. *The New Deal and the Last Hurrah: Pittsburgh and Machine Politics*. Pittsburgh: University of Pittsburgh Press, 1970.

Stein, Judith. *Running Steel, Running America: Race, Economic Policy, and the Decline of Liberalism*. Chapel Hill: University of North Carolina Press, 1998.

———. *The World of Marcus Garvey: Race and Class in Modern Society*. Baton Rouge: Louisiana State University Press, 1986.

Stout, Mike. "Reindustrialization from Below: The Steel Valley Authority." *Labor Research Review* 5, no. 2 (Fall 1986): 9–34.

Streater, John Baxter, Jr. "The National Negro Congress, 1936–1947." PhD diss., University of Cincinnati, 1981.

Strickland. Arvarh E., and Robert Weems, eds. *The African American Experience: An Historiographical and Bibliographical Guide*. Westport, CT: Greenwood Press, 2001.

Sugrue, Thomas J. "Affirmative Action from Below: Civil Rights, the Building Trades, and the Politics of Racial Equality in the Urban North, 1945–1969." *Journal of American History* 91, no. 1 (June 2004): 148–51.

———. *The Origins of the Urban Crisis: Race and Inequality in Postwar Detroit*. Princeton: Princeton University Press, 1996.

Tarr, Joel A. *Growth, Stability, and Decline in an Urban Area: One Hundred Years of Hazelwood*. Pittsburgh: Carnegie Mellon University, 1976.

Taylor, Cynthia. *A. Philip Randolph: The Religious Journey of an African American Labor Leader*. New York: New York University Press, 2006.

Taylor, Quintard. *The Forging of a Black Community: Seattle's Central District from 1870 Through the Civil Rights Era*. Seattle: University of Washington Press, 1994.

Temin, Peter. *Iron and Steel in Nineteenth-Century America: An Economic Inquiry*. Cambridge, MA: Massachusetts Institute of Technology Press, 1964.

Terry, Wallace. *Bloods: An Oral History of the Vietnam War*. New York: Random House, 1984.

Theoharis, Jeanne F., and Komozi Woodard. *Freedom North: Black Freedom Struggles Outside the South, 1940–1980*. New York: Palgrave Macmillan, 2003.

Thomas, Richard W. *Life for Us Is What We Make It: Building Black Community in Detroit, 1915–1945*. Bloomington: Indiana University Press, 1992.

Thompson, Heather. *Whose Detroit: Politics, Labor and Race in a Modern American City*. Ithaca: Cornell University Press, 2001.

Thornbrough, Emma Lou. *T. Thomas Fortune: Militant Journalist*. Chicago: University of Chicago Press, 1972.

Toker, Franklin. *Pittsburgh: An Urban Portrait*. University Park: Pennsylvania State University Press, 1986.

Trotter, Joe William, Jr. *The African American Experience*. Boston: Houghton Mifflin Company, 2001.

———. *Black Milwaukee: The Making of an Industrial Proletariat, 1915–45*. Urbana: University of Illinois Press, 1985.

———, ed. *The Great Migration in Historical Perspective: New Dimensions of Race, Class, and Gender*. Bloomington: Indiana University Press, 1991.

———. "Reflections on the Great Migration to Western Pennsylvania." *Pittsburgh History* (Winter 1995–96): 156.

———. *River Jordan: African American Urban Life in the Ohio Valley*. Lexington: University Press of Kentucky, 1998.

Trotter, Joe William, Jr., and Earl Lewis, eds. *African Americans in the Industrial Age: A Documentary History, 1915–1945*. Boston: Northeastern University Press, 1996.

Trotter, Joe William, Jr., Earl Lewis, and Tera W. Hunter, eds. *The African American Urban Experience: Perspectives from the Colonial Era to the Present*. New York: Palgrave Publishing Company, 2004.

Trotter, Joe William, Jr., and Eric Ledell Smith, eds. *African Americans in Pennsylvania: Shifting Historical Perspectives*. University Park: Pennsylvania State University, 1997.

Trotter, Joe William, Jr., with H. LaRue Trotter. "The Caribbean Experience in Pittsburgh: An Interview with Myrven Caines, M.D." *Pittsburgh History: A Magazine of the City and Its Region* (Winter 1995/96): 193–96.

Vale, Lawrence J. *Reclaiming Public Housing: A Half Century of Struggle in Three Public Neighborhoods*. Cambridge, MA: Harvard University Press, 2002.

Van Deburg, William L. *New Day in Babylon: The Black Power Movement and American Culture, 1965–1975*. Chicago: University of Chicago, 1992.

Wallace, Phyllis A. *Black Women in the Labor Force*. Cambridge, MA: MIT Press, 1980.

Warren, Kenneth. *The American Steel Industry, 1850–1970: A Geographical Interpretation*. Oxford: Clarendan Press, 1973.

Waters, Oliver G. "Smoky City: Part I." *Colored American Magazine* 3, no. 6 (Oct. 1901): 419–21.

———. "Smoky City: Part II." *Colored American Magazine* 3, no. 7 (Nov. 1901): 15–17.

Weaver, Robert. *The Negro Ghetto*. New York: Russell & Russell, 1948.

Weber, Michael P. *Don't Call Me Boss: David L. Lawrence: Pittsburgh's Renaissance Mayor*. Pittsburgh University of Pittsburgh Press, 1988.

Weiss, M. A. "The Origins and Legacy of Urban Renewal." In *Federal Housing Policy and Programs: Past and Present*, edited by J. P. Mitchell, 253–76. New Brunswick: Rutgers University Press, 1985.

Whatley, Warren C. "African American Strikebreaking from the Civil War to the New Deal." *Social Science History* 17, no. 4 (Winter 1993): 525–58.

Whitaker, Matthew C. *Race Work: The Rise of Civil Rights in the Urban West*. Lincoln: University of Nebraska Press, 2005.

Wideman, John Edgar. *Brothers and Keepers*. New York: Penguin Books, 1984.

Wiese, Andrew. *Places of Their Own: African American Suburbanization in the Twentieth Century*. Chicago: University of Chicago Press, 2004.

Williams, Dana, and Sandra Shannon, eds. *August Wilson and Black Aesthetics*. New York: Palgrave MacMillan, 2004.

Williams, Lillian Serece. *Strangers in the Land of Paradise: The Creation of an African American Community, Buffalo, New York, 1900–1940*. Bloomington: Indiana University Press, 1999.

Williams, Melvin. "Childhood in an Urban Black Ghetto: Two Life Histories." *UMOJA* 2, no. 3 (Fall 1978): 168–82.

———. *On the Street Where I Lived.* New York: Holt, Rinehart, and Winston, 1981.

Williams, Rhonda. *The Politics of Public Housing: Black Women's Struggles Against Urban Inequality.* New York: Oxford University Press, 2004.

Wilson, August. *Fences.* New York: Penguin Books USA, Inc., 1986.

———. *Gem of the Ocean.* New York: Theatre Communications Group, Inc., 2003.

———. *Jitney.* Woodstock, NY: The Overlook Press, Peter Mayer Publishers, Inc., 2003.

———. *Joe Turner's Come and Gone.* New York: Penguin Books USA, Inc., 1988.

———. *King Hedley II.* New York: Theatre Communications Group, Inc., 2005.

———. *Ma Rainey's Black Bottom.* New York: Penguin Books USA, Inc., 1985.

———. *The Piano Lesson.* New York: Penguin Books USA, Inc., 1990.

———. *Radio Golf.* New York: Theatre Communications Group, Inc., 2007.

———. *Seven Guitars.* New York: Penguin Books USA, Inc., 1997.

———. *Two Trains Running.* New York: Penguin Books USA, Inc., 1993.

Wilson, William J., *The Declining Significance of Race: Blacks and Changing American Institutions.* Chicago: The University of Chicago Press, 1978.

———. *The Truly Disadvantaged: The Inner City, the Underclass, and Public Policy.* Chicago: The University of Chicago Press, 1987.

———. *When Work Disappears: The World of the New Urban Poor.* New York: Alfred A. Knopf, 1996.

Wilson, William J., Peter I. Rose, and Stanley Rothman, eds. *Through Different Eyes: Black and White Perspectives on American Race Relations.* New York: Oxford University Press, 1973.

Wolseley, Roland E. *The Black Press U.S.A.* Ames: The Iowa State University Press, 1990.

Wolters, Raymond. *Negroes and the Great Depression: The Problem of Economic Recovery.* Westport, CT: Greenwood Publishing Company, 1970.

Wright, R. R. *The Negro in Pennsylvania: A Study in Economic History.* 1912. Reprint, New York: Arno Press, 1969.

Wright, Richard, and Edwin Rosskam. *12 Million Black Voices.* New York: Thunder's Mouth Press, 1941.

Youngner, Rina C. *Industry in Art: Pittsburgh, 1812 to 1920.* Pittsburgh: University of Pittsburgh Press, 2006.

Newspapers

Ackerman, Jan. "Black Leaders' Suit Challenges At-Large Voting." *Pittsburgh Post-Gazette,* 23 Jan. 1986.

Ackerman, Jan, and Jan Schmitz. "Verdict Ends First of 2 Criminal Prosecutions in Traffic Stop Death." *Pittsburgh Post-Gazette,* 14 Nov. 1996.

"Activism/Rent Strike: PHA Threatened by Rent Strike." *Pittsburgh Post-Gazette,* 19 Feb. 1971.

"A. M. E. Woman's Missionary Society Spurs Campaign for Permanent FEPC." *Pittsburgh Courier,* 19 Jan. 1946.

Anderson, Dorothy. "Ban Race Nurses: Montefiore Says 'No' to Local Girl." *Pittsburgh Courier*, 1 June 1946.

"Anti-Trust Suit Hits Pgh. Multi-list." *New Pittsburgh Courier*, 8 Apr. 1967.

"Appoint Two More Negro Teachers Here." *Pittsburgh Courier*, 31 Aug. 1946.

"Arena Improves Hiring Policy: *Courier*, NAACP, NALC Protests Bring Results." *Pittsburgh Courier*, 28 Oct. 1961.

Artis, Bryant. "Brutality Is Charged to Northview Mob." *Pittsburgh Post-Gazette*, 21 June 1968.

Barbour, George E. "City, Union 'Pass Buck' on Negro Electrician." *Pittsburgh Courier*, 25 Nov. 1961.

———. "H'wood Leaders Ask Has City Quit Us?" *Pittsburgh Courier*, 23 Nov. 1963.

———. "Pittsburgh: 1900–2000." *New Pittsburgh Courier*, 5 Feb. 2000.

Barnes, Tom. "Blacks, Women Lacking in Office: Underrepresented in Elected Posts by Large Margins in Pittsburgh Area." *Pittsburgh Post-Gazette*, 16 April 2003.

"Begin Drive in State for Fair Housing." *Pittsburgh Courier*, 9 Mar. 1957.

"Bell Says 'No' to UNPC: Telephone Co. Refuses to Sign Job Agreement." *New Pittsburgh Courier*, 26 Aug. 1967.

Benic, Thomas P. "Perils and the Project Housing Authority Aim's Security." *Pittsburgh Post-Gazette*, 1 Dec. 1975.

"Bidwell Graduates First Cable Class." *New Pittsburgh Courier*, 3 Jan. 1981.

"Big March Vowed." *Pittsburgh Post-Gazette*, 16 Aug. 1969.

"Black Leaders Hit Alleged Cop Brutality." *Pittsburgh Post-Gazette*, 4 May 1971.

"Black Population Shifting East." Clippings file, Ethnic Groups, African Americans, No. 3. Senator John Heinz History Center, Pittsburgh.

"Black Teachers at Pitt Urge Student Rally." *New Pittsburgh Courier*, 21 Nov. 1970.

"Blacks Confront Slusser with Brutality Charges." *New Pittsburgh Courier*, 22 Mar. 1969.

"Blacks Increase Share of Public Housing" *Pittsburgh Press*, 26 Apr. 1970.

"Blacks Push for Assistant Police Boss." *Pittsburgh Post-Gazette*, 30 Mar. 1969.

"Blacks Quit Barr's Riot Task Force: NAACP Head Raps City's Civil Disorder Probe, Mayor Faces Negro Revolt in City Hall" *Pittsburgh Courier*, 20 Apr. 1968.

"Blacks Uniting in Fight to Get Building Jobs." *Pittsburgh Press*, 17 Aug. 1969.

Blotzer, Jane. "King Is Missed: Frustration, Loss of Hope Still is Felt." *Pittsburgh Post-Gazette*, 4 Apr. 1988.

"Board Ducks Local Meeting with Gladstone Parent Groups." *New Pittsburgh Courier*, 25 Jan. 1969.

Bolden, Frank E. "People in Ghettos." *Pittsburgh Courier*, 26 May 1951.

"Bouie Haden's Family Cherishes His Memory." *New Pittsburgh Courier*, 18 February 1978.

Bradford, Gary. "Black Leaders Here See Threat of Violent Protest Like Miami's." *Pittsburgh Press*, 1 June 1980.

"Break Job Barriers in Pittsburgh Department Stores: Intensive Citizens' Campaign Brings New Opportunities." *Pittsburgh Courier*, 8 Feb. 1947.

Brem, Ralph. "More Negro Leaders Needed to Equalize Housing and Jobs." *Pittsburgh Press*, 24 June 1963.

Brown, Charles N. "Pennsylvania Tops Prison Disparity." *New Pittsburgh Courier*, 1 Aug. 2001.

Bryant, Jean. "Discrimination Limits Blacks' Housing Choices." *Pittsburgh Post-Gazette*, 14 Apr. 1996.

———. "Fearful Mothers Rely on Faith, Communication." *Pittsburgh Post-Gazette*, 29 June 1994.

Bruce, Aubrey. "March Organizers Say Event Will Resurrect Black Pride." *New Pittsburgh Courier*, 7 Oct. 1995

"Budget Cut Kills FEPC Here; Closes 5 Offices; Drops 66 Workers." *Pittsburgh Courier*, 4 Aug. 1945.

Bull, John M. R. "Patterns of Racial Division: Pittsburgh's Housing Projects among Nation's Most Segregated." *Pittsburgh Post-Gazette*, 14 Apr. 1996.

"C. Kohlman Clears the Air." *New Pittsburgh Courier*, 26 May 1973.

"Cabbie Bias Bared Here: Jitneys Under Fire Too." *Pittsburgh Courier*, 29 Jan. 1966.

"Caravan of Pittsburghers Ready for FEPC Hearings." *Pittsburgh Courier*, 24 Mar. 1945.

"Careathers Tells Why He Became Communist Voice." *Pittsburgh Courier*, 23 May 1953.

Carter, Ulish. "News Media Draws Wrath of Angry Black Leaders Who Support Kohlman." *Pittsburgh Courier*, ca. Aug. 1973, newsclippings file, Carnegie Library of Pittsburgh.

———. "Teacher Asserts Blacks Need to Aid Own Destiny." *New Pittsburgh Courier*, 7 May 1977.

"Case History of Fight for Negro Street Car Operators." *Pittsburgh Courier*, 7 Apr. 1945.

"Catholics Support Dep't Store Fight." *Pittsburgh Courier*, 14 Dec. 1946.

"Cause Seen for Concern at J&L." *Pittsburgh Courier*, 3 Aug. 1946.

Chappell. Edna. "Seeking Permanent Anti-Bias Job Law." *Pittsburgh Courier*, 20 Jan. 1954.

Charles, N. "Udin's Pittsburgh Works Gets Council's Preliminary OK." *New Pittsburgh Courier*, 21 Apr. 2001.

Chute, Eleanor. "Walking in Circles: 50 Years Later, Many Children Still Go to Schools That Are Nearly All White or All Black." *Pittsburgh Post-Gazette*, 16 May 2004.

"Citizens Plan 'March' for Fair Housing Bill." *Pittsburgh Courier*, 10 Oct. 1959.

"City, Brutality Group Seek Police Solution." *Pittsburgh Post-Gazette*, 4 Nov. 1965.

"City Escapes Planned Riot: Informer Tells Cops of Plan." *New Pittsburgh Courier*, 12 Aug. 1967.

"City Housing Agency Plans Security Hike." *Pittsburgh Press*, 21 Jan. 1972.

"City Uses NAACP Vote to Bolster Position in Suit Against Crusade." *New Pittsburgh Courier*, 14 Mar. 1987.

"City's Fair-Housing Law to Be Explained." *Pittsburgh Courier*, 4 Apr. 1959.

"Civil Rights Group List Demands for Housing." *New Pittsburgh Courier*, 15 July 1967.

Clark, John L. "Brown's Bill Wins 'First Round': 2,000 at Hearing in State Capital." *Courier* Harrisburg Bureau, 31 Mar. 1945.

———. "Political Power at Stake in Tuesday's Primary Election." *Pittsburgh Courier*, 16 Jun 1945.

Clemetson, Lynette. "Revival for a Black Enclave." *New York Times*. 9 Aug. 2002.

"Cmdr. Bill Moore Cools Militant Students." *Pittsburgh Courier*, 22 Feb. 1969.

"Communist Candidate Here 28: William Z. Foster to Speak in Labor Lyceum on Miller Street." *Pittsburgh Courier*, 27 Oct. 1928.

"Community Action Council Continues Store Picketing." *Pittsburgh Courier*, 21 Dec. 1946.

"Community Applauds School Hiring Policy." *Pittsburgh Courier*, 7 March 1964.

"Confrontation and Change." *Pittsburgh Press*, 17 Oct. 1982.

"Cops Force Calm at Gladstone." *Pittsburgh Courier*, 22 Feb. 1969.

"Copters Over Hill Open New Horizon." *Pittsburgh Courier*, 14 Apr. 1969.

"County Rights Unit Asks Police Force Aid." *Pittsburgh Post-Gazette*, 3 May 1969.

"Court Battle Blocks Housing; Aids Slums; North Side 'Pioneers' Create New Hazards for Redevelopment." *Pittsburgh Courier*, 29 Aug. 1953.

"Court Limits, OKs Stadium Pickets: Big March Vowed." *Pittsburgh Post-Gazette*, 16 Aug. 1969.

"'Coy' Gov. Shafer Sends 'Feeler' He Would Like Talks with City's Miffed Rights Leaders." *New Pittsburgh Courier*, 12 Aug. 1967.

"Craig Credits Police 5-Year Plan with Keeping Riots Here Bloodless: Tactical Platoons Modeled in 1963." *New Pittsburgh Courier*, 14 Apr. 1969.

Crutchfield, James. "Housing Issue: Black vs. White." *Pittsburgh Press*, ca. June 1970, newsclippings file, Carnegie Library of Pittsburgh.

Cunningham, James V., and Patricia W. Murphy. "Get Everybody on Board." *Pittsburgh Post-Gazette*, 26 Feb. 1995.

Davis, Ed. "Explosive Homicide Statistics Alarm Afro-American Community" *New Pittsburgh Courier*, 9 Dec. 1992.

———. "Nation of Islam Looks to Become Part of Total Black Perspective" *Pittsburgh Courier*, 10 Nov. 1990.

"Democracy and Diversity: Politics in the Pittsburgh Region Is Pale and Male." *Pittsburgh Post-Gazette*, 20 Apr. 2003.

"Derrick Bell Says Conditions Make Muslims: NAACP Leader Decries Hate, but Believes Muslims and Others Thrive on Injustice." *Pittsburgh Courier*, 5 Sept. 1959.

DeWitt, Karen. "Pittsburgh Moves to Integrate Schools." *New York Times*, 13 Dec. 1979.

"Dick Jones New School Bd. Veep." *New Pittsburgh Courier*, 19 Nov. 1966.

"Districts and Dissenters." *Pittsburgh Post-Gazette*, 5 Feb. 1987.

"Diversified Jobs Given Negroes in Housing Program." *Pittsburgh Courier*, 21 Sept. 1940.

Donalson, Al. "Fear Part of the Bargain at Housing Projects." *Pittsburgh Press*, 21 Sept. 1973.

———. "Group Vows Police Watch: Seeks to Prevent Alleged Abuse." *Pittsburgh Press*, ca. 20 July 1974, newsclippings file, Carnegie Library of Pittsburgh.

Dunlop, Beth. "To Residents, Housing Patrol Means Cop When You Need One." *Pittsburgh Press*, 13 May 1973.

"Duquesne Light Agrees to Hire 350 Negroes." *New Pittsburgh Courier*, 28 Oct. 1967.

"Duquesne Light Picketed." *Pittsburgh Post-Gazette*, 13 Aug. 1963.

Dyer, Ervin. "Bankrupt Lemington Home Empties Out at Last." *Pittsburgh Post-Gazette*, 15 July 2005.

———. "Revisiting the Great Migration: Senior Citizens Remember the Mass Exodus of Southern Blacks to Northern Cities in the Early to Mid-20th Century." *Pittsburgh Post-Gazette*, 25 Feb. 2001.

———. "The Sweet Life for Black Pittsburghers: Sugar Top." *Pittsburgh Post-Gazette*, 17 July 2005.

"An Economic Crisis of Shocking Proportions for Region's Black Males." *Pittsburgh Post-Gazette*, 28 Apr. 1996.

Editorial. *Pittsburgh Courier*, 11 Sept. 1932.

Editorial. *Pittsburgh Courier*, 14 Sept. 1946.

"Education, Role Models Are Key to Progress." *Pittsburgh Post-Gazette*, 28 Apr. 1996.

Espo, David. "Obama Wins . . . Elected Nation's 44 President: Landslide Victory a Triumph Over Racial Barriers." *New Pittsburgh Courier*, 4 Nov. 2008.

Farrish, Jean S. "Women's Political Crusade Expands Focus." *Pittsburgh Courier*, 25 Feb. 1995.

"Fear New Wave of Job Bias Here: Powerless USES and Lack of FEPC 'Protects' Firms." *Pittsburgh Courier*, 15 Sept. 1945.

"Fear of Black Militancy Terror: Threatens to Close H-B Stores." *New Pittsburgh Courier*, 9 Dec. 1967.

"FEPC Opens Office Here." *Pittsburgh Courier*, 3 Feb 1945.

"15,000 Sign Udin's Pittsburgh Works Petition." *Pittsburgh Courier*, 21 Aug. 1999.

"Fight for Urban Survival." *Pittsburgh Press*, 24 June 1963.

Fitzpatrick, Dan. "Rate of Pittsburgh Women Working Evens Up: Region Had Long Trailed Nation." *Pittsburgh Post-Gazette*, 12 Aug. 2003.

Florida, Richard. "Pittsburgh's Prosperity Depends on Diversity." *Pittsburgh Post-Gazette*, 15 Oct. 2000.

"For Blacks and Whites in Our Region, School Desegregation Gets a Failing Grade." *Pittsburgh Post-Gazette*, 21 Apr. 1996.

"For Blacks and Whites in Our Region, the Workplace Yields." *Pittsburgh Post-Gazette*, 28 Apr. 1996.

"For Blacks and Whites in the Region, the Issue Is . . . The Color of the Law." *Pittsburgh Post-Gazette*, 5 May 1996.

Foster, Pamela. "Gloria Spearman: Destined Businesswoman." *New Pittsburgh Courier*, 3 Mar. 1990.

"Four Area Hospitals Charged with Bias." *Pittsburgh Post-Gazette*, 7 Aug. 1964.

Franklin, Stephen. "Guardians Still Hope for More Black Police." *Pittsburgh Post-Gazette*, n.d.

———. "Housing Authority's Security Force OKd." *Pittsburgh Post-Gazette*, 30 Sept. 1972.

Garland, Phyl. "City's Redevelopers Admit Shortcomings." *Pittsburgh Courier*, 23 Dec. 1961.

Gagetta, Vince. "Hill's Businessmen Demand Payments for Riots' Losses." *Pittsburgh Post-Gazette*, 17 Apr. 1968.

"Gas Co. to Hire 100 Negroes. Lerner's May Face Boycott." *New Pittsburgh Courier*, 15 July 1967.

"Gladys McNairy First Black School Board Head." *New Pittsburgh Courier*, 13 Nov. 1971.

"Glass Bandits Hit Crew Offices of Hill Realty." *New Pittsburgh Courier*, 1 Apr. 1967.

Golightly, John. "City Housing Probe Resumes Today." *Pittsburgh Post-Gazette*, 16 May 1974.

"Guardians Ask Asst. Supt. Job." *New Pittsburgh Courier*, 5 Apr. 1969.

Haley, Leon L. "Urban League of Pittsburgh: A Statement on Violence." *New Pittsburgh Courier*, 22 Sept. 1993.

Hamm, Sandy. "History Made in Pittsburgh: Former School Board President Becomes 1st Afro-American [Woman] on City Council." *New Pittsburgh Courier*, 26 Nov. 1994

———. "Residents Can't Get Straight Answers to Honest Questions." *New Pittsburgh Courier*, 16 July 1994

———. "Sala Udin Emerges as the 6 District Front Runner." *Pittsburgh Courier*, 15 Feb. 1995.

Hart, Rahmon. "Million Man March: It's Time for the Black Man to Do His Part." *New Pittsburgh Courier*, 18 Jan. 1995.

"Has Homewood Become a Pgh. Vice Center?" *Pittsburgh Courier*, 16 Nov. 1963.

Haynes, Sonya M. "Gammage Case Brings National NAACP to City." *New Pittsburgh Courier*, 23 Nov. 1996.

———. "Jury Acquits Vojtas." *New Pittsburgh Courier*, 16 Nov. 1996.

———. "Stevens: Trial Littered with Injustices" *New Pittsburgh Courier*, 16 Nov. 1996.

———. "A Tragic Loss." *New Pittsburgh Courier*, 17 May 1997.

"H-B Med. Center Approved." *Pittsburgh Courier*, 8 Apr. 1967.

"HCIA Prexy Says Neighborhood Burdened with Taverns, No Police and Youth Mobs." *Pittsburgh Courier*, 19 Oct. 1957.

Hennessy, Thomas A. "Urban League Hits Doctor 'Inequality': Local Committee Regrets Lack of Integration in All Hospitals." *Pittsburgh Post-Gazette*, 10 July 1963.

Heuck, Douglas. "Surviving St. Clair Village." *Pittsburgh Post-Gazette*, 4 Mar. 1990.

Heuck, Douglas, Cindi Lash, Bill Schackner, Bill Hetzel, and Tom Barnes. "Justice Delay Brings Letdown." *Pittsburgh Post-Gazette*, 20 Oct. 1996.

"Highlights of Council's Housing Authority Inquiry." *New Pittsburgh Courier*, 24 May 1974.

"'Hire More Negroes at Arena!'—NAACP." *Pittsburgh Courier*, 7 Oct 1961.

"Hold Meeting to Spur Passage of Brown Bill." *Pittsburgh Courier*, 21 Apr. 1945.

Holt, Ernestine. "Status of Steelworkers Presents Sorry Picture: Negroes Refused Supervisory Jobs." *Pittsburgh Courier*, 24 Aug. 1946.

"Homewood Boycott On: Pickett Homewood Avenue Merchants." *New Pittsburgh Courier*, 3 June 1967.

"Homewood Merchants Face Boycotts: Group Demand Managers, Issue Ultimatum." *New Pittsburgh Courier*, 27 May 1967.

"Homewood Renewal Unit Launches War for Work." *Pittsburgh Courier*, 26 Oct. 1963.

Hopkins, Marc. "Advocacy Groups wants Superintendent Who Will Help Blacks Achieve." *New Pittsburgh Courier*, 25 July 1992.

"Housing Authority, Tenants Reach Agreement on Five Crucial Issues." *New Pittsburgh Courier*, 13 Mar. 1971.

"Housing Board Votes to Dismiss Tronzo." *Pittsburgh Post-Gazette*, 27 Feb. 1970.

"Housing, Jobs, Representation: Basic Issues in Outgoing 1970." *New Pittsburgh Courier*, 2 Jan. 1971.

"Interracial Plan Submitted to Detroit Mayor: 'Live Together in Peace,' Slogan for Detroit Club Plan." *Pittsburgh Courier*, 10 July 1943.

"Isaly's Promises Negro Manager by Sept. 15." *New Pittsburgh Courier*, 24 June 1967.

"It's Still a House Divided for Blacks and Whites in the Region." *Pittsburgh Post-Gazette*, 14 Apr. 1996.

Jackson, Kent. "FEPCC Killed by GOP in City, State." *Pittsburgh Courier*, 11 May 1946.

Jensen, Edward. "Duquesne Light Picketed by 300 in Racial Case." *Pittsburgh Post-Gazette*, 13 Aug. 1963.

"Jobs First, Immigrants Second." *Pittsburgh Post-Gazette*, 10 June 2001.

Johnson, C. Denise. "Obama Makes Pittsburgh Debut as Candidate." *New Pittsburgh Courier*, 27 June 2007.

Jones, Diana Nelson. "Surviving Oliver High's Racial Divide." *Pittsburgh Post-Gazette*, 28 Apr. 1996.

Jones, Paul L. "Housing Upheavals; How to Meet Them?" *Pittsburgh Courier*, 13 May 1950.

Jones, R. LaMont, Jr. "City Should Have Read the Gang Signs Years Ago." *Pittsburgh Post-Gazette*, 27 June 1994.

"Jury Finds Communist Defendants Guilty!" *Pittsburgh Courier*, 22 Aug. 1953.

"Jury Selection Under Fire at Red Trial." 21 Mar. 1953.

Karamcheti, Deepak. "'Journey' Marchers Meet with Justice Department." *New Pittsburgh Courier*, 19 Feb. 1997.

"Kaufmann's Asks Reprieve from NAACP and Pickets: Pledges to Upgrade Negroes." *Pittsburgh Courier*, 2 Dec. 1961.

"Keeping African American Males in High School Should Be a Top Priority." Editorial, *New Pittsburgh Courier*, 13 Oct. 1993.

Keith, Harold L. "Who's Who in Labor: Independent Refuse Haulers in Debut." *Pittsburgh Courier*, 22 Apr. 1950.

Kelley, Holland F. "Hand Bills Swamp Downtown District." *Pittsburgh Courier*, 7 Dec. 1946.

———. "Plans to 'Work On' Department Stores: Interracial Council." *Pittsburgh Courier*, 3 Feb. 1945.

———. "Spur Dept. Store Fight." *Pittsburgh Courier*, 9 Nov. 1946.

Kendrick, Louis "Hop." "Blame White Folks? Not This Time." *New Pittsburgh Courier*, 27–31 July 2005.

Koger, Ralph. "Sears Boycott Ends, HRC Plays Key Role." *New Pittsburgh Courier*, 8 Mar. 1970.

"Kohlman Quitting Housing Post." *Pittsburgh Press*, 13 Aug. 1973.

"Kohlman's Exit: Pete's Opening." *Pittsburgh Post-Gazette*, 22 Aug. 1973.

Korol, Paul S. "A Brief History of the Hill." *Pittsburgh Senior News*, 4 Feb. 2002.

Lapin, Adam. "Negro America Acts to Build Steel Unions." *Daily Worker*, 8 Feb. 1937.

"Law Inequality View Is Backed." *Pittsburgh Post-Gazette*, 21 Oct. 1970.

Lee, Carmen. "Survey to Study Student Decline." *Pittsburgh Post-Gazette*, 10 Apr. 1995.

———. "Trying for the Best of Both Worlds: Area's Black Private Schools Offer Safe Environment, Cultural Focus." *Pittsburgh Post-Gazette*, 21 Apr. 1996.

Letter to the editor. *Homestead Daily Messenger*, 28 Feb. 1944.

"Level Blast at Cops' Laxity: Youth, 16, Beaten in E. Liberty. No Probe." *Pittsburgh Courier*, 3 June 1961.

Levin, Steve. "Census Shows Changing Racial Makeup of County." *Pittsburgh Post-Gazette*, 13 Mar. 2001.

———. "Region Sees More Blacks Buying Their Own Homes." *Pittsburgh Post-Gazette*, 26 Aug. 2001.

Lindsey, Robert. "School Integration Looks More Than Ever Like a Lost Horizon." *New York Times*, 24 Aug. 1980.

"List of Demands to Sears." *New Pittsburgh Courier*, 20 Dec. 1969.

"Local FEPC Fight On: Leaders' Views Differ: Homer Brown, Mon Lead Opposition Against Job Law." *Pittsburgh Courier*, 8 Dec. 1945.

"Local FEPC Law Urged." *Pittsburgh Courier*, 24 Nov. 1945.

"Local Group Formed to Fight Police Brutality." *New Pittsburgh Courier*, 20 July 1974.

"Local Race Areas Would Be Targets for Hostile Armies: Defense Council Appeals for Race Co-Operation Here." *Pittsburgh Courier*, 13 Dec. 1941.

Lyman, Brian. "Growing Diversity: More Minorities Call Northern Towns Home, But Their Numbers Are Still Small." *Pittsburgh Post-Gazette*, 28 Jan. 2001.

Mackey, David "City Housing Entry Rules Hit." *Pittsburgh Press*, 7 Oct. 1971.

Maeroff, Gene I. "Magnet Schools Used as Tool for Equity." *New York Times*, 31 Jan. 1984.

Majors, Dan. "Pittsburgh Rated 'Most Livable City' Once Again." *Pittsburgh Post-Gazette*, 26 Apr. 2007.

"Many Changes in the Offing for Housing Authority." *New Pittsburgh Courier*, 28 Apr. 1973.

"March for Jobs." *New Pittsburgh Courier*, 3 July 1999.

Marshall, Elizabeth C. "Deltas Will Promote Improved Social Laws: Back Drive for FEPC PA, Better Housing." *Pittsburgh Courier*, 4 May 1946.

Martinez, Andrew. "On the Brink? City's Economic Decline May Be Tough to Stop." *Pittsburgh Post-Gazette*, 15 Feb. 1995.

"Massive 'Black Monday' Protest Set Against Sears." *New Pittsburgh Courier*, 15 Nov. 1969.

"Mayor Calls for New Dep't Store Meeting: Parlay Set for New Year's Eve" *Pittsburgh Courier*, 21 Dec. 1946.

"Mayor Criticized for No Fair Housing Laws." *Pittsburgh Courier*, 9 Nov. 1957.

"Mayor Fears City FEPC Court Test." *Pittsburgh Courier*, 20 Sept. 1952.

"Mayor Proud of Racial Amity Here." *Pittsburgh Courier*, 14 Feb. 1959.

McCarron, James. "Negro Wins Realty Berth: Multilist Eliminating Bias from By-Laws." *Pittsburgh Press*, 3 Oct. 1968.

McKay, Jim."Backslide: Jobs, Programs Haven't Fulfilled Promises for Blacks." *Pittsburgh Post-Gazette*, 28 Apr. 1996.

———. "Blacks Lost Jobs and a Generation with Manufacturing's Demise." *Pittsburgh Post-Gazette*, 15 Nov. 1994.

———. "An Economic Crisis of Shocking Proportions for Region's Black Males." *Pittsburgh Post Gazette*, 28 Apr. 1996.

———. "Unequal Payback: For Blacks and Whites in Our Region." *Pittsburgh Post-Gazette*, 28 Apr. 1996.

McKay, Jim, and Tawanda Williams. "What Can Be Done?" *Pittsburgh Post-Gazette*, 28 Apr. 1996.

McNulty, Timothy. "Two Black Districts or Three?: City Council Panel Revising Boundaries." *Pittsburgh Post-Gazette*, 25 June 2002.

Mellon-Vann, Esther, and Alma Thompson-Han. "Background on Braddock School Fight." *Pittsburgh Courier*, 15 Oct. 1955.

Michelmore, David. "The Color of Money: Loan Statistics Continue to Indicate Discrimination Against Blacks." *Pittsburgh Post-Gazette*, 12 May 1994.

"Million Man March." *New Pittsburgh Courier*, 18 Jan. 1995.

Mims, Greg. "Black Populace Gathers for Haden's Final Rites." *New Pittsburgh Courier*, 10 August 1974.

———. "Community Slighted in Kohlman Issue." *Pittsburgh Courier*, 22 Sept. 1973.

———. "Kohlman Answers Latest Accusations." *Pittsburgh Courier*, 10 Nov. 1973.

———. "McIlvane Charges 'End Run' Behind Back of Citizens." *Pittsburgh Courier*, 20 Oct. 1973.

Molloy, Tim. "Study Says PA Minorities Four Times as Likely to Be Imprisoned for Drugs." *Associated Press and Local Wire*, 5 Aug. 2000.

"Montefiore May Change Policy." *Pittsburgh Courier*, June 8, 1946.

Morris, Carl. "The Black Mood in Pittsburgh." *New Pittsburgh Courier*, series, 2–16 Mar. 1968.

———. "Bob Lavelle's Lawsuit." *Pittsburgh Courier*, 8 Apr. 1967.

———. "The Circus Comes to Homewood." *Pittsburgh Courier*, 23 Dec. 1967.

"Mortgaging Inequality—Blacks Still Have Less Chance of Getting a Home Loan." *Pittsburgh Post-Gazette*, 13 May 1994.

Moushey, Bill. "Gangs Are All They Have." *Pittsburgh Post-Gazette*, 26 June 1994.

"Multi-List Meeting with Negro Realtor: Lavelle to Try for Membership Again." *Pittsburgh Post-Gazette*, 24 June 1966.

"NAACP Campaign Closes July 28, Center City Leads." *New Pittsburgh Courier*, 15 July 1967.

"NAACP Demonstration Targets Weitz." *Pittsburgh Courier*, 12 Jan. 1985.

"NAACP Maps Its Battle Here on U.S. Steel Hiring Setup." *Pittsburgh Press*, 6 June 1966.

"NALC Bristles." *Pittsburgh Courier*, 8 Sept. 1962.

"NALC Mass Protest Wins: Arena to Improve Job-Hiring Policy." *Pittsburgh Courier*, 16 Sept 1961.

"Negro Homeowners Fight for Stiff Zoning Ordinance." *New Pittsburgh Courier*, 1 Apr. 1967, 27 Aug. 1974.

"Negroes to Stage Mass Protest at Civic Arena: NAACP, NALC Spark Move." *Pittsburgh Courier*, 21 Oct. 1961.

"New Homewood Property Improvement Group to Meet." *Pittsburgh Courier*, 17 Sept. 1955.

"New Police, Citizens Unit Is Formed." *Pittsburgh Post-Gazette*, 16 Dec. 1970.

"No Jim Crow for Pitt's New Nurses School." *Pittsburgh Courier*, 29 Nov. 1945.

"North Side 'Pioneers' Create New Hazards for Redevelopment." *Pittsburgh Courier*. 29 Aug. 1953.

"Northview School Mothers March on Board of Education." *New Pittsburgh Courier*, 28 Oct. 1967.

"Nurses Pledge Cooperation in Hospital Fight." *Pittsburgh Courier*, 1 June 1946.

"Obituary: Justin L. Johnson: Prominent Attorney and Son of Superior Court Judge." *Pittsburgh Post-Gazette*, 25 Aug. 2004.

"One Negro Physician Among 67 Negroes on Staff of 1,102 Kane Hospital Workers." *Pittsburgh Courier*, May 1961.

"Oppose Hiring Police." n.d., in authors' possession, newsclippings file, Carnegie Library of Pittsburgh.

O'Toole, James. "Historic Wave Sweeps Obama to Victory." *Pittsburgh Post-Gazette*, 5 Nov. 2008.

———. "A Torch Is Passed, a Barrier Broken: Barack Obama Is Sworn in as 44th President." *Pittsburgh Post-Gazette*, 21 Jan. 2009.

"Ouster of Bouie Haden Is Hailed by Many Whites in Area." *New Pittsburgh Courier*, 12 July 1969.

Pace, Laura. "Mt. Lebanon's Past of Not Selling to Minorities Is Highlighted." *Pittsburgh Post-Gazette*, February 21, 2001.

"Panther Unit Scores Negro Moderates." *New Pittsburgh Courier*, 25 Apr. 1970.

"'Panthers No Threat': Says U. S. Atty.-Gen." *New Pittsburgh Courier*, 23 May 1970.

"Parents Picket Wilkinsburg Schools." *New Pittsburgh Courier*, 17 Apr. 1971.

"Part of Frankstown Avenue Seen as Homewood Slums." *Pittsburgh Courier*, 10 August 1957.

"People Assured Voice in Homewood Renewal Plan." *Pittsburgh Courier*, 6 Jan. 1962.

Perlman, Marla. "It Is Income, Not Race, That Is the Marker of Infant Mortality." *Pittsburgh Post-Gazette*, 5 Dec. 1993.

Perry, Diane. "Black Panther Party Opens H'Wood Office." *New Pittsburgh Courier*, 18 Apr. 1970.

———. "Black Teacher Fights Boro School System." *New Pittsburgh Courier*, 3 April 1971.

———. "The Coming Crisis in Pittsburgh Schools." *New Pittsburgh Courier*, 29 Aug. 1970.

———. "Golden Triangle Is Hit with COP Brutality, Mass Arrests: Thousands See Blacks Clubbed." *Pittsburgh Courier*, 30 Aug. 1969.

"PHA Board Members Get Wide Support." *New Pittsburgh Courier*, 7 Feb. 1970.

"Phil Murray Urges Negro Workers to Join Great Steel Industry Union." *Pittsburgh Courier*, 13 Feb. 1937.

"Picketing Stops Work at 3 Homewood Sites." *Pittsburgh Press*, 23 Aug. 1969.

Pierce, Henry W. "Negro MD Plight 1 More Problem: Varied Aspects of Discrimination Bring Wide List of Observations." *Pittsburgh Post-Gazette*, 11 July 1963.

"'Pigeon' Cvetic Names Careathers and Wright." *Pittsburgh Courier*, 25 Feb. 1950.

"Pitt Medical School Charged with Race Bias." *New Pittsburgh Courier*, 15 July 1967.

"Pittsburgh Album: A Hill Comes Tumbling Down." *Pittsburgh Press*, magazine section, 17 Feb. 1957, 6.

"Pittsburgh Blacks Ask to Patrol Own Neighborhoods." *Valley Daily News—Daily Dispatch*, 16 July, 1971.

"Pittsburgh Panther Posters." *New Pittsburgh Courier*, 2 May 1970.

"Pittsburgh Works Referendum." *New Pittsburgh Courier*, 7 June 2000.

"Pittsburgh Works! Gets Mixed Reaction." *New Pittsburgh Courier*, 3 Mar. 1999.

"Pittsburgh Works! Passes, Still Faces Challenges." *New Pittsburgh Courier*, 6 Nov. 1999.

"Pittsburgher Named Top Executive for Warner." *New Pittsburgh Courier*, 27 June 1981.

"Pittsburgh's Housing Projects among Nation's Most Segregated." *Pittsburgh Post-Gazette*, 14 Apr. 1996.

Pitz, Marylynne. "Lawyer Byrd Brown Dies: Giant in Civil Rights Struggle." *Pittsburgh Post-Gazette*, 4 May 2001.

Place, John. "Police to Put Crime Office in Homewood." *Pittsburgh Post-Gazette*, 11 Apr. 1969.

"Powerful Groups Back Department Store Fight: Hand Bills Swamp Downtown District." *Pittsburgh Courier*, 7 Dec. 1946.

Prattis, P. L. "Profiles etc." *Pittsburgh Courier*, 12 Jan. 1963.

———. "Profiles etc." *Pittsburgh Courier*, 19 Jan. 1963.

———. "Profiles etc.: For Teachers' Scrapbooks." *Pittsburgh Courier*, 22 Dec. 1962.

Princiotto, Ted. "Alex Wright Reveals Secret Cabal of Local Red Plotters." *Pittsburgh Courier*, 24 Dec. 1955.

"Property Upkeep Group Plans Mass Meeting in Homewood." *Pittsburgh Courier*, 8 Oct. 1955.

"R. Williamson Can't Move to Davenport St." *Pittsburgh Courier*, 9 November 1957.

"Randolph Named Labor Honoree." *New Pittsburgh Courier*, 15 July 1967.

"Red-Vested Black Militants Volunteer to Help 'Cool It.'" *New Pittsburgh Courier*, 13 Apr. 1968.

"Reflections on Bouie Haden." *New Pittsburgh Courier*, 3 August 1974.

Reid, Gene. "Local Group Formed to Fight Brutality." *Pittsburgh Courier*, ca. late 1960s, newsclippings file, Carnegie Library of Pittsburgh.

Reiland, Ralph. "Pittsburgh: First in Shrinkage." *New Pittsburgh Courier*, 28 Oct. 1998.

"Resident Named to Housing Board." *Pittsburgh Post-Gazette*, 7 Aug. 1970.

Ritter, Bernard L. "NAACP Working at Achieving 'The Dream.'" *New Pittsburgh Courier*, 10 Dec. 1988.

Robertson, Michele D. "Blacks Shocked, Express Disbelief." *New Pittsburgh Courier*, 16 Nov. 1996.

———. "Justice Probe Requested by National NAACP." *New Pittsburgh Courier*, 14 Dec. 1996.

———. "Youth on the March." *New Pittsburgh Courier*, 27 Nov. 1996.

Robinson, A. Vivienne. "Adams Meets NAACP Challenges with Commitment, Compassion." *New Pittsburgh Courier*, 10 Dec. 1988.

———. "Protestor Calls Attention to Plight of City's Homeless, Housing Problems." *New Pittsburgh Courier*, 28 June 1989.

———. "Reflections of a Former NAACP President." *New Pittsburgh Courier*, 10 Dec. 1988.

Roddy, Dennis. "The Gammage Case: Brentwood Waits, Prepares for Trouble." *Pittsburgh Post-Gazette*, 14 Nov. 1996.

Rosensweet, Alvin. "Race Pressure in City Called 'Rough' on Kids: Discrimination from Birth Is Lot of Non-Whites Here, Says President of NAACP." *Pittsburgh Post-Gazette*, 10 Sept. 1963.

Rowland, Debran. "Committee Investigates Area Hiring Practices." *New Pittsburgh Courier*, 10 Dec. 1988.

———. "Committees Keep In Touch with Community." *New Pittsburgh Courier*, 10 Dec. 1988.

———. "Early NAACP Efforts Set Stage for Future Successes." *New Pittsburgh Courier*, 10 Dec. 1988.

———. "Harvey Adams Jr. . . . The Voice of the NAACP Speaks to the Community." *New Pittsburgh Courier*, 10 Dec. 1988.

Schalk, Johnson Toki. "Pittsburgh Neighborhood Units Coping with Urban Renewal Migrations." *Pittsburgh Courier*, 29 Nov. 1958.

"School Board Guilty of Flagrant Discrimination." *Pittsburgh Courier*, 5 June 1937.

"School Board Picketing to Continue." *Pittsburgh Post-Gazette*, 24 Aug. 1965.

"School Busing Plan Case Reset." *New Pittsburgh Courier*, 28 Oct. 1967.

Scott, Marjorie. "Readers Write." *Pittsburgh Courier*, 13 Sept. 1963.

Scott, Michelle. "Hill District Once a Beacon of Culture." *Pitt News*, 20 Oct. 2004.

"Sears Now Ready for Negotiations." *New Pittsburgh Courier*, 13 Dec. 1969.

"Sears Stores Here Facing Black Boycott." *New Pittsburgh Courier*, 8 Nov. 1969.

"Seeking Permanent Anti-Bias Law." *Pittsburgh Courier*, 20 Jan 1945.

Sharpe, Jerry. "Northview Tenants Seek Housing Project Control." *Pittsburgh Press*, 23 Sept. 1974.

Shropshire, Carolyn. "New Industry Old Story: Like Other Industries, High-Tech Sector Lacks African American Managers, Workers." *Pittsburgh Post-Gazette*, 22 Feb. 2001.

Shropshire, Philip. "City, Crusade Agree to Consent Decree: District Election Reapportionment Under Federal Court Control." *New Pittsburgh Courier*, 6 June 1987.

———. "Judge Denies Injunction: Grants Earlier Trial Date." *New Pittsburgh Courier*, 28 Feb. 1987.

———. "NAACP's Stance Key Factor in Lawsuit" *New Pittsburgh Courier*, 21 Mar. 1987.

Snyder, Thomas P. "Negroes Charge County with Job Discrimination." *Pittsburgh Post-Gazette*, 26 June 1963.

"Still Few Blacks in Unions." *Pittsburgh Post-Gazette*, 15 Aug. 1969.

Stokes, Tom. "Blacks Rally for Support, Kohlman to Stay—for Now." *Pittsburgh Courier*, 18 Aug. 1973.

"Store Fight Spurred: 10 Seek Positions." *Pittsburgh Courier*, 9 Nov. 1946.

"Store Heads 'Mum' About Race Issue." *Pittsburgh Courier*, 24 Oct. 1947.

"Store Heads Still Dodge Race Issue." *Pittsburgh Courier*, 16 Nov. 1946.

"Store Pickets Will Not Quit: Talks with Mayor Called Fruitless." *Pittsburgh Courier*, 14 Dec. 1946.

Strikameswaran, Anita. "Minorities Lag in Receiving Transplants and Heart Surgeries." *Pittsburgh Post-Gazette*, 23 July 2002.

Stuart, Roger. "Black Injustice Charge Disputed." *Pittsburgh Press*, 21 Oct. 1970.

Stuart, Roger, and Jack Grochot. "Hiring Under Kohlman Authority 'All in the Family.'" *Pittsburgh Press*, 16 Dec. 1973.

Suber, Ron. "Homewood Parents Rally to Boycott Baxter School." *New Pittsburgh Courier*, 30 Aug. 1975.

"Survey Shows Negroes Paying More for Less." *Pittsburgh Courier*, 15 Jan. 1966.

Taylor, Woodrow. "Housing Authority Borders on Chaos in Land of Plenty." *Pittsburgh Courier*, 6 Oct. 1973.

———. "State, Realtors Reach Anti-Bias Housing Pact." *New Pittsburgh Courier*, 27 July 1974.

"They Fight for Democracy." Editorial, *Homestead Daily Messenger*, 28 Feb. 1944.

Thomas, Clarke. "As Different as Black and White: Why Don't Minorities Get the Same Benefit from Pittsburgh's Health-Care System?" *Pittsburgh Post-Gazette*, Apr. 7, 2004.

———. "Neighborhood City: Tending the Pieces that Make Up Pittsburgh's Still Key." *Pittsburgh Post-Gazette*, 3 Apr. 1996.

Toler, Sonya. "Bush: State of Black Pittsburgh 'Dismal.'" *New Pittsburgh Courier*, 28 Oct. 2000.

"Traffic Snarls Add to Furor in Job Protest." *Pittsburgh Press*, 6 Aug. 1969.

"Transplant Recipient Nears One-Month Mark." *New York Times*, 27 Nov. 1987.

"Tronzo and Janitor Issue Resurrected." *Pittsburgh Press*, 9 Nov. 1971.

"Two Local Organizations Announce Platforms." *Pittsburgh Courier*, 1 Aug. 1931.

"UBPC, Sears Set Meeting." *New Pittsburgh Courier*, 10 Jan. 1970.

"Udin's Pittsburgh Works Supporters Jam Council Hearing." *New Pittsburgh Courier*, 13 Feb. 1999.

"UNIA meeting in Pittsburgh." *Negro World*, 26 Sept. 1919.

"UNPC Calls for Resignations at Housing Auth." *New Pittsburgh Courier*, 25 Nov. 1967.

"UNPC Making Headway on Jobs in Dairy Industry." *New Pittsburgh Courier*, 29 Jan. 1966.

"UNPC Schedules More Job Talks." *New Pittsburgh Courier*, 19 July 1969.

"UNPC to Meet with Murphy's A&P on Jobs" *New Pittsburgh Courier*, 12 Aug. 1967.

"Urban League Opposes Local FEPC Campaign." *Pittsburgh Courier*, 22 Dec. 1945.

"Vow More Protests on Jobs." *Pittsburgh Press*, 20 Aug. 1969.

Wallsten, Peter. "Analysis: Whites Boost Obama Victory." *Pittsburgh Post-Gazette*, 6 Nov. 2008.

Walsh, Lawrence. "Barr Years: This Family's Influence on the City." *Pittsburgh Press*, 28 Dec. 1969.

Warner, David. "Housing Pete's Pawn, Tronzo Says." *Pittsburgh Press*, 18 May 1974.

Warnick, Mark S. "Gangs Triggering Fear in their Neighborhoods." *Pittsburgh Post-Gazette*, June 30, 1994.

Washington, Jesse. "Obama's Color: Is He Black, White . . . or Neither? Racial Categories Are Falling Apart." *New Pittsburgh Courier*, 31 Dec. 2008.

"'We're Not Subversive': Malcolm X." *Pittsburgh Courier*, 1 Sept. 1960.

"West End Resident Fight Public Housing." *New Pittsburgh Courier*, 14 Oct. 1967.

"White 'Establishment' Secretly Rooting for Blacks on Jobs." *Pittsburgh Press*, 20 Aug. 1969.

"White Officers Patrol Troubled Oliver High." *New Pittsburgh Courier*, 22 Feb. 1969.

"White Students, Cop Arrested in Gladstone School Crisis, Hill Constables Make Arrests." *New Pittsburgh Courier*, 1 Mar. 1969.

Wilkes. "Nathaniel K. Angry Confrontation at Broadhead Manor." *New Pittsburgh Courier*, 6 Sept. 1996.

Williams, Tawanda. "Both Races Feel Victimized." *Pittsburgh Post-Gazette*, 28 Apr. 1996.

Willis, Marty. "All-White Council Ceremony Draws Protest." *New Pittsburgh Courier*, 18 Jan. 1986.

———. "Black Groups Unify Around District Elections Effort." *New Pittsburgh Courier*, 11 Apr. 1987.

———. "B-PEP Endorses District Council Elections." *New Pittsburgh Courier*, 11 Apr. 1987.

———. "B-PEP Support Mounts for Voter Registration." *New Pittsburgh Courier*, 4 Jan. 1986.

———. "D.C. Rally Hits New Issues." *New Pittsburgh Courier*, 17 Apr. 1985.

———. "Jan. 6 Demonstration to Greet All-White City Council." *New Pittsburgh Courier*, 11 Jan. 1986.

———. "School Board Links to South Africa." *New Pittsburgh Courier*, 12 Jan. 1985.

Wintermantel, Ed, and Al Schriner. "From Slaves to Statesmen: A History of Blacks in Pittsburgh." *Pittsburgh Press*, 17 Oct. 1982.

"Wylie Avenue." *Pittsburgh Courier*, 17 June 1933.

Yoland, Bill. "NAACP Convention Zeroes in on Voting." *Pittsburgh Post-Gazette*, 13 July 2004.

Zapinski, Ken. "Housed But Hopeless." *Pittsburgh Post-Gazette*, 11 July 1993.

Zemel, Jane. "Finding Her Way in the World." *Pittsburgh Post-Gazette*, 21 Apr. 1996.

———. "Upper St. Clair Teen Takes on Role as a Representative of His Race." *Pittsburgh Post-Gazette*, 21 Apr. 1996.

———. "Words That Hurt: Blatant or Subtle, Racist Comments and Actions Can Be Damaging." *Pittsburgh Post-Gazette*, 21 Apr. 1996.

Film, Television, Internet Sites

Al-Qahtani, Haroon. *An Oral History of Islam in Pittsburgh*. Pittsburgh: Pittsburgh Muslim Media, 2007. Film. Available at http://ia331333.us.archive.org/1/items/ An_Oral_History_of_Islam_in_Pittsburgh/an_oral_history_of_ islam_in_pittsburgh-hi.mp4 (accessed 9 Dec. 2008).

Black Political Empowerment Project. http://www.b-ep.net/police_accountability .htm (accessed 8 December 2008).

Bolin, Doug, Christopher Moore, and Nancy Levin. *Wylie Avenue Days: Pittsburgh's Hill District.* Pittsburgh QED Communications, Inc., 1991. Film.

"Getting to Know Alma Illery Medical Center/Primary Care Health Services." *Networks: Caring for the Whole Person,* Nov. 2001. http://www. coordinatedcarenetwork.org/CCN/newsletters/November.pdf (accessed 2 October 2009).

Glasco, Laurence. "The Civil Rights Movement in Pittsburgh: To Make This City 'Some Place Special.'" Freedom Corner. http://www.freedomcorner.org/ downloads/glasco.pdf. (accessed 5 October 2009).

Henderson, Ray, and Tony Buba. *Struggles in Steel: The Fight for Equal Opportunity.* San Francisco: California Newsreel, 1996. Film.

The Kingsley Association. "Who We Are." http://kingsleyassociation.org/who_we_ are.html (accessed 2 October 2009).

Landmark Education Program. "Tim Stevens: Black Political Empowerment Project, Community Action Builds African-American Voter Impact." http://www. landmarkeducation.com/display_content.htm (accessed December 2008).

Love, Kenneth. *One Shot: The Life and Work of Teenie Harris.* California Newsreel, 2001. Film.

Manchester Craftsmen's Guild. "MCG History." http://www.manchesterguild.org/ MCG_History.htm (accessed 10 December 2009).

Nelson, Stanley. *The Black Press: Soldiers without Swords.* PBS Television, 1999. Film.

"Reverend Jimmy Joe Robinson." Civil Rights Digital Library, University of Georgia, http://crdl.usg.edu/people/r/robinson_jimmy_joe/ (accessed 3 Dec. 2009).

Washington Legal Foundation, commentary on *Michael Hopp, et al. v. City of Pittsburgh.* U. S. Court of Appeals for the Third Circuit, 1999, case nos. 98–3411, 98–3427, http://openjurist.org/194/f3d/434/michael-hopp (accessed January 2009).

INDEX

Note: Page numbers in italic type indicate photographs. Tables are indicated by a "t" following a page number.